Early Release in International Criminal Law

Early Release in International Criminal Law

Róisín Mulgrew

Lecturer in Criminology and Criminal Justice, School of Law and Irish Centre for Human Rights, University of Galway, Ireland

Edward Elgar
PUBLISHING

Cheltenham, UK • Northampton, MA, USA

Cover image: Markus Spiske on Unsplash.

Published by
Edward Elgar Publishing Limited
The Lypiatts
15 Lansdown Road
Cheltenham
Glos GL50 2JA
UK
Edward Elgar Publishing, Inc.

William Pratt House
9 Dewey Court
Northampton
Massachusetts 01060
USA

Authorised representative in the EU for GPSR queries only: Easy Access System Europe – Mustamäe tee 50, 10621 Tallinn, Estonia, gpsr.requests@easproject.com

A catalogue record for this book
is available from the British Library

Library of Congress Control Number: 2024951209

This book is available electronically in the **Elgar**online
Law subject collection
https://doi.org/10.4337/9781786433213

MIX
Paper | Supporting responsible forestry
FSC® C013604

ISBN 978 1 78643 320 6 (cased)
ISBN 978 1 78643 321 3 (eBook)

Printed and bound by CPI Group (UK) Ltd, Croydon, CR0 4YY

Contents

1. Introduction to *Early Release in International Criminal Law*

1. EARLY RELEASE IN INTERNATIONAL CRIMINAL LAW

Criminal punishment and sanctions are increasingly viewed as essential means for dealing with collective violence and upholding the rights of victims of atrocities.[1] All contemporary international criminal courts impose sentences of imprisonment as their primary penalty.[2] Without an international prison, these sentences are (usually) enforced by cooperating states.[3] The states that enforce sentences on behalf of international courts are bound by the length of the international sentences imposed.[4] In other words, release decision-making is retained by the sentencing court or tribunal.[5] In contrast to the relative conformity of law and policy in relation to sanctions and the modalities of sentence enforcement in international criminal law, however, there have been significant divergences in the law, policy and practice of international criminal courts and tribunals in relation to early release.

It is important to clarify at the outset that none of the statutes of the contemporary international courts actually provide for early release. The statutes of the temporary courts, for example, refer only to pardon and commutation

1 See Elena Maculan and Alicia Gil Gil, 'The Rationale and Purposes of Criminal Law and Punishment in Transitional Contexts' (2020) 40(1) *Oxford Journal of Legal Studies* 132157 at 132–134.

2 See Article 24(1) ICTYSt; Article 23(1) ICTRSt; Article 77(1) ICCSt; Article 19(1) SCSLSt. Other penalties (fines, forfeiture and compensation) can only be imposed in addition to imprisonment and have not been used to date.

3 See Article 27 ICTYSt; Article 26 ICTRSt; Article 25(1) MICTSt; Article 103(1)(a) ICCSt; Article 22(1) SCSLSt. For a more detailed discussion of this decentralised system of enforcement for international sentences of imprisonment, see Róisín Mulgrew, *Toward the Development of the International Penal System* (CUP, 2013) 33–102.

4 See for example Article 110(1) ICCSt.

5 See for example Article 110(2) ICCSt.

of sentence.[6] In practice, however, only early release, that is release before the end of the sentence originally imposed, has been granted. As it is not an explicit power, it is not surprising that there is very little statutory detail on the purpose of, process for or factors to consider when contemplating granting release. The release practice of the post-World War II military tribunals did not provide the contemporary courts with much guidance. For those convicted by the International Military Tribunal, Nuremberg (IMTN), early release was only granted to those with serious health conditions due to fears that they would be viewed as martyrs should they die in prison.[7] The expectation was that sentences would be served in full. In fact, Spandau prison, which housed IMTN prisoners, only closed following the suicide of its last, solitary inmate, six years before the establishment of the International Criminal Tribunal for the former Yugoslavia (ICTY).[8] In sharp contrast, all persons convicted by the International Military Tribunal for the Far East, even those sentenced to life imprisonment, were granted clemency and released by 1958.[9] Yet, over the years, the regulatory and policy detail, documentation and practice in relation to early release has grown significantly, which each contemporary international court adopting its own distinct approach.

Until recently, however, sentence management was viewed as an accessory function and non-critical aspect of the mandate of international criminal courts.[10] With the movement to the residual stage of operations of the temporary international courts, however, the institutional, media and victim focus has shifted from arrests, prosecutions and trials to focus on sentence enforcement, release and reintegration. This shift in focus has happened at a time when a prevalent counter-impunity discourse is generating critique of not only the length of sentences imposed, but the length of sentences actu-

---

[6] See Article 28 ICTYSt; Article 27 ICTRSt; Article 26 MICTSt; Article 23 SCSLSt; Article 24 RSCSLSt. The Rome Statute of the ICC also only refers to reduction of sentence and not early release – see Article 110 ICCSt.

[7] See Norman Goda, *Tales from Spandau: Nazi Criminals and the Cold War* (CUP, 2007) 132, 193; Filip Votja, 'Punishment and Sentence Enforcement for Serious Violations of International Humanitarian Law Committed in the Former Yugoslavia' in AM Getoš Kalac, HJ Albrecht and M Kilchling (eds) *Mapping the Criminological Landscape of the Balkans* (Duncker and Humblot, 2014) 401–428.

[8] Filip Vojta, 'From West Berlin, with Love: The Legacy of the Spandau Prison in the Contemporary International Sentence Enforcement Practice' Leuven Transitional Justice Blog, 2 November 2021.

[9] Sandra Wilson, 'The Sentence is Only Half the Story: From Stern Justice to Clemency for Japanese War Criminals, 1945–1958' (2015) 13 *JICJ* 745–761 at 746.

[10] Gert Vermeulen and Eveline Dewree, *Offender Reintegration and Rehabilitation as a Component of International Criminal Justice?* (Antwerpen, Maklu 2014) at 11, 71.

ally being served by persons convicted of international crimes.[11] Release is being reframed as central to international criminal justice, on the basis of the growing recognition of the impact that the outcome of release decisions has for convicted persons, victims, society and indeed the credibility of the international court or tribunal.[12] Accordingly, release decisions have become significant legacy indicators for temporary international courts. Likewise, sentence reduction decisions have been and will remain a vitally important aspect of the work of the permanent International Criminal Court (ICC).

Release represents not only a 'defining feature of the carceral experience'[13] but also the penal system that grants or denies it. This book is dedicated to understanding how early release can (re)define the scope, reach and impact of international punishment. This introductory chapter sets out the substantive, institutional and temporal scope of this study, its objectives and contribution to knowledge and the structure and content of the following chapters.

2. SCOPE OF THE STUDY

This book is concerned with *early release* in international criminal law. The focus is on post-conviction release. It is not concerned with interim or provisional release from international custody that may be granted prior to conviction.[14] Early release law comprises a complex corpus of statutory, regulatory and policy provisions and an extensive body of international jurisprudence. Early release law has experienced substantial change and expansion over the last two decades. This monograph explores the evolution of early release policy and early release practice, in light of the institutional, legal, and political contexts in which they operate.

The book charts the development of the law, jurisprudence and practice in relation to three forms of release that may be granted by international criminal courts and tribunals prior to the completion of the original (final) sentence

---

[11] See Marion V Dubray, 'Impunity and Atrocity Punishment after Mass Violence and Conflict: Questioning the Admissibility of Leniency Measures in (Post)Transition Contexts' in R Mulgrew and MJ Christensen, *Research Handbook on the Punishment of Atrocity Crimes* (Edward Elgar Publishing, 2024).

[12] Cristina Fernández-Pacheco Estrada, 'What we talk about when we talk about early release in international criminal law: the sui generis nature of the reduction of sentence under the Rome Statute' (2022) 22 *ICLR* 539–567 at 541.

[13] Thomas Guiney, 'Parole, parole boards and the institutional dilemmas of contemporary prison release' (2022) *Punishment and Society* 1–20 at 1–2.

[14] See Andrew Trotter, 'Provisional release from international remand detention' in R Mulgrew and D Abels (eds) *Research Handbook on the International Penal System* (Edward Elgar Publishing, 2016) 23–53.

imposed – *unconditional early release, conditional early releas*e and *sentence reduction.* Unconditional early release was granted by the ICTY, the International Criminal Tribunal for Rwanda (ICTR) and the International Residual Mechanism for Criminal Tribunals (MICT) until 2018. The Special Court for Sierra Leone (SCSL) introduced a system of conditional early release in 2013, which is now implemented by the Residual Special Court for Sierra Leone (RSCSL). The MICT adopted a conditional early release system in 2018. Despite being residual mechanisms, the sentence management role of the RSCSL and MICT is likely to continue for at least two decades.[15] The only permanent court, the ICC, relies on a system of sentence reduction.

The goal was to produce a *comprehensive depiction* of early release law and policy, release practice and the implications thereof for a wide range of international criminal justice stakeholders. All known laws, policies, decisions and case-law of the ICTY, ICTR, MICT, SCSL, RSCSL and ICC on early release from the outset of sentence management operations at the various courts up to May 2024 have been analysed.

The book seeks to answer what may, at first glance, seem to be quite basic questions. What form does early release take in international criminal law? Who makes international release decisions? What factors are taken into consideration? Who can influence release decisions? What happens when international criminals are released before the end of their sentence? Are conditions attached to their release? Who supervises released prisoners? Can international prisoners be released if they become very ill or very old? The study of early release in international criminal law is, however, complex. It involves the analysis of changing laws and often conflicting principles against a backdrop of shifting political, penological, ethical, humanitarian, diplomatic, security, legacy and logistical considerations. Early release in international criminal law can only be understood by adopting a number of methodological approaches, and synthesising findings within a broad frame of multi-disciplinary scholarship. The initial part of the book contains doctrinal accounts of particular release systems, focusing on the analysis of legal and policy frameworks in light of jurisprudential pronouncements and decisions. Later chapters provide socio-legal, comparative and critical perspectives and, overall, a more systemic approach to the analysis of early release in international criminal law, drawing on international and comparative legal, rights, criminology and penology literature.

---

[15] Letter dated 14 April 2022 from the President of the International Residual Mechanism for Criminal Tribunals addressed to the President of the Security Council, S/PRST/2022/2, para. 50.

3. OBJECTIVES AND CONTRIBUTION TO KNOWLEDGE

International criminal law consists of different components: substantive law, procedural law and sanctioning law.[16] The goal of this book is to contribute to knowledge about the latter element. It does so in recognition of the fact that a sentence of imprisonment remains 'a mere abstraction until given effect in the correctional context'.[17] It is therefore important to extend the study of 'war crime justice to the post-sentencing phase' as 'no criminal sentence can be fully understood if we stop at the moment of sentencing'.[18] Indeed, as Wilson rightly acknowledges, the 'relative certainty' of the sentences pronounced can become 'undermined by a complex mixture of political considerations, competing conceptions of justice, bureaucratic imperatives and legal pragmatism'.[19] Furthermore, 'victims care deeply about what ultimately happens to the persons convicted of serious international crimes'.[20] For these reasons, sentence management (focusing on release, conditional release and recall) should be seen as an 'autonomous legal field'.[21] Despite this, early and conditional release are often a 'neglected aspect of penality' and domestic and international criminal law scholarship.[22] The true scope and meaning of punishment cannot, however, be understood without also contemplating the effect of release forms, supervision and outcomes.

The primary objective of this book is to describe, compare and critique international systems of early release, and by doing so, contribute to knowledge about the reach, depth and impact of international punishment. It is hoped that this study will strengthen recognition of (the value of) post-conviction

---

[16] See R Mulgrew and D Abels, *Research Handbook on the International Penal System* (Edward Elgar Publishing, 2016) at xiii.

[17] Joan Petersilia and Kevin R Reitz, 'Sentencing and Corrections: Overlapping and Inseparable Subjects' in J Petersilia & K Reitz (eds) *The Oxford Handbook of Sentencing and Corrections* (OUP, 2014) 3–20 at 3.

[18] Wilson, note 9 at 745.

[19] Ibid at 761.

[20] Mark Drumbl, 'Penalties and Punishment' in M deGuzman and V Oosterveld, *The Elgar Companion to the International Criminal Court* (Edward Elgar Publishing, 2020) at 128.

[21] Martine Herzog-Evans, 'French early release: McProcedures and McReentry' (2019) 11(3) *European Journal of Probation* 188–201 at 188.

[22] Nicola Carr and Ester Blay 'Parole and prisoner release: Exploring rationalities across time and place' (2019) 11(3) *European Journal of Probation* 119–123 at 119.

studies as a distinct sub-field of international criminal law.[23] Scholarship on international punishment has often focused on penalties and sentencing.[24] But, as Sexton stresses, the judicial pronouncement of a term of imprisonment only relays the 'articulated or abstract' form of 'the penalty, not the punishment'.[25] It is encouraging to see that the literature on international sentence enforcement and sentence management has been growing.[26] In particular, increased

---

[23] Claus Kreß, *Towards a Truly Universal Invisible College of International Criminal Lawyers* (TOAEP, 2014) at 10.

[24] Shahram Dana, 'The Sentencing Legacy of the Special Court for Sierra Leone' (2014) 42(3) *Georgia Journal of International and Comparative Law* 615–686; Marek Szydło, 'Reduction of Life Sentences Imposed by International Criminal Tribunals after the Galić Decision: Is There Need for Further Improvement?' (2015) 13 *JICJ* 1099–1120; Joseph W Doherty and Richard H Steinberg, 'Punishment and Policy in International Criminal Sentencing: An Empirical Study' (2016) 110(1) *AJIL* 49–81; Dirk van Zyl Smit, 'Determinate and Indeterminate Sentences of Imprisonment in International Criminal Justice' in R. Mulgrew and D. Abels (eds) *Research Handbook on the International Penal System* (Edward Elgar Publishing, 2016) 80–101; Dragana Spencer, 'Overview of Language Rights in the International Criminal Law Sentencing Models' (2018) 31 Int J Semiot Law 787–804; Shahram Dana, 'Reimagining Punishment for Atrocity Crimes: An Innovative Sentencing Framework for International Criminal Law' (2020) V(i) *Cambridge Law Review* 49–78; Florian Jeßberger and Julia Geneuss (eds) *Why Punish Perpetrators of Mass Atrocities?: Purposes of Punishment in International Criminal Law* (CUP, 2020); Mark Drumbl, 'Penalties and Punishment' in M deGuzman and V Oosterveld, *The Elgar Companion to the International Criminal Court* (Edward Elgar Publishing, 2020) 128–146.

[25] Lori Sexton, 'Penal Subjectivities: Developing a Theoretical Framework for Penal Consciousness' (2015) 17(1) *Punishment and Society* 114–136 at 115, 131, 133.

[26] See Mark Drumbl, *Atrocity, Punishment and International Law* (CUP, 2007); Róisín Mulgrew, *Towards the Development of the International Penal System* (CUP, 2013); Barbora Holá, Róisín Mulgrew and Maja Munivrana (eds), Symposium on 'Post-trial (In)Justice: Reflections on the Legacies and Impacts of Atrocity Crime Prosecutions' (2023) 21(1) *Journal of International Criminal Justice*; Marina Maier, 'Offender Rehabilitation in International Criminal Justice: Towards Implementation of Tailored Rehabilitation Programs' (2021) 53 *Case W. Res. J. Int'l L* 269; Barbora Holá and Maja Munivrana, 'There is Something Special about War Criminals: Constructing and Assessing the Rehabilitation of War Criminals at the ICTY/IRMCT and in Croatia' (2023) *JICJ* 1–23.

attention has been paid to release[27] and post-release[28] issues over the last decade. International sentence management deserves to be interrogated in its own right. Insights into how release systems work, and how they evolve, are important for deeper understandings about the parameters and implications of international punishment. In addition to the contribution to knowledge, it is also hoped that the detail and findings of this book will constitute a valuable resource for international lawyers and contemporary international courts, as well as future temporary international(ised) criminal courts and authorities involved in the domestic punishment of atrocity crime.

4. STRUCTURE OF THE BOOK

This book examines the evolution of early release in the international criminal justice context over time and across judicial institutions through an exploration of law, policy and practice. To gain a deep understanding of the development and impact of early release law and practice, it is necessary to first explore the distinct systems in place at each international court. This approach facilitates an understanding of the evolution of early release within the law and practice of particular international courts, but also within international criminal law more generally. In addition to substantive chapters setting out the law, practice and jurisprudence relevant to each early release system, the book also analyses

---

[27] See Jessica M Kelder, Barbora Holá and Joris van Wijk, 'Rehabilitation and Early Release of Perpetrators of International Crimes: A Case Study of the ICTY and ICTR' (2014) 14 *ICLR* 1177–1203 at 1180; Barbora Holá, Joris van Wijk, Francesca Constantini and Armi Korhonnen, 'Does Remorse Count? ICTY Convicts' Reflections on Their Crimes in Early Release Decisions' (2018) 28(4) *International Criminal Justice Review* 349–331; Priyamvada Yarnell, 'Relativising Atrocity Crimes: The Message of Unconditional Early Release of Perpetrators Convicted by the ICTY (1998–2018)' (2021) 21 *International Criminal Law Review* 67–96. Estrada, note 12; Róisín Mulgrew, 'Terminal Illness and Compassionate Release: Lessons for the ICC from the UN Tribunals and National Jurisdictions' (2023) 21(1) *JICJ* 61–87; Cristina Fernández-Pacheco Estrada, 'Gravity of the Crime and Early Release: A Comparative Study of Early Release Practices in International Tribunals' (2024) *LJIL* 1–22.

[28] Elies van Sliedregt, 'International Outlaws' (2020) *LJIL* 535–540; Lina Strupinskienė, 'Life after Conviction at the International Criminal Tribunal for the former Yugoslavia' (2023) 21(1) *JICJ* 113–135; Cécille Lecolle, 'Relocation Issues of Released and Acquitted at International Criminal Courts and Tribunals – a Defence Perspective' (2023) 21(1) *JICJ* 167–184; Kate Gibson and Bonnie Johnson, 'Acquitted, released and homeless: The crisis of stateless of former defendants' in R Mulgrew and MJ Christensen, *Research Handbook on the Punishment of Atrocity Crimes* (Edward Elgar Publishing, 2024).

these early release systems from a comparative and critical perspective. In other words, this book explores the issue of early release from both institutional and systemic viewpoints. Accordingly, the first half of the book focuses on the law, policy and practice of specific international courts structured around the chronological adoption of particular models of early release. The second half of the book adopts a more holistic, comparative and critical approach to the evolution of early release forms, factors, influences and challenges.

4.1 Institutional Forms and Modalities of Early Release

The book begins with detailed discussions of release law, policy and practice at the UN Tribunals for the former Yugoslavia and Rwanda, MICT, (Residual) SCSL and ICC, focusing on the legal framework, eligibility, factors and procedures involved in release decision-making. Chapter 2 traces the development and application of the law and policies on unconditional early release at the ICTY, ICTR and MICT from the beginning of operations until 2018. Chapter 3 examines the legal framework for and practice in relation to sentence reduction at the ICC. Chapter 4 analyses the creation and operation of the conditional early release system introduced by the (R)SCSL. In addition to the focus of the chapters so far, Chapter 4 also details the conditions that can be imposed, the consequences of breaching conditions of release and the processes for monitoring and recalling persons subject to supervision in the community. Chapter 5 traces the introduction and challenges of developing a conditional early release system at the MICT, and the impact of Presidential interpretations of relevant law and policy for its scope and reach.

4.2 Comparative and Critical Perspectives on Release in International Criminal Law

Building on the insights gained from the institutional or release specific evaluations of the preceding chapters, Chapters 6 to 9 adopt a comparative and critical approach to the analysis of release law, policy and practice in international criminal law. Chapter 6 focuses on the evolution of conditional early release in international criminal law, comparing and contrasting the approaches to introducing this form of release, the conditions that govern it, means for supervising the service of an international sentence in the community and dealing with (alleged) breaches of conditions of release at the MICT and RSCSL. Chapter 7 explores the variations and developments in relation to the factors that international judges consider when making release decisions. This chapter pays particular attention to how rehabilitation has been (re)conceptualised in international criminal law and applied within the international criminal justice context. Chapter 8 identifies a range of potentially influential voices in release decision-making procedures (judges, victims, prosecutors and states) and examines the extent of their role and the impact and merit of taking their views into account. Chapter 9 addresses the significance of health and advanced age for release decision-making with particular consideration given to possibilities and challenges of granting compassionate release and providing palliative care for internationally convicted persons. The book concludes with a review of some notable, often conflicting, findings of this study in Chapter 10.

2. Unconditional early release at the UN Tribunals and the International Residual Mechanism for Criminal Tribunals

1. EARLY RELEASE AT THE UN TRIBUNALS AND THE INTERNATIONAL RESIDUAL MECHANISM FOR CRIMINAL TRIBUNALS

The statute of the first international criminal tribunal, the International Criminal Tribunal for the former Yugoslavia (ICTY), did not refer to early release. Nor did the Statute of the International Criminal Tribunal for Rwanda (ICTR). Both statutes referred instead to pardon and commutation of sentence.[1] Part Nine of both the ICTY and ICTR's Rules of Procedure and Evidence (and the rules therein) also only refer to pardon and commutation of sentence. The term early release first appeared when President McDonald of the ICTY, following consultations with the Bureau, Prosecutor and Registrar, issued a Practice Direction in April 1999 to 'establish an internal procedure for the determination of applications for pardon, commutation of sentences and early release'.[2] Although the ICTY Practice Direction contained the statutory power for the President to grant pardon or commute a sentence,[3] neither option was ever used. In practice, what was granted at the ICTY (and ICTR) was early release.

One of the key roles of the International Residual Mechanisms for Criminal Tribunals (MICT) is to supervise the sentences imposed by not only the

---

1 Art. 28 ICTYSt; Art. 27 ICTRSt.

2 Introduction, Practice Direction on the Procedure for the Determination of Applications for Pardon, Commutation of Sentence and Early Release of Persons Convicted by the International Tribunal Practice Direction (hereafter ICTY PDER). The ICTR did not publish its practice direction, but the same terms were used – see para. 1 MICT PDER.

3 ICTY PDER Rev. 1 (7 April 1999), para. 7; ICTY PDER Rev. 2 (1 September 2009), para. 8; ICTY PDER Rev. 3 (16 September 2010), para. 8.

Mechanism itself, but also those imposed by the ICTY and ICTR.[4] Despite the practice of the ICTY and ICTR, Article 26 of the MICT Statute only refers to pardon and commutation of sentence. Unlike its predecessors, however, Part Nine of the MICT Rules, and the rules therein, referred to early release from the outset.[5] In July 2012, President Meron, in consideration of the ICTY and ICTR Practice Directions, and following consultations with the Prosecutor and Registrar, adopted a Practice Direction setting out the procedure for determining applications for 'pardon, commutation of sentence and early release'.[6] All versions of the Practice Direction retained the power to grant pardon or to commute a sentence.[7] President Meron did not grant either. Until the UN Security Council intervened in 2018 to request the adoption of a conditional release system at the MICT,[8] early release granted by the UN Tribunals, and by President Meron at the MICT, was unconditional.[9] This chapter explores the key aspects of the unconditional early release systems applied by the UN Tribunals and the MICT until 2018: eligibility for release, the factors considered in reaching a decision on release, and the procedure for making such decisions.

2. ELIGIBILITY FOR PARDON, COMMUTATION OF SENTENCE OR EARLY RELEASE

The statutes of the UN Tribunals appear to locate responsibility for triggering eligibility for release in the domestic law of enforcing states. Articles 28 (ICTY) and 27 (ICTR) state that 'if, pursuant to the applicable law of the state in which the convicted person is imprisoned, he or she is eligible for pardon or commutation of sentence, the state concerned shall notify' the Tribunal. Article 26 MICT replicates this approach, although enforcing states must notify the Mechanism if persons convicted by the ICTY, ICTR or the Mechanism become eligible for pardon or commutation.[10] Release decisions, however, demonstrate that Presidents of the UN Tribunal, based on the

---

4 Articles 25(2) and 26 MICTSt.

5 See Rules 149–151 MICT RPE, MICT/1, 8 June 2012.

6 Practice Direction on the Procedure for the Determination of Applications for Pardon, Commutation of Sentence, and Early Release of Persons Convicted by the ICTR, the ICTY or the Mechanism, MICT/3, 5 July 2012.

7 MICT PDER, 2012, para. 9; MICT PDER, 2018 Rev. 1, para. 9; MICT PDER, 2019, Rev. 2, para. 10.

8 See UN Security Council Resolution 2422, 27 June 2018 and Chapter 5.

9 See Chapter 9 for a discussion of provisional release and conditional release granted to terminally ill prisoners by President Meron.

10 See also Rule 149 MICT RPE.

statutory stipulation that the Tribunals supervise the sentences,[11] retained control over sentence enforcement by imposing their own standards for eligibility.

Even though the ICTY and ICTR statutes contain identical statutory provisions, their eligibility policies diverged. At the ICTY, release decisions for determinate sentences were made on the basis of a presumption of release at the two-thirds point unless there were significant negative factors militating against release. The ICTR initially operated on the basis of a presumption against release, though later decisions demonstrated a growing trend towards release at the three-quarters stage. This changed in 2012 when President Meron adopted a standardised approach to determinate sentences imposed by the ICTY, ICTR and MICT. The question of eligibility for indeterminate sentences imposed by any UN Tribunal remained unresolved until 2015.

2.1 Determinate Sentences

2.1.1 ICTY

Although eligibility in accordance with enforcing state domestic law was often cited as an essential precondition for release in ICTY release decisions,[12] the temporal threshold was in fact determined by ICTY Presidents. To equalise the treatment of prisoners convicted by the Tribunal, ICTY Presidents adopted a rule of thumb whereby prisoners only became eligible for release when they had served two-thirds of their sentence.[13] This threshold was considered to reflect the approach of the majority of states of enforcement.[14] There are, of course, exceptions to this practice in the domestic law of cooperating states.

---

[11] Art. 27 ICTYSt; Art. 26 ICTRSt; Art. 25 MICTSt.

[12] *Prosecutor v Josipović*, Decision of the President on the Application for Pardon or Commutation of Sentence of Drago Josipović, IT-95-16-ES, 30 January 2006, paras 6–7; *Prosecutor v Šantić*, Decision of the President on the Application for Pardon or Commutation of Sentence of Vladimir Šantić, IT-95-16-ES, 16 February 2009, para. 6; *Prosecutor v Martinović*, Decision of the President on the Application for Pardon or Commutation of Sentence of Vinko Martinović, IT-98-34-ES, 22 January 2010, para. 9.

[13] See *Prosecutor v Vuković*, Decision of the President on Commutation of Sentence, IT-96-23 & 23/1-ES, 11 March 2008, para. 11.

[14] See ICTY *Manual of Developed Practice* (2009), section D.4.4, para. 52 at 162.

Belgium for example facilitates release after one-third of a sentence[15] and prisoners in the UK,[16] Austria,[17] and France[18] can become eligible after serving half of their sentences. Spanish prisoners, in contrast, must typically serve three-quarters of their sentences before being considered for release: the Spanish penal code only permits release after two-thirds in exceptional and enumerated circumstances.[19] The domestic law of some enforcing states does not provide guidance on eligibility. Finland's implementing legislation, for example, disapplies domestic release provisions to prisoners convicted by international tribunals[20] and Mali's domestic law does not contain a fixed temporal point for release consideration.[21]

---

15 *Prosecutor v Dragan Zelenović*, Public Redacted Version of the 28 August 2015 Decision of the President on the Early Release of Dragan Zelenović, MICT-15-89-ES, 18 September 2015, para. 11.

16 See *Prosecutor v Krajišnik*, Decision of the President on Early Release of Momčilo Krajišnik, IT-00-39-ES, 26 July 2010, para. 1.

17 *Prosecutor v Kordić*, Decision of President on Application for Pardon or Commutation of Sentence of Dario Kordić, IT-95-14/2-ES, 13 May 2010, para. 2; *Prosecutor v Žigić*, Public Redacted Version of the 10 November 2014 Decision of the President on the Early Release of Zoran Žigić, MICT-14-81-ES.1, 23 December 2014, para. 12.

18 *Prosecutor v Radić*, Decision of President on Application for Pardon or Commutation of Sentence of Mlado Radić, IT-98-30/1-ES, 23 April 2010, para. 2.

19 See *Prosecutor v Josipović*, Decision of the President on the Application for Pardon or Commutation of Sentence of Drago Josipović, IT-95-16-ES, 30 January 2006, para. 4; *Prosecutor v Šantić*, Decision of the President on the Application for Pardon or Commutation of Sentence of Vladimir Šantić, IT-95-16-ES, 16 February 2009, para. 7. See José Cid and Beatriz Tébar, 'Spain' in Nicola Padfield, Dirk van Zyl Smit, Frieder Dünkel *Release from Prison: European Policy and Practice* (Cullompton: Willan Publishing, 2010).

20 *Prosecutor v Momir Nikolić*, Public Redacted Version of the 14 March 2014 Decision on the Early Release of Momir Nikolić, MICT-14-65-ES, 12 October 2015, para. 12 discussing Section 14 of the 1987 Finnish Act on International Cooperation in the Enforcement of Certain Penal Sanctions. See also *Prosecutor v Radivoje Miletić*, Decision of the President on the Early Release of Radivoje Militić, MICT-15-85-ES.5, 23 October 2018, para. 21.

21 In Mali, Article 35 of Law no. 1–003 of 27 February 2001 on the Prison System and Supervised Education, in conjunction with Rule 25 of Decision No. 10–002 MJ-DNAPES of 6 August 2010 on the Internal Regulations of Prisons and Supervised Education, stipulates that a convicted person may be eligible for *provisional release, or semi-custodial treatment* 'upon sufficient proof of their improvement [...]' and receive 'favourable consideration' for conditional release where his or her 'conduct and work has been satisfactory'. Cited in *Prosecutor v Youssof Munyakazi*, Public Redacted Version of the 22 July 2015 Decision of the

The ICTY rejected arguments that it was bound by enforcing state law on eligibility in situations where it appears to entitle prisoners to release before the two-thirds point of their sentence on the basis of the statutory stipulation that the enforcement of ICTY sentences was 'subject to the supervision of the Tribunal' (Article 27) and the regulatory requirement for Presidents to take the treatment of similarly situated prisoners into account (Rule 125).[22] It was affirmed that the 'two-thirds practice has [therefore] been applied consistently … notwithstanding the domestic law in enforcement states'.[23] The application of this interpretation of the ICTY's legal framework meant that prisoners eligible for release in the enforcing states in which they were serving their sentences were not considered eligible for release by ICTY Presidents as they had not yet served two-thirds of their sentence.[24]

Introduced to ensure equality of treatment of convicted persons, the rule of thumb also ensured that ICTY prisoners served a minimum period of time in prison before they could be considered for release. Release discretion enabled Presidents to achieve what was considered to be beyond the powers of a trial chamber. The ICTY Appeal Chamber in Stakić concluded that as the legal framework stated that eligibility for pardon, commutation of sentence or early release was to be determined by the national law of enforcing states, the trial chamber's direction that the prisoner must serve a minimum of twenty years before he could be considered for early release was *ultra vires*.[25]

Though not considered to be a rule in 2008 by President Pocar,[26] the threshold became so ingrained in ICTY release practice that serving two-thirds of a

---

President on the Early Release of Youssof Munyakazi, MICT-12-18-ES.1, 22 July 2015, para. 11.

22 *Prosecutor v Radić*, Decision of President on Application for Pardon or Commutation of Sentence of Mlado Radić, IT-98-30/1-ES, 23 April 2010, paras 2, 12–15.

23 *Prosecutor v Simić*, Decision of the President on Early Release of Blagoje Simić, IT-95-9-ES, 15 February 2011, para. 20.

24 *Prosecutor v Radić*, Decision of President on Application for Pardon or Commutation of Sentence of Mlado Radić, IT-98-30/1-ES, 23 April 2010, paras 2, 5, 12; *Prosecutor v Žigić*, Decision of President on Early Release of Zoran Žigić, IT-98-30/1-ES, 8 November 2010, paras 12–13; *Prosecutor v Krajiśnik*, Decision of the President on Early Release of Momčilo Krajišnik, IT-00-39-ES, 11 July 2011, para. 21.

25 See *Prosecutor v Stakić*, Appeals Chamber, Judgment, IT-97-24-A, 22 March 2006, paras 392–393; *Prosecutor v Stakić,* Trial Chamber II, Judgment, IT-97-24-T, 31 July 2003 at 253–254.

26 See *Prosecutor v Vuković*, Decision of the President on Commutation of Sentence, IT-96–23 & 23/1-ES, 11 March 2008, para. 11.

sentence became an almost absolute requirement for release.[27] The only exception to the rule was substantial cooperation with the Prosecutor.[28] Despite the insistence on the application of this rule of thumb to all persons convicted by the ICTY, prisoners were considered for release 'only after'[29] or when 'at least'[30] two thirds of the sentence had been served. While the two-thirds point marks eligibility for consideration for release, and not an entitlement to release,[31] the majority of prisoners were granted release at this point.[32]

2.1.2 ICTR

The ICTR, in contrast, appeared to operate on the basis of a presumption against granting release at all. All ICTR prisoners, whether serving their sentences at the UN Detention Facility in Arusha or in enforcing states, served their sentences in full until 2011.[33] Presidents declined to grant early release due to the gravity of crimes, the fact that factors had already been taken into account in

---

[27] See *Prosecutor v Sikirica*, Decision of the President on Early Release of Duško Sikirica, IT-95-8-ES, 21 June 2010, para. 13; *Prosecutor v Gvero*, Decision of the President on Early Release of Milan Gvero, IT-05-88-ES, 28 June 2010, para. 8; See *Prosecutor v Krajišnik*, Decision of the President on Early Release of Momčilo Krajišnik, IT-00-39-ES, 26 July 2010, para. 14; *Prosecutor v Bala*, Decision on Application of Haradin Bala for Sentence Remission, IT-03-66-ES, 15 October 2010, para. 14; *Prosecutor v Žigić*, Decision of President on Early Release of Zoran Žigić, IT-98-30/1-ES, 8 November 2010, para. 14; *Prosecutor v Rajić*, Decision of President on Early Release of Ivica Rajić, IT-95-12-ES, 31 January 2011, para. 14; *Prosecutor v Simić*, Decision of the President on Early Release of Blagoje Simić, IT-95-9-ES, 15 February 2011, para. 20; *Prosecutor v Tarčulovski*, Decision of the President on Early Release of Johan Tarčulovski, IT-04-82-ES, 23 June 2011, para. 13.

[28] See *Prosecutor v Obrenović*, Decision of the President on Early Release of Dragan Obrenović, IT-02-60/2-ES, 21 September 2011; *Prosecutor v Krajišnik*, Decision of the President on Early Release of Momčilo Krajišnik, IT-00-39-ES, 8 November 2012, paras 27, 43.

[29] *Prosecutor v Dragan Zelenović*, Decision of the President on the Early Release of Dragan Zelenović, MICT-15-89-ES, 10 June 2010, para. 13.

[30] *Prosecutor v Krajišnik*, Decision of the President on Early Release of Momčilo Krajišnik, IT-00-39-ES, 26 July 2010, para. 14.

[31] *Prosecutor v Simić*, Decision of the President on Early Release of Blagoje Simić, IT-95-9-ES, 15 February 2011, para. 20; *Prosecutor v Obrenović*, Decision of the President on Early Release of Dragan Obrenović, IT-02-60/2-ES, 21 September 2011, para. 16.

[32] See Barbora Holá and Joris van Wijk, 'Life after Conviction at International Criminal Tribunals' (2014) 12 *JICJ* 109–132 at 112.

[33] See for example ICTR Press Release 'Vincent Rutaganira Released After Completing his Sentence' ICTR/INFO-9-2–556.EN, 3 March 2008.

mitigation during sentencing, and that the term remaining to be served did not militate in favour of release.[34] One notable exception was Ruggiu: he was the first person to be granted early release from an enforcing state due to acceptance of the remission granted to him by the Italian authorities.[35] The first grant of early release by an ICTR President occurred in October 2011. Bagaragaza, serving his sentence in Sweden, was released after serving three-quarters of his sentence.[36] President Khan stressed that this decision was 'not intended to create a precedent for early release at three quarters' and that 'future decisions will continue to be determined on a case-by-case basis'.[37] Just four months later, however, Rugambarara was also granted early release by President Khan at the three-quarters point.[38] In both cases, their guilty pleas and significant cooperation with the Prosecutor were strong factors supporting release.[39] Just a month later, Muvunyi was released from the UN Detention Facility at the three-quarters point on the basis of this practice,[40] even though he had not cooperated with the Prosecutor.[41] President Joensen, granting release, emphasised the amount of time served by similarly situated prisoners: noting he had served an amount of time in prison that was 'equal to or exceeds that of prisoners who were sentenced at the lesser end of the spectrum for similar crimes'.[42] These cases indicated that there may have been an acceptance or movement towards a three-quarters rule of thumb at the ICTR. With the movement of sentence supervision to the MICT, however, things changed again.

2.1.3 MICT

When faced with making the first release decision as President of the MICT, President Meron had to decide whether Rule 151's reference to similarly situated persons referred to persons convicted by the same Tribunal or to persons

---

[34] See Damien Scalia, 'Long-term sentences in international criminal law: do they meet the standards set out by the European Court of Human Rights?' (2011) 9(3) *JICJ* 669–687 at 676.

[35] *Prosecutor v Ruggiu*, Decision of the President on the Application for Early Release of Georges Ruggiu, ICTR-97-32-S, 12 May 2005.

[36] *Prosecutor v Bagaragaza*, Decision on the Early Release of Michel Bagaragaza, ICTR-05-86-S, 24 October 2011, para. 8.

[37] Ibid, para. 17.

[38] *Prosecutor v Rugambarara*, Decision on the Early Release Request of Juvénal Rugambarara, ICTR-00–59, 8 February 2012, para. 17.

[39] Ibid, paras 10, 13.

[40] *Prosecutor v Muvunyi,* Decision on the Early Release of Tharcisse Muvunyi, ICTR-00-055A-T, 6 March 2012, paras 11–12.

[41] Ibid, para. 7.

[42] Ibid, para. 13.

sentenced by the ICTY, ICTR and MICT.[43] He opted for the latter interpretation, and significantly, in doing so, adopted the ICTY rule of release eligibility at the two-thirds point of the sentence. President Meron based this choice on the need to ensure equality among all persons supervised by the MICT irrespective of which court they had been sentenced by.[44] While recognising the divergent practice of the ICTY and ICTR,[45] and conceding that this may 'constitute a benefit not previously recognised for persons convicted by the ICTY',[46] he stressed that the requirements of fairness dictated that the ICTY practice should be applied uniformly to all prisoners supervised by the MICT.[47] Moreover, he emphasised that the two-thirds rule represented a threshold for consideration for early release and not an entitlement to release.[48] Decisions show that provisionally recognised remission can be taken into account in the determination of whether two-thirds of a sentence has been served.[49] A failure to demonstrate extraordinary circumstances warranting release prior to the two-thirds point of a sentence, however, will result in a denial of early release.[50]

43 *Prosecutor v Bisengimana,* Decision on the Early Release Request of Paul Bisengimana, MICT-12–07, 11 December 2012, para. 16.

44 Ibid, paras 16–17.

45 Ibid, paras 18–19.

46 Ibid, para. 21.

47 Ibid, para. 20; *Prosecutor v Serushago*, Public Redacted Version of Decision of the President on the Early Release of Omar Serushago, MICT-12-28-ES, 13 December 2012, para. 17.

48 *Prosecutor v Bisengimana,* Decision on the Early Release Request of Paul Bisengimana, MICT-12–07, 11 December 2012, para. 21; *Prosecutor v Serushago*, Public Redacted Version of Decision of the President on the Early Release of Omar Serushago, MICT-12-28-ES, 13 December 2012, para. 18.

49 *Prosecutor v Jelisić*, Public Redacted Version of 22 May 2017 Decision of the President on Recognition of Commutation of Sentence, Remission of Sentence and Early Release of Goran Jelisić, MICT-14-63-ES, 11 August 2017, para. 58.

50 *Prosecutor v Ntawukukikyayo*, Decision of the President on the Early Release of Dominique Ntawukulilyayo, MICT-13-34-ES, 8 July 2016, paras 36–37; *Prosecutor v Semanza*, Public Redacted Version of the Decision of the President on the Early Release of Laurent Semanza, MICT-13-36-ES, 9 June 2016, paras 36–37; *Prosecutor v Lukić*, Decision of the President on the Early Release of Sreten Lukić, MICT-14-67-ES.4, 17 September 2018, para. 37.

2.2 Indeterminate Sentences

The ICTY, ICTR and MICT were all permitted by their statutes to impose life sentences.[51] And indeed, a significant number of life sentences were imposed. As with determinate sentences, the statutes and rules did not set a temporal point for release eligibility, referring only to notification from enforcing states. The adoption of the two-thirds rule for determinate sentences did not solve the issue. As Van Zyl Smit observes, 'no logical assumptions can be made about what is 2/3 of a human life'.[52] The lack of a temporal threshold for consideration for release is particularly problematic in the context of life sentences for international prisoners, given the wide disparity of minimum terms and means by which prisoners serving such sentences can become eligible for parole and release under domestic law. Scholarly analysis reveals the substantial differences that emerge from the domestic law of enforcing states even within Europe: prisoners serving life sentences can become eligible for release after 10 years in Belgium, 15 years in Austria, 26 years in Poland, and 30 years in Italy.[53] The domestic law of other enforcing states, such as Mali and Benin, does not provide mechanisms that enable life prisoners to apply for parole or early release and rely instead on applications for executive pardon that are rarely granted.[54] Szydło notes that this has detrimental consequences for a release system dependent on eligibility notification by the enforcing state.[55] Reliance on domestic eligibility requirements would also create significant disparities between international prisoners serving determinate and indeterminate sentences. For example, an international prisoner sentenced to life imprisonment serving their sentence in Germany would become eligible

---

[51] Art. 24(1) ICTYSt; Art. 23(1) ICTRSt; Art 22(1) MICTSt.

[52] Dirk van Zyl Smit, 'Determinate and indeterminate sentences of imprisonment in international criminal justice' in R. Mulgrew and D. Abels (eds) *Research Handbook on the International Penal System* (Edward Elgar Publishing, 2016) 80–101 at 92.

[53] See Frieder Dünkel, Dirk van Zyl Smit and Nicola Padfield, 'Concluding Thoughts' in Nicola Padfield, Dirk van Zyl Smit and Frieder Dünkel, *Release from Prison: European Policy and Practice* (Cullompton: Willan Publishing, 2010) 395–444 at 408, 420; Van Zyl Smit, note 52 at 92.

[54] Marek Szydło, 'Reduction of Life Sentences Imposed by International Criminal Tribunals after the Galić Decision: Is There Need for Further Improvement?' (2015) 13 *JICJ* 1099–1120 at 1100, 1108 citing Penal Code of Mali, Law No. 01–079 of 20 August 2001; Penal Code of Benin, known as Code Bouvenet, Decree of 6 May 1877, as amended and Clemency Law of Mali, No. 82-117/AN-RM, 23 December 1982; Art 130 of the Constitution of Benin.

[55] Ibid at 1100, 1108.

for consideration for release under national law after serving 15 years.[56] This means they would become eligible for release under domestic law before an international prisoner serving a determinate sentence over 23 years would if serving their sentence elsewhere.[57]

The question of eligibility for prisoners serving indeterminate sentences was addressed for the first time by President Meron at the MICT in *Galić* in June 2015. From the outset, Meron clarified that, despite the lack of explicit guidance in the statutes or rules, persons sentenced to life imprisonment by the ICTY, ICTR and MICT were eligible for consideration for early release.[58] This decision was supported by the fact that the statutory grant of power to the President to order release was not restricted to a particular type of sentence, and that jurisprudence from the ICTY and ICTR implied the possibility of release by granting credit for time served by those sentenced to life imprisonment with recognition of the potential impact on future release decisions.[59] President Meron also noted that the emphasis placed on rehabilitation and reintegration by international penal standards (the Nelson Mandela Rules, International Covenant on Civil and Political Rights) and decisions of the Grand Chamber of the European Court of Human Rights (ECtHR)[60] would be 'rendered meaningless if a prisoner is not afforded the possibility of having his sentence reviewed'.[61] The principle of equality was also invoked to support this decision; this principle would be violated if persons sentenced to life imprisonment were 'denied, in a blanket fashion, the possibility of review of their sentences and the prospect of release available to those who received determinate sentences'.[62]

---

56 *Prosecutor v Galić*, Public Redacted, Reasons for the President's Decision to Deny the Early Release of Stanislav Galić and Decision on Prosecution Motion, MICT-14-83-ES, 23 June 2015, para. 13.

57 R. Mulgrew, *Towards the Development of the International Penal System* (CUP: Cambridge, 2013) at 59.

58 Reasons for the President's Decision to Deny the Early Release of Stanislav Galić and Decision on Prosecution Motion, MICT-14-83-ES, 23 June 2015, paras 18–19, 24.

59 Ibid at paras 20–21.

60 Citing *Vinter and Others v UK*, 9 July 2013 paras 110–119, and para. 114 in footnote 38: 'indeed there is also now clear support in European and international law for the principle that all prisoners, including those serving life sentences, be offered the possibility of rehabilitation and the prospect of release if that rehabilitation is achieved'.

61 Reasons for the President's Decision to Deny the Early Release of Stanislav Galić and Decision on Prosecution Motion, MICT-14-83-ES, 23 June 2015, para. 22.

62 Ibid, para. 23.

The principle of equality would also guide his determination of the more challenging question of *when* they would become eligible for release and specifically how he could 'apply the existing two-thirds framework of the Mechanism to cases involving sentences of life imprisonment'.[63] He accepted the Prosecutor's suggestion of adopting a hypothetical fixed-term sentence reflecting a term greater than the highest determinate sentence imposed by the UN tribunals to reflect the qualitative difference of a life sentence and uphold the principle of gradation in sentencing.[64] He did not accept the Prosecutor's suggestion of adopting a term meaningfully longer than 52 years, as this was based on reference to SCSL sentencing practice.[65] The statutory bar on the imposition of indeterminate sentences[66] had impacted on the length of the sentence imposed by the SCSL.[67] As the ICC barred consideration of applications for release from life-sentenced prisoners prior to 25 years,[68] its law and practice provided limited guidance: ICC review occurred at a 'higher ratio' of five-sixths of the maximum determinate sentence, and the MICT could consider direct petitions from prisoners at any time.[69]

While the Grand Chamber of the ECtHR supported mandatory review after no more than 25 years (*Vinter v UK*), President Meron felt this should be considered in the context of the margin of appreciation states had to set their own systems and the wide range of practice within European domestic systems.[70] Without international consensus or consistent national practice, he concluded there was no customary legal norm on a temporal eligibility threshold for release for life prisoners.[71] Consequently, 'the most relevant and principled basis' for a temporal threshold was the sentencing practice of the UN Tribunals as this represented the sentences imposed on similarly situated prisoners.[72] This approach would ensure equality and fairness among prisoners

---

63 Ibid, para. 29.

64 Ibid, paras 26, 29.

65 Ibid, para. 26.

66 Art. 19(1) SCSLSt.

67 Reasons for the President's Decision to Deny the Early Release of Stanislav Galić and Decision on Prosecution Motion, MICT-14-83-ES, 23 June 2015, para. 30.

68 Art. 110(3) ICCSt.

69 Reasons for the President's Decision to Deny the Early Release of Stanislav Galić and Decision on Prosecution Motion, MICT-14-83-ES, 23 June 2015, para. 31.

70 *Prosecutor v Galić*, Public Redacted, Reasons for the President's Decision to Deny the Early Release of Stanislav Galić and Decision on Prosecution Motion, MICT-14-83-ES, 23 June 2015, para. 32.

71 Ibid.

72 Ibid, para. 33.

supervised by the MICT as well as ensuring the coherence and consistency of the Mechanism's legal regime.[73]

President Meron therefore decided that a life sentence would be treated (for release purposes) as equivalent to the longest sentence imposed by a UN Tribunal at that point – 45 years.[74] Using this hypothetical baseline, prisoners would only become eligible for release when they had served *at least* 30 years of their life sentence.[75] This hypothetically equivalent sentence was fixed and would not change even if a longer determinate sentence was imposed by a UN Tribunal at a later stage. This approach was necessary to uphold the interests of justice, the principles of legal certainty, equality and fairness, and the legitimate expectations of the prisoner and the enforcing state.[76] Any equality issues created by the imposition of a longer sentence of 45 years would have to be considered at a later point.[77] As with determinate sentences, this threshold did not create an entitlement to release, only an entitlement to a review, and release prior to this two-thirds point would only occur in exceptional circumstances such as extraordinary cooperation with the Prosecutor and humanitarian emergencies.[78]

The determination of a fixed hypothetical equivalent sentence did not, however, provide the certainty or equality that the two-thirds rule provides for prisoners serving determinate sentences: the 'extent to which the life sentence will be considered to exceed the fixed term sentence of 45 years' for release purposes will be considered 'on a case-by-case basis'.[79] As Szydło highlights, the uncertainty around what more than 30 years requires means that there was still no single eligibility threshold for life prisoners supervised by the MICT, and it remained unclear at what point in the sentence this individual eligibility would be determined.[80] It seemed that this eligibility will only be determined following an application for release to the President. In *Beara,* this specific point was not considered: early release was denied, inter alia, due to the fact that only 13 years of the sentence had been served, and conditional release was granted instead.[81]

---

73 Ibid, para. 33.
74 Ibid, para. 35.
75 Ibid, para. 36.
76 Ibid, paras 37–38.
77 Ibid, para. 38.
78 Ibid, para. 39.
79 Ibid, para. 35.
80 Szydło, note 54 at 1111–1112, 1116–1117.
81 *Prosecutor v Beara*, Public Redacted Version of the 7 February 2017 Decision of the President on the Early Release of Ljubiša Beara, MICT-15-85-ES.3, 16 June 2017, paras 26–27.

3. FACTORS CONSIDERED IN THE DETERMINATION OF THE APPROPRIATENESS OF EARLY RELEASE

The statutes, rules and practice directions set out the factors considered by Presidents of the UN Tribunals when making release decisions. The statutory direction that decisions should be made in the 'interests of justice and based on general principles of law'[82] provided little concrete guidance. The Rules provide a checklist of four factors that should be discussed in release decisions: the gravity of crimes, the treatment of similarly situated persons, the demonstration of rehabilitation, and any substantial cooperation with the Prosecutor.[83] These regulatory lists were not exhaustive, and practice directions confirmed that the President may consider any other information deemed relevant.[84] The main additional factor that was considered was humanitarian considerations. This section analyses the jurisprudential interpretation and application of these factors at each UN tribunal.

3.1 ICTY

Despite the fact that *gravity* was an explicit factor to be considered by Presidents, early release was regularly granted 'notwithstanding' the high gravity of the crimes committed.[85] Even in decisions that discussed the observations of trial and appeals chambers in relation to the gravity of the crimes applicants were convicted of, and it was considered that gravity was a factor weighing against release,[86] early release was still granted.[87] The only time gravity appeared to act as a determinative factor militating against release were cases in which the

[82] Article 28 ICTY St; Article 27 ICTR St; Article 26 MICTSt.

[83] Rule 125 ICTY RPE; Rule 126 ICTR RPE; Rule 151 MICT RPE.

[84] See para. 8 ICTY PDER; para. 9 MICT PDER.

[85] See *Prosecutor v Tadić*, Decision of the President on the Application for Pardon or Commutatino of Sentence of Duśko Tadić, IT-94-1-ES, 17 July 2008, para. 17; *Prosecutor v Banović*, Decision of the President on Commutation of Sentence, IT-02-65/1-ES, 3 September 2008, para. 15; *Prosecutor v Plavšic*, Public Redacted Decision of the President on the Application for Pardon or Commutation of Sentence of Mrs Biljana Plavšić, IT-00-39& 40/1-ES, 14 September 2009, para. 10; ICTY *Manual of Developed Practice*, para. 48 at 162.

[86] *Prosecutor v Rajić*, Decision of President on Early Release of Ivica Rajić, IT-95-12-ES, 22 August 2011, paras 13–16.

[87] See *Prosecutor v Simić*, Decision of the President on Early Release of Blagoje Simić, IT-95-9-ES, 15 February 2011.

convicted person had not yet served two-thirds of their sentence.[88] The *treatment of similarly-situated persons* factor was interpreted and applied as a prerequisite and standard temporal eligibility threshold to ensure equal treatment of prisoners by requiring that they serve two-thirds of their sentence before they became eligible for early release.

The President was required, however, to form an opinion on whether prisoners had demonstrated signs of *rehabilitation*. ICTY decisions show that Presidents considered a wide range of information and elements under this factor including behaviour in detention, participation in work, education and activities, relations with staff and prisoners, expressions of remorse, acknowledgements of responsibility, the prisoner's psychological condition, risk of recidivism, and ability to reintegrate into society upon release.[89] With regards

---

[88] See *Prosecutor v Kordić*, Decision of President on Application for Pardon or Commutation of Sentence of Dario Kordić, IT-95-14/2-ES, 13 May 2010, para. 23; *Prosecutor v Krajišnik*, Decision of the President on Early Release of Momčilo Krajišnik, IT-00-39-ES, 26 July 2010, paras 23–24; *Prosecutor v Žigić*, Decision of President on Early Release of Zoran Žigić, IT-98-30/1-ES, 8 November 2010, paras 12–13; *Prosecutor v Rajić*, Decision of President on Early Release of Ivica Rajić, IT-95-12-ES, 31 January 2011, para. 14; *Prosecutor v Stakić*, Decision of President on Early Release of Milomir Stakić, IT-97-24-ES, 15 July 2011, para. 27; *Prosecutor v Zelenović*, Decision of President on Early Release of Dragan Zelenović, IT-96-23/2-ES, 21 October 2011, para. 32.

[89] See *Prosecutor v Josipović*, Decision of the President on the Application for Pardon or Commutation of Sentence of Drago Josipović, IT-95-16-ES, 30 January 2006, paras 11–12; *Prosecutor v Vuković*, Decision of the President on Commutation of Sentence, IT-96-23 & 23/1-ES, 11 March 2008, paras 4, 6, 11; *Prosecutor v Delić,* Decision on Hazim Delić's Motion for Commutation of Sentence, IT-96-21-ES, 24 June 2008 (Public Redacted 15 July 2008) paras 7, 20; *Prosecutor v Tadić*, Decision of the President on the Application for Pardon or Commutation of Sentence of Duśko Tadić, IT-94-1-ES, 17 July 2008, paras 8, 16; *Prosecutor v Banović*, Decision of the President on Commutation of Sentence, IT-02-65/1-ES, 3 September 2008, paras 6, 8, 12–13; *Prosecutor v Šantić*, Decision of the President on the Application for Pardon or Commutation of Sentence of Vladimir Šantić, IT-9S-16-ES, 16 February 2009, paras 11–12; Decision of the President on the Application for Pardon or Commutation of Sentence of Milorad Krnojelac, IT-97-25-ES, 9 July 2009, para. 20; *Prosecutor v Plavšic*, Public Redacted Decision of the President on the Application for Pardon or Commutation of Sentence of Mrs Biljana Plavšić, IT-00-39& 40/1-ES, 14 September 2009, paras 8, 9; *Prosecutor v Vasiljević*, Public Redacted Version of Decision of President on Application for Pardon or Commutation of Sentence of Mitar Vasiljević, IT-98-32-ES, 12 March 2010, para. 21; *Prosecutor v Radić*, Decision of President on Application for Pardon or Commutation of Sentence of Mlado Radić, IT-98-30/1-ES, 23 April 2010, para. 18; *Prosecutor v Kordić*, Decision of President on Application for Pardon or

to *cooperation with the Prosecutor*, testimony at the ICTY, other international or domestic trials, and active cooperation with the Prosecutor were held to be factors in favour of early release.[90] If the convicted person merely made himself or herself available to the Prosecutor or expressed a willingness to testify, such cooperation was considered a neutral factor in early release decisions.[91]

In addition to the four factors listed in Rule 125, ICTY Presidents were also willing to consider other information and issues they deemed relevant.[92] This included media material and information provided by third parties,[93] the suffering of the prisoner's family due to their loved one's conviction and imprisonment,[94] the physical and mental health of the prisoner, and the

---

Commutation of Sentence of Dario Kordić, IT-95-14/2-ES, 13 May 2010, paras 19–20; *Prosecutor v Krajišnik*, Decision of the President on Early Release of Momčilo Krajišnik, IT-00-39-ES, 26 July 2010, paras 21, 23; *Prosecutor v Rajić*, Decision of President on Early Release of Ivica Rajić, IT-95-12-ES, 31 January 2011, paras 18–19; Prosecutor v Mrd*a*, Public Redacted Version of Decision of President on Early Release of Darko Mrda, IT-02-59-ES, 18 December 2023, paras 23–25; *Prosecutor v Simić*, Decision of the President on Early Release of Blagoje Simić, IT-95-9-ES, 15 February 2011; *Prosecutor v Šljivančanin*, Decision of President on Early Release of Veselin Šljivančanin, IT-95-13/1-ES, 5 July 2011, paras 22, 24–25, 28–29; *Prosecutor v Stakić*, Decision of President on Early Release of Milomir Stakić, IT-97-24-ES, 15 July 2011,paras 29, 30, 32, 33; *Prosecutor v Zelenović*, Decision of President on Early Release of Dragan Zelenović, IT-96-23/2-ES, 21 October 2011, paras 22, 27, 29.

90 See *Prosecutor v Banović*, Decision of the President on Commutation of Sentence, IT-02-65/1-ES, 3 September 2008, para. 14; *Prosecutor v Šantić*, Decision of the President on the Application for Pardon or Commutation of Sentence of Vladimir Šantić, IT-9S-16-ES, 16 February 2009, para. 13; *Prosecutor v Plavšic*, Public Redacted Decision of the President on the Application for Pardon or Commutation of Sentence of Mrs Biljana Plavšić, IT-00-39& 40/1-ES, 14 September 2009, para. 12; ICTY *Manual of Developed Practices*, para. 51 at 162.

91 *Prosecutor v Josipović*, Decision of the President on the Application for Pardon or Commutation of Sentence of Drago Josipović, IT-95-16-ES, 30 January 2006, para. 10; *Prosecutor v Strugar*, Decision of the President on the Application for Pardon or Commutation of Sentence of Pavle Strugar, IT-01-42-ES, 16 January 2009, para. 13.

92 Para. 8 ICTY PDER.

93 *Prosecutor v Krajišnik*, Decision of the President on Early Release of Momčilo Krajišnik, IT-00-39-ES, 26 July 2010, para. 22; *Prosecutor v Bala*, Decision on Application of Haradin Bala for Sentence Remission, IT-03-66-ES, 15 October 2010, paras 23–24.

94 *Prosecutor v Delić*, Decision on Hazim Delić's Motion for Commutation of Sentence, IT-96-21-ES, 24 June 2008 (Public Redacted 15 July 2008) para. 21.

adequacy of medical care.[95] Age, by itself, and time spent in isolation due to harassment were not, however, considered pertinent to rehabilitation assessments.[96]

3.2 ICTR

Though the *gravity* of crimes was cited in early ICTR decisions not to grant early release,[97] later decisions stated that the high gravity of crimes would not *per se* bar consideration of release if it was otherwise appropriate.[98] In applying the *treatment of similarly situated persons* factor, ICTR Presidents did not feel bound by the ICTY's two-thirds practice, and in the few cases where early release was granted, a three-quarters threshold was considered more appropriate for persons convicted of genocide-related offences.[99] In relation to *rehabilitation*, factors previously considered in mitigation (surrender, guilty pleas, confessions, remorse, acknowledgment of responsibility) were considered to be positive factors,[100] as was good behaviour (during trial and in detention) and

---

[95] See Decision of the President on the Application for Pardon or Commutation of Sentence of Milorad Krnojelac, IT-97-25-ES, 9 July 2009, para. 20; *Prosecutor v Plavšic,* Public Redacted Decision of the President on the Application for Pardon or Commutation of Sentence of Mrs Biljana Plavšić, IT-00-39& 40/1-ES, 14 September 2009, para. 11; *Prosecutor v Radić,* Decision of President on Application for Pardon or Commutation of Sentence of Mlado Radić, IT-98-30/1-ES, 23 April 2010, para. 19.

[96] *Prosecutor v Radić,* Decision of President on Application for Pardon or Commutation of Sentence of Mlado Radić, IT-98-30/1-ES, 23 April 2010, para. 19; *Prosecutor v Krajišnik,* Decision of the President on Early Release of Momčilo Krajišnik, IT-00-39-ES, 26 July 2010, para. 22.

[97] See *Prosecutor v Serushago,* Decision of the President on the Application for Early Release of Omar Serushago, ICTR-98-39-S, 12 May 2005.

[98] *Prosecutor v Bagaragaza,* Decision on the Early Release of Michel Bagaragaza, ICTR-05-86-S, 24 October 2011, para. 7; *Prosecutor v Rugambara,* Decision on the Early Release Request of Juvénal Rugambarara, ICTR-00-59, 8 February 2012; *Prosecutor v Muvunyi,* Decision on the Early Release of Tharcisse Muvunyi, ICTR-00-055A-T, 6 March 2012, para. 9.

[99] *Prosecutor v Bagaragaza,* Decision on the Early Release of Michel Bagaragaza, ICTR-05-86-S, 24 October 2011, paras 8–10; *Prosecutor v Rugambara,* Decision on the Early Release Request of Juvénal Rugambarara, ICTR-00-59, 8 February 2012, para. 11; *Prosecutor v Muvunyi,* Decision on the Early Release of Tharcisse Muvunyi, ICTR-00-055A-T, 6 March 2012, para. 11.

[100] *Prosecutor v Bagaragaza,* Decision on the Early Release of Michel Bagaragaza, ICTR-05-86-S, 24 October 2011, paras 5-6, 11–12; *Prosecutor v*

reintegration potential.[101] The overriding consideration in the first two release decisions appeared to have been the significant value attached to the prisoners' voluntary, substantial and long-term *cooperation with the Prosecutor.*[102] This is in stark contrast to the first application for early release, when President Møse declined to consider the applicant's cooperation with the Prosecutor, voluntary surrender and guilty plea as they had already been considered as mitigating factors during sentencing.[103]

3.3 MICT

Discussions of *gravity* in MICT release decisions recalled the details of the scale of specific crimes, the applicants' roles in and liability for such crimes, the impact the crimes had on victims, and any particular vulnerabilities of the victims.[104] In every case, President Meron noted that the (very) high gravity

---

Rugambara, Decision on the Early Release Request of Juvénal Rugambarara, ICTR-00-59, 8 February 2012, para. 13.

101 *Prosecutor v Bagaragaza*, Decision on the Early Release of Michel Bagaragaza, ICTR-05-86-S, 24 October 2011, paras 11–12; *Prosecutor v Rugambara*, Decision on the Early Release Request of Juvénal Rugambarara, ICTR-00-59, 8 February 2012, paras 13–15; *Prosecutor v Muvunyi,* Decision on the Early Release of Tharcisse Muvunyi, ICTR-00-055A-T, 6 March 2012, para. 6.

102 *Prosecutor v Bagaragaza*, Decision on the Early Release of Michel Bagaragaza, ICTR-05-86-S, 24 October 2011, para. 13; *Prosecutor v Rugambara*, Decision on the Early Release Request of Juvénal Rugambarara, ICTR-00-59, 8 February 2012, paras 10, 13.

103 *Prosecutor v Serushago*, Decision of the President on the Application for Early Release of Omar Serushago, ICTR-98-39-S, 12 May 2005.

104 *Prosecutor v Galić*, Public Redacted, Reasons for the President's Decision to Deny the Early Release of Stanislav Galić and Decision on Prosecution Motion, MICT-14-83-ES, 23 June 2015, paras 14–15; *Prosecutor v Češić*, Public Redacted Version of the 30 April 2014 Decision of the President on the Early Release of Ranko Češić, MICT-14-66-ES, 28 May 2014, paras 13–14; *Prosecutor v Munyakazi*, Public Redacted Version of the 22 July 2015 Decision of the President on the Early Release of Youssof Munyakazi, MICT-12-18-ES.1, 22 July 2015, para. 12; *Prosecutor v Nikolić*, Public Redacted Version of the 20 July 2015 Decision of the President on the Application for Early Release or Other Relief of Drago Nikolić, MICT-15-85-ES.4, 13 October 2015, para. 16; *Prosecutor v Nikolić*, Public Redacted Version of the 14 March 2014 Decision on the Early Release of Momir Nikolić, MICT-14-65-ES, 12 October 2015, paras 14–15; *Prosecutor v Šainović*, Public Redacted Version of the 10 July 2015 Decision of the President on the Early Release of Nikola, MICT-14-67-ES.1, 27 August 2015, para. 14; *Prosecutor v Zelenović*, Public Redacted Version of the 28 August 2015 Decision of the President on the Early Release of Dragan Zelenović, MICT-15-89-ES, 18

of the applicants' crimes militated against the grant of release.[105] In *Jelisić*,

September 2015, para. 12; *Prosecutor v Žigić*, Public Redacted Version of the 10 November 2014 Decision of the President on the Early Release of Zoran Žigić, MICT-14-81-ES.1, 23 December 2014, para. 13; *Prosecutor v Miletić*, Decision of the President on the Early Release of Miletić, MICT-15-85-ES.5, 23 October 2018, paras 27–29; *Prosecutor v Kunarac*, Public Redacted Decision of the President on the Early Release of Dragoljub Kunarac, MICT-15-88-ES.1, 2 February 2017, paras 18–19; *Prosecutor v Borovčanin*, Public Redacted Version of the 14 July 2016 Decision of the President on the Early Release of Ljubomir Borovčanin, MICT-15-85-ES.6, 2 August 2016, para. 15; *Prosecutor v Ntawukukikyayo*, Decision of the President on the Early Release of Dominique Ntawukulilyayo, MICT-13-34-ES, 8 July 2016, paras 16–17; *Prosecutor v Semanza*, Public Redacted Version of the Decision of the President on the Early Release of Laurent Semanza, MICT-13-36-ES, 9 June 2016, paras 14–15; *Prosecutor v Ljubiša Beara*, Public Redacted Version of the 7 February 2017 Decision of the President on the Early Release of Ljubiša Beara, MICT-15-85-ES.3, 16 June 2017, para. 20.

105 *Prosecutor v Bisengimana,* Decision on the Early Release Request of Paul Bisengimana, MICT-12-07, 11 December 2012, para. 14; *Prosecutor v Serusahago*, Public Redacted Version of Decision of the President on the Early Release of Omar Serushago, MICT-12-28-ES, 13 December 2012, para. 15; *Prosecutor v Galić*, Public Redacted, Reasons for the President's Decision to Deny the Early Release of Stanislav Galić and Decision on Prosecution Motion, MICT-14-83-ES, 23 June 2015, para. 17; *Prosecutor v Češić*, Public Redacted Version of the 30 April 2014 Decision of the President on the Early Release of Ranko Češić, MICT-14-66-ES, 28 May 2014, para. 15; *Prosecutor v Munyakazi*, Public Redacted Version of the 22 July 2015 Decision of the President on the Early Release of Youssof Munyakazi, MICT-12-18-ES.1, 22.07.2015, para. 13; *Prosecutor v Nikolić*, Public Redacted Version of the 20 July 2015 Decision of the President on the Application for Early Release or Other Relief of Drago Nikolić, MICT-15-85-ES.4, 13 October 2015, para. 17; *Prosecutor v Nikolić*, Public Redacted Version of the 14 March 2014 Decision on the Early Release of Momir Nikolić, MICT-14-65-ES, 12 October 2015, para. 16; *Prosecutor v Šainović*, Public Redacted Version of the 10 July 2015 Decision of the President on the Early Release of Nikola Šainović, MICT-14-67-ES.1, 27 August 2015, para. 16; *Prosecutor v Zelenović*, Public Redacted Version of the 28 August 2015 Decision of the President on the Early Release of Dragan Zelenović, MICT-15-89-ES, 18 September 2015, para. 13; *Prosecutor v Žigić*, Public Redacted Version of the 10 November 2014 Decision of the President on the Early Release of Zoran Žigić, MICT-14-81-ES.1, 23 December 2014, para. 14; *Prosecutor v Kunarac*, Public Redacted Decision of the President on the Early Release of Dragoljub Kunarac, MICT-15-88-ES.1, 2 February 2017, para 20; *Prosecutor v Miletić*, Decision of the President on the Early Release of Radivoje Miletić, MICT-15-85-ES.5, 23 October 2018, para. 30; *Prosecutor v Borovčanin*, Public Redacted Version of the 14 July 2016 Decision of the President on the Early Release of Ljubomir Borovčanin, MICT-15-85-ES.6, 2 August 2016,

for example, the bestial and sadistic nature of the crimes and his profound contempt for the right to life weighed 'strongly' against early release.[106] The negative impact of the gravity of the crimes on the decision to grant release remained even in cases that noted numerous acquittals and the reversal of convictions on appeal[107] and findings of the limited involvement of the applicant in the crimes, the pursuit of justifiable military objectives, and actions to save the lives of thousands of others.[108]

As stated above, President Meron interpreted the *treatment of similarly situated prisoners* factor to mean that all convicted persons supervised by the MICT would become eligible for early release after serving two-thirds of their sentence, irrespective of the domestic law of their enforcing state or the tribunal that sentenced them.[109] Time spent on provisional release was not counted as time in detention for the purposes of sentence calculation,[110] including time

---

para. 16; *Prosecutor v Ntawukukikyayo*, Decision of the President on the Early Release of Dominique Ntawukulilyayo, MICT-13-34-ES, 8 July 2016, para. 18; *Prosecutor v Semanza*, Public Redacted Version of the Decision of the President on the Early Release of Laurent Semanza, MICT-13-36-ES, 9 June 2016, para. 16; *Prosecutor v Nteziryayo*, Public Redacted, Decision of the President on the Early Release of Alphonse Nteziryayo, MICT-15-90, 9 March 2016, paras 13–14; *Prosecutor v Lazaerić*, Public Redacted Version of the 7 September 2015 Decision of the President on the Early Release of Vladimir Lazarević, MICT-14-67-ES.3, 3 December 2015, para. 12; *Prosecutor v Šainović*, Public Redacted version of the 10 July 2015 Decision of the President on the Early Release of Nikola Šainović, MICT-14-67-ES.1, 27 August 2015, para. 16; *Prosecutor v Beara*, Public Redacted Version of the 7 February 2017 Decision of the President on the Early Release of Ljubiša Beara, MICT-15-85-ES.3, 16 June 2017, para. 21.

[106] *Prosecutor v Jelisić*, Public Redacted Version of the 22 May 2017 Decision of the President on Recognition of Commutation of Sentence, Remission of Sentence and Early Release of Goran Jelisić, MICT-14-63-ES, 11 August 2017, para. 32.

[107] *Prosecutor v Lukić*, Decision of the President on the Early Release of Sreten Lukić, MICT-14-67-ES.4, 17 September 2018, paras 23–24.

[108] *Prosecutor v Pandurević*, Public Redacted Version of the 9 April 2015 Decision of the President on the Early Release of Vinko Pandurević, MICT-15-85-ES.1, 10 April 2015, paras 13–15, 18–19.

[109] *Prosecutor v Bisengimana*, Decision on the Early Release Request of Paul Bisengimana, MICT-12-07, 11 December 2012, para. 22; *Prosecutor v Serusahago*, Public Redacted Version of Decision of the President on the Early Release of Omar Serushago, MICT-12-28-ES, 13 December 2012, para. 19.

[110] *Prosecutor v Miletić*, Decision of the President on the Early Release of Radivoje Miletić, MICT-15-85-ES.5, 23 October 2018, para. 24.

spent in hospital under police surveillance.[111] The creation of a temporal eligibility threshold did not prohibit enforcing states from notifying the MICT if and when convicted persons became eligible for pardon, commutation of sentence, or early release under domestic law before the two-thirds point; though early release would only be granted in exceptional circumstances before this point, such as extraordinary cooperation with the Prosecution or humanitarian emergencies if other factors in favour of early release also existed.[112] This temporal requirement was applied in all cases, with the caveat that service of this period resulted in mere eligibility and not entitlement to release: decisions were a matter of presidential discretion to be made after consideration of the totality of circumstances in each case.[113] Decisions usually stated the date at which the convicted person would have served two-thirds of the sentence under this factor: if the date had been reached, either nothing else was

---

111 *Prosecutor v Lazaerić*, Public Redacted Version of the 7 September 2015 Decision of the President on the Early Release of Vladimir Lazarević, MICT-14-67-ES.3, 3 December 2015, para. 16.

112 *Prosecutor v Nikolić*, Public Redacted Version of the 20 July 2015 Decision of the President on the Application for Early Release or Other Relief of Drago Nikolić, MICT-15-85-ES.4, 13 October 2015, para. 21; *Prosecutor v Lukić*, Decision of the President on the Early Release of Sreten Lukić, MICT-14-67-ES.4, 17 September 2018, paras 16, 18; *Prosecutor v Pušić*, Public Redacted Version of the 20 April 2018 Decision of the President on the Early Release of Berislav Pušić, MICT-17-112-ES.1, 24 April 2018, para. 34.

113 *Prosecutor v Češić*, Public Redacted Version of the 30 April 2014 Decision of the President on the Early Release of Ranko Češić, MICT-14-66-ES, 28 May 2014, paras 16–17; *Prosecutor v Munyakazi*, Public Redacted Version of the 22 July 2015 Decision of the President on the Early Release of Youssof Munyakazi, MICT-12-18-ES.1, 22.07.2015, para. 14; *Prosecutor v Nikolić*, Public Redacted Version of the 20 July 2015 Decision of the President on the Application for Early Release or Other Relief of Drago Nikolić, MICT-15-85-ES.4, 13 October 2015, paras 19–20; *Prosecutor v Nikolić*, Public Redacted Version of the 14 March 2014 Decision on the Early Release of Momir Nikolić, MICT-14-65-ES, 12 October 2015, para. 18; *Prosecutor v Miletić*, Decision of the President on the Early Release of Radivoje Miletić, MICT-15-85-ES.5, 23 October 2018, para. 23; *Prosecutor v Lukić*, Decision of the President on the Early Release of Sreten Lukić, MICT-14-67-ES.4, 17 September 2018, para. 17; *Prosecutor v Pušić*, Public Redacted Version of the 20 April 2018 Decision of the President on the Early Release of Berislav Pušić, MICT-17-112-ES.1, 24 April 2018, para. 35; *Prosecutor v Nteziryayo*, Public Redacted, Decision of the President on the Early Release of Alphonse Nteziryayo, MICT-15-90, 9 March 2016, para. 16; *Prosecutor v Lazaerić*, Public Redacted Version of the 7 September 2015 Decision of the President on the Early Release of Vladimir Lazarević, MICT-14-67-ES.3, 3 December 2015, paras 14–15.

stated[114] or the decision stated that this weighed in favour of early release.[115] If this date was in the future, it was usually stated that the amount of time served did not weigh in favour of early release.[116] In some decisions, release was granted in advance but would only take effect on the date upon which (or as soon as practicable after) two-thirds of the sentence would be served.[117] As discussed above, this factor was interpreted by President Meron to mean that life prisoners must serve more than 30 years before they become eligible for consideration for release.[118]

---

114 *Prosecutor v Češić*, Public Redacted Version of the 30 April 2014 Decision of the President on the Early Release of Ranko Češić, MICT-14-66-ES, 28 May 2014, para. 18; *Prosecutor v Pandurević*, Public Redacted Version of the 9 April 2015 Decision of the President on the Early Release of Vinko Pandurević, MICT-15-85-ES.1, 10 April 2015, para. 22; *Prosecutor v Žigić*, Public Redacted Version of the 10 November 2014 Decision of the President on the Early Release of Zoran Žigić, MICT-14-81-ES.1, 23 December 2014, para. 17; *Prosecutor v Zelenović*, Public Redacted Version of the 28 August 2015 Decision of the President on the Early Release of Dragan Zelenović, MICT-15-89-ES, 18 September 2015, para. 15.

115 *Prosecutor v Šainović*, Public Redacted Version of the 10 July 2015 Decision of the President on the Early Release of Nikola Šainović, MICT-14-67-ES.1, 27 August 2015, para. 19.

116 *Prosecutor v Munyakazi*, Public Redacted Version of the 22 July 2015 Decision of the President on the Early Release of Youssof Munyakazi, MICT-12-18-ES.1, 22.07.2015, para. 15; *Prosecutor v Nikolić*, Public Redacted Version of the 20 July 2015 Decision of the President on the Application for Early Release or Other Relief of Drago Nikolić, MICT-15-85-ES.4, 13 October 2015, para. 22; *Prosecutor v Nikolić*, Public Redacted Version of the 14 March 2014 Decision on the Early Release of Momir Nikolić, MICT-14-65-ES, 12 October 2015, para. 19; *Prosecutor v Jelisić*, Public Redacted Version of the 22 May 2017 Decision of the President on Recognition of Commutation of Sentence, Remission of Sentence and Early Release of Goran Jelisić, MICT-14-63-ES, 11 August 2017, para. 54; *Prosecutor v Ntawukukikyayo*, Decision of the President on the Early Release of Dominique Ntawukulilyayo, MICT-13-34-ES, 8 July 2016, para. 22; *Prosecutor v Semanza*, Public Redacted Version of the Decision of the President on the Early Release of Laurent Semanza, MICT-13-36-ES, 9 June 2016, para. 20.

117 *Prosecutor v Šainović*, Public Redacted version of the 10 July 2015 Decision of the President on the Early Release of Nikola Šainović, MICT-14-67-ES.1, 27 August 2015, paras 26–27; *Prosecutor v Lazaerić*, Public Redacted Version of the 7 September 2015 Decision of the President on the Early Release of Vladimir Lazarević, MICT-14-67-ES.3, 3 December 2015, paras 28–29.

118 *Prosecutor v Galić*, Public Redacted, Reasons for the President's Decision to Deny the Early Release of Stanislav Galić and Decision on Prosecution Motion, MICT-14-83-ES, 23 June 2015, para. 36; *Prosecutor v Beara*, Public Redacted

The discussion of *rehabilitation* became more detailed over the years, particularly when applicants spent longer periods of time in prisons in enforcing states (rather than international detention centres). President Meron acknowledged reports and recommendations in relation to release from national prison authorities and considered prisoners' views.[119] Behaviour in prison, expressions of remorse or acknowledgement of responsibility, signs of rehabilitation, the prisoner's mental state, potential for successful reintegration after release (in terms of work, family support, etc.), and recidivism risks were important factors in the consideration of rehabilitation.[120] Good behaviour in prison was

---

Version of the 7 February 2017 Decision of the President on the Early Release of Ljubiša Beara, MICT-15-85-ES.3, 16 June 2017, paras 24, 26.

[119] *Prosecutor v Bisengimana,* Decision on the Early Release Request of Paul Bisengimana, MICT-12-07, 11 December 2012, paras 6, 24; *Prosecutor v Serusahago,* Public Redacted Version of Decision of the President on the Early Release of Omar Serushago, MICT-12-28-ES, 13 December 2012, paras 20–21; *Prosecutor v Miletić,* Decision of the President on the Early Release of Radivoje Miletić, MICT-15-85-ES.5, 23 October 2018, para. 32; *Prosecutor v Kunarac,* Public Redacted Decision of the President on the Early Release of Dragoljub Kunarac, MICT-15-88-ES.1, 2 February 2017, para. 42.

[120] *Prosecutor v Bisengimana,* Decision on the Early Release Request of Paul Bisengimana, MICT-12-07, 11 December 2012, para. 25; *Prosecutor v Galić,* Public Redacted, Reasons for the President's Decision to Deny the Early Release of Stanislav Galić and Decision on Prosecution Motion, MICT-14-83-ES, 23 June 2015, paras 41–44; *Prosecutor v Češić,* Public Redacted Version of the 30 April 2014 Decision of the President on the Early Release of Ranko Češić, MICT-14-66-ES, 28 May 2014, paras 19–21; *Prosecutor v Munyakazi,* Public Redacted Version of the 22 July 2015 Decision of the President on the Early Release of Youssof Munyakazi, MICT-12-18-ES.1, 22 July 2015, paras 16–19; *Prosecutor v Nikolić,* Public Redacted Version of the 20 July 2015 Decision of the President on the Application for Early Release or Other Relief of Drago Nikolić, MICT-15-85-ES.4, 13 October 2015, paras 23–24; *Prosecutor v Nikolić,* Public Redacted Version of the 14 March 2014 Decision on the Early Release of Momir Nikolić, MICT-14-65-ES, 12 October 2015, paras 21–23; *Prosecutor v Pandurević,* Public Redacted Version of the 9 April 2015 Decision of the President on the Early Release of Vinko Pandurević, MICT-15-85-ES.1, 10 April 2015, paras 23–25; *Prosecutor v Šainović,* Public Redacted Version of the 10 July 2015 Decision of the President on the Early Release of Nikola Šainović, MICT-14-67-ES.1, 27 August 2015, paras 20–22; *Prosecutor v Zelenović,* Public Redacted Version of the 28 August 2015 Decision of the President on the Early Release of Dragan Zelenović, MICT-15-89-ES, 18 September 2015, paras 16–19; *Prosecutor v Žigić,* Public Redacted Version of the 10 November 2014 Decision of the President on the Early Release of Zoran Žigić, MICT-14-81-ES.1, 23 December 2014, paras 18–19; *Prosecutor v Kunarac,* Public Redacted Decision of the President on the Early Release of

indicated by compliance with rules, participation in the regime, education and training, respectful behaviour towards staff and other prisoners, a lack of aggression or self-harm, and good behaviour during supervised excursions.[121] While some applicants accepted responsibility for their crimes and their role in them,[122] and expressed remorse for their crimes,[123] others referred more

---

Dragoljub Kunarac, MICT-15-88-ES.1, 2 February 2017, para. 53; *Prosecutor v Lukić*, Decision of the President on the Early Release of Sreten Lukić, MICT-14-67-ES.4, 17 September 2018, para. 26; *Prosecutor v Miletić*, Decision of the President on the Early Release of Radivoje Miletić, MICT-15-85-ES.5, 23 October 2018, para. 32; *Prosecutor v Jelisić*, Public Redacted Version of the 22 May 2017 Decision of the President on Recognition of Commutation of Sentence, Remission of Sentence and Early Release of Goran Jelisić, MICT-14-63-ES, 11 August 2017, para. 36; *Prosecutor v Borovčanin*, Public Redacted Version of the 14 July 2016 Decision of the President on the Early Release of Ljubomir Borovčanin, MICT-15-85-ES.6, 2 August 2016, paras 21–22, 24. *Prosecutor v Semanza*, Public Redacted Version of the Decision of the President on the Early Release of Laurent Semanza, MICT-13-36-ES, 9 June 2016, para. 25.

[121] *Prosecutor v Lukić*, Decision of the President on the Early Release of Sreten Lukić, MICT-14-67-ES.4, 17 September 2018, para. 26; *Prosecutor v Miletić*, Decision of the President on the Early Release of Radivoje Miletić, MICT-15-85-ES.5, 23 October 2018, para. 32; *Prosecutor v Pušić*, Public Redacted Version of the 20 April 2018 Decision of the President on the Early Release of Berislav Pušić, MICT-17-112-ES.1, 24 April 2018, para. 38; *Prosecutor v Jelisić*, Public Redacted Version of the 22 May 2017 Decision of the President on Recognition of Commutation of Sentence, Remission of Sentence and Early Release of Goran Jelisić, MICT-14-63-ES, 11 August 2017, paras 34–35; *Prosecutor v Borovčanin*, Public Redacted Version of the 14 July 2016 Decision of the President on the Early Release of Ljubomir Borovčanin, MICT-15-85-ES.6, 2 August 2016, paras 21, 24; *Prosecutor v Ntawukukikyayo*, Decision of the President on the Early Release of Dominique Ntawukulilyayo, MICT-13-34-ES, 8 July 2016, para. 24; *Prosecutor v Lazaerić*, Public Redacted Version of the 7 September 2015 Decision of the President on the Early Release of Vladimir Lazarević, MICT-14-67-ES.3, 3 December 2015, para. 18; *Prosecutor v Šainović*, Public Redacted version of the 10 July 2015 Decision of the President on the Early Release of Nikola Šainović, MICT-14-67-ES.1, 27 August 2015, para. 20.

[122] *Prosecutor v Borovčanin*, Public Redacted Version of the 14 July 2016 Decision of the President on the Early Release of Ljubomir Borovčanin, MICT-15-85-ES.6, 2 August 2016, paras 22–23.

[123] *Prosecutor v Jelisić*, Public Redacted Version of the 22 May 2017 Decision of the President on Recognition of Commutation of Sentence, Remission of Sentence and Early Release of Goran Jelisić, MICT-14-63-ES, 11 August 2017, para. 41.

vaguely to regret for events and the fate of victims in a general sense.[124] Some offered to promote reconciliation[125] or help establish the truth and locate missing remains.[126] There were examples of national prison and psychiatric reports noting that the prisoner had been deemed capable of reintegration into society if released.[127] However, in numerous decisions, President Meron simply referred to good behaviour in prison and the maintenance of contact with family to demonstrate that the applicant was 'capable of reintegrating into society if released'.[128] In one case, compliance with ICTY orders while on provisional release was taken to indicate the ability to reintegrate into society.[129]

The vast majority of MICT decisions stated that the applicant had demonstrated (some) signs of rehabilitation and/or capability for reintegration. Accordingly, this factor nearly always weighed in favour of early release.[130]

---

124 *Prosecutor v Ntawukukikyayo*, Decision of the President on the Early Release of Dominique Ntawukulilyayo, MICT-13-34-ES, 8 July 2016, paras 24–26.

125 Ibid., para. 24; *Prosecutor v Semanza*, Public Redacted Version of the Decision of the President on the Early Release of Laurent Semanza, MICT-13-36-ES, 9 June 2016, para. 24.

126 *Prosecutor v Jelisić*, Public Redacted Version of the 22 May 2017 Decision of the President on Recognition of Commutation of Sentence, Remission of Sentence and Early Release of Goran Jelisić, MICT-14-63-ES, 11 August 2017, para. 41.

127 *Prosecutor v Ntawukukikyayo*, Decision of the President on the Early Release of Dominique Ntawukulilyayo, MICT-13-34-ES, 8 July 2016, para. 27; *Prosecutor v Semanza*, Public Redacted Version of the Decision of the President on the Early Release of Laurent Semanza, MICT-13-36-ES, 9 June 2016, para. 26.

128 *Prosecutor v Miletić*, Decision of the President on the Early Release of Radivoje Miletić, MICT-15-85-ES.5, 23 October 2018, para. 36; *Prosecutor v Lukić*, Decision of the President on the Early Release of Sreten Lukić, MICT-14-67-ES.4, 17 September 2018, para. 28; *Prosecutor v Ljubomir Borovčanin*, Public Redacted Version of the 14 July 2016 Decision of the President on the Early Release of Ljubomir Borovčanin, MICT-15-85-ES.6, 2 August 2016, para. 25; *Prosecutor v Nteziryayo*, Public Redacted, Decision of the President on the Early Release of Alphonse Nteziryayo, MICT-15-90, 9 March 2016, para. 21; *Prosecutor v Šainović*, Public Redacted version of the 10 July 2015 Decision of the President on the Early Release of Nikola Šainović, MICT-14-67-ES.1, 27 August 2015, para. 22; *Prosecutor v Lazaerić*, Public Redacted Version of the 7 September 2015 Decision of the President on the Early Release of Vladimir Lazarević, MICT-14-67-ES.3, 3 December 2015, para. 20.

129 *Prosecutor v Pušić*, Public Redacted Version of the 20 April 2018 Decision of the President on the Early Release of Berislav Pušić, MICT-17-112-ES.1, 24 April 2018, para. 39.

130 *Prosecutor v Galić*, Public Redacted, Reasons for the President's Decision to Deny the Early Release of Stanislav Galić and Decision on Prosecution Motion,

The weight of this factor was stronger in some cases, for example, where an applicant had not appealed the judgment or the sentence, he was considered to have demonstrated 'consistent and sustained' signs of rehabilitation that weighed 'significantly' in favour of release.[131] A finding of signs of rehabilitation occurred even where the prisoner had a 'somewhat ambivalent' attitude

---

MICT-14-83-ES, 23 June 2015, para. 44; *Prosecutor v Češić*, Public Redacted Version of the 30 April 2014 Decision of the President on the Early Release of Ranko Češić, MICT-14-66-ES, 28 May 2014, para. 21; *Prosecutor v Munyakazi*, Public Redacted Version of the 22 July 2015 Decision of the President on the Early Release of Youssof Munyakazi, MICT-12-18-ES.1, 22.07.2015, para. 19; *Prosecutor v Nikolić*, Public Redacted Version of the 20 July 2015 Decision of the President on the Application for Early Release or Other Relief of Drago Nikolić, MICT-15-85-ES.4, 13 October 2015, para. 25; *Prosecutor v Nikolić*, Public Redacted Version of the 14 March 2014 Decision on the Early Release of Momir Nikolić, MICT-14-65-ES, 12 October 2015, para. 24; *Prosecutor v Pandurević*, Public Redacted Version of the 9 April 2015 Decision of the President on the Early Release of Vinko Pandurević, MICT-15-85-ES.1, 10 April 2015, para. 25; *Prosecutor v Šainović*, Public Redacted Version of the 10 July 2015 Decision of the President on the Early Release of Nikola Šainović, MICT-14-67-ES.1, 27 August 2015, para. 22; *Prosecutor v Žigić*, Public Redacted Version of the 10 November 2014 Decision of the President on the Early Release of Zoran Žigić, MICT-14-81-ES.1, 23 December 2014, para. 20; *Prosecutor v Zelenović*, Public Redacted Version of the 28 August 2015 Decision of the President on the Early Release of Dragan Zelenović, MICT-15-89-ES, 18 September 2015, para. 20; *Prosecutor v Miletić*, Decision of the President on the Early Release of Radivoje Miletić, MICT-15-85-ES.5, 23 October 2018, para. 36; *Prosecutor v Lukić*, Decision of the President on the Early Release of Sreten Lukić, MICT-14-67-ES.4, 17 September 2018, para. 28; *Prosecutor v Pušić*, Public Redacted Version of the 20 April 2018 Decision of the President on the Early Release of Berislav Pušić, MICT-17-112-ES.1, 24 April 2018, para. 39; *Prosecutor v Jelisić*, Public Redacted Version of the 22 May 2017 Decision of the President on Recognition of Commutation of Sentence, Remission of Sentence and Early Release of Goran Jelisić, MICT-14-63-ES, 11 August 2017, para. 55; *Prosecutor v Semanza*, Public Redacted Version of the Decision of the President on the Early Release of Laurent Semanza, MICT-13-36-ES, 9 June 2016, para. 26; *Prosecutor v Lazaerić*, Public Redacted Version of the 7 September 2015 Decision of the President on the Early Release of Vladimir Lazarević, MICT-14-67-ES.3, 3 December 2015, para. 20; *Prosecutor v Nteziryayo*, Public Redacted, Decision of the President on the Early Release of Alphonse Nteziryayo, MICT-15-90, 9 March 2016, para. 21.

[131] *Prosecutor v Borovčanin*, Public Redacted Version of the 14 July 2016 Decision of the President on the Early Release of Ljubomir Borovčanin, MICT-15-85-ES.6, 2 August 2016, para. 25.

towards his crimes[132] or the prisoner claimed in the release submission that he had nothing on his conscience and hoped the truth would come out one day.[133]

In a rare break from practice, President Meron denied Kunarac early release after he had served two-thirds of the sentence due to his failure to demonstrate sufficient signs of rehabilitation.[134] The prison authority report described Kunarac as a very demanding prisoner who had been subject to numerous disciplinary proceedings for a 'striking history of breaches and offences' (possession of drugs and phones, conflict with other prisoners).[135] Although his behaviour improved after 2014[136] and his psychiatric report noted that he was very unlikely to commit similar crimes again,[137] Kunarac told the prison authorities that he had not committed the crimes he had been convicted for and explicitly claimed that a woman he was accused of raping had, in fact, raped him.[138] The prison social worker did not support his application for release.[139] President Meron noted that despite some improvements in behaviour, the breaches of prison rules, the denial of responsibility for crimes, and his failure to use his time in prison in a positive manner meant he had failed to demonstrate sufficient signs of rehabilitation.[140] Consequently, early release would be 'premature at this stage'.[141]

In the application of the *cooperation with the Prosecutor* factor, several issues were discussed. The entry of a guilty plea and subsequent cooperation favoured release due to the positive impact they had on the efficient administration of

---

132 *Prosecutor v Zelenović*, Public Redacted Version of the 28 August 2015 Decision of the President on the Early Release of Dragan Zelenović, MICT-15-89-ES, 18 September 2015, para. 18.

133 *Prosecutor v Ntawukukikyayo*, Decision of the President on the Early Release of Dominique Ntawukulilyayo, MICT-13-34-ES, 8 July 2016, para. 27 (release was denied as he hadn't served two-thirds of the sentence).

134 *Prosecutor v Kunarac*, Public Redacted Decision of the President on the Early Release of Dragoljub Kunarac, MICT-15-88-ES.1, 2 February 2017, paras 55, 68, 71.

135 Ibid, paras 25–27.

136 Ibid, para. 33.

137 Ibid, para. 48.

138 Ibid, para. 37.

139 Ibid, para. 42.

140 Ibid, para. 55.

141 Ibid, para. 54. Judge Meron agreed with President Agius that release should be denied again in December 2020, inter alia, on the basis that he had failed to demonstrate sufficient signs of rehabilitation. *Kunarac*, 31 December 2020, see paras 85–87.

justice.[142] Prosecutors objected to this approach on the basis that cooperation was required by plea agreements and it had already been taken into account in mitigation during sentencing.[143] President Meron defended this stance, noting that another significant factor that influences sentencing, namely the gravity of offences, is considered in early release decisions.[144] President Meron reiterated that an accused person is under no obligation to plead guilty or, in the absence of a plea agreement, to cooperate with the Prosecutor, and that consequently, a lack of cooperation is a neutral factor.[145] There has been no engagement with

---

142 *Prosecutor v Bisengimana,* Decision on the Early Release Request of Paul Bisengimana, MICT-12-07, 11 December 2012, paras 30–31; *Prosecutor v Serusahago,* Public Redacted Version of Decision of the President on the Early Release of Omar Serushago, MICT-12-28-ES, 13 December 2012, para. 30; *Prosecutor v Češić,* Public Redacted Version of the 30 April 2014 Decision of the President on the Early Release of Ranko Češić, MICT-14-66-ES, 28 May 2014, para. 24; *Prosecutor v Nikolić,* Public Redacted Version of the 14 March 2014 Decision on the Early Release of Momir Nikolić, MICT-14-65-ES, 12 October 2015, para. 28; *Prosecutor v Zelenović,* Public Redacted Version of the 28 August 2015 Decision of the President on the Early Release of Dragan Zelenović, MICT-15-89-ES, 18 September 2015, para. 21.

143 *Prosecutor v Bisengimana,* Decision on the Early Release Request of Paul Bisengimana, MICT-12-07, 11 December 2012, para. 29; *Prosecutor v Serusahago,* Public Redacted Version of Decision of the President on the Early Release of Omar Serushago, MICT-12-28-ES, 13 December 2012, para. 25; *Prosecutor v Češić,* Public Redacted Version of the 30 April 2014 Decision of the President on the Early Release of Ranko Češić, MICT-14-66-ES, 28 May 2014, para. 22; *Prosecutor v Lukić,* Decision of the President on the Early Release of Sreten Lukić, MICT-14-67-ES.4, 17 September 2018, para. 30; *Prosecutor v Kunarac,* Public Redacted Decision of the President on the Early Release of Dragoljub Kunarac, MICT-15-88-ES.1, 2 February 2017, para. 57; *Prosecutor v Borovčanin,* Public Redacted Version of the 14 July 2016 Decision of the President on the Early Release of Ljubomir Borovčanin, MICT-15-85-ES.6, 2 August 2016, para. 27.

144 *Prosecutor v Šainović,* Public Redacted Version of the 10 July 2015 Decision of the President on the Early Release of Nikola Šainović, MICT-14-67-ES.1, 27 August 2015, para. 25.

145 *Prosecutor v Galić,* Public Redacted, Reasons for the President's Decision to Deny the Early Release of Stanislav Galić and Decision on Prosecution Motion, MICT-14-83-ES, 23 June 2015, para. 47; *Prosecutor v Munyakazi,* Public Redacted Version of the 22 July 2015 Decision of the President on the Early Release of Youssof Munyakazi, MICT-12-18-ES.1, 22.07.2015, para. 21; *Prosecutor v Nikolić,* Public Redacted Version of the 20 July 2015 Decision of the President on the Application for Early Release or Other Relief of Drago Nikolić, MICT-15-85-ES.4, 13 October 2015, para. 28; *Prosecutor v Pandurević,* Public Redacted Version of the 9 April 2015 Decision of the President on the Early Release of

the term 'substantial' used in the rules: it does not seem to act as a threshold. Either cooperation was present, in which case this acted in favour of release, or it was not, in which case it was a neutral factor.

President Meron also took *humanitarian considerations* into account when making release decisions on the basis of paragraph 9 of the Practice Direction. This provided precedent for considering requests for early release on the basis of medical reasons and jurisprudence that determined that a serious illness may make continued detention inappropriate.[146] Information was often heavily redacted, so it was often unclear on which precise (humanitarian or medical) grounds the decision had been taken.[147] Medical reports indicating treatment for illnesses have been considered and appear to have been factors in favour of release.[148] If injuries or illnesses could be managed from prison, they were

---

Vinko Pandurević, MICT-15-85-ES.1, 10 April 2015, para. 28; *Prosecutor v Žigić*, Public Redacted Version of the 10 November 2014 Decision of the President on the Early Release of Zoran Žigić, MICT-14-81-ES.1, 23 December 2014, para. 22; *Prosecutor v Miletić*, Decision of the President on the Early Release of Radivoje Miletić, MICT-15-85-ES.5, 23 October 2018, para. 40; *Prosecutor v Pušić*, Public Redacted Version of the 20 April 2018 Decision of the President on the Early Release of Berislav Pušić, MICT-17-112-ES.1, 24 April 2018, para. 42.

146 *Prosecutor v Nikolić*, Public Redacted Version of the 14 March 2014 Decision on the Early Release of Momir Nikolić, MICT-14-65-ES, 12 October 2015, para. 30; *Prosecutor v Nikolić*, Public Redacted Version of the 20 July 2015 Decision of the President on the Application for Early Release or Other Relief of Drago Nikolić, MICT-15-85-ES.4, 13 October 2015, para. 29; *Prosecutor v Bisengimana*, Decision on the Early Release Request of Paul Bisengimana, MICT-12-07, 11 December 2012, paras 32–35; *Prosecutor v Serusahago*, Public Redacted Version of Decision of the President on the Early Release of Omar Serushago, MICT-12-28-ES, 13 December 2012, para. 31; *Prosecutor v Munyakazi*, Public Redacted Version of the 22 July 2015 Decision of the President on the Early Release of Youssof Munyakazi, MICT-12-18-ES.1, 22 July 2015, para. 22.

147 *Prosecutor v Munyakazi*, Public Redacted Version of the 22 July 2015 Decision of the President on the Early Release of Youssof Munyakazi, MICT-12-18-ES.1, 22 July 2015, para. 23; *Prosecutor v Galić*, Public Redacted, Reasons for the President's Decision to Deny the Early Release of Stanislav Galić and Decision on Prosecution Motion, MICT-14-83-ES, 23 June 2015, paras 48–50; *Prosecutor v Nikolić*, Public Redacted Version of the 14 March 2014 Decision on the Early Release of Momir Nikolić, MICT-14-65-ES, 12 October 2015, paras 31–34; *Prosecutor v Nikolić*, Public Redacted Version of the 20 July 2015 Decision of the President on the Application for Early Release or Other Relief of Drago Nikolić, MICT-15-85-ES.4, 13 October 2015, paras 30–31.

148 *Prosecutor v Bisengimana*, Decision on the Early Release Request of Paul Bisengimana, MICT-12-07, 11 December 2012, para. 33; *Prosecutor v Serusahago*,

not considered serious enough to weigh in favour of release.[149] Likewise, if the applicants' health or age-related conditions were not serious enough to constitute exceptional circumstances, they were considered to be neutral factors.[150] In some situations, illnesses that affected the prisoner's well-being, even though not serious, were ascribed limited weight in favour of release.[151]

Terminally ill prisoners have been released from international and national custody. However, early release was denied.[152] Controversially, President Meron used provisional release to do so in the case of *Dragan Nikolić* and conditional release in the case of *Ljubiša Beara*. These cases are examined in detail in Chapter 9. As both cases involved a grant of release before two-thirds of the sentence had been completed, the dying prisoners were obliged to remain under armed guard at their homes (or in hospital) in Serbia.[153] Given the early stage of his sentence (13 years into a life sentence), Meron also

---

Public Redacted Version of Decision of the President on the Early Release of Omar Serushago, MICT-12-28-ES, 13 December 2012, para. 33.

[149] *Prosecutor v Kunarac*, Public Redacted Decision of the President on the Early Release of Dragoljub Kunarac, MICT-15-88-ES.1, 2 February 2017, para. 67; *Prosecutor v Lukić*, Decision of the President on the Early Release of Sreten Lukić, MICT-14-67-ES.4, 17 September 2018, paras 34–36.

[150] *Prosecutor v Ntawukukikyayo*, Decision of the President on the Early Release of Dominique Ntawukulilyayo, MICT-13-34-ES, 8 July 2016, para. 35; *Prosecutor v Semanza*, Public Redacted Version of the Decision of the President on the Early Release of Laurent Semanza, MICT-13-36-ES, 9 June 2016, para. 35; *Prosecutor v Lazaerić*, Public Redacted Version of the 7 September 2015 Decision of the President on the Early Release of Vladimir Lazarević, MICT-14-67-ES.3, 3 December 2015, para. 27; *Prosecutor v Munyakazi*, Public Redacted Version of the 22 July 2015 Decision of the President on the Early Release of Youssof Munyakazi, MICT-12-18-ES.1, 22 July 2015, para. 24.

[151] *Prosecutor v Nteziryayo*, Public Redacted, Decision of the President on the Early Release of Alphonse Nteziryayo, MICT-15-90, 9 March 2016, para. 27.

[152] *Prosecutor v Nikolić*, Public Redacted Version of the 20 July 2015 Decision of the President on the Application for Early Release or Other Relief of Drago Nikolić, MICT-15-85-ES.4, 13 October 2015, paras 33, 35; *Prosecutor v Beara*, Public Redacted Version of the 7 February 2017 Decision of the President on the Early Release of Ljubiša Beara, MICT-15-85-ES.3, 16 June 2017, paras 48–49.

[153] *Prosecutor v Nikolić*, Public Redacted Version of the 20 July 2015 Decision of the President on the Application for Early Release or Other Relief of Drago Nikolić, MICT-15-85-ES.4, 13 October 2015, para. 44; *Prosecutor v Beara*, Public Redacted Version of the 7 February 2017 Decision of the President on the Early Release of Ljubiša Beara, MICT-15-85-ES.3, 16 June 2017, para. 52(i)(a–d).

required that Beara's abbreviated life expectancy be independently verified by the UN Detention Unit's medical team.[154]

4. PROCEDURE FOR EARLY RELEASE DECISIONS

According to the Tribunals' statutes, the procedure was to be initiated following receipt of a notification of eligibility for release from an enforcing state.[155] Notifications, informing the tribunals about prisoner eligibility for release under domestic law, were communicated directly by national ministries of justice or prison services, or received through the enforcing state's embassies. The notifications were usually accompanied by a range of supporting documentation, including prison reports on the conditions of detention and the behaviour of the prisoner, medical reports, psychological evaluations, psycho-social reports, sentence enforcement plans and (pending) deportation orders.[156] They sometimes contained recommendations on whether the prisoner should be released.[157]

It became apparent that this approach needed to be adapted to permit the initiation of the procedure following the receipt of applications from convicted persons.[158] The change was necessary due to the delay or failure of some

---

[154] *Prosecutor v Beara*, Public Redacted Version of the 7 February 2017 Decision of the President on the Early Release of Ljubiša Beara, MICT-15-85-ES.3, 16 June 2017, para. 36.

[155] Art. 28 ICTYSt; Rule 123 ICTY RPE; para. 1 ICTY PDER; Art. 2 ICTRSt; Rule 124 ICTR RPE; Article 26 MICTSt; Rule 149 MICT RPE; para. 2 MICT PDER.

[156] See *Prosecutor v Munyakazi*, Public Redacted Version of the 22 July 2015 Decision of the President on the Early Release of Youssof Munyakazi, MICT-12-18-ES.1, 22 July 2015, para. 4; *Prosecutor v Nikolić*, Public Redacted Version of the 14 March 2014 Decision on the Early Release of Momir Nikolić, MICT-14-65-ES, 12 October 2015, para. 5; *Prosecutor v Galić*, Public Redacted, Reasons for the President's Decision to Deny the Early Release of Stanislav Galić and Decision on Prosecution Motion, MICT-14-83-ES, 23 June 2015, para. 4; *Prosecutor v Žigić*, Public Redacted Version of the 10 November 2014 Decision of the President on the Early Release of Zoran Žigić, MICT-14-81-ES.1, 23 December 2014, para. 5; *Prosecutor v Zelenović*, Public Redacted Version of the 28 August 2015 Decision of the President on the Early Release of Dragan Zelenović, MICT-15-89-ES, 18 September 2015, para. 4.

[157] See *Prosecutor v Češić*, Public Redacted Version of the 30 April 2014 Decision of the President on the Early Release of Ranko Češić, MICT-14-66-ES, 28 May 2014, paras 4, 11.

[158] See ICTY, Manual of Developed Practices, paras 41–43 at 161; Prosecutor v Tadić, Decision of the President on the Application for Pardon or Commutation

enforcing states to notify the tribunal of an international prisoner's eligibility for release and the fact that some convicted persons were serving their entire sentences in international detention centres without being transferred to enforcing states.[159] The ICTY Practice Direction was revised to acknowledge the right of direct petition.[160] On receipt of a direct petition, the enforcing state (if applicable) would be asked for its opinion on eligibility.[161] The MICT Practice Direction also permits direct petitions.[162] Direct petitions for early release were received from convicted persons serving their sentences not only

of Sentence of Miroslav Tadić, IT-95-9-T, 3 November 2004, paras 2–4; Decision of the President on the Application for Pardon or Commutation of Sentence of Milorad Krnojelac, IT-97-25-ES, 9 July 2009, para. 5; *Prosecutor v Josipović*, Decision of the President on the Application for Pardon or Commutation of Sentence of Drago Josipović, IT-95-16-ES, 30 January 2006, paras 1, 4, 6; *Prosecutor v Tadić*, Decision of the President on the Application for Pardon or Commutation of Sentence of Duśko Tadić, IT-94-1-ES, 17 July 2008, para. 3; *Prosecutor v Banović*, Decision of the President on Commutation of Sentence, IT-02-65/1-ES, 3 September 2008, para. 10; *Prosecutor v Strugar*, Decision of the President on the Application for Pardon or Commutation of Sentence of Pavle Strugar, IT-01-42-ES, 16 January 2009, paras 5, 6, 9; *Prosecutor v Šantić*, Decision of the President on the Application for Pardon or Commutation of Sentence of Vladimir Šantić, IT-9S-16-ES, 16 February 2009, para. 1; Decision of the President on the Application for Pardon or Commutation of Sentence of Milorad Krnojelac, IT-97-25-ES, 9 July 2009, para. 1; *Prosecutor v Martinović*, Decision of the President on the Application for Pardon or Commutation of Sentence of Vinko Martinović, IT-98-34-ES, 22 January 2010, para. 1; *Prosecutor v Tarčulovski*, Decision of the President on Early Release of Johan Tarčulovski, IT-04-82-ES, 23 June 2011, paras 1, 10, 19; *Prosecutor v Šljivančanin*, Decision of President on Early Release of Veselin Šljivančanin, IT-95-13/1-ES, 5 July 2011, paras 1, 14; *Prosecutor v Muvunyi,* Decision on the Early Release of Tharcisse Muvunyi, ICTR-00-055A-T, 6 March 2012, paras 3, 10.

[159] R. Mulgrew, *Towards the Development of the International Penal System* (CUP: Cambridge, 2013) at 56.

[160] Para. 2 ICTY PDER, Rev. 2, 1 September 2009.

[161] See para. 2(b) ICTR PDER.

[162] Para. 3 MICT PDER.

in the UNDU (The Hague)[163] and the UNDF (Arusha),[164] but also in a variety of enforcing states (Denmark, Finland, Mali, Sweden, Belgium, Italy and Germany).[165]

---

[163] *Prosecutor v Pandurević*, Public Redacted Version of the 9 April 2015 Decision of the President on the Early Release of Vinko Pandurević, MICT-15-85-ES.1, 10 April 2015, paras 1, 5, 11; *Prosecutor v Pušić*, Public Redacted Version of the 20 April 2018 Decision of the President on the Early Release of Berislav Pušić, MICT-17-112-ES.1, 24 April 2018, paras 17, 20; *Prosecutor v Nikolić*, Public Redacted Version of the 20 July 2015 Decision of the President on the Application for Early Release or Other Relief of Drago Nikolić, MICT-15-85-ES.4, 13 October 2015, paras 1, 4, 11, 14; *Prosecutor v Lazaerić*, Public Redacted Version of the 7 September 2015 Decision of the President on the Early Release of Vladimir Lazarević, MICT-14-67-ES.3, 3 December 2015, paras 1–3, 9.

[164] *Prosecutor v Sagahutu*, Public Redacted Version of the 9 May 2014 Decision of the President on the Early Release of Innocent Sagahutu, MICT-13-43-ES, 13 May 2014, paras 1, 6, 11–12; *Prosecutor v Alphonse Nteziryayo*, Public Redacted Decision of the President on the Early Release of Alphonse Nteziryayo, MICT-15-90, 9 March 2016, paras 1, 5, 11.

[165] *Prosecutor v Bisengimana,* Decision on the Early Release Request of Paul Bisengimana, MICT-12-07, 11 December 2012, paras 1, 4–5; *Prosecutor v Serushago*, Public Redacted Version of Decision of the President on the Early Release of Omar Serushago, MICT-12-28-ES, 13 December 2012, paras 1, 6, 12; *Prosecutor v Češić*, Public Redacted Version of the 30 April 2014 Decision of the President on the Early Release of Ranko Češić, MICT-14-66-ES, 28 May 2014, para. 1; *Prosecutor v Munyakazi*, Public Redacted Version of the 22 July 2015 Decision of the President on the Early Release of Youssof Munyakazi, MICT-12-18-ES.1, 22 July 2015, para. 1; *Prosecutor v Nikolić*, Public Redacted Version of the 14 March 2014 Decision on the Early Release of Momir Nikolić, MICT-14-65-ES, 12 October 2015, para. 2; *Prosecutor v Šainović*, Public Redacted Version of the 10 July 2015 Decision of the President on the Early Release of Nikola Šainović, MICT-14-67-ES.1, 27 August 2015, paras 1–2; *Prosecutor v Zelenović*, Public Redacted Version of the 28 August 2015 Decision of the President on the Early Release of Dragan Zelenović, MICT-15-89-ES, 18 September 2015, para. 1; *Prosecutor v Borovčanin*, Public Redacted Version of the 14 July 2016 Decision of the President on the Early Release of Ljubomir Borovčanin, MICT-15-85-ES.6, 2 August 2016, para. 1; *Prosecutor v Ntawukukikyayo*, Decision of the President on the Early Release of Dominique Ntawukulilyayo, MICT-13-34-ES, 8 July 2016, para. 1; *Prosecutor v Semanza*, Public Redacted Version of the Decision of the President on the Early Release of Laurent Semanza, MICT-13-36-ES, 9 June 2016, para. 1; *Prosecutor v Jelisić*, Public Redacted Version of the 22 May 2017 Decision of the President on Recognition of Commutation of Sentence, Remission of Sentence and Early Release of Goran Jelisić, MICT-14-63-ES, 11 August 2017, para. 1; *Prosecutor v Kunarac*, Public Redacted Decision of the President on the Early Release of Dragoljub Kunarac, MICT-15-88-ES.1, 2 February 2017, para. 8.

Following receipt of notification of eligibility or a direct application, the Registrar was responsible for preparing a file for the President with reports on behaviour during incarceration, conditions of imprisonment, the prisoner's mental condition, cooperation of the convicted person with the Office of the Prosecution, and any other information the President considered relevant.[166] Whether or not the convicted person had consented to the disclosure of their medical information was rarely discussed, although there are examples of explicit references to the grant of consent.[167] The Registrar was also charged with informing the convicted person of their eligibility for release, advising him or her about the steps that would be taken, and providing him or her with a copy of the file prepared for the President.[168] The prisoner had ten days to examine the file and send written submissions or make oral submissions to the President by video link or telephone.[169] This right of response was usually exercised by prisoners, though not always.[170] In some instances, it seems that the MICT had been willing to assign legal counsel to convicted persons to assist them in reviewing the materials sent by the Registry and preparing their response.[171]

President Meron consistently denied the Prosecutor standing to make recommendations as to whether a convicted person should be released.[172] He was only willing to consider Prosecutor submissions made in relation to the President's discretion under the practice direction to take any other relevant

---

166 Para. 3(b)-(d) ICTR PDER; para. 4(b)-(d) MICT PDER.

167 *Prosecutor v Nikolić*, Public Redacted Version of the 20 July 2015 Decision of the President on the Application for Early Release or Other Relief of Drago Nikolić, MICT-15-85-ES.4, 13 October 2015, para. 7.

168 Paras 3(a), 4–5 ICTY PDER; paras 4(a), 5, 6 MICT PDER.

169 Para. 5 ICTY PDER; para. 6 MICT PDER.

170 See *Prosecutor v Munyakazi*, Public Redacted Version of the 22 July 2015 Decision of the President on the Early Release of Youssof Munyakazi, MICT-12-18-ES.1, 22 July 2015, para. 5.

171 *Prosecutor v Zelenović*, Public Redacted Version of the 28 August 2015 Decision of the President on the Early Release of Dragan Zelenović, MICT-15-89-ES, 18 September 2015, para. 5.

172 *Prosecutor v Pušić*, Public Redacted Version of the 20 April 2018 Decision of the President on the Early Release of Berislav Pušić, MICT-17-112-ES.1, 24 April 2018, para. 24; *Prosecutor v Galić*, Public Redacted, Reasons for the President's Decision to Deny the Early Release of Stanislav Galić and Decision on Prosecution Motion, MICT-14-83-ES, 23 June 2015, para. 5; *Prosecutor v Miletić*, Decision of the President on the Early Release of Radivoje Miletić, MICT-15-85-ES.5, 23 October 2018, para. 18.

information into account (para. 9), and even then, only if there were compelling reasons or special circumstances to do so in specific cases.[173]

The Presidents of the ICTY and ICTR were obliged, by statute, to consult with other judges in reaching their decision.[174] The precise scope of this obligation changed over time. For example, the ICTY rules were amended in 2001 to specify that this consultation should be with 'permanent' judges[175] and in 2005 to require the President to consult with members of the Bureau[176] and the permanent judges of the sentencing Chamber who remain Judges of the Tribunal.[177] Although the MICT Statute does not refer to consultation, its rules and practice direction reflected this approach, specifying that the President should consult with any judges of the sentencing Chamber who are judges of the MICT about the appropriateness of granting release.[178] This formulation, however, at times resulted in President Meron only being required to consult with one other judge[179] or having no obligation to consult other judges given that no judge from the Sentencing Chamber remained.[180] Consequently,

---

173 *Prosecutor v Galić*, Public Redacted, Reasons for the President's Decision to Deny the Early Release of Stanislav Galić and Decision on Prosecution Motion, MICT-14-83-ES, 23 June 2015, para. 8; *Prosecutor v Nikolić*, Public Redacted Version of the 20 July 2015 Decision of the President on the Application for Early Release or Other Relief of Drago Nikolić, MICT-15-85-ES.4, 13 October 2015, para. 7; *Prosecutor v Pušić*, Public Redacted Version of the 20 April 2018 Decision of the President on the Early Release of Berislav Pušić, MICT-17-112-ES.1, 24 April 2018, para. 23.

174 Article 28 ICTYSt; Article 27 ICTRSt.

175 Rule 124 ICTY RPE, Rev. 20, 12 April 2001.

176 The Bureau is composed of the President, Vice-President and the Presiding Judge of the Trial Chambers. Rule 23(A) ICTY/ICTR RPE.

177 Rule 124 ICTY RPE, Rev. 34, 11 February 2005.

178 Rule 150 MICT RPE; para. 7 MICT PDER.

179 *Prosecutor v Lazaerić*, Public Redacted Version of the 7 September 2015 Decision of the President on the Early Release of Vladimir Lazarević, MICT-14-67-ES.3, 3 December 2015, para. 6; *Prosecutor v Borovčanin*, Public Redacted Version of the 14 July 2016 Decision of the President on the Early Release of Ljubomir Borovčanin, MICT-15-85-ES.6, 2 August 2016, para. 7; *Prosecutor v Šainović*, Public Redacted version of the 10 July 2015 Decision of the President on the Early Release of Nikola Šainović, MICT-14-67-ES.1, 27 August 2015, para. 9.

180 See *Prosecutor v Serushago*, Public Redacted Version of Decision of the President on the Early Release of Omar Serushago, MICT-12-28-ES, 13 December 2012, para. 7; *Prosecutor v Jelisić*, Public Redacted Version of the 22 May 2017 Decision of the President on Recognition of Commutation of Sentence, Remission of Sentence and Early Release of Goran Jelisić, MICT-14-63-ES, 11 August 2017, para. 18.

in April 2018, the judges amended Rule 150 to require the President to consult with at least two other judges if none of the judges who imposed the sentence were judges of the Mechanism. Irrespective of the precise consultation requirement, it is important to note that the President was not bound by the views of the other judges.[181] It is often implicit in these discussions that there was unanimous agreement on the final decision. Release decisions also outlined if the President's view that release should be granted or denied was shared by the judge(s) consulted with.[182]

In cases of disagreement, the details of the consultations on the merits (or otherwise) of granting release were set out in greater detail. In *Miletić*, for example, Judge Agius 'strongly objected' to early release on the basis of the high gravity of the crimes, the lack of even 'the slightest sign of rehabilitation,' the 'cold, challenging and uncompromising stance' taken by the applicant throughout his trial, and his appeal to others not to provide information to the ICTY in relation to Srebrenica.[183] Judge Agius argued that he could not be

---

[181] Para. 8 ICTY PDER; ICTY *Manual of Developed Practice*, para. 45 at 161; para. 9 MICT PDER. See *Prosecutor v Vuković*, Decision of the President on Commutation of Sentence, IT-96-23 & 23/1-ES, 11 March 2008, para. 12; *Prosecutor v Plavšic*, Public Redacted Decision of the President on the Application for Pardon or Commutation of Sentence of Mrs Biljana Plavšić, IT-00-39& 40/1-ES, 14 September 2009, para. 13.

[182] *Prosecutor v Galić*, Public Redacted, Reasons for the President's Decision to Deny the Early Release of Stanislav Galić and Decision on Prosecution Motion, MICT-14-83-ES, 23 June 2015, para. 51; *Prosecutor v Češić*, Public Redacted Version of the 30 April 2014 Decision of the President on the Early Release of Ranko Češić, MICT-14-66-ES, 28 May 2014, para. 25; *Prosecutor v Munyakazi*, Public Redacted Version of the 22 July 2015 Decision of the President on the Early Release of Youssof Munyakazi, MICT-12-18-ES.1, 22 July 2015, para. 25; *Prosecutor v Nikolić*, Public Redacted Version of the 20 July 2015 Decision of the President on the Application for Early Release or Other Relief of Drago Nikolić, MICT-15-85-ES.4, 13 October 2015, para. 35; *Prosecutor v Nikolić*, Public Redacted Version of the 14 March 2014 Decision on the Early Release of Momir Nikolić, MICT-14-65-ES, 12 October 2015, para. 35; *Prosecutor v Šainović*, Public Redacted Version of the 10 July 2015 Decision of the President on the Early Release of Nikola Šainović, MICT-14-67-ES.1, 27 August 2015, para. 26; *Prosecutor v Zelenović*, Public Redacted Version of the 28 August 2015 Decision of the President on the Early Release of Dragan Zelenović, MICT-15-89-ES, 18 September 2015, para. 22; *Prosecutor v Pandurević*, Public Redacted Version of the 9 April 2015 Decision of the President on the Early Release of Vinko Pandurević, MICT-15-85-ES.1, 10 April 2015, para. 29.

[183] *Prosecutor v Miletić*, Decision of the President on the Early Release of Radivoje Miletić, MICT-15-85-ES.5, 23 October 2018, para. 41.

considered 'equal to those who were correctly granted early release in the past' and that granting him release at the two-thirds stage would show 'complete disregard to the ongoing process of reconciliation and insensitivity to the pain of the victims of the Srebrenica 1995 events and genocide'.[184] President Meron noted that the applicant's conduct at trial was taken into account at sentencing as an aggravating factor and that his behaviour in detention had generally been positive and focused on rehabilitation.[185] President Meron stated that consultations with other judges were a 'meaningful part of the President's assessment', and outlined that the practice at all UN Tribunals had been that early release should be granted if a majority were in favour and should be denied if a majority were opposed (absent any compelling circumstances indicating otherwise).[186] As both remaining judges of the Sentencing Chamber, and therefore the majority of judges consulted, strongly objected to release being granted, early release was denied despite the fact that the prisoner had served two-thirds of the sentence and showed some signs of rehabilitation.[187]

In all cases, however, the President's decision was final and was not subject to appeal.[188] If the President decided to grant early release, the Registry was tasked with sending the decision to the enforcing state, the convicted person and other interested parties.[189] The President could also direct the Registry to inform persons who testified at the convicted person's trial about the destination the prisoner would travel to upon release and any other information considered relevant by the President.[190] Decisions were usually made public, although the President could decide to withhold publication.[191]

5. CONCLUSION

This chapter traced the development and application of the law and policies relevant to early release decision-making at the ICTY, ICTR and MICT up to 2018. It outlined how a statutory system designed to facilitate the Presidential grant of pardon or commutation of sentence became instead a system for the almost routine grant of unconditional early release. The Presidential creation of a temporal threshold for eligibility for consideration for release at two-thirds of the sentence became its dominant feature. Choi argues that this

184 Ibid, para. 42.
185 Ibid, para. 43.
186 Ibid, para. 44.
187 Ibid, paras 44–46.
188 Para. 10 ICTY PDER; para. 12 MICT PDER.
189 Para. 11 ICTY PDER; para. 13 MICT PDER.
190 Para 12 ICTY PDER; para. 13 MICT PDER.
191 Para. 8 ICTY PDER; para. 9 MICT PDER.

interpretation and application of the 'similarly-situated persons' factor resulted in the two-thirds rule becoming 'essentially dispositive' in release decisions.[192] To substantiate his argument, Choi gives the example of Mlađo Radić.[193] Even though his crimes were of high gravity, he had displayed little or no evidence of rehabilitation and did not cooperate with the Prosecutor, President Meron explicitly stated he was granting (deferred) release solely on the basis that he had served two-thirds of his sentence.[194]

Factors already considered during sentencing – the gravity of crimes and cooperation with the Prosecutor – had become mostly irrelevant other than in exceptional cases, and the remaining factor – rehabilitation – though discussed in greater detail in later cases, was almost invariably found to be a positive factor.[195] Votja argues that the low influence of the gravity of the crimes in release decision-making was contrary to expectations given the focus on gravity and culpability of the prisoners convicted by the International Military Tribunal, Nurnberg.[196] The practice of the UN Tribunals, up until 2018, prioritised (at the expense of logic in humanitarian emergency cases) the equal treatment of prisoners. This equality of treatment was understood to mean they served the same proportion of the sentences imposed on them prior to release. The application of this principle to those serving indeterminate sentences did not have quite the same impact as the rule that they must serve 'more than' 30 years, which left room for interpretation and Presidential discretion. The ICC system differs in this regard with more detailed rules on eligibility for release and a requirement for release decisions to be made by three judges.

---

192 Jonathan H. Choi, 'Early Release in International Criminal Law' (2014) 123 *Yale Law Journal* 1784–1828 at 1795. He noted the only exception in ICTY decisions to deny release after the two-thirds point was a reluctant decision in *Banović* by President Pocar on the basis of a technicality of French law.

193 Ibid. at 1797.

194 *Prosecutor v Radić*, Public Redacted Version of 13 February 2012 Decision of the President on the Release of Mlado Radić, IT-98-30/1-ES, 9 January 2013, para. 30. Release was denied at the point at which he had served two-thirds of his sentence, but granted effective from a later stated date (four months later).

195 See Jessica M Kelder, Barbora Holá and Joris van Wijk, 'Rehabilitation and Early Release of Perpetrators of International Crimes: A Case Study of the ICTY and ICTR' (2014) 14(6) *International Criminal Law Review* 117–1203.

196 Filip Votja, 'Punishment and Sentence Enforcement for Serious Violations of International Humanitarian Law Committed in the Former Yugoslavia' in Kalac, Albrecht and Kilchling (eds) *Mapping the Criminological Landscape of the Balkans* (Duncker and Humblot, 2014) at 417.

3. Reduction of sentence at the International Criminal Court

1. SENTENCE REDUCTION AT THE INTERNATIONAL CRIMINAL COURT

The Rome Statute makes it abundantly clear that sentences imposed by the ICC are binding on enforcing States[1] and that the right to decide on the reduction of sentences is reserved exclusively by the Court.[2] Specifically, 'the State of enforcement shall not release the person before the expiry of the sentence pronounced by the Court'.[3] The Rome Statute and the ICC Rules of Procedure and Evidence provide a more detailed legal framework to govern release than those of the ad hoc Tribunals or MICT. The principal statutory provision on release, Article 110, creates statutory temporal eligibility thresholds for both determinate and indeterminate sentences,[4] sets out the procedure for the review of sentences and two explicit factors that must be considered during sentence review.[5] Additional factors and procedures to be followed for initial and subsequent sentence reviews are to be found in Rules 223 and 224 of Section V of the Rules of Procedure and Evidence.

Unlike the ad hoc Tribunals, MICT and SCSL, the ICC has not issued a practice direction to govern sentence review. This may be due to the sentiment expressed by the Appeal Chamber judges in sentence review decisions that, read together, Articles 110(3), (4), (5) and Rule 223 provide a 'comprehensive framework for the purposes of sentence review'.[6] These judges further

[1] Article 105(1)–(2) ICCSt.

[2] Article 110(2) ICCSt.

[3] Article 110(1) ICCSt.

[4] Article 110(3) ICCSt.

[5] Article 110 (2), (4)–(5) ICCSt.

[6] Situation in the DRC, *Prosecutor v Thomas Lubanga Dyilo*, Decision on the review concerning reduction of sentence of Mr Thomas Lubanga Dyilo, ICC-01/04-01/06, 22 September 2015, para. 19 (hereafter *Lubanga* First Sentence Review); Situation in the DRC, *Prosecutor v Thomas Lubanga Dyilo*, Second Decision on the review concerning reduction of sentence of Mr Thomas Lubanga Dyilo, ICC-01/04/01/06, 3 November 2017, para. 28 (hereafter *Lubanga* Second

highlighted that the statutory reference to 'other factors' in Article 110(4)(c) was qualified by the words 'as provided in the Rules of Procedure and Evidence' and accordingly interpreted the phrase to mean the factors set out in Rule 223(a)-(e). In other words, 'the factors that can be taken into account for purposes of considering whether to reduce a sentence are, in principle, those set out in the Court's legal texts'.[7] These decisions imply that the statutory and regulatory factors are exhaustive and the only factors that will or indeed can be considered by the ICC during sentence reviews.

This chapter examines eligibility for a sentence reduction review at the ICC, the procedures governing initial and subsequent reviews, the statutory and regulatory factors considered during such reviews and the decision-making process.

2. STATUTORY ELIGIBILITY FOR REVIEW CONCERNING REDUCTION OF SENTENCE

Article 110(3) provides that 'when a person has served two thirds of the sentence, or 25 years in the case of life imprisonment, the Court shall review the sentence to determine whether it should be reduced. Such a review shall not be conducted before that time'. The Rome Statute therefore provides temporal eligibility requirements for sentence review for both determinate and indeterminate sentences. Importantly, this means that 'the initial review of sentence… is not triggered by an application of a sentenced person, but rather it is an automatic and mandatory review once the threshold of having served two thirds of a sentence has been met'.[8] This statutory trigger avoids the potential disparity of treatment that could arise from reliance on domestic law on eligibility and the lack of certainty for convicted persons serving indeterminate sentences. In so doing, the statutory trigger introduces transparency, predictability and consistency. Van Zyl Smit praises the ICC framework for upholding important principles of proportionality, legal clarity and legal certainty, arguing that linking the release provisions 'specifically to sentences that may be imposed

---

Sentence Review); Situation in the DRC, *Prosecutor v Germain Katanga*, Decision on the review concerning reduction of sentence of Mr Germain Katanga ICC-01/04/01/07, 13 November 2015, para. 19 (hereafter *Katanga* Sentence Review; Situation in the Republic of Mali, *Prosecutor v Ahmad Al Faqi Al Mahdi*, Public Redacted Version of the Decision on the Review concerning reduction of sentence of Mr Ahmad Al Faqi Al Mahdi, ICC-01/12-01/15, 25 November 2021, para. 15 (hereafter *Al Mahdi* Sentence Review).

[7] *Lubanga*, First Sentence Review, para. 25; *Katanga* Sentence Review, para. 19.

[8] *Lubanga* First Sentence Review, para. 20.

signals up front that the determination of the actual term of imprisonment to be served depends not only on the initial sentencing decision of the court, but also on its decision on release'.[9]

Scalia notes that the introduction of a statutory requirement for the mandatory review of *indeterminate sentences*[10] provides a 'possibility to moderate the lengthy or perpetual character' of a life sentence.[11] Draft versions of the Rome Statute had previously set eligibility for consideration for sentence review for persons sentenced to life imprisonment at 20 years but this was increased to 25 years to create a clear distinction between persons serving determinate and indeterminate sentences.[12] This change reflected the fact that the longest possible determinate sentences that can be imposed by the ICC is 30 years,[13] with subsequent eligibility for release arising at 20 years. The 25 year eligibility point was therefore intended to reflect the statutory requirement that life sentences can only be imposed where justified by the extreme gravity of the crime committed and the individual circumstances of the convicted person.[14] Van Zyl Smit has conceded that while '25 years is a long minimum period… its length is probably justifiable' in the context of the 'extremely serious nature of crimes that the ICC tries and the restrictions... on the use of life imprisonment'.[15] Moreover, he notes that the ICC's procedure 'in the sense of judicial review after a fixed period of 25 years' was endorsed by the Grand Chamber of the European Court on Human Rights.[16]

3. SENTENCE REVIEW HEARINGS

The Statute and Rules set out the procedure for reviews concerning reduction of sentence. The foundational principle governing such reviews is that 'the Court alone shall have the right to decide any reduction of sentence'.[17]

---

9 Van Zyl Smit, 'Determinate and Indeterminate Sentences of Imprisonment in International Criminal Justice' in Mulgrew and Abels (eds) *Research Handbook on the International Penal System* (2016) 80–101 at 97.

10 Article 110(3), (5) ICCSt; Rule 224(3) ICC RPE.

11 D Scalia, 'Long-term Sentences in International Criminal Law' (2011) 9(3) *JICJ* 669–687 at 687.

12 See Mulgrew, *Towards the Development of the International Penal System* (2013) at 60.

13 Art. 77(1)(a) ICCSt.

14 Art. 77(1)(b) ICCSt.

15 Van Zyl Smit, note 9, at 97.

16 Ibid, referring to *Vinter and Others v UK*, App. Nos 66069/09, 130/10 and 3896/10, 9 July 2013.

17 Article 110(2) ICCSt.

3.1 Initial Sentence Review Hearing

Rule 224(1) sets out the procedure for initial sentence review hearings pursuant to Article 110(3) ICCSt. Three judges from the Appeals Chamber must be appointed by the Appeals Chamber to hold a review hearing with the convicted person assisted by counsel and interpreters (where required).[18] The convicted person's right to be heard prior to decisions on sentence reduction is enshrined in the Statute.[19] The Rules note that, in exceptional circumstances, the hearing can be conducted using video-conferencing or in an enforcing State by a judge delegated by the Appeals Chamber.[20] Sentence review hearings are scheduled at or shortly after the date at which the convicted person has served the requisite amount of time,[21] though delays may occur. In *Lubanga*, for example, the hearing appears to have been delayed due to accusations of witness interference and a request for the disqualification of a judge from the Panel.[22]

The Rules require the Review Panel to invite the Prosecutor, States enforcing penalties or reparations, and (to the extent possible) victims and their legal representatives who participated in proceedings to attend the sentence review hearing or submit written observations.[23] Panels have also requested written observations from the Registrar and country of origin of the convicted person.[24] A request to participate in the hearing may not result in an enforcing state or state of origin attending.[25]

3.2 Nature of the Proceedings and the Burden of Proof

During the ICC's first sentence review, the Panel was forced to address the contention raised by the Prosecutor that the burden of proof rests 'squarely on the person seeking release' and further, if the convicted person failed to demonstrate the presence of a statutory factor in favour of release in clear and conclusive terms, that no reduction of sentence could be ordered.[26] Indeed it is

---

18 Rule 224(1) ICC RPE.

19 Article 110(2) ICCSt.

20 Rule 224(1) ICC RPE.

21 See *Lubanga* First Sentence Review, para. 4; *Katanga* Sentence Review, paras 5, 13.

22 *Lubanga* First Sentence Review, paras 5–6, 10–14.

23 Rule 224(1) ICC RPE.

24 *Katanga* Sentence Review, paras 6, 12; *Al Mahdi* Sentence Review, para. 3.

25 See *Al Mahdi* Sentence Review, paras 8–9.

26 See *Lubanga* First Sentence Review Situation, para. 31.

unclear from the Court's legal texts where the burden of proof lies (generally or in regard to particular factors) or what type of proof is required.[27]

The Panel was quick to dismiss the Prosecutor's contention on the basis that it misconceived the nature of the sentence review proceedings at the ICC. The Panel made it clear that unlike procedure at the *ad hoc* tribunals and in domestic jurisdictions, where the process may be triggered by the sentenced person, the review of sentences at the ICC is a 'mandatory *proprio motu* review undertaken by the panel of judges appointed by the Appeals Chamber for that purpose'.[28] Accordingly, '[w]hile a sentenced person clearly has a strong interest in presenting information sufficient to establish the presence of factors justifying a reduction of his or her sentence, this does not equate to a burden of proof'.[29] Moreover, the sentenced person 'may not have access to or be able to provide all of the necessary information relevant to factors'. This practicality justified the request for information from a wider range of sources specified in the rules (Registrar and state authorities). The Panel concluded that ***all participants*** were 'required to provide any information in their possession, whether weighing for or against release'[30] and that their decision would be based on all information provided.[31]

The reasoned decision must be communicated to all review participants as soon as possible.[32]

3.3 Subsequent Review(s)

In addition to establishing the point at which convicted persons become eligible for an initial review concerning reduction of sentence, the Rome Statute also establishes a mandatory process for subsequent reviews.[33] The Rules introduce a mandatory three-year interval for such reviews.[34] As argued previously,[35] three years seems to be a disproportionately long period between

---

27 See R. Mulgrew, 'Releasing International Prisoners' in M Herzog-Evans (ed.) *Offender release and supervision: The role of Courts and the use of discretion* (Wolf Legal Publishers, 2014) 21–51 at 43.

28 *Lubanga* First Sentence Review, para. 32.

29 *Lubanga* First Sentence Review, para. 32; see also *Katanga* Sentence Review, para. 21.

30 *Lubanga* First Sentence Review, para. 32; see also *Katanga* Sentence Review, para. 21.

31 See *Al Mahdi* Sentence Review, para. 17.

32 Rule 224(2) ICC RPE.

33 Art. 110(5) ICCSt.

34 Rule 224(3) ICC RPE.

35 See R. Mulgrew, note 27 at 32.

reviews given that those serving the longest determinate sentence of 30 years will become eligible for a sentence review after 20 years. This would mean a denial of sentence reduction at the 20 year point would result in service of a third of the remaining term before a subsequent review could occur. Given that most determinate sentences reviewed to date have been much less than this 30-year maximum term (Lubanga (14 years), Katanga (12 years) Al Mahdi (9 years)), the three year interval seems even more excessive. In most European countries, subsequent reviews are permitted after a few months.[36] Moreover it seems from the drafting history of the provision that the three-year interval was intended to be applied to persons serving life sentences.[37]

The Rules do, however, enable the judges to hold subsequent reviews before the three-year period in two situations: firstly, where there has been a significant change in circumstances and secondly, if a shorter review period was set by the decision denying sentence reduction pursuant to Article 110(3).[38] There has been no practice in relation to the former situation to date so it is not clear what will be required to constitute a significant chance of circumstances.

The judicial setting of an earlier and pre-determined review date occurred in the first *Lubanga* sentence review. Following the unanimous denial of sentence reduction in September 2015, the three judges decided to review the sentence again in two years.[39] This timeframe was determined by reference to the length of the original sentence of 14 years: with only 4.5 years remaining to be served from the date of denial of sentence reduction, the Panel thought a three-year interval would not be appropriate.[40] Further reasons for this decision were not given. The subsequent review took place less than halfway through the remaining term to be served.

An order scheduling the second review called for written submissions from the convicted person, the Prosecutor, Victims, the Democratic Republic of the Congo (the enforcing State) and the Registrar.[41] It was made clear that the

---

36 See D. van Zyl Smit and Spencer 'The European Dimension to the Release of Sentenced Prisoners' in N Padfield, D van Zyl Smit, F Dünkel (eds) *Release from Prison: European Policy and Practice* (Routledge, 2010) 9–48 at 18; F Dünkel, D Van Zyl Smit and N Padfield, 'Concluding Thoughts' in N Padfield, D van Zyl Smit, F Dünkel (eds) *Release from Prison: European Policy and Practice* (Routledge, 2010) 395–444 at 427.

37 W Schabas, *The ICC: A Commentary on the Rome Statute* (OUP, 2010) at 1104.

38 Rule 224(3) ICC RPE.

39 *Lubanga* First Sentence Review, para. 2.

40 *Lubanga* First Sentence Review, para. 79.

41 Situation in the DRC, *Prosecutor v Thomas Lubanga Dyilo*, Scheduling Order for the second review concerning reduction of sentence of Mr Thomas

second review would be limited to consideration of whether there have been any changed circumstances since the first sentence review and if this change had been significant.[42] Any actions discussed during the previous sentence review or actions that may occur in the future would not be considered.[43] Accordingly, written submissions could only address the specific intervening period between the last sentence review and the commencement of the subsequent review. Subsequent reviews will typically to be conducted through the means of written representations,[44] although the three judge panel may decide to hold a hearing.[45] Subsequent review decisions follow the structure of initial sentence review decisions – setting out the applicable law, the factor being considered in terms of both the participants' submissions and the panel's determination, along with the decision – though they also include details on the consideration of and decisions in relation to each factor from the initial sentence review.

It is interesting to note that in denying a reduction of sentence in the second *Lubanga* review, the Panel decided that there was no reason to schedule a further review before the completion of his sentence on 15 March 2020. The Panel stressed, however, that 'this is without prejudice to Mr Lubanga's right under rule 224(3) to apply for a new review of his sentence in case of a significant change of circumstances'.[46] Specifically, the rule enables the sentenced person to apply for a review 'within the three-year period or such shorter period as may have been set'. This decision highlights the right of sentenced persons to directly petition the court for review of sentence at any time following a review if there has been a significant change of circumstances from the time of the decision of the previous review.

3.4 Postponement of Subsequent Reviews

In the second *Lubanga* review, the Panel held that it had the power to modify the timing of a review decision.[47] However, it rejected the request from the legal representatives of victims to postpone the review for six months to allow for meetings to agree on the best way for Lubanga to deliver his proposed public apologies,[48] arguing a postponement was not warranted given the

Lubanga Dyilo, ICC-01/04-01/06, 7 August 2017.

[42] *Lubanga* Second Sentence Review, paras 30–31.

[43] See *Lubanga* Second Sentence Review, paras 32, 42, 55–56, 84.

[44] See *Lubanga* Second Sentence Review, paras 5–10.

[45] Rule 224(4) ICC RPE.

[46] *Lubanga* Second Sentence Review, para. 95.

[47] *Lubanga* Second Sentence Review, para. 20.

[48] *Lubanga* Second Sentence Review, paras 11–14.

uncertainty surrounding the timing and occurrence of the proposed actions.[49] Moreover, the Panel felt postponement was unnecessary given the sentenced person's regulatory right to apply for another review if there was a significant change of circumstances following the decision (rule 224(3)).[50]

4. ICC STATUTORY RELEASE FACTORS

The factors considered during a sentence review are to be found in both the Statute and the Rules of Procedure and Evidence. In Sentence Review Decisions, the oral and written submissions of the parties are summarised before the determination of the panel on the presence or otherwise of each factor is discussed. A declaration is made after the discussion of each factor whether the factor is present for the purposes of weighing it against other present factors to determine whether it is appropriate to reduce sentence.

The Rome Statute sets out two explicit factors to be considered in sentence review proceedings in Article 110(4): (a) the early and continuing willingness of the person to cooperate with the Court in its investigations and prosecutions, and (b) the voluntary assistance of the person in enabling the enforcement of the judgments and orders of the Court in other cases, and in particular providing assistance with locating assets subject to orders of fine, forfeiture or reparation which may be used for benefit of victims. The sentence review decisions outline how these factors have been interpreted and applied to the facts of each case.

4.1 Article 110(4)(a): Early and Continuing Willingness of the Person to Cooperate with the Court in its Investigations and Prosecution

This statutory factor requires consideration of two cooperation elements: the early willingness of the person to cooperate **and** their continuing willingness to cooperate.

During the first *Lubanga* review, the Panel ruled that the fact that Lubanga's cooperation during the trial was considered in sentencing as a mitigating factor did not mean that it could not be taken into account in a sentence review *per se*. However, as no evidence of any post-sentence cooperation had been identified, the trial-based cooperation alone could not qualify as early and continuing cooperation for the purposes of Article 110(4)(a).[51] The Panel stressed that

49 *Lubanga* Second Sentence Review, paras 20–21, 23.

50 *Lubanga* Second Sentence Review, para. 22.

51 *Lubanga* First Sentence Review, para. 36.

while cooperation that does not continue post-conviction will not generally be considered for sentence reduction purposes, the fact that the cooperation was taken into account in mitigation in sentencing will not always result in its automatic non-consideration at sentence reduction. This approach is based on recognition that the full impact of such cooperation may only become apparent post-sentence and the original sentence, therefore, may not fully capture the extent of assistance provided, any benefit to victims or the degree to which it furthered the Court's investigations and prosecutions. Accordingly, whether information taken into account at sentencing is relevant at sentence reduction review is to be assessed on case-by-case basis.[52]

The fact that cooperation is also a potential mitigating circumstance in sentencing[53] was further discussed by the Panel in the *Katanga* sentence review. The Panel accepted that cooperation for sentence review purposes under Article 110(4)(a) and cooperation as a potential mitigating factor in sentencing had the same meaning.[54] Moreover, deference would generally be given to the trial chambers' findings on whether or not conduct during trial qualified as cooperation.[55] It noted that the Trial Chamber expected cooperation at trial to exceed mere good behaviour and attendance as these are to be expected.[56] The Trial Chamber did however put weight on Katanga's decision to testify in a manner that incriminated himself.[57] The Panel accepted that these findings established early cooperation for the purposes of Article 110(4)(a). The question remained if (other) cooperation began or continued after the imposition of the sentence.[58]

The *Katanga* Panel reiterated the stance taken by the first *Lubanga* Sentence Review Panel, that cooperation that does not continue post-conviction (and was considered in sentencing) will not generally be taken into account in sentence review. This statement was qualified by recognition that this may not always result in non-consideration of such cooperation: rather a case-by-case assessment would be undertaken.[59] On the facts in *Katanga*, the focus of arguments centred on whether Katanga's withdrawal of his appeal of conviction and sentence constituted cooperation for the purposes of sentence reduction. The Panel appeared dismissive of the Prosecutor's oral submission that the withdrawal of

52 *Lubanga* First Sentence Review, para. 30.
53 Rule 145(2)(a)(ii) ICC RPE.
54 *Katanga* Sentence Review, para. 29.
55 *Katanga* Sentence Review, para. 28.
56 *Katanga* Sentence Review, paras 29–30.
57 *Katanga* Sentence Review, para. 31.
58 *Katanga* Sentence Review, para. 32.
59 *Katanga* Sentence Review, para. 26.

appeal should be construed as a mere strategic choice of counsel,[60] noting that this contention was at odds with the Prosecutor's written submission and did not explain why 'a withdrawal of appeal, coupled with a public apology and acknowledgement of crimes committed does not equate to the examples cited in the written submission as qualifying as cooperation, particularly in regards to a guilty plea'.[61] The Panel agreed with the Prosecutor's contention that cooperation for the purposes of sentence review should contribute to the efficient administration of justice.[62] The Panel noted while a convicted person has a statutory right to appeal his conviction, the non-exercise of this right would not automatically and by itself constitute cooperation. However, it noted that if the right was not exercised due to an acknowledgement of guilt, was accompanied by a public apology, prevented the 'unnecessary prolongation of proceedings' and enabled the reparations phase of proceedings to begin in a timely manner – then this would advance the efficient administration of justice in the same manner as a guilty plea prior to sentence and in this case, constituted *continuing cooperation* for the purposes of Article 110(4)(a). Continuing cooperation was defined as cooperation that occurred after the end of trial and the imposition of sentence.[63] Only when both elements – early and continuous willingness to cooperate – are found, will Article 110(4)(a) be deemed to be present. Cooperation with the Court was an important element in the *Al Mahdi* sentence review decision. Al Mahdi submitted that he had cooperated fully, unconditionally and unequivocally from the time of his arrest and pleaded guilty, thereby providing an 'invaluable contribution to the pursuit of the truth' about what happened in Timbuktu.[64] The Prosecutor supported Al Mahdi's submission that he had demonstrated early and continuing cooperation with the Court.[65] The Panel reiterated that cooperation must contribute to the efficient administration of justice and while cooperation taken into account in mitigation of sentence will not generally be revisited, whether conduct prior to sentence imposition qualifies as an indicator of early cooperation for sentence review purposes will be determined on a case-by-case basis.[66] The Panel noted the Trial Chamber had found his cooperation to be honest, substantial and spontaneous from the first interviews with the Prosecution and that this conduct qualified as early cooperation for sentence reduction review purposes.[67]

60 *Katanga* Sentence Review, para. 25.
61 *Katanga* Sentence Review, para. 33.
62 *Katanga* Sentence Review, para. 24.
63 *Katanga* Sentence Review, para. 34.
64 *Al Mahdi* Sentence Review, para. 19.
65 *Al Mahdi* Sentence Review, para. 21.
66 *Al Mahdi* Sentence Review, paras 24–25.
67 *Al Mahdi* Sentence Review, paras 26–27.

The Panel also found that Al Mahdi had demonstrated continued cooperation with the Court on the basis of his continued adherence to his admission of guilt, continued compliance with the terms of his Agreement and post sentence cooperation as indicative of continued cooperation.[68] Accordingly, the factors set out in Article 110(4)(a) were found to be present.[69]

Cooperation may also occur in other proceedings before the Court. In the second *Lubanga* sentence review, cooperation was considered in relation to participation in reparation proceedings.[70] While the Panel recognised Lubanga's active participation in such proceedings, it felt that this participation was confined to the exercise of his right to defend his interests and that the exercise of procedural rights does not demonstrate, *per se*, a change of circumstances required by this statutory factor.[71]

4.2 Article 110(4)(b): Voluntary Assistance in Enabling the Enforcement of Judgments and Orders of the Court – in Particular Providing Assistance in Locating Assets Subject to Orders of Fine, Forfeiture or Reparations Which May be Used for the Benefit of Victims

This statutory factor reflects the ICC's statutory power to impose fines or the forfeiture of proceeds, property or assets[72] and to order convicted persons to make reparations to, or in respect of, victims.[73] As no information has been presented by convicted persons in relation to this factor, it has not been found to be present in any sentence review case to date.[74]

Notably in *Al Mahdi*, while the Defence argued that the factor was not applicable as the convicted person had been deemed indigent,[75] the Prosecutor argued that the factor was present on account of the convicted person's voluntary assistance to the Prosecutor.[76] The Panel was not convinced by the Prosecutor's submission, arguing the facts referred to related to cooperation under Article 110(4)(a) and not (b).[77]

---

68 *Al Mahdi* Sentence Review, para. 31.

69 *Al Mahdi* Sentence Review, para. 31.

70 *Lubanga* Second Sentence Review, para. 41.

71 *Lubanga* Second Sentence Review, paras 43–44.

72 Article 77(2) ICCSt.

73 Article 75(2) ICCSt.

74 *Katanga* Sentence Review, paras 36–37; *Lubanga* First Sentence Review, para. 40; *Al Mahdi* Sentence Review, para. 36.

75 *Al Mahdi* Sentence Review, para. 32.

76 *Al Mahdi* Sentence Review, para. 33.

77 *Al Mahdi* Sentence Review, para. 35.

The Panels in *Lubanga's* first and second review declined to comment further on the relevance of the Prosecutor's submissions in relation to Lubanga's alleged involvement in witness interference in the *Ntaganda* case[78] due the finding that the factor was not present. However, it would seem from their reasoning that if the factor (voluntary assistance) was (first) found to be present, then administration of justice offences may become a relevant consideration.[79]

5. RULE 223 AND THE REGULATORY CRITERIA FOR REVIEW CONCERNING REDUCTION OF SENTENCE

Article 110(4)(c) of the Rome Statute facilitated the creation of additional criteria to be considered in the sentence review process in the Rules. Its reference to 'other factors' has been interpreted to mean those set out in Rule 223(a)–(e). This statutory provision also added a threshold for the consideration of these further regulatory criteria. Even where such factors are present, they must establish 'a clear and significant change of circumstances sufficient to justify a reduction of sentence'.

However, sentence review jurisprudence has established that as two of these five factors (prospects for resocialisation and successful resettlement and whether early release could give rise to significant social instability) will only be considered for the first time during the sentence review process, the requirement to establish a clear and significant change in circumstances is only applicable to the following three factors: conduct in detention showing genuine dissociation from his crime; significant action taken by the sentenced person for benefit of victims and impact of release on victims and their families; and individual circumstances.[80]

Even in situations where one of the two factors has been taken into consideration previously, the Panel will only consider it for the first time at sentence review proceedings. For example, in *Katanga*, the Trial Chamber had taken the convicted person's age and family situation into consideration as mitigating factors during sentencing as circumstances that could facilitate reintegration.[81]

---

78 *Lubanga* First Sentence Review, para. 38; *Lubanga* Second Sentence Review, paras 45–46.

79 *Lubanga* First Sentence Review, para. 40; *Lubanga* Second Sentence Review, para. 48.

80 *Katanga* Sentence Review, para. 19; *Lubanga* First Sentence Review, para. 28; *Al Mahdi* Sentence Review, para. 16.

81 Situation in the DRC, *Prosecutor v Germain Katanga*, TCII, Decision on Sentence pursuant to Article 76 of the Statute, ICC-01/04/01/07, 23 May 2014, para. 144.

The Sentence Review Panel felt that as reintegration and resocialisation are not ordinarily taken into account in the determination of sentence length, and that it is more appropriate to consider these factors at sentence review (given the possibility of release), this factor would continue to be considered for the first time to determine whether sentence reduction is justified.[82]

In relation to the statutory threshold to be applied to the discussion of changes in circumstances, review decisions have defined the term 'clear' as meaning 'free from doubt, unambiguous and very obvious' and the term 'significant' to mean 'large enough to be noticed or have an effect' or 'of a measurable large amount'.[83] This section examines each of these regulatory factors in more detail with a focus on their jurisprudential interpretation and application.

5.1 Rule 223(a): Conduct of the Sentenced Person While in Detention, Which Shows a Genuine Dissociation from His or Her Crime

The Sentence Review Panels have been clear that the plain meaning of this factor means mere good conduct in detention or towards detainees or staff is insufficient for the purposes of sentence review as it does not establish 'the necessary connection between this conduct and dissociation from crimes'.[84] Moreover, it has been made clear that there is a 'difference between expressing opposition to a particular criminal act in the abstract and that person accepting responsibility and expressing remorse for having committed those criminal acts:' only the latter is relevant for sentence review purposes.[85]

The factor will not be found to be present in the absence of acts in addition to good behaviour in detention, including acknowledgement of responsibility for the crime convicted of or an expression of remorse or regret to the victims of the crimes for which the applicant was convicted.[86] For this reason, the factor was not found to be present in either the first[87] or second[88] *Lubanga* Sentence Reviews: generalised expressions of remorse or opposition to crimes in the abstract do not suffice.

---

82 *Katanga* Sentence Review, para. 57.

83 *Katanga* Sentence Review, para. 47; *Al Mahdi* Sentence Review, para. 16.

84 *Lubanga* First Sentence Review, para. 45; *Katanga* Sentence Review, para. 47; *Al Mahdi* Sentence Review, para. 41.

85 *Lubanga* First Sentence Review, para. 45. See also *Katanga* Sentence Review, para. 47; *Lubanga* Second Sentence Review, para. 54.

86 See *Lubanga* First Sentence Review, para. 46.

87 *Lubanga* First Sentence Review, para. 47.

88 *Lubanga* Second Sentence Review, para. 57.

This factor was found to be present for the first time in *Katanga*. Katanga noted that his time in detention had had a profound effect on him and enabled him to reconsider his behaviour, culminating in his withdrawal of his appeal against conviction and sentence (and the acceptance of this conclusion of his conviction) and expressions of remorse.[89] Katanga also noted at the Sentence Review Hearing that 'when an accused person is found guilty his very value as a human being collapses' and that 'in the course of the trial I had to come to terms with the role that I personally played in the attack in Bogoro as well as with the degree or scope of suffering inflicted upon the victims of the attack'.[90] The Prosecutor supported a finding of this factor being present, drawing parallels with the *Dragoljub Ojdanić* case at the ICTY, highlighting his conduct and statements post-sentencing (acceptance of responsibility and expressions of remorse) that demonstrated genuine dissociation from his crimes.[91] The victims were more cautious arguing that good conduct in detention may be a 'simple survival strategy'[92] that the expressions of remorse and apologies were too general (and not specific to the relevant victims) and that the withdrawal of his appeal was a strategic decision to avoid a harsher sentence.[93] While noting, with reference to the Trial Chamber's reasoning, that a statement of remorse must be sincere and more than mere convention,[94] the Panel directly rejected the victims' submissions that Katanga's apologies were general – stating that Katanga has 'repeatedly and publicly taken responsibility for crimes convicted for and expressed regret for harm caused'. [95] It found that while Katanga had not dissociated from his crimes at the time of the imposition of sentence, the determinative issue in sentence review proceedings is whether circumstances have changed since that time.[96] Accordingly, it felt that the combined effect of his decision to withdraw his appeal against conviction, his acceptance of the Trial Chamber's findings in relation to his role and conduct with respect to the crimes he was convicted for, his expression of regret to the direct victims of his crimes and the recording of an apology to victims constituted a clear and significant change in circumstances that demonstrated post-sentence dissociation from his crimes.[97]

---

89 *Katanga* Sentence Review, para. 40.
90 *Katanga* Sentence Review, para. 46.
91 *Katanga* Sentence Review, paras 42–43.
92 *Katanga* Sentence Review, para. 44.
93 *Katanga* Sentence Review, para. 45.
94 *Katanga* Sentence Review, para. 48.
95 *Katanga* Sentence Review, para. 50.
96 *Katanga* Sentence Review, para. 49.
97 *Katanga* Sentence Review, paras 50–51.

The factor was not found to be present in *Al Mahdi*. While the Panel accepted that the convicted person had expressed remorse for his crimes post-sentencing, those made in detention had not been public and, though welcome, his personal address to victims and Malian society at the sentence review hearing asking for forgiveness was not sufficient to represent a clear and significant change of circumstances to justify a sentence reduction under Rule 223(b).[98]

5.2 Rule 223(b): The Prospect of the Resocialisation and Successful Resettlement of the Sentenced Person

The determination of the presence of this factor has rested on a number of elements including regular contact with family during detention, plans to enrol in further education courses post-release, plans to return to the army or farming on family land, place of resettlement and young age.[99]

Given the relatively short length of sentences considered for sentence reduction to date, and the length of time spent in custody before the finalisation of sentence and transfer to an enforcing State, the ICC convicted persons were in a similar situation to other international prisoners in that they did not have access to rehabilitation programmes during their time at the ICC Detention Centre. The ICC Registrar explained that as the ICC Detention Centre's mandate is limited to the detention of suspects and accused persons, no rehabilitation programmes are available.[100] Consequently (as the Prosecutor and victims have noted[101]) the Panels had to rely on the stated intentions of convicted persons[102] rather than any prison reports based on completion of relevant programmes, training or counselling. Psychological, psychiatric or risk assessments do not appear to have featured in this analysis either.

Despite this, the Prosecutor supported *Katanga*'s release on this ground, stating it was possible for him to be successfully resettled but also noting the fact that Katanga may face national proceedings upon return to DRC which may have an impact on resettlement.[103] The Panel, however, ruled that potential future criminal prosecutions post-release were irrelevant to sentence

---

[98] *Al Mahdi* Sentence Review, para. 45. See also paras 37, 42–44.

[99] *Lubanga* First Sentence Review, para. 52; *Katanga* Sentence Review, para. 58.

[100] *Lubanga* First Sentence Review, para. 49. See also *Katanga* Sentence Review, para. 52.

[101] See *Lubanga* First Sentence Review, para. 50; *Katanga* Sentence Review, para. 54.

[102] See *Lubanga* First Sentence Review, para. 48; *Katanga* Sentence Review, para. 54.

[103] *Katanga* Sentence Review, para. 55.

review proceedings as this was not a factor for consideration under Article 110(4) or Rule 223.[104]

Ultimately, in the cases to date, as convicted persons have not been able to show resocialisation in the traditional sense of analysis, Panels have required convicted persons to demonstrate that they have a feasible resettlement plan.[105] The DRC authorities cautioned against accepting the view expressed by the ICC Registrar – that a convicted person's interaction with fellow detainees and staff does not suggest an impediment to resocialisation[106] – arguing that the attitude of a detainee does not always reflect the real possibility of resocialisation and successful resettlement and that such behaviour can be intentionally deceptive.[107] Nevertheless, this factor was found to be present in all cases to date.[108]

There has been some discussion of the views of victims in relation to resettlement. In *Katanga*, for example, the victims rejected Katanga's submission that he had the support of (particular) victim communities,[109] arguing that these communities were not direct victims of the crimes for which he had been convicted.[110] The Panel accepted this observation but noted that he did have the support of Hema communities from areas closer to where he wished to resettle.[111] In *Al Mahdi*, the Panel highlighted the convicted person's intention to educate young people about the dangers of extremism.[112] However, the heavily redacted nature of the discussion of rehabilitation (submissions from the enforcing state, Prosecutor and Defence as well as the Panel's discussion[113]) make it very difficult to understand the grounds that influenced the decision to find there was a prospect for his resocialisation and successful resettlement and therefore that the factor was present.[114] It is interesting to note that where this factor has been found to exist in a prior sentence review, and if there is no indication of a significant change in circumstances in a subsequent review, the factor will be found to still exist.[115]

---

104 *Katanga* Sentence Review, para. 60.
105 *Katanga* Sentence Review, para. 58.
106 *Katanga* Sentence Review, para. 52.
107 *Katanga* Sentence Review, para. 53.
108 *Lubanga* First Sentence Review, para. 53; *Katanga* Sentence Review, para. 61.
109 *Katanga* Sentence Review, para. 54.
110 *Katanga* Sentence Review, para. 56.
111 *Katanga* Sentence Review, para. 59.
112 *Al Mahdi* Sentence Review, para. 50.
113 *Al Mahdi* Sentence Review, paras 46–47, 50, 52.
114 *Al Mahdi* Sentence Review, para. 53.
115 *Lubanga* Second Sentence Review, para. 61.

5.3 Rule 223(c): Whether the Early Release of the Sentenced Person Would Give Rise to Significant Social Instability

Rule 223(c) is a negative factor and, if found to be present, it can weigh against the reduction of sentence.[116] Decisions have outlined factors identified by the Registrar that can be taken into account when making this determination, which include the timing of any potential release particularly when elections are approaching; the convicted person's links with, position in and political strength of former associated political or military groups; and the views of the local community.[117]

Panels, referring to Oehmichen's commentary on the Rules, have noted that significant social instability may be demonstrated by information indicating that an individual's release would undermine public safety, cause social unrest (riots or ethnic-based violence), lead to the commission of new international crimes by that individual or his or her supporters or undermine public confidence in the domestic legal system.[118] The submissions from the parties appear to be important factors in this discussion.

In the first *Lubanga* review, the national authorities (DRC) expressed concerns, but these appeared to be related more to perceptions about the actual conviction and sentence (rather than release), and the impact of release on other international and domestic criminal prosecutions.[119] Lubanga urged caution in relation to such assessments given the unverified nature of the claims and reliance on opinion in relation to social and political stability. He drew attention to the distance of his proposed relocation site from the direct victims' communities, arguing that his resettlement could help promote reconciliation, and noting that Mr Ngudjolo's (acquitted on all charges) return had not caused any difficulties.[120] Victims were worried that his release would not only give rise to tensions but possibly result in the resumption of armed conflict and, potentially, new war crimes.[121]

In his submissions, Katanga argued that there was no objective evidence that he posed any threat to stability in the region he wished to resettle in, that he had no connection with the former militia group and that he had no intention of resuming military activity.[122] He expressed a wish to assist with peace

---

116 *Al Mahdi* Sentence Review, para. 58.

117 *Lubanga* First Sentence Review, paras 54–57; *Katanga* Sentence Review, paras 63–65.

118 *Katanga* Sentence Review, para. 74; *Al Mahdi* Sentence Review, para. 58.

119 *Lubanga* First Sentence Review, para. 58.

120 *Lubanga* First Sentence Review, paras 59–60.

121 *Lubanga* First Sentence Review, para. 62.

122 *Katanga* Sentence Review, paras 66–67.

talks and drew attention to the lack of victim opposition to his resettlement in his designated area.[123] He further argued that the timing of elections should not be directly related to sentence reduction given the speculative nature of this discussion and the fact that any potential instability would not be attributable to him.[124] The Prosecutor noted the reconciliation of relevant communities and felt there was no indication that the former militia group would reorganise around Katanga if released.[125] The victims were of the view that reconciliation was not as deep as it had been suggested due to land disputes and the ongoing presence of militia and the dissatisfaction felt in relation to the length of Katanga's sentence.[126] The DRC authorities reiterated serious reservations but again linked these to the length of the sentence imposed by the ICC and the potential impact of release on perceptions of other international and domestic criminal proceedings.[127] In *Katanga*, the Panel noted that the victims' negative feelings in relation to the length of the sentence were not relevant to considerations of social instability but may be relevant under Rule 223(d).[128] In relation to the DRC's submissions on the potential detrimental impact of release on domestic proceedings, the Court declined to comment given that no information was provided other than this 'bald assertion'.[129]

Sentence Review Panels seem to have adopted a cautious approach to this factor. The first *Lubanga* Review Panel referred to the challenges faced during the drafting of the Court's legal texts 'to capture the concept of considering the political conditions' of a country as a factor in sentence reduction review.[130] A cautious approach is further warranted by the practical reality that available information to date has been inconclusive[131] and conflicting[132] and the fact that the reality on the ground is beyond the convicted person's control. This has been demonstrated by the delays in relation to elections and the lack of a clear timeline for the next elections admitted in the second *Lubanga* review.[133]

---

123 *Katanga* Sentence Review, paras 67–68.

124 *Katanga* Sentence Review, para. 69.

125 *Katanga* Sentence Review, para. 70.

126 *Katanga* Sentence Review, para. 71.

127 *Katanga* Sentence Review, para. 72.

128 *Katanga* Sentence Review, para. 77.

129 *Katanga* Sentence Review, para. 78.

130 *Lubanga* First Sentence Review, para. 63; *Katanga* Sentence Review, para. 74.

131 *Lubanga* First Sentence Review, para. 54; *Katanga* Sentence Review, para. 62; *Lubanga* Second Sentence Review, para. 63.

132 *Lubanga* First Sentence Review, para. 64; *Katanga* Sentence Review, para. 75; *Lubanga* Second Sentence Review, para. 73.

133 *Lubanga* Second Sentence Review, paras 63–64.

The factor acts as an excluding criterion. If a reduction in sentence would not cause any social instability then the factor would weigh in favour of release. If found to be present, it weighs against other factors.[134] In all reviews to date, while Panels have considered it necessary to acknowledge the possibility of some level of social instability, they have been hesitant to find that such instability could be categorised as significant, as required by the rule.[135] For example, in the first *Lubanga* review, it was felt that any potential disturbances would remain localised and could be sufficiently controlled by national authorities or UN peacekeepers.[136] In the second *Lubanga* review, the Panel felt that the circumstances had changed slightly in the DRC since the first review but that the changes were not significant.[137] In *Katanga*, the Panel went further in its discussion and noted that while the potential social instability was not significant as required by the rule, it had not found that a sentence reduction would be beneficial for social stability or that it would not cause any social instability, and accordingly it would be a neutral factor weighing neither for or against a sentence reduction.[138]

The *Al Mahdi* decision further highlights the difficulties presented by the need to consider this factor. The sentence reduction review had to be conducted in light of the challenging political and security situation in Mali.[139] On the one hand, the Registrar stated there was no information to suggest his case had created unrest or that his release would give rise to social instability in Mali or elsewhere.[140] On the other hand, Mali opposed a sentence reduction on the basis that the people of Mali and Timbuktu 'had not fully healed from the wounds caused by' Al Mahdi's crimes.[141] The victims consulted expressed concerns that a return to Timbuktu might result in a renewal of ties with armed groups but 'were unable to discern' if his release would result in significant social insecurity.[142] Al Mahdi responded to submissions on this factor noting that his release would cause the least amount of disturbance to society if he was received by a country other than Mali.[143] Even though the Panel confirmed that 'it was not possible to provide a definite assessment' as to

134 *Katanga* Sentence Review, para. 74.
135 *Lubanga* First Sentence Review, para. 64; *Katanga* Sentence Review, para. 76; *Lubanga* Second Sentence Review, para. 73.
136 *Lubanga* First Sentence Review, para. 57.
137 *Lubanga* Second Sentence Review, paras 72–73.
138 *Katanga* Sentence Review, para. 79.
139 *Al Mahdi* Sentence Review, para. 54.
140 *Al Mahdi* Sentence Review, para. 54.
141 *Al Mahdi* Sentence Review, para. 55.
142 *Al Mahdi* Sentence Review, para. 56.
143 *Al Mahdi* Sentence Review, para. 57.

whether there was a risk of significant social instability, the Panel appears to put weight on concerns expressed by victims of the possibility of renewing ties with armed groups in Mali.[144] Victims also requested that any release should be monitored to ensure 'the process of individual and collective reparations… proceeds smoothly'.[145] The Panel seems to have accepted these views as sufficient to constitute evidence of risk of an impact on the reparations process if a sentence reduction was granted.[146] The Panel ultimately concluded that as release could happen during the reparation phase, Rule 223(c) was present and therefore weighed against a sentence reduction.[147]

5.4 Rule 223(d): Any Significant Action Taken by the Sentenced Person for the Benefit of the Victims as well as any Impact on the Victims and Their Families as a Result of the Early Release

Rule 223(d) contains two limbs: (1) any *significant* action taken by the sentenced person for the benefit of victims and (2) any impact on the victims and their families as a result of early release.

In the first *Lubanga* review, no information was presented to demonstrate the presence of the first limb of this factor.[148] Moreover, the Panel noted that instead of responding to the victims' suggestions in relation to acts he could take that they would consider being for their benefit, Lubanga's counsel challenged the status of these victims.[149] In relation to the second limb, the Panel noted that the information provided outlined the potential detrimental impact a sentence reduction and subsequent release would have on victims and their families.[150] Accordingly the factor was not found to be present.[151]

In the second *Lubanga* review, the Panel considered a number of possible actions including a proposal to organise a public ceremony to meet victims and offer apologies and a statement not to ask for a reduced sentence if it would affect the well-being of victims. In relation to the public ceremony, the Panel noted that while this constituted a change in circumstances, it was not sufficient as there was no indication as to when it would occur. It remained a proposal and not an action.[152] In relation to the statement, this was also ruled

---

144 *Al Mahdi* Sentence Review, para. 59.
145 *Al Mahdi* Sentence Review, para. 56.
146 *Al Mahdi* Sentence Review, para. 59.
147 *Al Mahdi* Sentence Review, para. 59.
148 *Lubanga* First Sentence Review, para. 69.
149 See *Lubanga* First Sentence Review, paras 67–69.
150 *Lubanga* First Sentence Review, paras 65, 70.
151 *Lubanga* First Sentence Review, para. 71.
152 *Lubanga* Second Sentence Review, para. 85.

to be an intention and not an action such as meaningful involvement in the reparation process or a sincere apology. [153] Overall, the Panel concluded it could not identify any significant change in circumstances and therefore the factor was not present.[154]

This factor received significant attention in *Katanga*. The Panel noted that while the first limb of this factor must be considered in conjunction with rule 223(a), as both may involve the same actions, such actions would be assessed differently under each heading. Under sub-paragraph (a), the actions were considered from the perspective of, or the impact on, the sentenced person (indicating a genuine dissociation from the crime), whereas under sub-paragraph (d), the actions were assessed from the perspective of the victims – whether such actions were considered by the victims to have benefitted them or were significant.[155] However, the Panel noted that caution should be taken in putting too much emphasis on the victims' subjective assessment of such actions given the risk of arbitrary and unequal results and accepted that while their views should be taken into account, assessments should be taken on a case-by-case basis taking into account 'an objective evaluation of actions balanced against the reasonableness of the victims' objections that they have not benefited from those actions'.[156]

In terms of what actions count, the Panel noted in general terms that involvement in the reparation process or a demonstration of regret would qualify as acts demonstrating significant action for the benefit of victims for his crimes.[157] In relation to the facts of the case at hand, the discussion focused on a number of actions taken by Katanga: the withdrawal of his appeal against conviction and his sentence, his support for the reparation process, the videoed apology and his offer to apologise to victims in person. In relation to the withdrawal of his appeal, the Panel felt that the specific circumstances of Katanga's case were of particular relevance. As a result of Katanga's withdrawal of appeal, the Prosecutor also withdrew her appeal against his acquittals on certain charges, increasing the frustration of victims already displeased by what they considered to be a lenient sentence. Consequently, the Panel felt that the withdrawal of the appeal could not be consider an action which benefitted the victims under rule 223(d).[158] The Panel also rejected aspirational statements for future action as qualifying actions.[159]

---

153 *Lubanga* Second Sentence Review, para. 86.
154 *Lubanga* Second Sentence Review, para. 87.
155 *Katanga* Sentence Review, para. 90.
156 *Katanga* Sentence Review, para. 91.
157 *Katanga* Sentence Review, para. 87.
158 *Katanga* Sentence Review, para. 93.
159 *Katanga* Sentence Review, para. 94.

The victims objected to the fact that reparations proceedings had not yet been concluded due to the short period of time that had elapsed since the completion of criminal proceedings and the commencement of the sentence review proceedings (1 year and 2 months). This timing had resulted in the victims rejecting Katanga's apology, stating that in Hema culture an apology should follow reparations and not precede them.[160] The Panel stressed that the timing of proceedings was not attributable to Katanga and accordingly this fact could not be held against him.[161] What the Panel felt was important to evaluate was whether his support of the victims' request for individual reparations, his filmed apology and offer to apologise personally were objectively significant actions, individually or collectively for the benefit of victims in the context of the ongoing reparations proceedings and whether the victims' objections that they have not benefitted from these actions were reasonable in the context of the reparations proceedings not being concluded.[162] The Panel decided that as Katanga's support for individual reparations derived from his required submission as part of the usual process: without more, this was only of marginal benefit to victims and not a significant action under Rule 223(d).[163] The Panel did suggest that the grant of a particular request of reparations under Rule 94 or the identification or location of assets to advance reparations would be of greater benefit for victims.[164]

In their analysis of the significance of the filmed apology and the offer to apologise personally to victims, the Panel took note of the observations of the Human Rights Centre at Queen's University Belfast and the Transitional Justice Institute at Ulster University made in their amicus curia submission which set out the steps a sentenced person can take to maximise the impact of and prospect of acceptance of their apology.[165] The Panel noted that the victims felt Katanga's apology was inadequate, and that more effort could be made to craft an apology acceptable to affected victims including dialogue with them.[166] The Panel stated that 'any steps taken by a sentenced person to attempt to ensure the broadest degree of acceptance and positive impact of that apology coupled with the reaction of victims to such steps may be relevant to determining whether such an apology or offer to apologise is a significant action that benefits victims'.[167] With regards to Katanga's filmed apology, it

---

160 See *Katanga* Sentence Review, paras 84–85.
161 *Katanga* Sentence Review, para. 96.
162 *Katanga* Sentence Review, para. 97.
163 *Katanga* Sentence Review, para. 98.
164 *Katanga* Sentence Review, para. 98.
165 *Katanga* Sentence Review, para. 99.
166 *Katanga* Sentence Review, para. 99.
167 *Katanga* Sentence Review, para. 100.

noted that, in principle, this may constitute a benefit to victims as viewing by the broader affected community including 'supporters' of the sentenced person may result in greater acceptance of the historical narrative as found by the ICC, and lead to broader recognition and acknowledgement of the harms done to victims.[168] However, this film was not intended for the broader community but for the direct victims of his crimes, and that it did not have any information to indicate that the manner of the delivery of the apology was informed by what was acceptable to these victims. Moreover, it was admitted by Katanga that the film was deliberately not shown to these victims due to concerns about negative reactions.[169] The Panel therefore found that the victims' rejection of the assertion that the filmed apology benefitted them to be reasonable and any indirect benefit that may accrue from viewing by the broader community was only minimal, if any at all, and therefore not significant for the purposes of rule 223(d).[170]

The Panel likewise acknowledged the potential benefit of personal apologies in face-to-face meetings but drew attention to the fact that it was unclear in the present case if the victims wished to have such an encounter or if such a meeting would cause further upset: therefore it was not a significant action for rule 223(d).[171] In relation to the second limb of the factor, the Panel noted in general terms only that it had considered submissions regarding the potential traumatising effect of Katanga's early release.[172] Its overall assessment was that while there had been limited benefit to victims from several actions, this did not amount to significant action for the benefit of victims within the meaning of rule 223(d). Moreover, early release could have a negative impact on victims and their families. Accordingly, rule 223(d) was found not to be present for the purposes of determining whether it was appropriate to reduce Katanga's sentence.[173]

This factor was also not found to be present in *Al Mahdi*.[174] The Panel reiterated the approach to the analysis of actions that may also have been considered under rule 223(a) that was set out in *Katanga*.[175] The Registrar reported that some victims had expressed fears about any potential release and their wish that Al Mahdi should serve his sentence in full, while others felt actions should be put in place to prevent any possible resumption of activities with

---

168 *Katanga* Sentence Review, para. 101.
169 See *Katanga* Sentence Review, para. 82.
170 *Katanga* Sentence Review, para. 102.
171 *Katanga* Sentence Review, para. 103.
172 *Katanga* Sentence Review, para. 104.
173 *Katanga* Sentence Review, para. 105.
174 *Al Mahdi* Sentence Review, para. 68.
175 *Al Mahdi* Sentence Review, para. 64.

terrorist groups.[176] The Legal Representative for Victims conveyed that victims were fearful for their safety and that of their families if he returned to the Timbuktu region on release, and the belief that Al Mahdi should serve his full sentence.[177] One group consulted however supported early release due to his expressions of remorse and apology though on the condition that he would not pose a threat to them or resume his activities.[178] The Panel concluded that although expressions of remorse had been made post-sentence they were of minimal benefit, if any, to victims as most were made in non-public settings and they did not constitute significant action.[179] In relation to the impact of release, the Panel noted the divergent views of consulted victims – some worried about the possible traumatising effect of release while others expressed forgiveness, and subsequently, assigned a neutral value to this factor.[180] Given the lack of significant action for the benefit of victims and the neutral impact on victims of release, the factor was not considered be present for the purposes of determining whether it was appropriate to reduce his sentence.[181]

5.5 Rule 223(e): Individual Circumstances of the Sentenced Person, Including a Worsening State of Physical or Mental Health or Advanced Age

The elements that might fulfil this factor were addressed for the first time in *Katanga*. The Panel reiterated that Katanga would have to demonstrate a clear and significant change in his circumstances since the imposition of his sentence. It recalled that his family situation and parental responsibilities were taken into account as mitigating circumstances during sentencing.[182] Moreover, it explicitly stated that it does not consider that the death of a family member constitutes a personal circumstance relevant to sentence reduction (though this is relevant for interim release).[183] However, where the death of a family member results in changed familial responsibilities (such as in Katanga's case where the death of his father and brother resulted in responsibilities for his mother, step-mother and three additional children[184]), this increased depend-

[176] *Al Mahdi* Sentence Review, para. 60.
[177] *Al Mahdi* Sentence Review, para. 62.
[178] *Al Mahdi* Sentence Review, para. 62.
[179] *Al Mahdi* Sentence Review, paras 65–66.
[180] *Al Mahdi* Sentence Review, para. 67.
[181] *Al Mahdi* Sentence Review, para. 68.
[182] *Katanga* Sentence Review, para. 108.
[183] *Katanga* Sentence Review, para. 109.
[184] *Katanga* Sentence Review, para. 107.

ency did represent a clear and significant chance in circumstances required by rule 223(e).[185]

The Panel rejected arguments from Lubanga that this factor could be used to provide a remedy in the form of sentence reduction for alleged violations of human rights that occurred prior to and during trial (detention in DRC and stays of proceedings due to Prosecutor's conduct[186]), stating that this was not possible in the given legal framework (sentence reduction) and that these arguments had been rejected by both the trial and appeal chambers during sentencing.[187] Without any further information being presented, this factor was not found to be present in first Lubanga review.[188] Lubanga again tried to seek a reduction in sentence for perceived rights violations in his second review under this factor. In this instance, he referred to the conditions of detention at Malaka Prison in the DRC, namely the security risks following an armed attack and the subsequent escape of 5,000 prisoners.[189] This argument was rejected as irrelevant to sentence reduction reviews on the same grounds as before but the Panel did note that any issue regarding the enforcement of sentence or conditions of imprisonment should be raised with the Presidency under Article 106 and rule 211.[190]

In *Al Mahdi*, the Defence submission focused on the harsh conditions endured in detention including the inability to see family members, isolation and assaults, and the fact that this made the time in detention 'tantamount to a longer term'.[191] The Panel rejected the argument that sentence reduction can be used as a remedy for harsh conditions as irrelevant to this assessment and appears to have pointed to support he had received.[192] As the enforcing state reported that he had no physical or mental health issues during his time in detention, the Panel felt there were no individual circumstances to consider.[193]

---

185 *Katanga* Sentence Review, para. 109–110.
186 *Lubanga* First Sentence Review, para. 72.
187 *Lubanga* First Sentence Review, para. 74–75.
188 *Lubanga* First Sentence Review, para. 76.
189 *Lubanga* Second Sentence Review, para. 89.
190 *Lubanga* Second Sentence Review, para. 92.
191 *Al Mahdi* Sentence Review, para. 69.
192 *Al Mahdi* Sentence Review, para. 71.
193 *Al Mahdi* Sentence Review, paras 70, 72.

6. PANEL DECISIONS ON THE APPROPRIATENESS AND EXTENT OF SENTENCE REDUCTION

Reasoned decisions must be communicated to all review participants as soon as possible.[194] All decisions reached by the three judge Panels (with a Presiding judge) to date have been unanimous.[195] It is unclear if all aspects of the decision are reached on a unanimous basis as no disagreements have been discussed. Panels have noted that all information received was considered even if it was not 'exhaustively summarised' in the published decision.[196]

The decisions stress that while the review itself is mandatory, the Panel's ultimate decision on whether it is appropriate to reduce the sentence is discretionary: Article 110(4) states that 'the Court may reduce' the sentence.[197] Moreover, the Panels have made clear that at least one factor must be found to be present before they will exercise their discretion to reduce a sentence but the presence of a factor in favour of reduction will not in itself result in a reduction.[198] This can be seen in the first *Lubanga* review where, although rule 223(c) (prospect for resocialisation and resettlement in DRC) was found to be present, a sentence reduction was not justified in the absence of any other factors.[199] In addition, the presence of a factor militating against a reduction (such as a finding of significant social instability under rule 223(c)) will not preclude the exercise of this judicial discretion.[200] The process involves weighing factors in favour of reduction against factors militating against reduction to determine whether a reduction of sentence is appropriate.[201] The Panel rejected the argument raised in the first *Lubanga* review (based on the practice of domestic and other international courts) that early release could only be refused where

194 Rule 224(2) ICC RPE.

195 *Lubanga* First Sentence Review, preamble; *Katanga* Sentence Review, preamble; *Lubanga* Second Sentence Review, preamble; *Al Mahdi* Sentence Review, preamble.

196 *Lubanga* First Sentence Review, para. 33; *Al Mahdi* Sentence Review, para. 18.

197 *Lubanga* First Sentence Review, para. 21; *Lubanga* Second Sentence Review, para. 28; *Katanga* Sentence Review, para. 20; *Al Mahdi* Sentence Review, para. 15.

198 *Al Mahdi* Sentence Review, para. 75.

199 *Lubanga* First Sentence Review, para. 77.

200 *Lubanga* First Sentence Review, para. 22; *Katanga* Sentence Review, para. 20.

201 *Lubanga* First Sentence Review, para. 22; *Katanga* Sentence Review, para. 20; *Al Mahdi* Sentence Review, para. 15.

exceptional circumstances exist, as the Statute ensures the primacy of the ICC's legal texts which did not contain this requirement.[202]

In *Katanga*, the Panel stated which factors found to be present that it considered to weigh in favour of a substantial reduction (cooperation and genuine dissociation)[203] and which factors (resocialisation and individual circumstances) supported 'a further reduction of sentence when considered together' with the other factors.[204] While the decision appears to rank and attribute relative weight to the factors found to be present, no corresponding reduction in sentence was given for the factors identified. In *Al Mahdi*, the Panel, with no elaboration on the relative weight of each factor, concluded that his cooperation and prospects for resocialisation and resettlement outweighed the factors militating against sentence reduction and therefore that it was appropriate to reduce the sentence.[205]

The Panels in *Katanga* and *Al Mahdi* stressed that as review can only occur after two-thirds of the original sentence has been served, any possible reduction can only be applied to the remaining one third of the sentence.[206] Further, the extent of any reduction would be determined by the information presented in each specific sentence review.[207] Where the Panel rules that a sentence reduction is appropriate, it states the amount by which the original sentence is to be reduced and the new date of completion of the sentence. For example, Katanga's original sentence was reduced by 3 years and 8 months, giving him a new sentence completion date of 18 January 2016 (rather than the original completion date of 18 September 2019).[208] This decision resulted in the grant of release four months after two-thirds of the sentence had been served. The *Al Mahdi* Panel noted the date on which two thirds of his nine-year sentence would be served, the date upon which the full sentence would be served, and concluded that due to the views expressed by Mali and a significant number of victims, a reduction could not be applied to the entirety of the remaining sentence.[209] But, without any further explanation, the Panel concluded that a reduction of two years was appropriate.[210] The decision set out the revised date

202 *Lubanga* First Sentence Review, para. 23.
203 *Katanga* Sentence Review, para. 114.
204 *Katanga* Sentence Review, para. 115.
205 *Al Mahdi* Sentence Review, paras 73–75.
206 *Katanga* Sentence Review, para. 113; *Al Mahdi* Sentence Review, para. 76.
207 *Katanga* Sentence Review, para. 113; *Al Mahdi* Sentence Review, para. 76.
208 *Katanga* Sentence Review, preamble and para. 116.
209 *Al Mahdi* Sentence Review, para. 77.
210 Ibid.

for the completion of sentence, which would occur one year after two-thirds of the sentence had been served.[211]

7. CONCLUSION

The ICC release system relies on a more detailed statutory and regulatory framework compared to the UN Tribunals, but it does not have a practice direction. At this point, there is a much smaller body of jurisprudence but the decisions to date have been consistent in their interpretation and application of the criteria set out in the legal framework. Since its first sentence review in 2015, the ICC has only conducted four sentence reviews for three convicted persons. One convicted person (Lubanga) was denied sentence reduction on two occasions and served his sentence in full. The two others were both granted sentence reductions (Katanga and Al Mahdi). In contrast to the UN system, a three-judge panel is obliged to conduct *proprio motu* sentence reviews at a statutorily established eligibility threshold (for both determinate and indeterminate sentences). The factors that the judicial panel must consider are set out in Article 110(4) and Rule 223. Of the ten different elements to be considered, some are cumulative tests, some have high thresholds and others must be demonstrated to represent a clear and significant change in circumstances since sentence imposition. These requirements demand a detailed application of the facts of each particular case.

Despite the detail of the legal framework, important issues remain unresolved. Can a serving prisoner apply for early release on humanitarian grounds prior to the two-thirds point? The plain wording of the ICC Statute would suggest they cannot. Further, it remains questionable how relevant or appropriate some of the factors that must be considered are for sentence reduction purposes given the difficulties in establishing an objective evidence base and the fact that the elements are beyond the control of the sentenced person. Aspects of the sentence reduction decisions are so heavily redacted it is very difficult to say on what factual basis the analysis of whether a factor is present or not has been made. Moreover, the decisions give virtually no detail as to why a particular reduction of sentence in terms of years has been deemed appropriate in the given case. Finally, although victims have expressed their view that a convicted person should be monitored upon release or actions put in place to ensure the released person cannot re-engage with former armed groups, the legal framework does not permit the imposition of conditions upon release. Sentence reduction at the ICC therefore results in unconditional release.

---

[211] Ibid.

4. Conditional early release at the Residual Special Court for Sierra Leone

1. THE CREATION OF A CONDITIONAL EARLY RELEASE SCHEME

The Special Court for Sierra Leone's (SCSL) statutory and regulatory framework governing release replicated that of the ad hoc UN Tribunals. Article 22(2) of the SCSL Statute on 'Enforcement of Sentences' stated that conditions of imprisonment, though governed by the law of the enforcing State, will be 'subject to the supervision of the Special Court'. Moreover, the enforcing State will be 'bound by the duration of the sentence, subject to article 23'. Article 23, entitled 'Pardon or Commutation of Sentences', stated that 'if, pursuant to the applicable law of the State in which the convicted person is imprisoned, he or she is eligible for pardon or commutation of sentence, the State concerned shall notify the Special Court accordingly. There shall only be pardon or commutation of sentence if the President of the Special Court, in consultation with the judges, so decides on the basis of the interests of justice and the general principles of law'. This provision is identical to Article 27 of the ICTY Statute and Article 28 of the ICTR Statute. The SCSL rules on pardon and commutation (Rules 123–124) were also identical to the ICTY and ICTR rules. This was not surprising given that Article 14 of the SCSL Statute stated that the Rules of Procedure and Evidence of the ICTR should apply *mutatis mutandis* to the conduct of legal proceedings before the SCSL.

Following the Legacy Conference in Freetown in 2007, however, the SCSL 'engaged in an examination of the theoretical and practical issues raised by the possibility of early release of sentenced prisoners'[1] and decided to appoint a Sub-Committee to make recommendations in relation to concerns and unresolved issues relevant to the implementation of Rules 123 and 124. This

[1] Teresa Anne Doherty and Shireen Avis Fisher, 'Enforcement of sentences and oversight of prisoners convicted by the SCSL' in R. Mulgrew and D. Abels (eds) *Research Handbook on the International Penal System* (Edward Elgar Publishing, 2016) 355–380 at 355.

included prisoner expectations of the possibility of remission of one-third of their sentence as permitted by Sierra Leonean law, the disparity of treatment if eligibility was determined by the national law of enforcing states, consultation requirements, and the criteria to be applied to release decisions.[2]

The legal framework governing release changed further with the passing of responsibility for the supervision of the enforcement of sentences to the Residual Special Court for Sierra Leone (RSCSL). In addition to a change in the numbering of the relevant articles,[3] a new provision was added to the statutory scheme. Article 23(3) empowers the RSCSL to 'supervise the enforcement of sentences, including the implementation of the sentence enforcement agreements, and other agreements with international and regional organisations and other appropriate organisations and bodies'. Moreover, Article 24 was amended to include a direction to consult with the judges who imposed the sentence where possible.

Rule 124 was amended in light of these statutory changes and further developed the consultation requirements relevant to release. Retitled to refer to early release in addition to pardon and commutation of sentence, it now states that 'there shall only be pardon, commutation or early release if the President of the Residual Special Court, in accordance with Article 24 of the RSCSL Statute and in consultation with the judges who imposed the sentence where possible, and after considering the position of the Prosecutor, which shall incorporate the interests of Prosecution witnesses and victims, as well as the convicted person individually or through counsel, so decides on the basis of the interests of justice and the general principles of law. An early release shall only occur after the prisoner has served a minimum of two-thirds of his or her original sentence'.

Given that the SCSL and RSCSL's statutory and regulatory framework mirrored those of the UN ad hoc Tribunals for the former Yugoslavia and Rwanda, it had been presumed that the release scheme would replicate their system of unconditional release. In October 2013, however, the RSCSL President introduced a Practice Direction which, for the first time in international penal law, introduced a conditional release system for persons convicted by an international(ised) criminal court.[4] The Practice Direction and its attached documents set out a detailed multi-stage system of conditional early release which includes a determination of eligibility for conditional early

---

2 Ibid at 357–358.

3 Article 23(2) RSCSLSt replicates Article 22(2) SCSLSt on Enforcement of Sentences, and Article 24 RSCSLSt replicates Article 23 SCSLSt on Pardon or Commutation of Sentence.

4 Practice Direction on the Conditional Early Release of Persons Convicted by the Special Court for Sierra Leone, 1 October 2013 (hereafter PDCER).

release, a decision on whether to grant conditional early release, the imposition of general and special conditions, the execution of the release decision, the supervision of released persons, the procedure for dealing with alleged or admitted breaches of release conditions, and the termination of conditional early release. Conditional release involves the service of a portion of a sentence of imprisonment outside of a prison establishment and therefore is a community sanction and measure.[5] Judicial decisions have further developed the principles, factors and procedures that apply to the supervision of convicted persons serving the remainder of their sentences in the community in Sierra Leone. This chapter explores the law, jurisprudence and practice in relation to each stage of the system in turn.

2. DETERMINATION OF ELIGIBILITY FOR CONSIDERATION FOR CONDITIONAL EARLY RELEASE

To progress to consideration for release, the President must first deem the convicted person eligible for consideration for conditional early release. Either the enforcing State or the prisoner can initiate the process 'in accordance with the applicable Enforcement of Sentence Agreement'.[6] The prisoner can apply to the enforcing State (copying his application to the Registrar)[7] or the enforcing State can notify the RSCSL of the prisoner's eligibility for release under domestic law.[8] The formal requirement of receipt of documents from the enforcing State appears to rule out direct applications from prisoners and, indeed, one prisoner's direct application to the Registrar was rejected 'due to non-compliance with the Practice Direction'.[9] During the 2016 revision of the Practice Direction, Article 3 (entitled 'Initiating the Process to Determine Eligibility for Consideration of Conditional Early Release) was amended from 'the Convicted Person may initiate the … review process' to 'initiation of the … review process' to reflect this approach.[10] If the relevant forms are forwarded in the correct manner, eligibility for consideration is determined on the basis of a list of cumulative criteria set out in Article 2(A)–(D) of the Practice

[5] Rule 9.2(c) UN Standard Minimum Rules on Non-Custodial Measures 1990 (Tokyo Rules); Recommendation CM/Rec (2017)3 on the European Rules on community sanctions and measures (ERCSM), Definitions.

[6] Art. 3(A) PDCER.

[7] Art. 3(A)(i) PDCER.

[8] Art. 3(A)(ii) PDCER.

[9] *Prosecutor v Senessie*, Decision of the President on Application for Conditional Early Release, SCSL-11-01-ES (580-589), 4 June 2014, para. 7.

[10] Art. 3(C) PDCER.

Direction. The prisoner must submit documentation establishing that he meets these requirements for eligibility.[11]

Rule 124 SCSL RPE was amended in November 2011 to add a regulatory threshold for eligibility for early release, noting that 'early release shall only occur after the prisoner has served a minimum of two-thirds of his original sentence'. The Practice Direction also requires that to be eligible for consideration for early release, the convicted person must show that he has served two-thirds of his sentence.[12] While it is clear from the Practice Direction that the process can only be initiated five months prior to the two-thirds point,[13] the current system appears to contain an internal inconsistency caused by the 2011 amendment. The fixed temporal point for eligibility was added to Rule 124 without amending or removing the current reference to notification following eligibility for release under national law in Article 23 of the Statute and Rule 123. This right of the enforcing State to notify the court when the prisoner becomes eligible for release under domestic law is therefore present in Form B attached to the PDCER. While the Rwandan legal position aligns with this 2/3 temporal threshold,[14] prisoners serving in the UK can become eligible for release after serving half of their sentence. Despite this, the Sub-Committee noted that due to the practice at other international tribunals, whereby the President can consider release applications *proprio motu* in the absence of domestic eligibility or indeed an enforcing State being involved in the implementation of the sentence, notice of eligibility from an enforcing State is not 'the exclusive trigger' for such considerations[15] and although notification of domestic eligibility 'may trigger … consideration and consultation by the President, but without presidential authorisation, the prisoner must remain incarcerated'.[16] Following this logic, the regulatory threshold, which fetters the President's discretion to grant release prior to the 2/3 point, would prevail over domestic eligibility. As demonstrated by Fofana's first submission, applications for release prior to the two-thirds point will be dismissed on the grounds of prematurity.[17]

---

11 Art. 3(B) PDCER. Art. 2 requires that the convicted person 'demonstrate' the criteria in 2(B) and 'shall provide proof' that the requirements in 2(C) have been met.

12 Art. 2(A) PDCER.

13 Art. 3(C) PDCER.

14 Art. 246 of the Law of Rwanda code of criminal procedure (Law No. 30/2013 of 24/5/2013).

15 Doherty and Fisher, note 1 at 363.

16 Ibid at 360.

17 *Prosecutor v Fofana and Kondewa*, Decision of the President on Application for Conditional Early Release, SCSL-04-14-ES (1270-1291), 11 August 2014, para. 3.

In contrast to the release systems at other contemporary international criminal courts, which only require service of two-thirds of the sentence, SCSL convicted persons must also demonstrate a range of cumulative factors (set out in Article 2(B)–(D)) before they can be deemed eligible for consideration for release.

It is compulsory for convicted persons to demonstrate their successful completion of any remedial, educational, moral, spiritual or other programmes they were referred to in prison.[18] This provision uses the terminology contained in rule 59 of the 1955 UN Standard Minimum Rules for the Treatment of Prisoners but fails to include the direction that such programmes should be appropriate and applied 'according to the individual treatment needs of the prisoners'.[19] It is also unclear what constitutes 'successful' completion. More problematically, insistence on completion in relation to moral and spiritual programmes may undermine the dignity of prisoners, violate their freedom of religion, and constitute compulsory moralisation.[20] Other factors listed in the Practice Direction appear difficult to prove. For instance, how do you demonstrate that you are not a danger to any member of the public?[21] What constitutes non-compliance with the terms and conditions of imprisonment?[22] It is also questionable if all of these factors should be mandatory requirements. Is it necessary for a convicted person to respect the fairness of the process by which they were convicted in order to be considered for release?[23] In contrast to the logical requirement to show they have not incited against the peace and security of the people of Sierra Leone during their time in prison,[24] it is more difficult for persons serving their sentences in Rwanda and the UK to demonstrate that they made a 'positive contribution to peace and reconciliation in Sierra Leone and the region' by means of public acknowledgment of

---

[18] Art. 2(B)(i) PDCER.

[19] Approved by ECOSOC resolutions 663 C (XXIV), 31 July 1957, and 2076 (LXII), 13 May 1977. This rule was refocused and repositioned during the 2015 revision of the Standard Minimum Rules. Rule 4(2), a basic principle of the Nelson Mandela Rules, now states that 'prison administrations and other competent authorities should offer education, vocational training and work, as well as other forms of assistance that are appropriate and available, including those of a remedial, moral, spiritual, social and health- and sports-based nature'. See GA Resolution 70/175, 17 December 2015, Annex.

[20] See Róisín Mulgrew, *Towards the Development of the International Penal System* (CUP, 2013) at 261.

[21] Art. 2(B)(ii) PDCER.

[22] Art. 2(B)(iii) PDCER.

[23] Art. 2(C)(i) PDCER.

[24] Art. 2(C)(ii) PDCER.

guilt, public support for peace projects, public apology to victims, or victim restitution.[25]

In addition to the requirements found in the Practice Direction, further (expanded) requirements are implied in the attached paperwork. Form A(1) requires the prisoner to show he has not posed a risk to the witnesses who testified against him and that not only did he not incite against the peace and security of Sierra Leone directly but that he did not do so through other persons.[26]

Finally, the convicted person must testify in their application that they will abide by the terms of a Conditional Early Release Agreement (CERA).[27] This is problematic given that only the general conditions, and not the special conditions that may be applied to the individual in question, are known. This is recognised in Form A(1) where the prisoner must 'acknowledge and accept that the President may impose further Special Conditions of Release'. While the scheme does ensure that convicted persons receive legal advice from the Principal Defender in relation to the conditions imposed and the potential consequences of breach, and that the voluntary and informed nature of the convicted person's agreement to abide by the terms must be attested to by two witnesses,[28] the convicted person must agree in principle to abide by terms of which they have no knowledge at this stage of the process.

While the forms annexed to the Practice Direction were intended to make the process as clear as possible, it became apparent that convicted persons required legal assistance to submit the required paperwork. Although there is no statutory or regulatory provision for legal representation during release proceedings, the President has granted legal counsel for this purpose. Further, a new provision was added to the revised Practice Direction, stating that 'the Principal Defender shall provide advice and assistance to the convicted persons if requested at any stage' during the release application process and proceedings.[29]

The decision on eligibility for consideration for conditional early release is made by the President in consultation with the sentencing judges, or if they are unavailable, at least two other judges. The President's decision is final: it is not

---

25 Art. 2(C)(iii) PDCER.

26 See Jamil Ddamulira Mujuzi, 'The Conditional Early Release of Offenders Transferred from the Special Court of Sierra Leone to Serve Their Sentences in Designated States: Some Observations and Recommendations' (2014) *African Yearbook of International Humanitarian Law* 154–170 at 160.

27 Art. 2(D) PDCER; *Prosecutor v Augustine Gbao,* Decision of the President on the application to determine eligibility for conditional early release, RSCSL-04-15-ES-1338, 10 January 2020.

28 Art. 10(A)-(B) PDCER.

29 Art. 2(G) PDCER.

subject to appeal or review.[30] If an application is denied, a convicted person can only reapply if he can demonstrate 'a change in circumstances warranting re-consideration'.[31] It is unclear what will constitute a sufficient change in circumstances in this regard. The President may also set a timeframe for permitted re-applications.[32]

Overall, while the factors set out in Article 2(B)–(C) represent an attempt to ensure a more purposeful release procedure that takes account of public safety, peace and reconciliation issues, they seem (on paper) difficult to prove, and their compulsory nature threatens to undermine any potential restorative or transitional effect. While they include factors that should rightly be taken into consideration when deciding whether to release an individual or not, the mandatory nature of these factors at the initial stage of determining eligibility for consideration for release appears to set the bar very high and stands in stark contrast to the law and practice at other international criminal courts, which only insist on temporal eligibility at this stage of the process.

In practice, however, it would seem that the threshold established by these cumulative objective criteria is not, in fact, too challenging to meet. It is difficult to say with any clarity, however, what each factor entails or what weight is given to the various factors. The *Senessie* decision appears to consider a factor not listed in Article 2 (favourable prospects for reintegration into society), and proceeds to find that the requirements in Article 2 had been met without discussing them at all.[33] The *Fofana* and *Kondewa* decisions merely state that the documentation submitted was 'sufficient to warrant … consideration for conditional early release and that [the applicant] has therefore met the requirements set out in Article 2 of the Practice Direction'.[34] The decisions refer to the forms of documentation considered – for example, danger to public safety was assessed on the basis of a psychological risk assessment, compliance with prison rules was based on disciplinary records and incitement against peace

30 Art. 2(F) PDCER.

31 Art. 2(E) PDCER.

32 Art. 2(F) PDCER.

33 *Prosecutor v Senessie*, Decision on Eric Senessie's Eligibility for Consideration for Conditional Early Release, SCSL-11-01-ES (307–310), 29 April 2014.

34 *Prosecutor v Fofana and Kondewa*, Decision on Moinina Fofana's Eligibility for Consideration for Conditional Early Release, SCSL-04-14-ES (1264–1267), 24 April 2014; *Prosecutor v Kondewa*, President's Decision on Allieu Kondewa's Eligibility for Consideration for Conditional Early Release, RSCSL-04-14-ES (1476–1480), The Hague, 2 December 2016.

and security was based on prison records.[35] The decisions do not discuss the content or conclusions of any of these assessments. But in relation to other mandatory factors, such as respect for the fairness of the process or contribution to peace and reconciliation, there was no discussion of what proof was submitted as required by Article 2(C) of the Practice Direction. President Kamanda in *Gbao* referred to documentation from the Rwandan Correctional Services and a medical professional, as well as Mr Gbao's written apology, promise to publicly apologise on national radio and television, and declarations made pursuant to Articles 2(B)(ii), 2(C)(i) and 2(C)(iii) of the Practice Direction.[36]

During the 2016 revision of the Practice Direction, Article 4(A) was revised to direct the President to specifically consult with the judges 'who imposed the sentence, if available, or if unavailable at least two other judges'. The decisions to date have simply stated that the consultations required under Article 4(A) occurred, without specifying with whom or what the views of the other judges were.[37]

3. PROCEDURE FOR DECISIONS ON CONDITIONAL EARLY RELEASE

As with other internationally convicted persons, persons convicted by the SCSL do not have a right to conditional early release.[38] In 2020, in a bid to counter misinformation, the RSCSL issued a statement emphasising that

---

[35] *Prosecutor v Fofana and Kondewa*, Decision on Moinina Fofana's Eligibility for Consideration for Conditional Early Release, SCSL-04-14-ES (1264–1267), 24 April 2014; *Prosecutor v Kondewa*, President's Decision on Allieu Kondewa's Eligibility for Consideration for Conditional Early Release, RSCSL-04-14-ES (1476–1480), The Hague, 2 December 2016.

[36] *Prosecutor v Augustine Gbao,* Decision of the President on the application to determine eligibility for conditional early release, RSCSL-04-15-ES-1338, 10 January 2020.

[37] *Prosecutor v Fofana and Kondewa*, Decision on Moinina Fofana's Eligibility for Consideration for Conditional Early Release, SCSL-04-14-ES (1264–1267), 24 April 2014; *Prosecutor v Senessie*, Decision on Eric Senessie's Eligibility for Consideration for Conditional Early Release, SCSL-11-01-ES (307–310), 29 April 2014; *Prosecutor v Kondewa*, President's Decision on Allieu Kondewa's Eligibility for Consideration for Conditional Early Release, RSCSL-04-14-ES (1476–1480), The Hague, 2 December 2016; *Prosecutor v Augustine Gbao,* Decision of the President on the application to determine eligibility for conditional early release, RSCSL-04-15-ES-1338, 10 January 2020.

[38] *Prosecutor v Senessie*, Decision of the President on Application for Conditional Early Release, SCSL-11-01-ES (580–589), 4 June 2014, para. 15.

release was a judicial decision made by the Residual Special Court President in line with RSCSL law, and neither the UN nor the Government of Sierra Leone had any role in such decision-making.[39]

To assist the President (and consulted judges) in reaching a decision on whether or not to grant CER to an individual, the Registrar must collect and collate a wide range of information and views through consultations.[40] A copy of this report is provided to the convicted person, the Prosecutor and the Principal Defender.[41] The Registrar must also provide the President with two potential Requested Areas of Residence (RAR) in the event that the first choice is deemed unsuitable, as well as reasons why they are suitable for resettlement, setting out the convicted person's connections with the area and how he will be supported financially.[42]

From the enforcing State, the Registrar may seek psychiatric evaluations and medical reports on the prisoner's general and mental health;[43] reports[44] on the convicted person's behaviour in prison (to include contact or threats with persons involved with SCSL prosecutions, any violent or threatening behaviour, violation of prison rules or SCSL orders, the commission, incitement or promotion of any crime[45] and any disrespect of law, rules or authority);[46] details of the convicted person's participation in prison programmes, acknowledgement of or remorse for his crimes, renunciation of violent ideology, willingness

---

39 RSCSL Press Release 'Statement by the Residual Special Court on the Conditional Early Release of Prisoners Convicted by the SCSL' Freetown, 12 October 2020.

40 Art. 5(B)–(H) PDCER.

41 Art. 5(I) PDCER; See *Prosecutor v Senessie,* Decision of the President on Application for Conditional Early Release, SCSL-11-01-ES (580–589), 4 June 2014, para. 10; *Prosecutor v Fofana and Kondewa*, Decision of the President on Application for Conditional Early Release, SCSL-04-14-ES (1270–1291), 11 August 2014, para. 6; *Prosecutor v Kondewa*, Decision of the President on Application for Conditional Early Release, RSCSL-04-14-ES (1581-1604), The Hague, 29 May 2017, para. 6.

42 Art. 5(B) PDCER.

43 Art. 5(C) PDCER.

44 In *Fofana*, a Prosecutor's challenge to the admissibility of a report from the Rwandan Prison Authorities was dismissed as there was no requirement for such a report to be an affidavit, and the President was satisfied that it came from an authorised person (*Prosecutor v Fofana and Kondewa*, Decision on Moinina Fofana's Eligibility for Consideration for Conditional Early Release, SCSL-04-14-ES (1264–1267), 24 April 2014, para. 39).

45 The 2016 Revision of the PDCER saw article 5(D)(i)(c) amended to the new 5(D)(i)(e) to include the commission of crimes outside the prison.

46 Art. 5(D)(i) PDCER.

to make restitution to victims or empathy towards them;[47] assessments of any likelihood to commit criminal offences, instigate or participate in discrimination or political unrest;[48] confirmation that the convicted person has demonstrated a commitment to agree to conditions of residency, behaviour and supervision if released;[49] any explanation offered by the convicted person for their offending behaviour[50] and any other information the President considers relevant.[51]

The Registrar must also ensure that the views of victims, witnesses and their families are provided to the President through either the Prosecutor or the Witnesses and Victims Section (WVS).[52]

Through communications with the WVS, the Home State Government, representatives of the RAR and other relevant persons and organisations[53] the Registrar must collect any information considered relevant by the President[54] but in particular on the following issues:

- the effect on the well-being and safety of the local community (especially victims, witnesses and their families, and others at risk on account of their testimony) if the convicted person is released;[55]
- any evidence of threatening behaviour or threats to victims, witnesses or SCSL Judges, Principals or personnel made directly or indirectly by the convicted person;[56]
- any evidence that CER would be used to incite members of the political or military factions with which he fought to use violence against the

47 Art. 5(D)(ii) PDCER.

48 Art. 5(D)(iii)(a)-(b) PDCER.

49 Art. 5(D)(iii)(iv) PDCER.

50 Art. 5(D)(iii)(v) PDCER.

51 Art. 5(D)(iii)(vi) PDCER.

52 Art. 5(E) PDCER.

53 The phrase 'other relevant persons and organisations' was added in the 2016 Revision.

54 Art. 5(F)(xiii) PDCER.

55 Art. 5(F)(i) PDCER. Expanded to include 'relevant witnesses, witnesses' and victims' families and any other that are at risk on account of testimony before SCSL' in the 2016 Revision.

56 Art. 5(F)(ii) PDCER. Rewritten from 'any evidence of threatening behaviour and in particular threats to victims, witnesses and Special Court judges, Principals or personnel made directly or indirectly by CP' to 'previous threats to victims, witnesses, SCSL/RSCSL judges, other Principals and personnel...' in the 2016 Revision.

community, victims, witnesses or their families, Special Court Judges, Principals or personnel;[57]
- the circumstances and attitudes of the convicted person's family to his release;[58]
- any risk to the safety of the convicted person; [59]
- the convicted person's response to any previous periods of community supervision;[60]
- the suitability of the RAR; [61]
- the willingness of the population of the community of the RAR to accept the convicted person as a resident;[62]
- the acknowledgement of the local community of the RAR that the convicted person is guilty of the crimes for which he was convicted, as well as the pain and suffering caused to the victims and their families by these crimes; [63]
- recommendations regarding conditions for release having regard to these factors;[64] and
- a proposed programme of supervision tailored to the convicted person based on information from the Monitoring Authority.[65]

The Registrar must request that the Prosecutor submit a report on his/her views on the CER request, and information relevant to the above factors and the convicted person's cooperation 'that was not a consideration in sentencing and the significance thereof in bringing other perpetrators to justice'.[66] Finally, a portfolio produced by the Registrar should contain the personal details and detention records of the convicted person, documentation on any previous CER applications, trial and appeal chamber sentencing comments and conclusions, pre-trial or pre-sentence reports, and periodic reports from the enforcing State.[67] Following receipt of the Registrar's portfolio, the convicted person has the right to submit any relevant information 'that may assist the President in

---

57 Art. 5(F)(iii) PDCER.
58 Art. 5(F)(iv) PDCER.
59 Art. 5(F)(v) PDCER.
60 Art. 5(F)(vi) PDCER.
61 Art. 5(F)(vii) PDCER.
62 Art. 5(F)(viii) PDCER.
63 Art. 5(F)(ix)–(x) PDCER - added during the 2016 Revision.
64 Art. 5(F)(xi) PDCER.
65 Art. 5(F)(xii) PDCER.
66 Art. 5(G) PDCER.
67 Art. 5(H) PDCER.

determining whether to grant CER'.[68] The President must take account of the Prosecutor's submissions that should incorporate the interests of Prosecution witnesses and victims.[69]

Foreseeably, the 'volume and amount of information' that the Registrar is required to obtain and collate from the enforcing State, the convicted person and his family, the government of the Home State, the SCSL Prosecutor, victims and witnesses (and their families), the Monitoring Authority, and residents from the requested areas of residence has led to delays.[70] However, this information is necessary to enable the President (and consulted judges) to assess key factors relevant for release: rehabilitation in the context of atrocity crimes, objective and subjective perspectives on the risk to public safety (broadly defined), and post-release considerations of residence, reintegration and the imposition of and compliance with conditions.

In addition to the information collated by the Registrar, the President can decide whether to hear the convicted person's views on these issues (either through a hearing in the prison or by video/phone-link) or to proceed on the basis of a written record.[71] In all decisions to date, the President has proceeded on the basis of written submissions from convicted persons.[72]

The President must issue a written and reasoned decision that evaluates a list of specific enumerated grounds[73] 'designed to explain, among other things, how he/she considered the safety of the public and the level of rehabilitation that has been accomplished by the convicted person'.[74] These grounds, listed in Article 8(D) of the Practice Direction, are as follows:

---

68 Art. 6(A), (C) PDCER.

69 Art. 6(B)-(D) PDCER.

70 Third Annual Report of the President of the RSCSL, January 2016 – December 2016 at 15. The Defence Office also had to request an extension as it was unable to contact members of the RAR communities during the festive season for consultations.

71 Art. 6(D) PDCER.

72 See the preambles of *Prosecutor v Senessie,* Decision of the President on Application for Conditional Early Release, SCSL-11-01-ES (580–589), 4 June 2014; *Prosecutor v Fofana and Kondewa*, Decision of the President on Application for Conditional Early Release, SCSL-04-14-ES (1270–1291), 11 August 2014; *Prosecutor v Kondewa*, Decision of the President on Application for Conditional Early Release, RSCSL-04-14-ES (1581–1604), The Hague, 29 May 2017; *Prosecutor v Gbao*, Decision of the President on Application for Conditional Early Release, RSCSL-04-15-ES, 8 September 2020, preamble and paras 5, 16.

73 Art. 8(D) PDCER.

74 Doherty and Fisher, note 1 at 373.

- the safety of victims, witnesses and their families, and others at risk on account of testimony before the Special Court;
- the safety of the community to which the convicted person will be released;
- the views and concerns of any victims, witnesses or their families, or others at risk on account of testimony before the SCSL;
- the effect of any conviction for contempt of court (which may alone justify a denial of CER);
- the convicted person's participation in prison programmes, demonstration of remorse, commitment to contribute to the restitution of victims, reconciliation, and the maintenance of peace in Sierra Leone; and
- the views, concerns and willingness and acknowledgements of the Requested Area of Release – their willingness to accept the convicted person as a resident; their acknowledgement that the convicted person is guilty of the crimes for which he was convicted, as well as the pain and suffering caused to victims and their families by these crimes.

The President's discretion is not absolute, as it is fettered by both the requirement to consider these grounds and the requirement to consult with the judges who imposed the sentence (or others if they are not available).[75] The Statute,[76] Rules[77] and Practice Direction[78] do not make it clear what weight the views of the consulted judges have on the final decision. Mujizi highlights that a duty to consult means a need to find consensus in some jurisdictions.[79] Case-law to date seems to suggest that these other judicial 'views form part of' the decision-making process:[80] that while the President makes the final decision, the views are one factor to be considered among others. Not all decisions have been explicit in relation to the consultation process. The *Senessie*, *Kondewa* and *Gbao* decisions simply state that consultations had taken place and that the views of the other judges would be considered or taken into account in reaching the final decision.[81] The *Fofana* decision, in contrast, demonstrated the

---

[75] Art. 8(A)–(B) PDCER.

[76] Art. 24 RSCSLSt.

[77] Rule 124 RSCSL RPE.

[78] Art. 8(A) PDCER.

[79] Mujuzi, note 26 at 161.

[80] *Prosecutor v Fofana and Kondewa*, Decision of the President on Application for Conditional Early Release, SCSL-04-14-ES (1270-1291), 11 August 2014, para. 18. See also para. 20.

[81] *Prosecutor v Senessie,* Decision of the President on Application for Conditional Early Release, SCSL-11-01-ES (580-589), 4 June 2014, para. 17; *Prosecutor v Kondewa*, Decision of the President on Application for Conditional Early Release, RSCSL-04-14-ES (1581–1604), The Hague, 29 May 2017, para. 12;

potential for disagreement between the consulted judges: one judge was supportive of CER, while the other expressed serious reservations due to Fofana's perceived failure to acknowledge his responsibility and leadership role in the armed conflict.[82] This reservation ultimately resulted in a delay in the grant of release.

Presidential discretion is further circumscribed by the mandatory list of explicit grounds upon which CER cannot be granted (see below).[83]

Ultimately, the President must decide if 'on the basis of the facts supplied and the applicable law, whether it is safe and proper for the convicted person to serve the remaining part of the sentence other than in prison'.[84] In other words, has the convicted person shown 'clear and convincing evidence that he will be a safe member of society and comply with the conditions imposed'.[85] Convicted persons have been assisted in the preparation of their applications by the Defence Office and pro bono counsel.[86] A right for convicted persons to be provided with advice and assistance from the Principal Defender 'at any stage' of the process was added to the Practice Direction in 2016.[87]

Release decisions have discussed the background and procedural history of the case, the applicable law, the judicial consideration of the Article 8 factors, the conclusion reached, and the disposition. Decisions should be made public, although the President retains the right to make some parts of the decision confidential for the protection or safety of any person.[88] As with the decision on eligibility for consideration, this decision is not subject to appeal or review.[89] If CER is denied, the convicted person can re-apply (although the President may specify the earliest point at which an application will be considered).[90]

Prosecutor v Gbao, Decision of the President on Application for Conditional Early Release, RSCSL-04-15-ES, 8 September 2020, paras 20, 81.

[82] *Prosecutor v Fofana and Kondewa*, Decision of the President on Application for Conditional Early Release, SCSL-04-14-ES (1270–1291), 11 August 2014, para. 18.

[83] Art. 8(C) PDCER.

[84] *Prosecutor v Fofana and Kondewa*, Decision of the President on Application for Conditional Early Release, SCSL-04-14-ES (1270–1291), 11 August 2014, para. 11.

[85] Art. 8(B) PDCER; *Prosecutor v Gbao*, Decision of the President on Application for Conditional Early Release, RSCSL-04-15-ES, 8 September 2020, para. 81.

[86] Third Annual Report of the President of the RSCSL, January 2016 – December 2016, at 26.

[87] Art. 2(G) PDCER, revised in 2016.

[88] Art. 9(A) PDCER.

[89] Art. 8(E) PDCER.

[90] Art. 9(B) PDCER.

Any grant of release is conditional upon the convicted person's agreement to abide by the terms of a Conditional Early Release Agreement, which contains 15 general conditions (contained in Annex C) and may also contain special conditions relevant to the individual in question.[91]

In reaching a decision, the President must consider a number of factors. President Waki noted in the *Senessie* decision that 'Article 8(D) of the Practice Direction, specifies in mandatory tone, the manner in which the President's decision shall be made and the factors that shall be considered'.[92] Rather than simply discuss the enumerated factors under Article 8(D), however, decisions also refer to the absolute prohibitions on release listed in Article 8(C).

4. GROUNDS FOR THE DENIAL OF RELEASE: ARTICLE 8(C)

The SCSL CER scheme differs from other international release systems in that the Practice Direction contains absolute prohibitions on release in certain circumstances (Article 8(C)), as well as an explicit discretionary ground for denying CER.

4.1 Refusal to Enter into or Comply with a CERA

The President cannot grant release if a convicted person will not enter into or agree to comply with the terms of the CERA specified by the President.[93] This means agreement to comply with both the general conditions and any special conditions attached. This factor has resulted in one grant of release being withdrawn and the prisoner serving his sentence in full.

On 4 June 2014, Senessie was granted CER conditional upon his completion and execution of a CERA (containing general conditions only).[94] Following the Registrar's assessment of the convicted person's willingness to comply with the terms of the CERA he had already signed, however, she determined that the prisoner did not understand the agreement when he signed it and that he was not willing to comply with its terms. This was despite the fact that the President had found that Senessie had agreed to comply with a CERA at both

---

[91] Art. 9(C) PDCER.

[92] *Prosecutor v Senessie*, Decision of the President on Application for Conditional Early Release, SCSL-11-01-ES (580–589), 4 June 2014, para. 16.

[93] Art. 8(C)(i) PDCER.

[94] *Prosecutor v Senessie*, Decision of the President on Application for Conditional Early Release, SCSL-11-01-ES (580–589), 4 June 2014, paras 38–39.

the eligibility for consideration[95] and consideration of release stages,[96] and indeed he had signed a CERA in the presence of witnesses.

Following notification of these facts under Article 10(E) of the Practice Direction, the President felt this situation had arisen either from the improper execution of Article 10(A) and (B) of the Practice Direction or the convicted person had reneged on his acceptance of the terms of the CERA which he had signed. In either case, the President ordered that the convicted person remain in custody until completion of his full term unless he freely decided to comply with the general conditions.[97] Senessie spent the nine remaining days of his two-year sentence in custody at the Special Court Detention Centre in Freetown.[98]

In order to avert the more serious consequences that could result in future cases, where much longer periods of time would remain on the sentence, the 2016 revision of the Practice Direction put some further steps in place to ensure there are no misunderstandings.[99] Moreover, in *Gbao*, release was suspended pending completion of additional training, which would include training on the conditions of his early release 'to ensure he thoroughly understands the conditions imposed'.[100]

4.2 Suitability of the Requested Area for Release

The President must reject an application for CER if there is no suitable programme of supervision in the RAR or the community is unwilling to accept the convicted person's return.[101] The suitability of supervision did become a pertinent issue in *Fofana* and this is discussed in more detail below. The second limb (community acceptance of the convicted person) has been discussed

---

95 *Prosecutor v Senessie*, Decision on Eric Senessie's Eligibility for Consideration for Conditional Early Release, SCSL-11-01-ES (307–310), 29 April 2014; *Prosecutor v Senessie*, Decision of the President on Application for Conditional Early Release, SCSL-11-01-ES (580-589), 4 June 2014, para. 8.

96 *Prosecutor v Senessie*, Decision of the President on Application for Conditional Early Release, SCSL-11-01-ES (580–589), 4 June 2014, paras 29, 37.

97 First Annual Report of the President of the RSCSL, January 2014–December 2014, at 22.

98 Ibid at 23.

99 See Art. 10(A)-(D) PDCER.

100 *Prosecutor v Gbao*, Decision of the President on Application for Conditional Early Release, RSCSL-04-15-ES, 8 September 2020, para. 82(b).

101 Art. 8(C)(ii)(a)–(b) PDCER.

at length in case-law under the heading 'Safety and Views of the Community' to which the convicted person wishes to be released.[102]

The term community is not defined in the Practice Direction, and it is not clear what 'unwilling to accept' actually means. It is also not apparent why decisions about such a fundamental right (liberty) should be delegated to the public. Contemporary standards view community participation as a means to provide support and ensure social inclusion;[103] not a ground to deny release. In practice, however, the community of the RAR has been defined broadly. This is demonstrated by the wide and diverse range of persons consulted by the Registrar (and Defence Office). In all cases to date, the consulted communities have been supportive of release. Unfortunately, it seems that this support may have created a new implicit (discretionary) ground for denial of release that is beyond the control of the convicted person. Due to the views expressed by some members of the communities in the RARs in *Fofana* and *Kondewa* that the convicted persons were viewed as heroes, the Practice Direction now requires the Registrar to gather information on 'the' acknowledgement by the RAR community that the convicted person is guilty of the crimes for which he was convicted, and the pain and suffering caused to the victims and their families by these crimes.[104]

Finally, the President must also deny release if he or she finds 'any other cause' which renders the RAR unsuitable.[105] This is an extremely vague and broad ground. In one sense, the Practice Direction tries to avoid this by instructing the Registrar to submit two potential RARs. While consideration of the place of residence post-release is an obvious and relevant factor for organising supervision and support, it should not be a decisive factor in the determination of whether to release an individual.

4.3 Inadequate Means of Financial Support

The same can be said about the provision allowing the automatic denial of CER to convicted persons who cannot provide evidence of adequate means of financial support.[106] Presidents have considered this element under the heading 'Safety and Views of the Community' to which the person wishes to be

---

[102] See *Prosecutor v Senessie*, Decision of the President on Application for Conditional Early Release, SCSL-11-01-ES (580–589), 4 June 2014, para. 18.

[103] See Rules 50–55 ERCSM.

[104] Art. 5(F)(ix)–(x) PDCER.

[105] Art. 8(C)(ii)(c) PDCER.

[106] Art. 8(C)(iii) PDCER.

released.[107] In practice, however, this seems to be little more than a rubber-stamping exercise with Presidents appearing to accept at face value the convicted persons' submissions in relation to their future employment intentions without analysing further the veracity or feasibility of these plans (despite prompts from the Prosecutor to do so). For example, on the basis of the future aspirations to continue working as a carver, Priest or Chairman of the Board of Governors (Senessie),[108] a fisherman and agriculturist (Fofana),[109] a farmer (Kondewa)[110] or to undertake agricultural or commercial activities (Gbao),[111] the Presidents all decided that the applicants had 'provided sufficient evidence of financial support'[112] or would be able to support themselves (and their family) financially.[113] In *Gbao*, for the first time, President Kamanda insisted that Gbao accept responsibility for the cost of his medical expenses during the duration of his conditional release (a special condition of his CERA).[114]

Mujizi questions the feasibility of some of these plans, in particular those that 'require high moral integrity' given that the individuals now have criminal records from an international criminal tribunal, and recommends that the Court 'scrutinise these submissions' more carefully.[115] However, the question of financial status is a question of support, not suitability for liberty. Boone and Herzog-Evans acknowledge that it is important for decision-makers to look at social resettlement factors to assess the credibility of release plans, but

---

107 See *Prosecutor v Senessie*, Decision of the President on Application for Conditional Early Release, SCSL-11-01-ES (580–589), 4 June 2014, para. 19.

108 Ibid, para. 20.

109 *Prosecutor v Fofana and Kondewa*, Decision of the President on Application for Conditional Early Release, SCSL-04-14-ES (1270–1291), 11 August 2014, para. 22.

110 *Prosecutor v Kondewa*, Decision of the President on Application for Conditional Early Release, RSCSL-04-14-ES (1581–1604), The Hague, 29 May 2017, paras 17–18.

111 *Prosecutor v Gbao*, Decision of the President on Application for Conditional Early Release, RSCSL-04-15-ES, 8 September 2020, para. 6(iv).

112 *Prosecutor v Senessie*, Decision of the President on Application for Conditional Early Release, SCSL-11-01-ES (580-589), 4 June 2014, para. 25.

113 *Prosecutor v Fofana and Kondewa*, Decision of the President on Application for Conditional Early Release, SCSL-04-14-ES (1270–1291), 11 August 2014, para. 28; *Prosecutor v Kondewa*, Decision of the President on Application for Conditional Early Release, RSCSL-04-14-ES (1581–1604), The Hague, 29 May 2017, para. 30; *Prosecutor v Gbao*, Decision of the President on Application for Conditional Early Release, RSCSL-04-15-ES, 8 September 2020, para. 62.

114 *Prosecutor v Gbao*, Decision of the President on Application for Conditional Early Release, RSCSL-04-15-ES, 8 September 2020, para. 83(ix).

115 Mujuzi, note 26 at 167.

argue that such factors should not be decisive as 'many offenders have limited social and human capital'.[116] A convicted person who has served a long sentence in a foreign prison may struggle to demonstrate sufficient means prior to release. Contemporary standards state that a lack of possibilities for work or the absence of regular accommodation should not constitute grounds for refusing or postponing conditional release.[117] What is required is support to find employment and accommodation, not continued detention. Van Zyl Smit and Snacken have argued that 'prisoners should not be disadvantaged by requirements that are beyond their control'.[118]

4.4 Refusal to Reconfirm Commitment to Comply with Protection Orders

The President must also refuse to grant release to convicted persons who refuse to (re)confirm their commitment to comply with protection orders issued pursuant to Rule 75 or to continue to refrain from revealing the identity of (potential) witnesses or contacting directly or indirectly any (potential) witness in his trial.[119] This issue has not arisen in case-law to date.

4.5 Contempt of Court Conviction

Unlike the other grounds, this ground is not a mandatory cause for the denial of an application for CER listed in Article 8(C). Rather, it is contained in the list of issues that must be evaluated in the President's decision in Article 8(D). Specifically, the President must discuss 'the effect of any conviction for contempt of court for any manner of interference or attempted interference with witnesses, bearing in mind that such a conviction **alone** *may* justify denial of CER'.[120] While this factor will not automatically result in the denial of CER, it may be the sole reason for a President's decision to deny an application.

---

[116] Miranda Boone and Martine Herzog-Evans 'Decision-Making and Offender Supervision' in Fergus McNeil and Kristel Beyens (eds) *Offender Supervision in Europe* (Palgrave Macmillan, 2013) 51–96 at 83.

[117] Recommendation Rec(2003) 22 of the Committee of Ministers to member states on conditional release (parole), 24 September 2003 (RCR), para. 19.

[118] Dirk van Zyl Smit and Sonja Snacken, *Principles of European Prison Law and Policy: Penology and Human Rights* (OUP: 2009) at 327.

[119] Art. 8(C)(iv) PDCER.

[120] Art. 8(D)(iv) PDCER.

In three cases to date, the individuals in question did not have convictions for contempt of court. Rather than being a neutral factor, the absence of such convictions was found to favour the grant of CER.[121]

Currently, two SCSL convicts (Kanu and Kamara) convicted of contempt of court offences must serve additional terms (1 year and 50 weeks) consecutively with their sentences for international crimes.[122] It is unclear how this factor will influence release decisions in these cases. This provision may be controversial on two grounds. Firstly, the Practice Direction setting out this potential sole ground for denial was issued one year after these convictions were handed down. Further, contemporary standards advocate the review and removal of formal legal obstacles that result in the denial of conditional release to persons convicted for particular offences.[123] It should be noted that in the one decided case where the convicted person *only* had convictions for contempt of court-related offences, the President found that as 'the effect of those convictions was taken into consideration by the Presiding Judge at the trial and in determining the appropriate sentence … this factor does not militate against the application for CER'.[124]

4.6 Conclusion

The inclusion of the unwillingness to abide by a supervision agreement or to reaffirm commitments to protection orders as grounds for denying CER is sensible and necessary in light of the objectives of the release scheme. Requiring the denial of CER on grounds beyond the prisoner's control (such as the suitability of supervision programmes and the views of community members) seems disproportionate. Permitting a denial of conditional release on the basis of a conviction obtained prior to the creation of the release scheme alone seems questionable on procedural fairness grounds. In addition to these grounds for

---

121 *Prosecutor v Fofana and Kondewa*, Decision of the President on Application for Conditional Early Release, SCSL-04-14-ES (1270–1291), 11 August 2014, para. 44; *Prosecutor v Kondewa*, Decision of the President on Application for Conditional Early Release, RSCSL-04-14-ES (1581–1604), The Hague, 29 May 2017, para. 56; *Prosecutor v Gbao*, Decision of the President on Application for Conditional Early Release, RSCSL-04-15-ES, 8 September 2020, para. 68.

122 *Independent Counsel v Bangura, Kargbo, Kanu and Kamara*, Sentencing Judgment in Contempt Proceedings, SCSL-11-02-T (669–703), TC-II, 11 October 2012.

123 Rule 19 ERCSM.

124 *Prosecutor v Senessie,* Decision of the President on Application for Conditional Early Release, SCSL-11-01-ES (580–589), 4 June 2014, para. 36.

denial of release, the Practice Direction also sets out specific factors that the President must consider.

5. ARTICLE 8(D) FACTORS

Release decisions have been structured around four topics: the safety and views of the community to which the convicted person seeks to be released; the views and concerns of victims, witnesses, their families and others at risk; reports from prison authorities; and the effect of any conviction for contempt of court (although this was considered under Conduct in Prison in *Gbao*). As this last factor was discussed above, this section will focus on the other elements of the release decisions to date. The judicial analysis of these elements includes discussions of some of the Article 8(C) factors outlined above.

5.1 The Safety of the Community to Which the Convicted Person Seeks to be Released

Under this heading, the President must assess two issues: whether the community to which he seeks to be released is suitable and whether it is safe for this community to release the convicted person into it.[125] The term 'potential for reintegration' is only used in *Senessie*.[126]

5.1.1 Suitability of the community

This first element requires consideration of the prohibitive ground discussed above relevant to the suitability of the RAR (supervision programme[127] and residents' acceptance of the convicted person) as set out in Article 8(C)(ii).[128] Since 2016, this discussion must also include an assessment of the views,

[125] *Prosecutor v Kondewa*, Decision of the President on Application for Conditional Early Release, RSCSL-04-14-ES (1581–1604), The Hague, 29 May 2017, para. 14.

[126] *Prosecutor v Senessie*, Decision of the President on Application for Conditional Early Release, SCSL-11-01-ES (580–589), 4 June 2014, para. 25.

[127] This was also discussed under the heading 'Views of Victims, Witnesses, their Families and Others at Risk' in *Kondewa*. See *Prosecutor v Kondewa*, Decision of the President on Application for Conditional Early Release, RSCSL-04-14-ES (1581–1604), The Hague, 29 May 2017, para. 31.

[128] See *Prosecutor v Fofana and Kondewa*, Decision of the President on Application for Conditional Early Release, SCSL-04-14-ES (1270–1291), 11 August 2014, para. 21; *Prosecutor v Senessie*, Decision of the President on Application for Conditional Early Release, SCSL-11-01-ES (580–589), 4 June 2014, para. 18.

concerns, willingness and acknowledgements of the RAR community in relation to the guilt of the individual in question for the crimes they were convicted for and the harm caused to the victims of such crimes.[129] Moreover, though the decisions do not cite the provision (explicitly[130]), this section is also used to assess another prohibitive ground – adequate means of financial support (Article 8(C)(iii)). The analysis of the safety of the community requires assessment of objective and subjective factors. The decisions outline the convicted person's connections to the proposed RARs, which to date have been through immediate or extended family connections, support from the community and past residence.[131]

To gauge the views of the communities on the proposed RARs, the Registrar and Outreach section have consulted with a diverse group of individuals and groups including community activists, opinion leaders, representatives of civil society, local government officials, traditional leaders, women's groups, youth groups, chiefs, police, ordinary citizens and victims.[132] Defence counsel and the Principal Defender have also added the views of a broad range of persons, including religious leaders, members of the applicant's family, paramount chiefs, victims, civil society members, youth groups, women's groups and former combatants.[133] These consultations have been conducted using a variety

---

[129] Art. 8(D)(vi) PDCER. See *Prosecutor v Kondewa*, Decision of the President on Application for Conditional Early Release, RSCSL-04-14-ES (1581–1604), The Hague, 29 May 2017, para. 20.

[130] *Prosecutor v Kondewa*, Decision of the President on Application for Conditional Early Release, RSCSL-04-14-ES (1581–1604), The Hague, 29 May 2017, para. 15 refers to the Registrar's duty to collect information on this element in Article 5.

[131] *Prosecutor v Fofana and Kondewa*, Decision of the President on Application for Conditional Early Release, SCSL-04-14-ES (1270–1291), 11 August 2014, para. 22; *Prosecutor v Kondewa*, Decision of the President on Application for Conditional Early Release, RSCSL-04-14-ES (1581–1604), The Hague, 29 May 2017, paras 17–18; *Prosecutor v Senessie*, Decision of the President on Application for Conditional Early Release, SCSL-11-01-ES (580–589), 4 June 2014, para. 20.

[132] *Prosecutor v Fofana and Kondewa*, Decision of the President on Application for Conditional Early Release, SCSL-04-14-ES (1270–1291), 11 August 2014, para. 23; *Prosecutor v Senessie*, Decision of the President on Application for Conditional Early Release, SCSL-11-01-ES (580–589), 4 June 2014, para. 21; *Prosecutor v Kondewa*, Decision of the President on Application for Conditional Early Release, RSCSL-04-14-ES (1581–1604), The Hague, 29 May 2017, para. 20.

[133] *Prosecutor v Fofana and Kondewa*, Decision of the President on Application for Conditional Early Release, SCSL-04-14-ES (1270–1291), 11 August 2014, para. 25; *Prosecutor v Kondewa*, Decision of the President on Application for Conditional Early Release, RSCSL-04-14-ES (1581–1604), The Hague, 29 May

of means, such as interviews, questionnaires, phone-in radio programmes, and town hall meetings.[134]

In all cases to date, consulted community members have expressed overall support for the release of applicants.[135] Support stemmed from the belief that the individuals were sorry for and would not repeat the crimes in question, they could be reintegrated into society, and they understood that they would be released under conditions and supervision. For example, in *Gbao*, the feedback from consulted communities was set out in detail over seven pages. Each consulted community supported the grant of CER and, moreover, showed a willingness to forgive Gbao and accept his apology.[136] This support is meaningful given that the consultations took place in areas where major atrocities had been committed, diamond mines had operated, and victims had been beheaded and amputated. Significantly, there were no expressions of widespread fears for victims or the wider community if he was released.[137] Where there had been some caution or opposition to Gbao's resettlement in certain consulted areas on account of the crimes he had been convicted of – these areas were not the RAR or the Proposed Alternative Address (PAA).[138] President Kambanda summarised the outcome of the community consultations: 'the communities consulted including victims and their families are largely receptive of Gbao's CER, are unconcerned for their safety or that of Gbao and are willing to accept Gbao back into the community'.[139] President Kambanda's conclusion that the RAR (Blama Town, Small Bo Chiefdom) was safe and suitable focused on the

---

2017, para. 20; *Prosecutor v Gbao*, Decision of the President on Application for Conditional Early Release, RSCSL-04-15-ES, 8 September 2020, para. 57.

[134] *Prosecutor v Fofana and Kondewa*, Decision of the President on Application for Conditional Early Release, SCSL-04-14-ES (1270–1291), 11 August 2014, para. 23; *Prosecutor v Kondewa*, Decision of the President on Application for Conditional Early Release, RSCSL-04-14-ES (1581–1604), The Hague, 29 May 2017, para. 20; *Prosecutor v Senessie*, Decision of the President on Application for Conditional Early Release, SCSL-11-01-ES (580–589), 4 June 2014, paras 21, 23.

[135] *Prosecutor v Fofana and Kondewa*, Decision of the President on Application for Conditional Early Release, SCSL-04-14-ES (1270–1291), 11 August 2014, para. 24; *Prosecutor v Kondewa*, Decision of the President on Application for Conditional Early Release, RSCSL-04-14-ES (1581–1604), The Hague, 29 May 2017, paras 19, 21, 24.

[136] See *Prosecutor v Gbao*, Decision of the President on Application for Conditional Early Release, RSCSL-04-15-ES, 08.09.20, paras 41, 43–48, 50, 52, 59.

[137] *Prosecutor v Gbao*, Decision of the President on Application for Conditional Early Release, RSCSL-04-15-ES, 8 September 2020, paras 41–42, 44, 59.

[138] Ibid, paras 45–46.

[139] Ibid, para. 61.

Article 5(F)(ix) and (x) acknowledgements of the convictions and pain caused by these crimes, the lack of any resident witnesses, Gbao's strong childhood and family connections to the area and plans for financial income, and the capability of the Sierra Leone Police as the Monitoring Authority.[140] In relation to Gbao's personal safety, the consulted communities had undertaken to inform the relevant authorities of any planned reprisals against Gbao.[141]

5.1.2 Safety of the community

In *Fofana*, the Prosecutor was 'totally opposed' to release on the basis of security fears of prosecution witnesses who were members of the community of the proposed RAR (though it must be stated that not all of these witnesses opposed release).[142] Some members of the community consulted felt Fofana was a 'hero of the CDF faction which protected civilians from rebel atrocities' and that his 'release would be greeted with jubilation'.[143] The Prosecutor argued that the interests of witnesses and victims should be given more weight than members of the community who viewed the applicant as a hero rather than a convicted war criminal who was responsible for their suffering.[144]

The President argued that, while this may be the case, these members of the community also understood that he had been convicted for crimes committed during the conflict and that he had paid the price for these crimes.[145] The President acknowledged that 'proximate physical and social ties in the community significantly increase the risk' of interference and stressed that he was not trying to 'downplay the concerns, interests and needs of witnesses and their families, a factor which must be a primary concern' in a release decision.[146] However, he felt that these safety fears 'can be ring-fenced by appropriate orders and conditions' [147] and in his assessment, he would not pose a risk to members of those communities if released.[148] Moreover, he stressed that 'a time will come, upon completion of sentence, when Fofana will unconditionally live in this community after paying his debt to society'.[149]

---

140 Ibid, para. 62. See also para. 6.

141 Ibid, paras 41, 43, 45, 48, 51–54.

142 *Prosecutor v Fofana and Kondewa*, Decision of the President on Application for Conditional Early Release, SCSL-04-14-ES (1270–1291), 11 August 2014, para. 29.

143 Ibid, para. 24.

144 Ibid, para. 29.

145 Ibid, para. 27.

146 Ibid, para. 28.

147 Ibid, para. 27.

148 Ibid, para. 28.

149 Ibid, para. 27.

Some members of the community consulted in *Kondewa* also expressed the view that the applicant was a 'hero'.[150] The Prosecutor again asked for the application to be denied on the basis of security concerns for witnesses who had testified at trial and the view that a grant of release would be 'contrary to the interests of justice and the proper administration of justice'.[151] This was despite the fact that the consulted prosecution witnesses were not from the proposed RAR communities and, in any case, the majority did not 'absolutely oppose' CER.[152] The President reiterated the primary nature of the 'concerns, interests and needs of witnesses and their families' but felt that in the absence of clear opposition from prosecution witnesses to the applicant's resettlement in the proposed RARs and the receptiveness of the communities of those RARs to such release, he would not pose a risk to these particular communities and that this factor favoured the grant of CER.[153]

In *Gbao*, the Prosecutor again opposed the application for conditional release on account of concerns expressed by witnesses, the gravity of the crimes, and concerns about the effectiveness of the Sierra Leone Police to act as the Monitoring Authority.[154] Of the 20 witnesses surveyed by the Prosecutor, however, only two opposed release completely.[155]

The Practice Direction was revised in 2016 to reflect these concerns that released persons were viewed as heroes rather than convicted criminals. Accordingly, not only must the Registrar collect information on 'the' acknowledgement by the local community of the RAR that the convicted person is guilty of the crimes for which he was convicted, and the pain and suffering caused to the victims and their families by these crimes,[156] but the President's decision must evaluate these required 'acknowledgements'.[157]

In the first case decided after this revision, the section setting out the applicable law erroneously cites Article 8(D) factors from the old version of the Practice Direction, which do not include this new requirement.[158] However,

---

150 *Prosecutor v Kondewa*, Decision of the President on Application for Conditional Early Release, RSCSL-04-14-ES (1581–1604), The Hague, 29 May 2017, para. 24.

151 Ibid, para. 25.

152 Ibid, paras 26–27.

153 Ibid, paras 29–30.

154 *Prosecutor v Gbao*, Decision of the President on Application for Conditional Early Release, RSCSL-04-15-ES, 8 September 2020, para. 14.

155 Ibid, para. 31.

156 Art. 5(F)(ix)–(x) PDCER.

157 Art. 8(D)(vi) PDCER.

158 *Prosecutor v Kondewa*, Decision of the President on Application for Conditional Early Release, RSCSL-04-14-ES (1581–1604), The Hague, 29 May

within the section dealing with the safety of the community, the revised Practice Direction's imperative to consider these required acknowledgements is stated.[159] Despite the fact that they are mentioned as particular elements that must be evaluated in a decision, the analysis of the consultations with members of the communities on the proposed RARs does not specifically mention either views on the individual's guilt or any acknowledgement of harm caused to victims by these crimes.[160]

Though the absence of these factors appears not to have negatively influenced the decision to release Kondewa, the revision appears to have created new implicit pre-conditions for release and potential implicit absolute grounds for denial given that the word 'the' rather than 'any' is used in Article 5(F)(ix)–(x), as well as the mandatory requirement for Presidential evaluation of this factor in Article 8(D)(vi).

In *Gbao*, it seems from the consultations, a 'hero' perception did not arise. The Article 5(F)(ix)–(x) PDCER requirements were simply deemed to have been met as a 'significant number of consultees and affiants … showed an understanding of the process by which he was convicted, acknowledged that he had been convicted for crimes committed during the civil conflict, and acknowledged the pain and suffering caused to the victims and their families'.[161]

5.2 Views and Concerns of Victims, Witnesses, their Families and Others Who are at Risk

Prior to the 2016 Revision, Article 8(D) required the President to evaluate the views and concerns of witnesses, victims and their families.[162] This was amended in 2016 to read 'relevant witnesses' and expanded to include the views and concerns of 'others who are at risk on account of testimony before the Special Court'.[163] The title of the heading in the 2017 *Kondewa* decision reflects this change. The 2016 Revision also resulted in the addition of a new objective aspect for consideration in the President's evaluation – 'the safety of victims, relevant witnesses, witnesses' and victims' families, and others who are at risk on account of testimony'.[164] These aspects tend to be dealt with in

2017, para. 11.

159 Ibid, para. 20.

160 Ibid, paras 20–24.

161 *Prosecutor v Gbao*, Decision of the President on Application for Conditional Early Release, RSCSL-04-15-ES, 8 September 2020, para. 62.

162 See Art. 8(D)(ii) 2013 PDCER.

163 Art. 8(D)(iii) PDCER.

164 Art. 8(D)(i) PDCER.

both this section and the section outlined above (safety of the community).[165] In *Kondewa*, the concerns of Prosecution witnesses were set out in detail under this heading. They included the perception that as Kondewa was still viewed as a gallant leader and war hero, he was in a position to garner significant political support that could result in their harassment from supporters. [166]

In addition to the Prosecutor's submissions on the safety of prosecution witnesses that are often detailed in the discussion of the safety of the community, this section also details reports from the Registry's Witness and Victims Section.[167] The prosecution witnesses consulted by the WVS in *Senessie* expressed security concerns but 'in their objectivity'[168] did not oppose CER being granted.[169] In *Fofana*, those consulted felt that while he was still a powerful and popular figure, he had lost his former status and the fact that many former fighters had testified against him had created divisions.[170] Most felt that release was appropriate as long as the SCSL protected their safety through the strict monitoring of conditionally released persons.[171] In *Kondewa*, the views of the prosecution witnesses consulted by the WVS were divided – though the majority supported CER with monitoring, visits by the Court to witness communities to build confidence and ensure safety, and a delay in granting CER until after the elections.[172]

In *Senessie*, the President felt that the 'concerns of victims, witnesses and their families will be adequately addressed'.[173] The President in the *Fofana*

---

[165] *Prosecutor v Fofana and Kondewa*, Decision of the President on Application for Conditional Early Release, SCSL-04-14-ES (1270–1291), 11 August 2014, para. 29.

[166] *Prosecutor v Kondewa*, Decision of the President on Application for Conditional Early Release, RSCSL-04-14-ES (1581–1604), The Hague, 29 May 2017, para. 32.

[167] *Prosecutor v Fofana and Kondewa*, Decision of the President on Application for Conditional Early Release, SCSL-04-14-ES (1270–1291), 11 August 2014, para. 29.

[168] *Prosecutor v Senessie*, Decision of the President on Application for Conditional Early Release, SCSL-11-01-ES (580–589), 4 June 2014, para. 28.

[169] Ibid, para. 26.

[170] *Prosecutor v Fofana and Kondewa*, Decision of the President on Application for Conditional Early Release, SCSL-04-14-ES (1270–1291), 11 August 2014, para. 29.

[171] Ibid, para. 32.

[172] *Prosecutor v Kondewa*, Decision of the President on Application for Conditional Early Release, RSCSL-04-14-ES (1581–1604), The Hague, 29 May 2017, para. 33.

[173] *Prosecutor v Senessie*, Decision of the President on Application for Conditional Early Release, SCSL-11-01-ES (580–589), 4 June 2014, para. 30.

decision did not feel that the 'legitimate' security issues raised were 'an overriding consideration' as they were 'not insurmountable … as there are sufficient safeguards in place'.[174] In *Kondewa*, the President felt that while the concerns were legitimate and 'serious enough to militate against the grant of CER', he would 'consider the factor further in my disposition'. It is unclear why this approach was taken, particularly given that a majority of consulted individuals were in favour of CER.[175]

It may be because the Kondewa case also raised the difficult question of whether future political participation should justify a delay in granting CER. The police, prosecutor and consulted witnesses voiced concerns about Kondewa's potential to re-enter politics in the volatile climate, particularly given the pending national elections.[176] The President felt that this was a 'serious factor that might militate against CER' and that the 'seriousness of the factor is further heightened by the current political climate'.[177] He also assumed however, that it was likely that divisions caused by former fighters testifying against him and others reduced the prospects for popularity.[178] In a bid to find a solution, the President referred to the Prosecutor's request that if CER be granted, it only be effected after the general elections.[179] Though the disposition states that Kondewa should remain in custody for further training, these concerns about political participation may have been the real reason behind the ten-month delay in Kondewa's release.

Concerns raised by prosecution witnesses in *Kondewa* in relation to his ability and sincerity to abide by imposed conditions were deferred for discussion under the 'Reports from Prison Authorities' section.[180] In *Gbao*, consultations with 25 prosecution witnesses from all regions of Sierra Leone by the Witness and Victims Section of the Registry revealed that none resided in the RAR and 60% had no objections to CER (20% were completely opposed).[181] A survey of a further 20 prosecution witnesses in the RUF trial in the Prosecutor's report

174 *Prosecutor v Fofana and Kondewa*, Decision of the President on Application for Conditional Early Release, SCSL-04-14-ES (1270-1291), 11 August 2014, para. 34.

175 *Prosecutor v Kondewa*, Decision of the President on Application for Conditional Early Release, RSCSL-04-14-ES (1581–1604), The Hague, 29 May 2017, para. 38.

176 Ibid, paras 21, 33, 35.

177 Ibid, para. 36.

178 Ibid, para. 37.

179 Ibid, para. 36.

180 Ibid, paras 46–47.

181 *Prosecutor v Gbao*, Decision of the President on Application for Conditional Early Release, RSCSL-04-15-ES, 8 September 2020, paras 12, 30.

showed that the vast majority (17/20) did not oppose CER, provided strict conditions were imposed to ensure the safety of the community.[182] President Kambanda reiterated the primacy accorded to the concerns, interests and needs of witnesses and their families in CER decisions but felt that the 'imposition of stringent conditions and a strict monitoring regime would adequately address these concerns'.[183]

5.3 Reports from Prison Authorities

Article 8(D)(v) requires the President to evaluate several distinct issues from the information contained in prison reports. These include:

- the convicted person's participation in any remedial educational, moral, spiritual or other programmes to which he has been referred in prison;
- any demonstration of remorse;
- the convicted person's commitment to contribute to the restitution of victims; and
- the convicted person's commitment to contribute to reconciliation and peace in Sierra Leone.

This information has been provided by both the designation report compiled by the SCSL Detention Facility (SCSLDF)/Residual Special Court Prison and reports from the prison authorities of enforcing States (Rwanda and Sierra Leone).[184] Assessments from the prison authorities of enforcing States directly address information required by the Practice Direction. This included discussions of whether the prisoner refrained from making prohibited contact or threats, violent or threatening behaviour; committed, incited or promoted crime; violated prison rules or orders; participated in prison programmes; expressed remorse for crimes for which he was convicted; had been a peaceful and well-disciplined prisoner who had not exhibited any continuing adherence to an ideology which is violent or contrary to peace and reconciliation and/or

---

182 Ibid, paras 12, 14, 31.

183 Ibid, para. 32.

184 *Prosecutor v Fofana and Kondewa*, Decision of the President on Application for Conditional Early Release, SCSL-04-14-ES (1270–1291), 11 August 2014, paras 35–36; *Prosecutor v Kondewa*, Decision of the President on Application for Conditional Early Release, RSCSL-04-14-ES (1581–1604), The Hague, 29 May 2017, paras 48–49, 51.

had agreed to conditions of residency, behaviour and supervision if granted CER.[185]

The designation reports compiled by the SCSLDF also addressed broader factors such as the security categorisation of the prisoner; participation in vocational and educational programmes; behaviour in prison; risk to the public; escape risk; potential for rehabilitation; and acceptance of conviction and responsibility for the crimes convicted for.[186] The report from the Residual Special Court Prison was more limited but referred to Senessie's desire not to repeat mistakes and his wish and ability to reintegrate into society.[187]

Concerns have been raised in relation to aspects discussed in prison reports or considered under this heading. In *Fofana*, the Prosecutor felt that the expression of remorse referred to was vague and self-serving, while following prison rules was not considered to be indicative of an intention to provide meaningful restitution.[188] The President, however, felt that as the positive reports from the prison authorities had confirmed good behaviour, a demonstration of rehabilitation and remorse, and a commitment to reconciliation and maintenance of peace, they militated in favour of granting CER.[189] In relation to concerns expressed by Prosecution witnesses in relation to Kondewa's ability to abide by conditions, the President felt he had 'no reason to doubt the prison officer's candour and neutrality' in this regard.[190] Overall, the positive reports indicating good behaviour in prison, participation in programmes, empathy

---

185 See *Prosecutor v Fofana and Kondewa*, Decision of the President on Application for Conditional Early Release, SCSL-04-14-ES (1270–1291), 11 August 2014, para. 38; *Prosecutor v Kondewa*, Decision of the President on Application for Conditional Early Release, RSCSL-04-14-ES (1581–1604), The Hague, 29 May 2017, para. 51; *Prosecutor v Gbao*, Decision of the President on Application for Conditional Early Release, RSCSL-04-15-ES, 8 September 2020, paras 8, 9, 11, 60.

186 *Prosecutor v Fofana and Kondewa*, Decision of the President on Application for Conditional Early Release, SCSL-04-14-ES (1270–1291), 11 August 2014, para. 37; *Prosecutor v Kondewa*, Decision of the President on Application for Conditional Early Release, RSCSL-04-14-ES (1581–1604), The Hague, 29 May 2017, para. 50.

187 *Prosecutor v Senessie*, Decision of the President on Application for Conditional Early Release, SCSL-11-01-ES (580–589), 4 June 2014, para. 32.

188 *Prosecutor v Fofana and Kondewa*, Decision of the President on Application for Conditional Early Release, SCSL-04-14-ES (1270–1291), 11 August 2014, para. 39.

189 Ibid, paras 42–43.

190 *Prosecutor v Kondewa*, Decision of the President on Application for Conditional Early Release, RSCSL-04-14-ES (1581–1604), The Hague, 29 May 2017, para. 52.

for victims, acknowledgment of his role in the crimes, public apology, and commitment to reconciliation and maintenance of peace militated in favour of CER.[191]

Even when records show that a prisoner has violated prison rules, such violations were considered against the overall report, with the President concluding in *Senessie* that the incidents reported did not 'irreversibly militate against a favourable assessment' and that in fact the 'balance tilts towards the conclusion that Senessie has been successfully rehabilitated in prison'.[192]

In *Gbao*, there appeared to be discrepancies between the reports submitted in relation to his conduct in detention. Whereas the Prison Director had certified that Gbao had not engaged in violent or threatening behaviour or violated the prison rules[193] and the periodic reports showed good behaviour, the detention records listed four incidents of alleged violations of the prison rules due to altercations with other prisoners and staff.[194] Though President Kambanda noted that 'it would have been helpful for the Director to remark on these exceptions as they pertain to … attitudinal and possible disciplinary issues', he nevertheless felt that such incidents did not 'irreversibly militate against a favourable assessment' and indeed that the 'balance tilts towards the conclusion that Gbao has largely conformed to prison directives and rules and been of good behaviour' in prison.[195]

The assessment of conduct in prison is supposed to determine whether the applicant will be a safe member of society if conditional release is granted.[196] In *Gbao*, the forensic psychiatric evaluation concluded that he did not pose any psychological risk to others.[197] The Prison Director, however, noted that he could not assess the risk of Gbao committing further offences or instigating or participating in political unrest, other than to state that Gbao had acted in compliance with the prison rules and was well behaved.[198] Despite this, President Kambanda felt Gbao had shown 'clear and convincing evidence that he will be a safe member of society'.[199]

---

191 Ibid, paras 53–55.

192 *Prosecutor v Senessie*, Decision of the President on Application for Conditional Early Release, SCSL-11-01-ES (580–589), 4 June 2014, paras 33–35.

193 *Prosecutor v Gbao*, Decision of the President on Application for Conditional Early Release, RSCSL-04-15-ES, 8 September 2020, para. 8.

194 Ibid, paras 64–66.

195 Ibid, paras 66–67.

196 Ibid, para. 63.

197 Ibid, para. 7(i).

198 Ibid, paras 10(i)–(ii), 74.

199 Ibid, para. 81.

To provide clear and convincing evidence that they are remorseful, applicants must both acknowledge their crimes and show sincere regret.[200] For example, the Prison Director certified that Gbao had demonstrated remorse for his crimes (although he had not discussed the reasons for their commission) and that he wished to apologise in person to the victims and the public.[201] Gbao also made declarations expressing regret for the crimes he committed as part of the CER application process, and his written apology to the victims of these crimes and the people of Sierra Leone in October 2019 was published and read out on national radio stations and at town hall meetings.[202] This public apology had positively influenced some consulted community members to accept him back into the community and traditional leaders felt this apology meant he had reformed and could serve as a role model for other ex-combatants.[203] President Kambanda felt these both weighed in favour of CER.[204] He also found that Gbao's stated regret for participating in the armed conflict and his crimes, his public renunciation of RUF ideology, and involvement in the peace process weighed in favour of CER.[205]

6. OTHER FACTORS

Despite the detailed framework of the conditional early release scheme, release decisions to date have considered and applied factors not provided for in the statute, rules, or the practice direction.

6.1 Gravity of the Offences

Neither the *Kondewa* nor the *Senessie* decisions discuss the gravity of the crimes for which the individuals were convicted as a distinct heading. This approach can be contrasted with the *Fofana* decision, where the gravity of the crimes committed was discussed at length under a separate heading (Gravity of the Crimes).[206] The President referred to the need to respect the totality principle, which, taking the gravity of the offences into account, guided the

200 Ibid, para. 69.
201 Ibid, paras 11, 71.
202 Ibid, para. 70.
203 Ibid, paras 51, 53.
204 Ibid, para. 72.
205 Ibid, paras 73, 75.
206 See *Prosecutor v Fofana and Kondewa*, Decision of the President on Application for Conditional Early Release, SCSL-04-14-ES (1270–1291), 11 August 2014 – Section IV(A), paras 15–17.

determination of the sentence imposed.[207] While this may have been a 'paramount consideration in … sentencing',[208] it is not clear why it remains relevant to the implementation or enforcement of the sentence – particularly in a conditional early release scheme where the original sentence is not modified.

After quoting extensively from the Appeals Chamber Disposition and its citation of the Trial Chamber sentencing judgment (recalling the large scale and distressing details of the brutality of the crimes committed, the targeting of innocent and vulnerable civilian victims, and the significant physical and psychological impact of the crimes on these victims[209]) the President decided that 'the high gravity of the crimes for which Fofana was convicted is a factor that weighs against granting the application for early release'.[210] This demonstrates that the President is doing more than simply recalling the gravity of the crime and has used it as a negative factor in decision-making without any legal basis for doing so.

It is not clear why President Waki adopted a different approach in deciding the *Senessie* and *Fofana* cases. The difference may lie in the fact that Senessie was not convicted for the commission of international crimes, but for contempt of court offences (offering a bribe to witnesses and interference with witnesses who had testified before the SCSL).[211] However, this does not explain why a different President (President Winter) did not find it necessary to discuss the gravity of crimes in the *Kondewa* decision. President Winter's approach is in line with the actual legal framework in place: the gravity of the crimes committed is not mentioned in the Statute, Rules or Practice Direction as a distinct ground for consideration. Though it did not result in a denial of release, the lack of legal basis should caution against following President Waki's approach and including gravity as an additional factor in release decisions.

Yet, President Kamanda also discussed gravity in *Gbao*, quoting extensively from the trial and appeal chambers' sentencing judgments, setting out their findings and aspects of the criminal offences that he was convicted for.[212] President Kamanda simply stated that 'I must recall the gravity of the offences for which Gbao was convicted'[213] without explaining the legal basis for doing so. However, he did end the section discussing gravity with the view that '[i]

---

207 Ibid, para. 45.

208 Ibid, para. 46.

209 Ibid, para. 15.

210 Ibid, para. 17.

211 *Prosecutor v Senessie*, Decision of the President on Application for Conditional Early Release, SCSL-11-01-ES (580–589), 4 June 2014, para. 3.

212 *Prosecutor v Gbao*, Decision of the President on Application for Conditional Early Release, RSCSL-04-15-ES, 8 September 2020, paras 22–28.

213 Ibid, para. 21.

n considering Gbao's application, the extent to which prison has led to the rehabilitation of the tendencies identified by the Special Court in the commission of his crimes will be relevant to determine whether it is safe for Gbao to serve part of his sentence in the community'.[214] In this way, it seems President Kamanda was framing the discussion as a precursor to understanding if Gbao has been sufficiently rehabilitated during the service of his sentence.

6.2 Additional Training Requirements

The Presidential decisions in *Fofana*, *Kondewa* and *Gbao* all resulted in the creation of an additional requirement or prerequisite: CER was granted 'subject to' and 'conditional upon' the completion of an additional set period of time in custody to facilitate the successful completion of further specific training.[215]

Fofana was required to spend an additional six months in prison in Rwanda to receive training on three elements:[216]

(a) The nature of his crimes under international law;
(b) Differentiating legitimate cause from illegal means; and
(c) His responsibility and leadership role in the armed conflict.

In *Fofana*, it seems that this additional requirement stemmed from the consultation process during which one judge was opposed to release based on reservations that Fofana had failed to acknowledge his 'responsibility and the leadership role he played in the armed conflict',[217] and concerns about the convicted person's view that acting with just cause justified illegal actions.[218] The consulted judge recommended, therefore, that the prisoner be denied release until he had undergone further training in prison on the nature of his crimes,

---

214 Ibid, para. 28.

215 *Prosecutor v Fofana and Kondewa*, Decision of the President on Application for Conditional Early Release, SCSL-04-14-ES (1270–1291), 11 August 2014, paras 47, 49; *Prosecutor v Kondewa*, Decision of the President on Application for Conditional Early Release, RSCSL-04-14-ES (1581–1604), The Hague, 29 May 2017, paras 59, 61; *Prosecutor v Gbao*, Decision of the President on Application for Conditional Early Release, RSCSL-04-15-ES, 8 September 2020, para. 82(a).

216 *Prosecutor v Fofana and Kondewa*, Decision of the President on Application for Conditional Early Release, SCSL-04-14-ES (1270–1291), 11 August 2014, paras 47, 49.

217 Ibid, para. 18.

218 Ibid, para. 19.

convictions and responsibility under international humanitarian law.[219] It is clear from the President's disposition that the reservations and recommendations expressed during the consultation process directly resulted in the six-month delay in Fofana's release.[220]

This extension is problematic as it ignores the previous findings by the President that Fofana had demonstrated rehabilitation through his willing and enthusiastic participation in the vocational, educational and remedial programmes he was referred to in prison (both in the SCSLDF and Rwanda).[221] The decision further ignores the prison reports from both the SCSLDF and Rwanda, which stated that Fofana had accepted his role and responsibility for his crimes and expressed remorse, which the President had accepted and concluded militated in favour of CER.[222]

Was the issue the appropriateness of the programmes he was referred to? If so, this failure would seem indefensible given the identified need to create specialist rehabilitation programmes from the initiation phase of the CER scheme. The subcommittee that created the scheme stressed the link between rehabilitation and public safety and argued that the CER scheme should ensure that convicted persons have 'undertaken and accomplished rehabilitation specific to atrocity crimes and his role in their commission'.[223] Accordingly, the Rwandan prison authorities 'agreed to work with the Court to provide rehabilitation programmes within the prison individualised according to the needs of the individual'.[224] Yet this does not seem to have occurred in a manner considered appropriate for the President. As Mujuzi points out, 'one would have expected that offenders who are serving sentences for gross violations of the law of war to at least be exposed to the basics of the laws of war when serving their sentence' and that the prison authorities should implement such programmes well in advance of the eligibility point for release.[225]

It is also not clear why a further spell in custody was required. While rehabilitation and reintegration potential are important elements of CER,[226] these aspects can be facilitated in a non-custodial setting. The Tokyo Rules foresee the possibility of including therapy, programmes and treatment developed to

---

219 Ibid, para. 19.

220 Ibid, para. 47.

221 Ibid, paras 37–38, 42–43.

222 *Prosecutor v Kondewa*, Decision of the President on Application for Conditional Early Release, RSCSL-04-14-ES (1581–1604), The Hague, 29 May 2017, paras 37–38, 42–43.

223 Doherty and Fisher, note 1 at 368.

224 Ibid at 371.

225 Mujuzi, note 26 at 163.

226 Rule 12.2 Tokyo Rules.

meet the needs of offenders in CER measures.[227] RSCSL jurisprudence and practice seem to take a different view, seeing rehabilitation in the custodial sentence and control in the non-custodial setting.

Kondewa was required by the decision granting CER to spend an additional ten months in prison to receive additional specific training on two elements:[228]

(a) human rights; and
(b) correct behaviour as a citizen of Sierra Leone.

This decision is problematic for a range of reasons. Firstly, the training requirement topics are broad and vague. Secondly, the need for such training was not supported by the release process. On the contrary (as in Fofana), the President had accepted that Kondewa had demonstrated rehabilitation by successfully completing all programmes he had been referred to in prison.[229] Thirdly, it is unclear why the training required by Kondewa would require four months longer to complete than the training required by Fofana. This additional time seems disproportionate, particularly given that the requirement for any additional training should have been assessed (and put in place) in light of the *Fofana* decision. Fourthly, as in the *Fofana* case, there does not appear to be any reason why the training could not occur in a non-custodial setting. Fifthly, the delay in the *Kondewa* case, in contrast to the *Fofana* case, was not attributable to statements made by the convicted person, but to fears expressed by witnesses that Kondewa was still viewed by others as a war hero rather than a convicted war criminal and that continuing support could result in his involvement in politics.[230] On this basis, the Prosecutor requested, in the alternative to the application being denied, that any release be deferred until after the general election.[231] This makes the delay seem unfair given that these perceptions were neither substantiated nor within the applicant's control. In fact, the President acknowledged that the fear that he would return to politics was *de minimis* as they were only expressed by one prosecution witness, and indeed

[227] Rule 13.1 Tokyo Rules.

[228] *Prosecutor v Kondewa*, Decision of the President on Application for Conditional Early Release, RSCSL-04-14-ES (1581–1604), The Hague, 29 May 2017, paras 59, 61(a).

[229] Ibid, paras 50–51, 54.

[230] RSCSL Press Release, 'CDF Convict Allieu Kondewa granted Conditional Early Release, with ten months delay' The Hague, the Netherlands, 30 May 2017.

[231] *Prosecutor v Kondewa*, Decision of the President on Application for Conditional Early Release, RSCSL-04-14-ES (1581–1604), The Hague, 29 May 2017, paras 7, 58.

that such fears were not 'insurmountable'.[232] Finally, these concerns could and should have been dealt with by additional conditions rather than extended time in custody in a foreign country. And indeed, the special conditions imposed on his release specifically stated that he should not join local or national politics.

President Winter stated that due to his 'possible political influence in his home district' Kondewa 'had a prolonged information and learning period concerning his rights and especially duties in order to strengthen and not to disturb the peace and reconciliation policy of the country'.[233] Worryingly, the training period was further prolonged due to Kondewa's ill-health:[234] President Winter extended Kondewa's required time in prison by three months to a total of 13 months on account of his inability to complete all the required modules.[235] However, the President received notification earlier than expected that Kondewa had successfully completed the required training and, after signing his CERA (6 June 2018) and the President's issuance of a Supervision and Transfer Order (STO) (18 June 2018), Kondewa returned to Sierra Leone to continue his sentence under supervision in the community until 2023.[236]

As with the *Fofana* case, the RSCSL was very much involved in the design, delivery and evaluation of the training. The Office of the Registrar 'consulted and coordinated' with the Rwandan prison authorities in relation to the design of the ten modules; the Principal Defender and an RSCSL expert facilitated and helped to deliver some of the training in Rwanda; and Kondewa's understanding of the training was evaluated by former and current SCSL officials.[237]

During his time in prison, Gbao benefited from traditional prison programmes (civic education, Kinyarwandan language courses, computer skills, and work schemes[238]) as well as the specialist training programmes designed with the RSCSL that focused on international humanitarian law, war crimes,

---

232 Ibid, para. 57.

233 Fifth Annual Report of the President of the RSCSL, January 2018–December 2018 at 6.

234 Fourth Annual Report of the President of the RSCSL, January 2017 to December 2017, at 29.

235 *Prosecutor v Kondewa*, Decision of the President on a Request for Extension of Time for Completion of Allieu Kondewa's Training as Ordered in the Decision of the President on Application for Conditional Early Release, RSCSL-04-14-ES, 22 March 2018.

236 Fifth Annual Report of the President of the RSCSL, January 2018–December 2018, at 10.

237 Fourth Annual Report of the President of the RSCSL, January 2017 to December 2017 at 19, 28; Fifth Annual Report of the President of the RSCSL, January 2018–December 2018 at 20.

238 *Prosecutor v Gbao*, Decision of the President on Application for Conditional Early Release, RSCSL-04-15-ES, 8 September 2020, para. 9.

crimes against humanity, human rights, and (respect for) the rule of law and order. This specialist training was 'directed towards a fuller understanding of Gbao's responsibility for the consequences of his crimes for which he was convicted'.[239] Despite this, President Kambanda also directed that Gbao remain in custody for a further period of three months to attend 'additional specific training geared towards his understanding of and acceptance of responsibility for the harm he inflicted … through the direct commission of enslavement, contributing his efforts and reputation to the commission of crimes pursuant to a Joint Criminal Enterprise, and by his actions in aiding and abetting the attack of the UN peacekeepers, its effect on the individuals involved and the harm to the peace process itself'.[240] The additional training was also to cover 'education on the conditions of his early release to ensure he thoroughly understands the conditions imposed'.[241] This aspect is problematic given that one of the special conditions of his release was to submit a plan of proposed community service, three months *after* his release (see below). Only once the training had been certified by the Registrar could Gbao be released in line with the conditions in the CERA.[242]

6.3 Equal Treatment

Granting Gbao conditional early release, President Kambanda noted that, based on the information available, the prison record and consultations, 'there seems to be no reason not to grant him CER'. Further, and importantly for the first time in RSCSL jurisprudence on release, he noted that this was particularly important 'in light of *equal treatment* with other former Special Court convicted persons'.[243]

7. THE EXECUTION OF DECISIONS AND THE IMPOSITION OF CONDITIONS

Release is conditional upon and accompanied by a Conditional Early Release Agreement (CERA). This section examines the procedural safeguards relevant to the execution of the CER decision and the general and special conditions that can and have been imposed on released persons.

[239] Ibid, para. 71.
[240] Ibid, para. 82(a).
[241] Ibid, para. 82(b).
[242] Ibid, para. 82(d).
[243] Ibid, para. 80.

7.1 Procedural Safeguards

The scheme contains procedural safeguards that aim to ensure the convicted person has fully understood the conditions he is agreeing to and is voluntarily undertaking to abide by them. This begins at the outset of the release process as the convicted person must submit a written and signed statement of understanding that release will be subject to entering into and complying with a CERA with his application for eligibility for consideration for CER.[244] Then, as part of the decision-making process on release, the prison authorities must confirm that the convicted person has demonstrated 'a commitment to agree to conditions of residency, behaviour and supervision' if conditionally released.[245]

The difficulty at these earlier stages is that it is not known whether any special conditions will be added or what they might contain. This undermines the validity of the acceptance of such supervision to a certain extent as 'where there is a formal legal precondition – justice requires that the individual do so in full knowledge of what they are consenting to'.[246] Further, the advice given to convicted persons in relation to the CERA is not complete given that it is unclear what consequences will result from noncompliance with particular terms.[247]

Following a grant of CER, however, the convicted person must testify that they have received advice from the Principal Defender in relation to the provisions of the PDCER, terms of the CERA and Supervision and Transfer Order, and the consequences of any breach of the CERA.[248] Moreover, they must testify that they understand the consequences of any breach of conditions contained therein, which will include detention and transfer to the RSCSL and may involve the revocation of the CERA and re-imprisonment for the remainder of the original prison term.[249] This involves accepting that under the Supervision and Transfer Order, the Monitoring Authority (MA) will detain and transfer the individual if they suspect that there has been a failure to comply with the CERA or if they pose a risk of harm to any person.[250] Two witnesses must attest to the voluntary nature of the convicted person's signing of the CERA (and understanding of its binding nature).[251]

---

244 Art. 2(D) PDCER.
245 Art. 5(D)(iii)(iv) PDCER.
246 Commentary on Rule 57 ERCSM.
247 See Rules 15, 57, 62 ERCSM.
248 Art. 10(A) PDCER; Pro Forma CERA, Annex C PDCER, para.1.
249 Pro Forma CERA, Annex C PDCER, paras 1–2, 4, 8.
250 Pro Forma CERA, Annex C PDCER, para. 8.
251 Art. 10(B) PDCER.

Fofana, for example, was interviewed by members of the RSCSL staff in his local language (through an interpreter), who submitted a report stating that they were satisfied that he understood the fundamental issues of the CER decision.[252] This complies with contemporary standards that require the offender's consent to the conditions be 'informed and explicit'[253] and that CER decisions and conditions be explained clearly to offenders in a language they understand.[254]

The system also includes a check by the Registrar. Since 2016, the convicted person must also 'reaffirm' his understanding and voluntary acceptance of the terms of the CERA and his intention to comply with it to the Registrar.[255] If the Registrar is not satisfied that the convicted person understands the CERA, intends to comply with its terms or has not entered into the CERA freely and voluntarily, then the convicted person must remain in custody in the enforcing State pending further consideration of the issue by the President.[256]

This procedure was amended in the 2016 Revision to reflect the problems that arose in the *Senessie* case and to prevent the individual from being transferred from the enforcing State before the check by the Registrar has occurred. The old provision only ensured that the check occurred 'upon arrival in the Home State' prior to release.[257] This did not result in logistical problems in *Senessie* as he was serving his sentence in Sierra Leone. However, for prisoners serving their sentences in a foreign country, this element of the process could create practical difficulties. For example, this meeting between the Registrar and Fofana occurred after his return to Freetown from Rwanda.[258] Kondewa also received further legal advice in relation to the conditions governing his release following his return to Freetown from personnel of the RSCSL Defence Office prior to his transfer to the Sierra Leone Police Monitoring Authority.[259] The PDCER now ensures that transfer from the enforcing State to the Home State shall only be organised after the Registrar is happy that the convicted person freely entered, understands, and intends to comply with the CERA.[260] The

252 Second Annual Report of the President of the RSCSL, January 2015–December 2015 at 20.

253 Rule 57 ERCSM.

254 Rules 30, 61 ERCSM; Rule 12.3 Tokyo Rules.

255 Art. 10(C) PDCER.

256 Art. 10(D) PDCER.

257 Art. 10(D) 2013 PDCER.

258 Second Annual Report of the President of the RSCSL, January 2015–December 2015 at 20.

259 Fifth Annual Report of the President of the RSCSL, January 2018–December 2018 at 28–29.

260 Art. 10(E) PDCER.

convicted person must also have a copy of the Supervision and Transfer Order served upon him prior to release.[261] If the Registrar is satisfied, the convicted person will be released under the terms of the CERA.

7.2 General Conditions

A decision to grant CER is conditional upon the convicted person entering into a Conditional Early Release Agreement (CERA). All released persons are subject to a list of general conditions contained in Annex C (Pro Forma CERA) that impose both positive and negative obligations and are subject to monitoring.[262]

In relation to supervision, the convicted person must agree to reside at a particular location,[263] accept the supervision of a specified monitoring authority (MA),[264] promise to keep in contact with that authority,[265] agree to visits from the MA at home, work or any other place,[266] to submit to searches of his person, possessions or property by the MA,[267] agree to report in person to the authority, its agent or the police[268] and promise to notify the authority if arrested or questioned by law enforcement officers or if they are required to take a drugs or alcohol test.[269]

The convicted person must also promise not to purchase, possess or consume alcohol, illegal drugs or weapons[270] (and to hand over such items found in his possession[271]), not to work in places or jobs not approved by the MA,[272] not to commit any offences[273] or incite or promote crime or behave in any way

---

[261] Art. 10(G) PDCER; *Prosecutor v Fofana and Kondewa*, Presidential Order for Detention and Transfer and for Hearing Pursuant to Article 12(F) of the Practice Direction on Conditional Early Release of Persons Convicted by the SCSL, RSCSL-04-14-ES (1297–1300), The Hague, 9 March 2015 at 3.

[262] Arts 8(F) and 9(C)(i) PDCER. See also Annex D (Pro Forma Draft SCSL Supervision and Transfer Order).

[263] Pro Forma CERA, Annex C PDCER, para. 5(b). This was amended in the 2016 revision to include a commitment not to leave this designated area without the express permission of the MA.

[264] Pro Forma CERA, Annex C PDCER, para. 5(c).

[265] Pro Forma CERA, Annex C PDCER, para. 5(d).

[266] Pro Forma CERA, Annex C PDCER, para. 5(g).

[267] Ibid.

[268] Pro Forma CERA, Annex C PDCER, para. 6.

[269] Pro Forma CERA, Annex C PDCER, para. 5(o).

[270] Pro Forma CERA, Annex C PDCER, para. 5(e)–(f).

[271] Pro Forma CERA, Annex C PDCER, para. 5(i).

[272] Pro Forma CERA, Annex C PDCER, para. 5(j).

[273] Pro Forma CERA, Annex C PDCER, para. 5(k).

that undermines public peace and security,[274] not to violate any protection order, identify or contact witnesses,[275] not to engage in violent, intimidating, threatening or coercive behaviour towards the MA, civilian or law enforcement officers of the Home State, any persons involved in the prosecution of crimes before the SCSL, Judges, personnel, witnesses or their families[276] and not to associate with persons he has been directed not to in writing by the MA.[277]

7.3 Special Conditions

The President may also impose special conditions 'relevant to the individual convicted person'.[278] The Pro Forma CERA contains a section that indicates that 5 special conditions may be added[279] – though there is no specified limit on the number of special conditions that the President may include.[280] While no special conditions were added in *Senessie*,[281] several identical conditions were added in *Fofana* and *Kondewa*.[282] These special conditions were further modified in *Fofana* following his breach of conditions (see below).

The RSCSL President noted that the conditions for Kondewa's early release 'had to be drafted with consideration of his own situation, and to assure a positive outcome for peace and reconciliation in Sierra Leone'.[283] The special conditions imposed on *Fofana* and *Kondewa* also seem to have been heavily influenced by recommendations made by the Prosecutor. For example, the requirement to publicly apologise, acknowledge guilt and show remorse; refrain from directly or indirectly approaching, harming, intimidating or interfering with any witness; an obligation to act honourably and peacefully; and a

---

274 Pro Forma CERA, Annex C PDCER, para. 5(l).

275 Pro Forma CERA, Annex C PDCER, para. 5(m).

276 Pro Forma CERA, Annex C PDCER, para. 5(n).

277 Pro Forma CERA, Annex C PDCER, para. 5(p).

278 Art. 9(C)(ii) PDCER.

279 Pro Forma CERA, Annex C PDCER, para. 1.

280 The number has exceeded this implied limit – see *Prosecutor v Gbao*, Decision of the President on Application for Conditional Early Release, RSCSL-04-15-ES, 8 September 2020, para. 83.

281 Mujuzi, note 26 at 163.

282 *Prosecutor v Fofana and Kondewa*, Decision of the President on Application for Conditional Early Release, SCSL-04-14-ES (1270–1291), 11 August 2014, para. 49 (Disposition); *Prosecutor v Kondewa*, Decision of the President on Application for Conditional Early Release, RSCSL-04-14-ES (1581–1604), The Hague, 29 May 2017, para. 61.

283 Fourth Annual Report of the President of the RSCSL, January 2017 to December 2017 at 6.

requirement not to engage in secret meetings intended to plan civil unrest—all mirror the recommendations made by the Prosecutor.[284] The special conditions in *Fofana* that relate to monitoring (a requirement to report in person at least twice a month and a duty placed on the Registrar to visit regularly) also seem to reflect concerns and requests made by the Prosecutor (and witnesses interviewed by the WVS Section).[285] Several of these special conditions overlap with the general conditions imposed in all cases, particularly in relation to interference with witnesses and monitoring requirements.[286]

It seems that the need to publicly apologise has also been wrongly framed as a post-release supervisory condition when in practice it appears to have been a prerequisite for release to occur.[287] Fofana complied with this order at a press conference in Freetown prior to his return to his community.[288] This additional requirement seems to undermine the criteria for CER already established in release eligibility and release stages of the process. This appears to be acknowledged in the Disposition in *Kondewa*, where he is ordered to apologise 'again'.[289]

Further, the special condition section has been used in *Fofana*, *Kondewa* and *Gbao* to place a duty on the Registrar to make regular visits 'to provide assurance' to vulnerable former witnesses.[290] In *Gbao*, the special condition section was also used to instruct the Registrar to submit a monitoring regime

---

[284] *Prosecutor v Fofana and Kondewa*, Decision of the President on Application for Conditional Early Release, SCSL-04-14-ES (1270–1291), 11 August 2014, para. 33.

[285] *Prosecutor v Fofana and Kondewa*, Decision of the President on Application for Conditional Early Release, SCSL-04-14-ES (1270–1291), 11 August 2014, paras 32–33. See also *Prosecutor v Kondewa*, Decision of the President on Application for Conditional Early Release, RSCSL-04-14-ES (1581–1604), The Hague, 29 May 2017, para. 61 (iv).

[286] See also Mujuzi, note 26 at 165.

[287] *Prosecutor v Fofana and Kondewa*, Decision of the President on Application for Conditional Early Release, SCSL-04-14-ES (1270–1291), 11 August 2014, para. 49; *Prosecutor v Kondewa*, Decision of the President on Application for Conditional Early Release, RSCSL-04-14-ES (1581–1604), The Hague, 29 May 2017, para. 61.

[288] Second Annual Report of the President of the RSCSL, January 2015–December 2015 at 20.

[289] *Prosecutor v Kondewa*, Decision of the President on Application for Conditional Early Release, RSCSL-04-14-ES (1581–1604), The Hague, 29 May 2017, para. 61(i).

[290] See *Prosecutor v Fofana and Kondewa*, Decision of the President on Application for Conditional Early Release, SCSL-04-14-ES (1270–1291), 11 August 2014, para. 49(v); *Prosecutor v Gbao*, Decision of the President on

plan for approval by the President.[291] A special condition should be applicable to the person subject to supervision and not be an obligation of a Court official. It is also not clear to whom such visits should be made – the applicant subject to CER or the witnesses. Moreover, it is unclear if this is a monitoring role or an outreach role.

The influence of consultations on the imposition of special conditions was demonstrated in *Gbao*. Witnesses and community members consulted by the Prosecutor, Registry and Defence Office recommended the imposition of a number of conditions: restricted mobility (to remain within the RAR); prevention of retaliation against witnesses, violence, and unrest; prohibition of contact with witnesses and victims; requirement to demonstrate remorse, apologies and the acknowledgement of specific crimes and the pain resulting from those crimes; obligation to stay peaceful and accept the court's verdict; and restrict associations, political activities and membership of secret societies.[292]

President Kambanda, noting the recommendations made by consultees,[293] imposed nine special conditions on Gbao (some of which are new in the jurisprudence and practice of the RSCSL)[294] and a very detailed direction to Gbao to give a personal and public apology to the victims of his crime and the people of Sierra Leone on radio and TV. This apology needed to include acceptance of responsibility for the harm he inflicted through direct perpetration of enslavement, through contributing his efforts and his reputation to the commission of crimes in Bo, Kono, Kailahun and Kenema and by his actions in aiding and abetting the attack on UN peacekeepers, its effect on the individuals involved and the harm to the peace process itself, an expression of remorse and of his commitment to reconciliation and maintenance of peace in Sierra Leone, and a renunciation of every political ideology, political affiliation and membership as well as membership in secret societies.[295]

The special conditions in *Gbao* also included a striking new requirement for the applicant to produce a community volunteer service plan for the President's approval within 90 days of release.[296] This requirement appears to have been directly influenced by consultations. While in prison, Gbao had indicated he would be willing to make restitution to victims, both individually

---

Application for Conditional Early Release, RSCSL-04-15-ES, 8 September 2020, para. 83(xi).

291 *Prosecutor v Gbao*, Decision of the President on Application for Conditional Early Release, RSCSL-04-15-ES, 8 September 2020, para. 83(x).

292 Ibid, paras 30–31, 54, 59.

293 Ibid, para. 60.

294 Ibid, para. 83.

295 Ibid, para. 83(i).

296 Ibid, para. 83(viii).

and collectively, without specifying how he would do this other than to claim he would serve the people of Sierra Leone in the fields of peace-building, conflict prevention, and resolution.[297] During consultations, RAR residents voiced their expectation that Gbao would help to rebuild the town, given that the RUF had burnt down houses. A traditional ruler suggested he volunteer with an international NGO, and another resident offered the services of an NGO to help him make restitution to victims.[298] President Kambanda felt Gbao had the 'skill and expertise to enable him to contribute to some amount of restitution to victims in the form of community service' and that this factor weighed in favour of granting CER.[299]

A final special condition that warrants attention relates to Gbao's health. Under the CERA, Gbao was required to undertake financial responsibility for his medical bills, allow the RSCSL to monitor his diabetes and blood pressure, and refrain from consuming alcohol or drugs not prescribed by his doctor.[300] It is unclear how this will operate as a condition of release. Could/should an inability to afford medical bills or a refusal to consent to access to medical records potentially result in a recall to prison? This would seem questionable on both rights and ethical grounds.

7.4 Review of Conditions

Despite the benefits attributed to allowing and encouraging offenders to make representations in conditional release decision-making,[301] the RSCSL does not allow convicted persons to contest the inclusion or applicability of initial conditions. In line with contemporary standards,[302] however, the scheme does provide for the review and adjustment of the nature and intensity of supervision during the period of conditional release. The President may review conditions *proprio motu*, or at the request of the convicted person, MA or Prosecutor.[303] Under the review process (where there has not been a breach), conditions contained in the CERA may only be modified with the convicted person's consent. The President must, however, take the views of the Prosecutor and the Monitoring Authority into account.

---

297 Ibid, para. 76.
298 Ibid, para. 77.
299 Ibid, para. 78.
300 Ibid, para. 83(ix).
301 Rule 29 ERCSM.
302 See Para. 9 RCR; Rule 10.3-4 Tokyo Rules.
303 Art. 10(A) PDCER.

8. THE SUPERVISION OF CONDITIONALLY RELEASED PERSONS

The convicted person's compliance with the terms and conditions of his CERA is overseen by a Monitoring Authority.[304] Following consultations with the Government of Sierra Leone, the RSCSL appointed the Sierra Leone Police as the Monitoring Authority to supervise conditional early release[305] and entered into a Monitoring Agreement to govern this relationship.[306] In addition to this general duty, it seems that localised units will be established in designated RARs for each released individual. For example, Fofana's conditional release was monitored by Bo East Police.[307]

The Special Court's legal framework facilitated this form of cooperation. Pursuant to Article 11 of the Agreement between the UN and the Government of Sierra Leone on the Establishment of the RSCSL, the Government of Sierra Leone had undertaken to 'comply without undue delay with any request for assistance... or any order issued' which may include the location, arrest or detention of persons and their transfer to the RSCSL. The Special Court Agreement (2002) (Ratification) Act 2002 also provided that 'for the purposes of execution, an order of the Special Court shall have the same force or effect as if it has been issued by a Judge, Magistrate or Justice of the Peace of a Sierra Leone Court'.[308] The functions of the MA under the CER scheme, however, are however also set out in detail in a bilateral agreement.[309]

The RSCSL CER scheme was also made possible by the fact that eight of the nine convicted persons are citizens of Sierra Leone and wished to return

---

304 Arts 9(C)(iii), 11(A) PDCER.

305 Second Annual Report of the President of the RSCSL, January 2015–December 2015 at 20.

306 Confidential Agreement to Perform the Duties of the Monitoring Authority, 2 March 2015. See *Prosecutor v Fofana*, Submission of the Registrar pursuant to Rule 33(B) as ordered in terms of Paragraph 81(v) of the Disposition on the matter of Moinina Fofana's violations of the terms of his conditional early release, RSCSL-04-14-ES (1468–1473), 26 May 2016, para. 5, footnote 6.

307 Second Annual Report of the President of the RSCSL, January 2015–December 2015 at 20; RSCSL Press Release, 'CDF Convict Moinina Fofana Returned to Bo,' Freetown, Sierra Leone, 16 March 2015.

308 Part V, Section 20.

309 An Agreement to Perform the Duties of the Monitoring Authority was signed on 27 February 2015 and 2 March 2015. See *Prosecutor v Fofana*, Disposition of the Matter of Moinina Fofana's Violations of the Terms of his Conditional Early Release, RSCSL-04-14-ES, (1416–1440) Freetown, 25 April 2016, para. 73.

there after completion of their sentence. The Pro Forma SCSL Supervision and Transfer Order (Annex D) refers to convicted persons as citizens of Sierra Leone. This creates an obvious gap for Mr. Taylor, a citizen of Liberia currently serving his sentence in the UK. The Practice Direction does define the MA more broadly as 'the authority in the Home State with which the Special Court enters an agreement to provide monitoring and supervision services'.[310] This perhaps leaves scope for an agreement to be entered into with Liberian or other authorities.

8.1 Efficacy of the Monitoring Authority

Despite having experience in overseeing the bail of accused persons,[311] the Prosecutor expressed concerns about the ability of the Sierra Leone Police (SLP) to act as the MA for the RSCSL, warning that the proposed system 'was wanting'.[312] The Prosecutor warned that stringent monitoring was necessary to 'maintain public confidence in the integrity of the SCSL and RSCSL judicial processes'.[313] Justice Waki dismissed these fears,[314] stating 'it is not in my province to second-guess the efficacy of the monitoring units'.[315] He felt satisfied by the fact that the scheme had been established by written agreement with the police, was supported by the Inspector General of the Police, that any orders issued by the RSCSL had the full force of the law, and the MA was under a duty to submit an annual report.[316] He further referred to the power of the President to review conditions and order the re-arrest of a convicted person on the basis of an alleged violation.[317]

---

310 Art. 1 PDCER.

311 *Prosecutor v Senessie*, Decision of the President on Application for Conditional Early Release, SCSL-11-01-ES (580–589), 4 June 2014, para. 29.

312 *Prosecutor v Fofana and Kondewa*, Decision of the President on Application for Conditional Early Release, SCSL-04-14-ES (1270–1291), 11 August 2014, para. 30.

313 Ibid, para. 33.

314 *Prosecutor v Senessie*, Decision of the President on Application for Conditional Early Release, SCSL-11-01-ES (580–589), 4 June 2014, para. 30.

315 *Prosecutor v Fofana and Kondewa*, Decision of the President on Application for Conditional Early Release, SCSL-04-14-ES (1270–1291), 11 August 2014, para. 31.

316 Ibid.

317 See Arts. 11(B), 12(A) PDCER. *Prosecutor v Fofana and Kondewa*, Decision of the President on Application for Conditional Early Release, SCSL-04-14-ES (1270–1291), 11 August 2014, para. 32.

Its envisaged integral role in implementing CER to achieve the goals of rehabilitation, public safety and protection of victims and witnesses,[318] and its undertaking of mandatory obligations in its agreement with the Special Court,[319] did not, however, prevent the MA's role in the breach of CERA conditions in the *Fofana* case. Justice Soloman therefore felt that it was necessary to publicly admonish the MA in the strongest possible terms for what she described as their complicity and dire failures in relation to Fofana's breach of violations.[320]

The complicity charge relates to the admission by a Monitoring Officer that he allowed Fofana to sign the register in advance of the date he was due to physically report to the police station.[321] The failings on the MA's behalf included a failure to require Fofana to report to the MA in other locations following travel; to immediately inform the Registrar about Fofana's failure to return to his RAR on the due date; and to intervene when Fofana attended an event in an unauthorised area.[322] This act of complicity and these omissions led Justice Soloman to conclude that the MA had not been performing its mandatory duties with 'the seriousness, commitment and diligence' required by the Practice Direction.[323] Justice Soloman reminded the MA of its mandatory duties and that its role should not be 'taken lightly if the objectives of Fofana's rehabilitation and meaningful reconciliation within the community are to be achieved'.[324] She therefore ordered the Registrar to contact the MA and enter into discussions, inter alia, about its failure to comply with its agreement with the Special Court and to assess the manner in which the MA proposed to ensure strict future enforcement of CERA conditions and adherence to its duties.[325]

The MA's complicity in Fofana's breach of conditions heightened the fears expressed by witnesses and the Prosecutor when consulted about Kondewa's

318 *Prosecutor v Fofana*, Disposition of the Matter of Moinina Fofana's Violations of the Terms of his Conditional Early Release, RSCSL-04-14-ES, (1416–1440) Freetown, 25 April 2016, para. 72.

319 Ibid, para. 73.

320 Ibid, paras 71, 74.

321 Ibid, para. 75.

322 Ibid, para. 76.

323 Ibid, paras 76–77.

324 Ibid, para. 77.

325 Ibid, para. 81(v); RSCSL Press Release, 'Moinina Fofana will face stricter conditions for violating terms of his Conditional Early Release', Freetown, Sierra Leone, 25 April 2016.

application for CER.[326] They felt that the Fofana incident meant that the MA 'still [had] to prove its merits'.[327] In contrast to the approach taken to such fears in the *Fofana* decision, the President readily admitted that this concern was 'a genuine one in light of ... Fofana's breach' and that the incident had been a 'matter of very grave concern' for the RSCSL.[328] Despite this, it was accepted that measures taken by the MA following the breach meant that concerns about the efficacy of the MA were not 'an overriding consideration against granting the application'.[329]

According to the Registrar's report,[330] a number of measures were taken following Fofana's breach to ensure the MA's future strict enforcement of CER. These included meetings and communication with the Inspector General and other senior police officials; the designation of a focal point within the MA to streamline communication and liaise with the MA in Bo City; the signing of a modified Monitoring Agreement; the provision of two weeks of intensive training for the local MA police officers on Fofana's modified conditions and general obligations; the use of these trained personnel as facilitators for broader national MA training; the agreement to train Local Unit Commanders throughout the country to supervise Monitoring Agents; and the requirement of a monthly assessment of Fofana's compliance from the Assistant Inspector General from the Southern Province and the designated focal point to Police HQ.[331] The National Witness Protection and Assistance Unit of the Sierra Leone Police was also tasked with conducting independent spot checks on Fofana to ensure the MA was carrying out its role.[332]

---

326 *Prosecutor v Kondewa*, Decision of the President on Application for Conditional Early Release, RSCSL-04-14-ES (1581–1604), The Hague, 29 May 2017, para. 31.

327 Ibid, para. 32.

328 Ibid, para. 39.

329 Ibid, para. 45.

330 As required by *Prosecutor v Fofana*, Disposition of the Matter of Moinina Fofana's Violations of the Terms of his Conditional Early Release, RSCSL-04-14-ES, (1416–1440) Freetown, 25 April 2016, para. 81(v).

331 See *Prosecutor v Fofana*, Submission of the Registrar pursuant to Rule 33(B) as ordered in terms of Paragraph 81(v) of the Disposition on the matter of Moinina Fofana's violations of the terms of his conditional early release, RSCSL-04-14-ES (1468-1473), 26 May 2016, paras 7–11, 13.1–13.2, 13.5, 13.8; *Prosecutor v Kondewa*, Decision of the President on Application for Conditional Early Release, RSCSL-04-14-ES (1581–1604), The Hague, 29 May 2017, paras 42–43; Third Annual Report of the President of the RSCSL, January 2016–December 2016 at 21.

332 See *Prosecutor v Fofana*, Submission of the Registrar pursuant to Rule 33(B) as ordered in terms of Paragraph 81(v) of the Disposition on the matter of

The efficacy of the Sierra Leone Police to act as the MA for the RSCSL was also raised by the Prosecutor when objecting to Gbao's application for conditional early release.[333] President Kambanda, however, felt that he was satisfied that the SLP would effectively perform its duties because of the 'extensive re-engagements' between the RSCSL and the MA, the reforms put in place by the SLP following Fofana's violation, the SLP's legal obligation to act in the event of any alleged violations of CER, and the re-assurance and commitments given by the Inspector General of the SLP in correspondence with the Registrar.[334] Further, President Kambanda noted that community consultations in the RAR and PAA did not expose any concerns about the SLP's ability to monitor Gbao's release.[335]

8.2 Joint Responsibility

The acceptance of these improvements by Justice Solomon was highly significant given that a lack of suitable supervision is a ground for the absolute prohibition of CER.[336] It should not be the responsibility of a convicted person housed in a foreign country to ensure that there is a suitable programme of supervision in the nominated areas of residence – the availability and suitability of programmes is the responsibility of the RSCSL and the Sierra Leonean Government.

Though this ground for prohibition still stands, it has become evident from the RSCSL jurisprudence and reports that the supervision of CER has become increasingly viewed as a joint responsibility or dual competency of the international(ised) court and the government of the Home State. In addition to public outreach activities relevant to CER (missions, documentation, radio programmes),[337] the MA and the RSCSL Registrar jointly determine reporting schedules; the Registrar conducts regular visits to assure concerned witnesses and the RSCSL has agreed to train MA personnel to improve their ability to implement the CER scheme.[338] For example, Justices Fisher and Doherty

---

Moinina Fofana's violations of the terms of his conditional early release, RSCSL-04-14-ES (1468–1473), 26 May 2016, paras 13.6, 13.7.

333 *Prosecutor v Gbao*, Decision of the President on Application for Conditional Early Release, RSCSL-04-15-ES, 8 September 2020, para. 14.

334 Ibid, para. 36.

335 Ibid, para. 37.

336 Art. 8(C)(ii) PDCER.

337 Second Annual Report of the President of the RSCSL, January 2015–December 2015 at 20.

338 *Prosecutor v Fofana and Kondewa*, Decision of the President on Application for Conditional Early Release, SCSL-04-14-ES (1270–1291), 11 August 2014, para.

provided training to the Principal Defender and a Defence Legal Associate on the provisions of the PDCER over two days in London, in order to both enhance their ability to assist RSCSL convicted persons applying for CER but also to assist with the training of MA personnel.[339]

More directly, the Registrar is responsible for conducting spot checks on a supervisee's compliance with conditions[340] and authorising travel outside the RAR.[341] The Registrar may also prohibit a conditionally released person from having contact with specified persons.[342] This means the Court is directly involved in monitoring conditionally released persons. In *Gbao*, the Registrar was directed by President Kamanda (under the heading of Special Conditions) to 'submit a complete and detailed document containing a robust monitoring regime to be put in place by the MA to ensure compliance with the conditions for my approval within six weeks' of the decision granting CER.[343] This instruction from President Kamanda ensured that the Registrar was involved from the outset in the design and detail of the monitoring regime to be implemented by the SLP. President Kamanda also dismissed the Prosecutor's concerns about the efficacy of the MA by stating that the SLP would exercise this role 'with the supervision of the RSC'.[344]

---

49 (Disposition); *Prosecutor v Kondewa*, Decision of the President on Application for Conditional Early Release, RSCSL-04-14-ES (1581–1604), The Hague, 29 May 2017, paras 43, 61; *Prosecutor v Gbao*, Decision of the President on Application for Conditional Early Release, RSCSL-04-15-ES, 08.09.20, para. 83(xi) (Disposition).

339 Third Annual Report of the President of the RSCSL, January 2016–December 2016 at 11, 23.

340 See *Prosecutor v Fofana*, Submission of the Registrar pursuant to Rule 33(B) as ordered in terms of Paragraph 81(v) of the Disposition on the matter of Moinina Fofana's violations of the terms of his conditional early release, RSCSL-04-14-ES (1468–1473), 26 May 2016, para. 13.6.

341 *Prosecutor v Fofana*, Disposition of the Matter of Moinina Fofana's Violations of the Terms of his Conditional Early Release, RSCSL-04-14-ES, (1416–1440) Freetown, 25 April 2016, para. 81(ii)(d)–(e); *Prosecutor v Gbao*, Decision of the President on Application for Conditional Early Release, RSCSL-04-15-ES, 8 September 2020, para. 83(ii).

342 Ibid, para. 83(v).

343 Ibid, para. 83(x).

344 Ibid, para. 37.

9. DEALING WITH ALLEGED OR ADMITTED BREACH(ES) OF CONDITIONAL EARLY RELEASE AGREEMENTS

The conditional release scheme sets out the procedures to be followed in the event of a breach of a condition by a convicted person serving the remainder of their sentence in the community. The operation of the CER system was tested when the first conditionally released person (Fofana) breached both general and special conditions in 2015. This incident resulted in 'adopted appropriate amendments' to the Practice Direction in 2016 after 'reviewing lessons learned'[345] and ongoing work with the Monitoring Authority to prevent the reoccurrence of such a breach. Dealing with allegations of a breach of conditions involves several stages and procedures including arrest and transfer to the RSCSL, determination of probable cause, admission of guilt, release pending the hearing, hearing on the merits, factors relevant to determinations, and consequences of a determination of a violation.

9.1 Arrest and Transfer

A convicted person should be immediately arrested and detained by the Monitoring Authority (pursuant to the Supervision and Transfer Order issued by the President) if it has reason to believe that the convicted person has breached any condition in their CERA (or poses a risk of harm to any person).[346] Once the individual is detained, the MA must immediately submit a list of the specific conditions alleged to have been violated to the Registrar using the Notice of Violation Form contained in Annex E to the Practice Direction.[347] The Registrar must report the detention of the convicted person and transfer the relevant documentation to the President, Prosecutor and Principal Defender within 24 hours.[348] The convicted person must be transferred to the custody of the RSCSL (or such other place as the President may decide) without delay.[349]

In early 2016, President Waki received a report from the Registrar containing evidence that supported allegations of a violation by Fofana of his CER

[345] Fourth Annual Report of the President of the RSCSL, January 2017 to December 2017 at 6.

[346] Art. 12(A) PDCER; Pro Forma Draft SCSL Supervision and Transfer Order, Annex D, para. A.

[347] Art. 12(C) PDCER. The 2013 version stated that the Prosecutor could submit the conditions that had been violated – this has now been removed.

[348] Art. 12(D) PDCER. The requirement to transmit the documentation to the Prosecutor and Principal Defender was added in the 2016 revision.

[349] Pro Forma Draft SCSL Supervision and Transfer Order, Annex D, para. D.

conditions. The Registrar's report included reports from the Sierra Leone Police and the RSCSL's Witness and Victim Section, as well as a Notice of Violation (Annex E PDCER).[350] On the basis of the Supervision and Transfer Order issued on 25 February 2015, the President ordered the MA (and Government authorities) to immediately detain the convicted person and transfer him to the RSCSL's custody.[351]

This Presidential order was necessary as the MA had failed to act in accordance with its duty to take steps to arrest and transfer Fofana to RSCSL custody 'despite having reason to believe that Mr. Fofana had violated the conditions of his early release'.[352] Due to this failure, the Practice Direction was revised in 2016 to include a provision that instructs the MA 'to consider any request from the Prosecutor' to arrest and transfer a convicted person for an alleged breach of the CERA, with any communication on such matters to be facilitated by the Registrar.[353] It should be noted, however, that while some provisions were amended to ensure that only the MA and not the Prosecutor should submit the specific conditions alleged to have been violated,[354] the Practice Direction still refers to the Prosecutor's role in making allegations of violations of CERA conditions.[355] In any case, Fofana voluntarily surrendered to the Sierra Leone Police on becoming aware of the President's Order for his arrest.[356] Fofana was detained on 10 March 2016 and spent 8 days in detention before his release pending his hearing.[357]

---

350 Third Annual Report of the President of the RSCSL, January 2016 – December 2016, at 10.

351 *Prosecutor v Fofana and Kondewa*, Presidential Order for Detention and Transfer and for Hearing Pursuant to Article 12(F) of the Practice Direction on Conditional Early Release of Persons Convicted by the SCSL, RSCSL-04-14-ES (1297–1300), The Hague, 9 March 2016 at 4.

352 *Prosecutor v Fofana*, Submission of the Registrar pursuant to Rule 33(B) as ordered in terms of Paragraph 81(v) of the Disposition on the matter of Moinina Fofana's violations of the terms of his conditional early release, RSCSL-04-14-ES (1468–1473), 26 May 2016, para. 5.5.

353 Art. 12(B) PDCER.

354 Art. 12(C) PDCER in contrast to Art. 12(B) 2013 PDCER.

355 Article 9(C)(iv) PDCER.

356 *Prosecutor v Fofana*, Disposition of the Matter of Moinina Fofana's Violations of the Terms of his Conditional Early Release, RSCSL-04-14-ES, (1416–1440) Freetown, 25 April 2016, para. 17.

357 RSCSL Press Release, 'Moinina Fofana Admits Violating Terms of his Conditional Early Release Agreement' Freetown, Sierra Leone, 18 March 2016.

9.2 Determination of Probable Cause

The President must decide whether there is probable cause to believe a violation has occurred within 48 hours of the convicted person's detention.[358] If the President determines there is no probable cause, the convicted person must be released on the conditions contained in the original CERA.[359] If, on the other hand, probable cause that the violation occurred is found, the President must designate a judge to hear the matter, direct the Prosecutor to prosecute the matter, direct the Principal Defender to represent the convicted person, and direct the Registrar to set a preliminary hearing within 7 days.[360] Having determined that there was probable cause to believe that a violation had occurred in the *Fofana* case, President Waki designated Justice Vivian M. Soloman to hear the matter pursuant to Article 13(3) of the RSCSL Statute.[361]

9.3 Admission of Guilt

If the convicted person admits to violating the conditions, the matter proceeds directly to disposition.[362] Fofana was accused of violating both general (5.d and 5.h) and special conditions (6.3 and 6.4) due to his failure to report to the MA when required or obtain permission for travel outside Bo Town and for joining in local politics.[363] He pretended to travel to Freetown but instead went to Makeni and attended a political conference. Moreover, he post-dated the register prior to his departure in order to falsely certify his physical presence on the required date and failed to return by the authorised date.[364] At his

---

358 Art. 12(A) PDCER.

359 Art. 12(F) PDCER.

360 Art. 12(G) PDCER. See *Prosecutor v Fofana and Kondewa*, Order for Detention and Transfer and For Hearing Pursuant to Article 12(F) of the Practice Direction on Conditional Early Release of Persons Convicted by the SCSL, RSCSL-04-14-ES (1297–1300) 9 March 2016.

361 *Prosecutor v Fofana and Kondewa*, Presidential Order for Detention and Transfer and for Hearing Pursuant to Article 12(F) of the Practice Direction on Conditional Early Release of Persons Convicted by the SCSL, RSCSL-04-14-ES (1297–1300), The Hague, 9 March 2016 at 4.

362 Art. 12(H) PDCER.

363 *Prosecutor v Fofana*, Disposition of the Matter of Moinina Fofana's Violations of the Terms of his Conditional Early Release, RSCSL-04-14-ES, (1416–1440) Freetown, 25 April 2016 at 4.

364 *Prosecutor v Fofana and Kondewa*, Decision on the Defence's Oral Application for the Release of Moinina Fofana from the Custody of the RSCSL pending the Disposition of the Matter of the Alleged Violations of his Conditional Early Release, RSCSL-04-14-ES (1305–1308) 18 March 2016; RSCSL Press

Preliminary Hearing on 16 March 2016, Fofana denied violating the terms of his conditional release.[365] During this hearing, the Prosecutor also notified the designated Judge of two further alleged violations (reporting obligations) that Fofana also denied.[366] At the next Preliminary Hearing, the Defence submitted that Fofana had not fully understood the allegations against him at the initial hearing and had now, with the benefit of further explanation from counsel, decided to admit all alleged violations.[367] Accordingly, the matter proceeded to disposition.[368]

9.4 Release Pending Hearing

An application for Fofana's temporary release by his pro bono counsel at the first Preliminary Hearing was denied by Justice Solomon.[369] During the second Preliminary Hearing (following an admission of guilt), Fofana's defence counsel made another oral application for his release from RSCSL custody pending the disposition of the matter. The Prosecution did not object to Fofana's release pending disposition provided certain additional conditions were imposed on him. Though the designated judge noted that the RSCSL must ensure that its jurisdiction 'is not frustrated and that proceedings do not lead to injustice', she acknowledged that the deprivation of liberty 'constitutes a fundamental aspect of due process recognised in international human rights treaties' (referring to UDHR and ICCPR).

Release, 'Moinina Fofana Admits Violating Terms of his Conditional Early Release Agreement' Freetown, Sierra Leone, 18 March 2016.

[365] *Prosecutor v Fofana*, Disposition of the Matter of Moinina Fofana's Violations of the Terms of his Conditional Early Release, RSCSL-04-14-ES, (1416–1440) Freetown, 25 April 2016 at 4 (refers to transcript at page 11.)

[366] Ibid at 4 (refers to transcript at page 14).

[367] *Prosecutor v Fofana and Kondewa*, Decision on the Defence's Oral Application for the Release of Moinina Fofana from the Custody of the RSCSL pending the Disposition of the Matter of the Alleged Violations of his Conditional Early Release, RSCSL-04-14-ES (1305–1308) 18 March 2016; *Prosecutor v Fofana*, Disposition of the Matter of Moinina Fofana's Violations of the Terms of his Conditional Early Release, RSCSL-04-14-ES, (1416–1440) Freetown, 25 April 2016, paras 4, 24 (refers to the Transcript 18th March at pp. 8, 10 and 16); RSCSL Press Release, 'Moinina Fofana Admits Violating Terms of his Conditional Early Release Agreement' Freetown, Sierra Leone, 18 March 2016.

[368] *Prosecutor v Fofana*, Disposition of the Matter of Moinina Fofana's Violations of the Terms of his Conditional Early Release, RSCSL-04-14-ES, (1416–1440) Freetown, 25 April 2016, para. 21.

[369] Third Annual Report of the President of the RSCSL, January 2016–December 2016, at 10.

She therefore granted the request for release on the condition that he comply with and reaffirm his understanding of his CERA, and, further that he

- obtain written permission from the Registrar for any travel outside Bo Town;
- report to the MA weekly;
- refrain from discussing any issue related to the proceedings with the Press, Media or third party;
- desist from influencing or bribing any potential witnesses that may be called at this hearing; and
- desist from the practice of signing forms in advance of his signing-on date.[370]

9.5 Hearing on the Merits

If the convicted person denies the allegation, either the President or the designated Judge will instruct the Registrar to set a date for a hearing on the merits during which the designated judge must decide whether the violation has been proven by a preponderance of the evidence.[371] A hearing on the merits is an adversarial setting with the Prosecutor ordered to prosecute the matter and the Principal Defender ordered to represent the convicted person.[372] In line with contemporary standards[373] and the revised PDCER,[374] Fofana was represented by the Principal Defender and was assigned a pro bono counsel.[375]

---

370 *Prosecutor v Fofana and Kondewa*, Decision on the Defence's Oral Application for the Release of Moinina Fofana from the Custody of the RSCSL pending the Disposition of the Matter of the Alleged Violations of his Conditional Early Release, RSCSL-04-14-ES (1305–1308) 18 March 2016; RSCSL Press Release, 'Moinina Fofana Admits Violating Terms of his Conditional Early Release Agreement' Freetown, Sierra Leone, 18 March 2016.

371 Art. 12(I) PDCER.

372 *Prosecutor v Fofana and Kondewa*, Presidential Order for Detention and Transfer and for Hearing Pursuant to Article 12(F) of the Practice Direction on Conditional Early Release of Persons Convicted by the SCSL, RSCSL-04-14-ES (1297–1300), The Hague, 9 March 2016 at 4.

373 Rule 69 ERCSM.

374 Art. 12(F)(iii) PDCER.

375 Third Annual Report of the President of the RSCSL, January 2016–December 2016, at 26.

If the allegation is not proven, the convicted person must be released on the conditions of the original CERA.[376] If the allegation is found to be proven, the matter will proceed to disposition.[377]

9.6 Dispositional Analysis

The Practice Direction does not contain any prescribed criteria that must be assessed or discussed in either a hearing on the merits or the disposition. As Fofana admitted all the alleged violations of his conditions, the matter proceeded to disposition.

Judge Solomon structured her disposition around the submissions of the parties (Prosecution and Defence), the applicable law, and her discussion of a range of issues: the alleged unintentional nature of the violations; the gravity of the violations (extent and impact of his participation in the conference and whether the violations were linked); whether the convicted person can continue to live in the community without posing a threat to victims, witnesses, and their families; and whether rehabilitation remains a viable option. Some factors were general (gravity, risk and rehabilitation), while others were based on or related to the facts of the breach. As this case proceeded to disposition following an admission of guilt, the breaches were not contested. The decision further analysed mitigating factors submitted by the Defence (health, admission of allegations, and remorse) before reaching a conclusion and proceeding to disposition.[378] No aggravating factors were discussed in this case.

9.6.1 Factors considered in Fofana

Judge Solomon dismissed Fofana's claim that he did not understand that his mere presence at a political conference would constitute joining in local politics in violation of his CERA as baseless and lacking merit, referring to his educational training in Mpanga prison, the fact that he twice affirmed his understanding of his CERA conditions prior to his release, and his own admission to the Court of the scope of this particular condition.[379] Moreover,

---

376 Art. 12(I)(ii) PDCER.

377 Art. 12(I)(i) PDCER.

378 The decision also contained a section setting out the complicity and failings of the MA.

379 *Prosecutor v Fofana*, Disposition of the Matter of Moinina Fofana's Violations of the Terms of his Conditional Early Release, RSCSL-04-14-ES, (1416–1440) Freetown, 25 April 2016, paras 16, 27–31. See also *Prosecutor v Fofana and Kondewa*, Presidential Order for Detention and Transfer and for Hearing Pursuant to Article 12(F) of the Practice Direction on Conditional Early Release of Persons Convicted by the SCSL, RSCSL-04-14-ES (1297–1300), The

referring to the numerous conflicting explanations forwarded by Fofana for his travel to Makeni and his presence at the political conference and the circumstances leading up to his request for permission to travel to Freetown, Judge Solomon concluded that as the violations were planned from the outset, Fofana had 'intentionally deceived the MA'.[380]

Judge Solomon rejected the Prosecutor's claims that Fofana had declared for one political party and remonstrated against another due to a lack of evidence.[381] She did however accept the Prosecutor's submission that the violations were inextricably linked and that their commission could not be viewed independently of each other.[382] The violations, she concluded, formed part of a 'continuing and eventual plan with the ultimate aim of attending the Conference'.[383]

When discussing the impact of Fofana's participation at the conference, Judge Solomon reiterated the President's acknowledgement that Fofana would, upon completion of his sentence, live in the community without conditions and that his previous status had been undermined by the divisions caused by the SCSL's use of former commanders and fighters as prosecution witnesses.[384] She concluded that Fofana's presence at the conference 'yielded minimal impact on the current political climate of Sierra Leone and its overall peace and security'.[385] However, she felt that 'his attendance and presence is significant as it reflects his general attitude of disregard and contempt for the orders of this Court and the terms of his CER'.[386]

Judge Solomon stated that the question of whether Fofana could continue to live in the community without posing a threat to victims, witnesses or their families was a 'paramount consideration' in assessing whether his CER should be revoked.[387] The risk assessment was concluded in light of the subjective views of the victims, witnesses and their families, the interests of the

Hague, 9 March 2016 at 3; Second Annual Report of the President of the RSCSL, January 2015–December 2015 at 20.

380 *Prosecutor v Fofana*, Disposition of the Matter of Moinina Fofana's Violations of the Terms of his Conditional Early Release, RSCSL-04-14-ES, (1416–1440) Freetown, 25 April 2016, paras 32–35, 52, 80.

381 Ibid, paras 2, 36, 42–45.

382 Ibid, paras 3, 36.

383 Ibid, para. 51.

384 Ibid, paras 48–49; *Prosecutor v Fofana and Kondewa*, Decision of the President on Application for Conditional Early Release, SCSL-04-14-ES (1270–1291), 11 August 2014, paras 27, 29.

385 Ibid, paras 50, 52, 80.

386 Ibid, paras 52, 80.

387 Ibid, para. 53.

RAR community, the number of violations committed by the offender while on CER, and the gravity of these violations.[388] Judge Solomon noted that all documentation from RSCSL officers working in witness protection supported the Defence's submission that Fofana did not pose any risk to such persons or indeed society at large.[389] Further, the fact that Fofana had not been charged or accused of any offence during his time on CER and had complied with the other terms of his CER meant there was nothing to suggest he was not reintegrating into society.[390] This balancing of positive and negative factors reflects the approach advocated by contemporary standards: where revocation is being considered, account should also be taken of compliance to date and positive aspects.[391]

Judge Solomon also asked whether Fofana's rehabilitation was still possible under conditional release. She noted that CER would 'cease to be a viable option' if violations were ongoing and continuing and of such a nature to suggest that the convicted person posed a threat to society or was otherwise not adjusting properly into the community … and therefore could not be counted on to comply with his CER'. As Judge Solomon had already found that Fofana did not pose a threat to anyone, had not been charged or accused of any offence during his time on CER, and had complied with the other terms of his CER, she felt there was nothing to suggest that he was not reintegrating into society.[392] Accordingly, she did not find it necessary to exclude CER as a viable option for Fofana's continued rehabilitation.[393]

9.6.2 Mitigating factors considered in Fofana

Both health and remorse were discussed in relation to possible mitigation. Although Judge Solomon noted that she could not make any assessment of Fofana's medical needs without appraisals from qualified and certified medical personnel, she observed that he appeared to be in pain with difficulties with his mobility. However, she felt that this would not prevent a return to prison, as there was no evidence that he would not receive adequate care.[394]

---

388 Ibid.

389 Ibid, paras 19, 54–58, 60.

390 *Prosecutor v Fofana*, Disposition of the Matter of Moinina Fofana's Violations of the Terms of his Conditional Early Release, RSCSL-04-14-ES, (1416–1440) Freetown, 25 April 2016, para. 59.

391 Rule 70 ERCSM.

392 *Prosecutor v Fofana*, Disposition of the Matter of Moinina Fofana's Violations of the Terms of his Conditional Early Release, RSCSL-04-14-ES, (1416–1440) Freetown, 25 April 2016, para. 59.

393 Ibid, para. 61.

394 Ibid, paras 13, 65–67.

Judge Solomon did, however, accept that Fofana's admission of the allegations was a mitigating factor.[395] She also considered that his sincere apology and expressions of remorse were mitigating factors.[396] The Prosecutor had argued that his expression of remorse should be attributed little weight given the circumstances in which they were given – as a prerequisite for CER and during his admission of the violations.[397]

10. POSSIBLE CONSEQUENCES FOR BREACHING CONDITIONS

Whether the convicted person admits the violation, or the designated judge finds the allegations to be proven by the preponderance of evidence, the disposition can be based on three possible consequences for the violation of CERA conditions: revocation and imprisonment, release on modified conditions, or release on the same conditions.[398] In *Fofana*, Judge Solomon stated that the 'determination of the appropriate disposition… must be made on a case-by-case basis having regard to the facts and circumstances of the case and the evidence at hand'.[399] This approach accords with contemporary European standards that advocate 'making a detailed examination of the facts' before modifying conditions or revoking CER.[400]

10.1 Revocation and Re-imprisonment

The designated judge can revoke the order for CER and order the re-imprisonment of the convicted person for the time remaining on the sentence at the date that the CERA went into effect, with credit for time served in detention pending disposition of the violation and any credit the judge may order for time served under the CERA.[401]

The RSCSL scheme complies with contemporary standards in that a violation does not automatically result in the conversion of conditional release to imprisonment.[402] This option does, however, raise questions of *proportionality*.

---

395 Ibid, para. 68.

396 Ibid, paras 15, 69.

397 Ibid, para. 10.

398 Art. 12(J) PDCER.

399 *Prosecutor v Fofana*, Disposition of the Matter of Moinina Fofana's Violations of the Terms of his Conditional Early Release, RSCSL-04-14-ES, (1416–1440) Freetown, 25 April 2016, para. 24.

400 Rule 67 ERCSM.

401 Art. 12(J)(i) PDCER.

402 Rules 12, 68 ERCSM; Rule 14.3 Tokyo Rules.

Consequential measures should be proportionate, governed by the principle of minimum intervention, and imprisonment should be a measure of last resort. Re-imprisonment is not appropriate for the breach of minor conditions or once-off transgressions that result from a misunderstanding in relation to the scope of the condition. It should be made clear that this option should only be used for the breach of particular conditions, or serious or continuing breaches of other conditions. The need to define the circumstances in which this is an appropriate penalty is heightened by the likelihood that it will result in the involuntary transfer of the prisoner abroad to serve the sentence: if re-imprisonment is ordered, the designated Judge must direct the Registrar to notify the enforcing State and arrange for the convicted person's transfer for imprisonment under the applicable Enforcement of Sentence Agreement.[403]

Moreover, the PDCER only appears to give the designated judge the option of re-imprisoning the offender for the 'time remaining on the sentence'. Given the length of the sentences imposed by the SCSL, this may also give rise to questions of proportionality. The Prosecutor in *Fofana* seems to acknowledge this challenge when it requested that, if Fofana was not returned to prison for the remainder of his sentence, he be returned for 'a specified period'.[404] It is also notable that the scheme grants the designated Judge discretion not to grant *credit for time served* in the community under a CERA. In other words, the Judge can order re-imprisonment for the time remaining on the sentence that was not spent in custody.

It is also unclear if a convicted person can *re-apply* for CER after re-imprisonment has been ordered. Given that CER is possible after two-thirds of the sentence has been served, and the judge might decide not to grant any credit for time served under supervision in the community, re-imprisonment could potentially be for one-third of the original sentence, which in some cases could be for sixteen years. There is currently neither a prohibition on such an application nor on the grant of CER for persons re-imprisoned following the violation of their CERA.

Although the original sentence constitutes the legal basis for re-detention until the full term has been served, the RSCSL should ensure that decisions to order re-imprisonment are taken with the objectives of the system in mind.[405] Such decisions have a significant impact on the rights, and in particular, the 'liberty interests,' of offenders.[406] To avoid any recall to prison being classed

---

403 Art. 12(K) PDCER.

404 *Prosecutor v Fofana*, Disposition of the Matter of Moinina Fofana's Violations of the Terms of his Conditional Early Release, RSCSL-04-14-ES, (1416–1440) Freetown, 25 April 2016, para. 11.

405 See Van Zyl Smit and Snacken, note 118 at 328.

406 Ibid at 329.

as arbitrary, it is important to ask if the conduct that resulted in the violation of conditions was of a 'sufficient nexus' to the underlying conviction to justify a return to custody in the interests of public safety.[407] In addition to ensuring the legality of the recall, it is also important that thought be given to the nature of this custody. As Campbell notes, despite the fact that recalled prisoners are deemed to have demonstrated the need for serious intervention, it is usually unclear what processes, interventions or preparation for later release should be applied to such persons.[408]

Contemporary standards also state that offenders should have the right to appeal the revocation (or modification) of non-custodial measures to a judicial or other competent independent authority.[409] The RSCSL should therefore introduce a *right to appeal* decisions to modify or revoke CER, particularly in the case of an order for re-imprisonment.[410]

10.2 Revocation and Release on Modified Conditions

The designated judge can revoke the order for CER and order the release of the convicted person subject to modified conditions.[411] In *Fofana*, Judge Solomon concluded that the aims of rehabilitation and reintegration would be best served by the revocation of Fofana's original CER and his continued release subject to stringent modified special conditions (and the MA's strict enforcement thereof).[412]

Some of the 'modified' conditions for Fofana remained unchanged. For example, the condition that Fofana or any person acting with his consent or authority shall not, directly or indirectly, approach any of the victims, witnesses, or their families in the future, to directly or indirectly try to harm, intimidate or otherwise interfere with them in any way[413] remains unchanged

[407] *Benjamin Manuel v NZ*, Communication No. 1385/2005, UN Doc. CCPR/C/91/D/1385/2005, para. 7.3.

[408] Christopher M. Campbell 'Rethinking Conditional Release as an Assumption-Based Test of Offender Readiness' (2018) 43(2) *Criminal Justice Review* 216–235 at 228.

[409] Rule 14.6 Tokyo Rules.

[410] See Rules 9.3, 14.6 Tokyo Rules.

[411] Art. 12(J)(ii) PDCER.

[412] *Prosecutor v Fofana*, Disposition of the Matter of Moinina Fofana's Violations of the Terms of his Conditional Early Release, RSCSL-04-14-ES, (1416–1440) Freetown, 25 April 2016, paras 80–81(i)–(ii).

[413] Ibid, para. 81(ii)(a).

from the special conditions imposed in the disposition of the decision to grant CER.[414]

The scope of the original special condition related to joining politics was extended: the obligation to 'conduct himself honorably and peacefully in the community and not to engage in secret meetings intended to plan civil unrest or join local politics[415] was amended to include a prohibition of his presence at any gathering aimed at a political purpose.[416]

The modified conditions increased the frequency of his reporting obligation from a twice-a-month requirement to visit a designated centre[417] to a weekly obligation on a specified day, time and at a specific location.[418]

The modified conditions also imposed new restrictions directly linked to his violations, which include a requirement to be physically present in Bo City for six months from the date of the disposition; to obtain authorisation for any travel outside Bo Town following this period from the Registrar, as well as a requirement to provide his exact location, purpose and return date for any requested travel; a requirement to immediately report to MA in authorised travel locations; and desistance from the practice of signing the register in advance of the required date.[419] Since the imposition of the new special conditions, the Registrar has issued written authorisations for Fofana to travel outside Bo Town for farming and family matters.[420]

This decision unfortunately copied the confusing use of the term 'special conditions' found in the decision to grant CER. Just as the original grant of CER included a 'special condition' directed to the Office of the Registrar to make regular visits to provide assurance of security to vulnerable former

---

414 *Prosecutor v Fofana and Kondewa*, Decision of the President on Application for Conditional Early Release, SCSL-04-14-ES (1270–1291), 11 August 2014, para. 49(ii) at 22–23.

415 Ibid, para. 49(iii) at 23.

416 *Prosecutor v Fofana*, Disposition of the Matter of Moinina Fofana's Violations of the Terms of his Conditional Early Release, RSCSL-04-14-ES, (1416–1440) Freetown, 25 April 2016, para. 81(ii)(b).

417 *Prosecutor v Fofana and Kondewa*, Decision of the President on Application for Conditional Early Release, SCSL-04-14-ES (1270–1291), 11 August 2014, para. 49(iv) at 23.

418 *Prosecutor v Fofana*, Disposition of the Matter of Moinina Fofana's Violations of the Terms of his Conditional Early Release, RSCSL-04-14-ES, (1416–1440) Freetown, 25 April 2016, para. 81(ii)(f).

419 Ibid, para. 81(ii)(c)–(e), (g).

420 Fourth Annual Report of the President of the RSCSL, January 2017 to December 2017 at 20, 29.

witnesses,[421] this disposition directed the MA and the RSCSL Registrar to conduct spot checks to ensure Fofana was in authorised locations at all times under the heading of special conditions.[422] This direction should have been included in the 'further orders' section, which required that the Registrar conduct an intensive two-week training course for Fofana on the modified special conditions (as well as the standard conditions) and that upon completion, the Registrar certify his satisfactory completion of the session.[423] Fofana's release was conditional on his understanding of the terms of his modified CERA and agreement to comply with them.[424] Fofana attended the required training from 5–18 May 2016. The training was conducted by the RSCSL Registrar, Principal Defender, Associate Defence Legal Officer, Monitoring Officer and Outreach Contractor.[425] The training was conducted in Krio, though a Mende interpreter was present so Fofana could follow proceedings in his own dialect.[426] It was also attended by ten Sierra Leone Police personnel from Bo City.[427] The training covered human rights law, international humanitarian law, the meaning and application of conditional early release, the meaning and import of Fofana's modified conditions, the consequences in the event of a breach of the modified conditions, and the role of the Sierra Leone Police in the enforcement of the modified conditions of release.[428]

11. TERMINATION OF CONDITIONAL EARLY RELEASE

An individual's CERA should contain provisions that explicitly set out the expiry date of the CERA (and the sentence) unless this CERA is revoked or modified.[429] The basic principle is that a convicted person will be discharged

---

[421] *Prosecutor v Fofana and Kondewa*, Decision of the President on Application for Conditional Early Release, SCSL-04-14-ES (1270–1291), 11 August 2014, para. 49(v) at 23.

[422] *Prosecutor v Fofana*, Disposition of the Matter of Moinina Fofana's Violations of the Terms of his Conditional Early Release, RSCSL-04-14-ES, (1416–1440) Freetown, 25 April 2016, para. 81(ii)(h).

[423] Ibid, para. 81(i)–(ii) at 25.

[424] Ibid, para. 81(iii)–(iv) at 25.

[425] See *Prosecutor v Fofana*, Submission of the Registrar pursuant to Rule 33(B) as ordered in terms of Paragraph 81(v) of the Disposition on the matter of Moinina Fofana's violations of the terms of his conditional early release, RSCSL-04-14-ES (1468–1473), 26 May 2016, paras 15, 17.

[426] See ibid, para. 16.

[427] See ibid, para. 15.

[428] Ibid, para. 16.

[429] Pro Forma CERA, Annex C PDCER, paras 3, 9.

from the control of the CERA at the expiration of his term of imprisonment.[430] On 28 May 2018, Fofana became the first person convicted by the SCSL to complete his sentence. Accordingly, he was 'relieved of all conditions imposed on him as a consequence of his conditional early release' and 'become a free citizen of Sierra Leone again'.[431] The Office of the Registrar felt that 'the successful completion of his sentence under these conditions (of CER) is a major achievement, demonstrating the value of the Residual Special Court's conditional early release policy'.[432]

This term of conditional release should include credit for each day of the sentence served under the CERA.[433] This has been complicated by the discretion awarded to judges to decide not to give credit for time served under CER in the case of a breach of a condition.[434] Contemporary standards state that where a violation has resulted in imprisonment, 'credit for any satisfactory compliance should be reflected in the length of the sentence'.[435]

The Practice Direction also lacks clarity in relation to the potential for the CERA to be revoked prior to the expiration of the term of imprisonment. Contemporary standards state that it should be possible to terminate supervision before it is due to end if the offender has responded favourably by observing conditions and it appears that CERA is no longer necessary to achieve its purpose.[436] Moreover, both the offender and the implementing authority should be able to apply to have the conditions terminated on these grounds.[437] Permitting progression from conditional to unconditional release could act as an additional incentive for the reintegrative, public safety, and reconciliation purposes outlined in the Practice Direction's preamble.

12. CONCLUSION

By introducing a conditional release system, the Special Court was the first international criminal court to extend international control over the sanction after release from custody. The decision to introduce a conditional early release scheme was based on the need to respect the totality of the sentences imposed and ensure the protection of public safety by reducing the risk of recidivism

430 Art. 13(B) PDCER.

431 Fifth Annual Report of the President of the RSCSL, January 2018–December 2018, at 22.

432 Ibid at 20.

433 Art. 13(A) PDCER.

434 Arts. 12(J)(i), 13(A) PDCER.

435 Rule 70 ERCSM.

436 See Rule 72 ERCSM; Rule 11.2 Tokyo Rules.

437 Rule 72 ERCSM.

and threats to reconciliation and peace.[438] The system was also designed to achieve penological goals of rehabilitation and reintegration.[439] The accompanying guidance and paperwork are detailed, and the system's application involves the broadest community-level consultations about the release of individuals to date in the international penal system. The responsiveness to the concerns of consulted individuals and groups has been reflected in the conditions imposed on released persons. The vague, general and mandatory nature of some of the conditions imposed, as well as the consequences that should be imposed for the breach of particular types of conditions, requires further scrutiny. The conditional release system has also faced challenges given the continued political volatility in Sierra Leone, concerns about the efficacy of the appointed monitoring authority, and the breach of conditions by the first person conditionally released. Moreover, it is unclear if or how the system can be applied to Charles Taylor, a Liberian citizen. Despite these challenges, the judicial decision to move away from the unconditional approach towards release practised by the UN Tribunals (despite having an identical legal framework) has resulted in widespread and documented support for the conditional release of convicted persons. The operation of this system led to the Rwandan Government requesting the introduction of a similar system for persons convicted by the ICTR at the MICT at the UN Security Council.

438 Doherty and Fisher, note 1 at 364–365.
439 Ibid at 366, 368.

5. Conditional early release at the International Residual Mechanism for Criminal Tribunals

Until 2018, virtually all persons convicted by the ICTY, ICTR and MICT were released on an unconditional basis. A Security Council debate in June 2018 provided the political catalyst for significant change to this international release system: from this point on, prisoners granted release have been granted a conditional form of release. In addition to the new form of release, the appointment of a new President in 2019 resulted in a broader procedural approach that allows for submissions from the Office of the Prosecutor (OTP) and States on sentence enforcement matters, increased engagement with and consideration of the impact on victims and witnesses and a deeper analysis of rehabilitative progress and reintegration potential in the context of atrocity crimes.

1. SECURITY COUNCIL RESOLUTION 2622

At the semi-annual debate on the MICT at the Security Council in June 2018, several countries voiced concerns about the release of persons convicted by the ICTR who had failed to express regret for their crimes and indeed went on to deny responsibility for or attempted to justify them.[1] Release in such cases, it was argued, would tarnish the legacy of the UN Tribunals and undermine the fight against impunity.[2] Some states suggested that this could be resolved by the introduction of a conditional early release system.[3] Other members highlighted the need to consult with and take account of the views of the states concerned, victims and the wider community.[4]

[1] Statements of the representatives of Peru, Bolivia and the USA, UN Security Council, 8278th Meeting, S/PV.8278, 6 June 2018 at 6, 14, 16.

[2] Statement of the representatives of Bolivia and the USA, UN Security Council, 8278th Meeting, S/PV.8278, 6 June 2018 at 6, 16.

[3] Statements of representatives of France and Kuwait, UN Security Council, 8278th Meeting, S/PV.8278, 6 June 2018 at 9, 11.

[4] Statements of the representative of Equatorial Guinea, Ethiopia, and the USA, UN Security Council, 8278th Meeting, S/PV.8278, 6 June 2018 at 12, 15–6.

The strongest call for change to the release system came from a non-Council member. Rwanda argued that the unconditional release of masterminds of the genocide in non-transparent circumstances and through inconsistent procedures meant the credibility of both the ICTR and MICT was seriously at stake. The Rwandan statement highlighted that Presidential decisions could be made without consulting with Rwanda or victim associations, and the lack of weight given to the lack of remorse by persons benefiting from early release. Rwanda claimed that some released persons had 'regrouped and formed an association denying the 1994 genocide against the Tutsi and repropagating the genocide ideology' without fear of any consequence due to the unconditional nature of their release.[5]

In light of these criticisms, the Rwandan government urged the MICT to consider adopting three of what it considered to be best practices of the RSCSL:[6] a requirement to demonstrate a positive contribution to peace and reconciliation in order to be considered eligible for release (public acknowledgments of guilt, support for peace projects, apology to victims or restitution); a need to obtain the opinions of witnesses, victims, the government of the home state, and residents of the requested area for release about the release of individuals; and accountability mechanisms such as stringent requirements for supervision, restitution to victims and the renunciation of ideologies contrary to peace and reconciliation. Ultimately, Rwanda wanted conditions placed on released persons that would prevent genocide convicts benefiting from early release from engaging in activities promoting genocide ideology and denial.[7]

On 27 June 2018, the UN Security Council adopted Resolution 2422.[8] In light of the 'views and concerns expressed by some Member States … about the approach of the Mechanism to the early release of persons convicted by the ICTR,' paragraph 10 of the resolution 'encouraged the Mechanism to consider an appropriate solution, including by considering putting in place conditions on early release in appropriate cases'.

2. THE INTRODUCTION OF A CONDITIONAL EARLY RELEASE SCHEME AT THE MICT

Even though the Resolution was not mandatory, referred only to persons convicted by the ICTR and not the ICTY, and only suggested using conditional

5 Statement of the representative of Rwanda, UN Security Council, 8278th Meeting, S/PV.8278, 6 June 2018 at 24.

6 Ibid at 24–25.

7 Statement of the representative of Rwanda, UN Security Council, 8278th Meeting, S/PV.8278, 6 June 2018 at 25.

8 The Russian Federation abstained from voting (14-0-1).

release in appropriate cases, release decisions since this resolution have only been granted on a conditional basis. The legality of the introduction of a conditional early release scheme was challenged in a motion to vary or remove conditions imposed (for the first time by the MICT) on a person convicted by the ICTY.[9]

2.1 Legal Challenge

Although the UNSC Resolution only requested consideration of conditional release for persons convicted by the ICTR, President Meron decided that it was necessary to also apply conditions to those convicted by the ICTY to 'harmonise the approach to early release across both branches of the Mechanism'.[10] The two main objections to the creation and implementation of the conditional early release scheme were that it was (a) ultra vires and (b) resulted in the unfair treatment of persons being supervised by the MICT.

2.1.1 Ultra vires

The central argument made by Ćorić was that the Rules of Procedure and Evidence could only be amended by the judges of the Mechanism and not unilaterally by the President.[11] The OTP had been recommending the amendment of Rule 151 in order to introduce a programme of conditional early release since 2016. This proposal was rooted in concerns that the 'vast majority of convicted persons have been released unconditionally upon or soon after serving only two-thirds of their sentences'.[12] This OTP proposal to amend Rule 151 was not, however, adopted by the judges sitting in plenary. While the plenary of judges in 2018 did amend the rules to incorporate changes to the release procedure, they opted not to adopt a conditional release scheme recommended

---

[9] *Prosecutor v Ćorić*, Urgent Motion Seeking Variation of Conditions of Early Release of 15 January 2019 and Request for Legal Aid, MICT-17-112-ES.4, 2 April 2019, para. 14.

[10] *Prosecutor v Ćorić*, Further Redacted Public Redacted Version of the Decision of the President on the Early Release of Valentin Ćorić and Related Motions, MICT-17-112-ES.4, 16 January 2019, para. 73.

[11] Art. 13 MICTSt.

[12] Para. 30, Progress report of the Prosecutor of the International Residual Mechanism for Criminal Tribunals, Serge Brammertz, for the period from 16 November 2018 to 15 May 2019 at 39, Annex II Letter dated 20 May 2019 from the President of the International Residual Mechanism for Criminal Tribunals addressed to the President of the Security Council, S/2019/417, 20 May 2019.

by the OTP.[13] This, Ćorić argued, demonstrated a lack of judicial support for conditional release. The imposition of conditions involved the use of powers not provided for in the Rules (or the Practice Direction), and as such constituted a unilateral and ultra vires amendment of the rules.[14] Further a consulted judge (Judge Liu) had expressed concerns that the imposition of conditions was contrary to the 'longstanding practice of the ICTY and the Mechanism not to do so'.[15]

Reliance on the UN Security Council Resolution as a legal basis for imposing conditions was also questioned given that the Resolution did not explicitly determine the existence of any threat to the peace, breach of peace or act of aggression which would be necessary to give it power to act under Articles 41 and 42 of the UN Charter.[16] Moreover, the Resolution itself only encourages (rather than orders) the Mechanism to adopt a change to the release scheme and contains no legal basis that would permit the President to override the sole authority granted by the Statute to judges to amend the Rules.[17] By 'taking upon himself the powers granted by the Statute to the judges of the Mechanism', the President, it was argued, had acted ultra vires.[18]

President Agius rejected these arguments on several grounds. Firstly, he noted that the release had been contingent on the acceptance of conditions: if the imposition of conditions was ultra vires, Ćorić would have to return to custody to serve his sentence.[19] Secondly, he dismissed the argument that he had unilaterally amended the Rules. He insisted that the imposition of conditions was within the President's statutory and sole discretion to decide whether to grant release, as granted by the Security Council.[20] This discretion was not affected in any way by the decision of the judges not to amend the Rules. Finally, there was a practice of the MICT President granting release subject

---

[13] *Prosecutor v Ćorić*, Urgent Motion Seeking Variation of Conditions of Early Release of 15 January 2019 and Request for Legal Aid, MICT-17-112-ES.4, 02.04.19, paras 15, 17–19.

[14] Ibid, paras 16, 20.

[15] Ibid, para. 16.

[16] Ibid, para. 21.

[17] Ibid, paras 22–23.

[18] Ibid, para. 23.

[19] *Prosecutor v Ćorić*, Decision on Motions Related to Valentin Ćorić's Request for Variation of Early Release Conditions, MICT-17-112-ES.4, 21.02.20, para. 38.

[20] Ibid, para. 39.

to conditions prior to the Security Council Resolution in the 2017 *Beara* decision.[21]

2.1.2 Unequal treatment

Ćorić also argued that he was not only being treated differently, inconsistently and unequally from other ICTY accused persons but also from similarly situated persons (persons from his case).[22] Berislav Pušić, he noted, had been released unconditionally a few months previously to the same city. Ćorić argued that this was unfair and unjust and that no 'cogent reasons' had been set out to justify the departure from established Rules and jurisprudence.[23] President Agius again rejected this argument, stating that all cases were addressed on their own merits and that conditions had been imposed in this case in line with recommendations made by the Victims and Witnesses Support Unit (WISP) (differentiating Ćorić's case from other unconditional release cases).[24]

2.2 Legal Framework

Unlike the Rules, the Practice Direction can be amended unilaterally by the President. In sharp contrast to the detailed Practice Direction and accompanying documentation created by the RSCSL,[25] the introduction of a conditional release system at the MICT happened with minimal changes to the legal framework governing release.

A revision of the Practice Direction that occurred after the UNSC Resolution did not result in any changes related to conditional release.[26] President Agius, however, informed the Security Council in May 2019 that he was exploring 'appropriate solutions' and changes to the Practice Direction to incorporate a conditional release system that would be 'consistent with the governing legal framework and applicable jurisprudence'.[27] Following consultations with the

---

21 This case dealt with an urgent and serious situation involving terminal illness – see Chapter 9.

22 *Prosecutor v Ćorić*, Urgent Motion Seeking Variation of Conditions of Early Release of 15 January 2019 and Request for Legal Aid, MICT-17-112-ES.4, 2 April 2019, para. 25.

23 Ibid, para. 26.

24 *Prosecutor v Ćorić*, Decision on Motions Related to Valentin Ćorić's Request for Variation of Early Release Conditions, MICT-17-112-ES.4, 21 February 2020, para. 40.

25 See Chapter 4.

26 MICT/3/Rev. 2, 20 February 2019.

27 Para 62, Annex I, Assessment and progress report of the President of the International Residual Mechanism for Criminal Tribunals, Judge Carmel Agius,

Prosecutor and the Registrar, the President revised the Practice Direction in May 2020 to introduce a conditional early release option at the MICT.[28] The solution was the insertion of one sentence: paragraph 20 simply states that '[e]arly release may be granted subject to conditions'.[29]

Accordingly, the Statute, Rules and Practice Direction do not discuss what conditions could or should be, how these conditions will be supervised or how (suspected) breaches of conditions will be dealt with either procedurally or punitively. The details of these fundamental aspects of a conditional release scheme are confined to basic discussions in release decisions.

3. ELIGIBILITY FOR CONDITIONAL EARLY RELEASE

The threshold for eligibility for those serving determinate sentences has remained the same, although it is now recognised as constituting a precondition for consideration for release. Eligibility for release for persons serving indeterminate sentences continues to lack a precise temporal reference point. Clarity has been introduced, however, in relation to the impact of the provisional recognition of sentence remission granted by domestic authorities.

3.1 Determinate Sentences

3.1.1 Two-thirds threshold

Eligibility for consideration for release has not altered under the conditional early release scheme. The temporal threshold of two-thirds has been retained and remains the sole factor considered in terms of the Rule 151 factor of 'treatment of similarly-situated prisoners'. Comparisons to release decisions in other cases have been rejected as being 'distinctly unhelpful'.[30] Rather than acting as a 'guiding principle',[31] this temporal threshold is now referred to and explicitly

---

for the period from 16 November 2018 to 15 May 2019, Letter dated 20 May 2019 from the President of the International Residual Mechanism for Criminal Tribunals addressed to the President of the Security Council, S/2019/417, 20 May 2019.

[28] Annual Report of the IRMCT to the Security Council (A/75/276; S/2020/763) 30 July 2021, para. 21.

[29] MICT/3/Rev. 3, 15 May 2020.

[30] *Prosecutor v Brdanin*, Decision on the Application of Radoslav Brdanin for Early Release, MICT-13-48-ES, 28 February 2020, para. 29.

[31] *Prosecutor v Simba*, Public Redacted Version of the President's 7 January 2019 Decision on the Early Release of Aloys Simba, MICT-14-62-ES.1, 7 January 2019, para. 31; *Prosecutor v Ćorić*, Further Redacted Public Redacted Version of

recognised as 'essentially a pre-condition'.[32] Consequently, Agius decided that in the 'interests of fairness and transparency', it was important to consider eligibility to be considered for early release (rather than eligibility to apply for early release) as a preliminary matter.[33]

The 2020 revision of the Practice Direction resulted in the insertion of two new provisions stating that, although an application can be lodged by a prisoner at any time, this was subject to the fact that, generally, a convicted person will be required to have served two-thirds of their sentence to be considered for early release.[34] This 'uniform eligibility threshold' was needed to ensure legal certainty and equal treatment between persons convicted by the various tribunals, serving their sentences in various states and international facilities, and the various methods of applying for release (direct petition or notification from an enforcing state).[35]

3.1.2 Notifications from enforcing states

The MICT continues to receive notifications from enforcing states outlining that prisoners have become eligible for release under national law.[36]

the Decision of the President on the Early Release of Valentin Ćorić and Related Motions, MICT-17-112-ES.4, 16 January 2019, para. 37.

[32] *Prosecutor v Bralo*, Decision on the Early Release of Miroslav Bralo, MICT-14-78-ES, 31 December 2019, para. 21; *Prosecutor v Krstić*, Decision on the Early Release of Radislav Krstić, MICT-13-46-ES.1, 10 September 2019, para. 18; *Prosecutor v Semanza*, Decision on Laurent Semanza's Application for Early Release, MICT-13-36-ES.2, 17 September 2020, para. 25.

[33] *Prosecutor v Krstić*, Decision on the Early Release of Radislav Krstić, MICT-13-46-ES.1, 10 September 2019, para. 18.

[34] See MICT/3/Rev. 3, 15 May 2020, paras 7–9.

[35] *Prosecutor v Brdanin*, Decision on the Application of Radoslav Brdanin for Early Release, MICT-13-48-ES, 28 February 2020, para. 29; *Prosecutor v Bralo*, Decision on the Early Release of Miroslav Bralo, MICT-14-78-ES, 31 December 2019, paras 22, 35; *Prosecutor v Krstić*, Decision on the Early Release of Radislav Krstić, MICT-13-46-ES.1, 10 September 2019, para. 16; *Prosecutor v Semanza*, Decision on Laurent Semanza's Application for Early Release, MICT-13-36-ES.2, 17 September 2020, para. 26; *Prosecutor v Stakić*, Decision on Sentence Remission and Early Release of Milomir Stakić, MICT-13-60-ES, 31 December 2020, para. 48.

[36] *Prosecutor v Simba*, Public Redacted Version of the President's 7 January 2019 Decision on the Early Release of Aloys Simba, MICT-14-62-ES.1, 7 January 2019, para. 6; *Prosecutor v Bralo*, Decision on the Early Release of Miroslav Bralo, MICT-14-78-ES, 31 December 2019, paras 1, 24; *Prosecutor v Krstić*, Decision on the Early Release of Radislav Krstić, MICT-13-46-ES.1, 10 September 2019, paras 1, 7, 20.

Notifications contain references to decisions of local courts on the formal entitlement of particular prisoners to apply for release under domestic law and applications by international prisoners to local courts for release.[37] The forms of possible release and the temporal threshold for such release vary between states. In Benin, a prisoner is eligible for either conditional or early release after serving just over half of the sentence if the prisoner has behaved and shown signs of social rehabilitation.[38] In Denmark, a prisoner is eligible for parole after serving two-thirds of the sentence if there is no major risk of recidivism, on the condition they will not commit a criminal offence for five years after release.[39] Prisoners serving in France may become eligible for conditional release after serving half of their sentence.[40] A State may also provide the President with information that a particular applicant does not meet the national conditions for release.[41]

Despite this process, it remains irrelevant how or when a person convicted by the ICTY, ICTR or MICT becomes eligible for release under the national law of enforcing states, or indeed what form of release they would be eligible for. Despite the existence of 'two concurrent thresholds',[42] eligibility and the form of release are determined solely by the MICT President in line with the MICT's legal framework and established practice.[43]

---

[37] *Prosecutor v Krstić*, Decision on the Early Release of Radislav Krstić, MICT-13-46-ES.1, 10 September 2019, paras 22–3.

[38] Article 810 of Law No. 2012–15 of 18 March 2013 in section III of Benin Code of Criminal Procedure; *Prosecutor v Simba*, Public Redacted Version of the President's 7 January 2019 Decision on the Early Release of Aloys Simba, MICT-14-62-ES.1, 7 January 2019, para. 29.

[39] *Prosecutor v Brdanin*, Decision on the Application of Radoslav Brdanin for Early Release, MICT-13-48-ES, 28 February 2020, paras 31–2.

[40] *Prosecutor v Stakić*, Decision on Sentence Remission and Early Release of Milomir Stakić, MICT-13-60-ES, 31 December 2020, para. 13.

[41] *Prosecutor v Ntawukulilyayo*, Decision on the Application of Dominique Ntawukulilyayo for Early Release, MICT-13-34-ES, 8 January 2020 at 4; *Prosecutor v Semanza*, Decision on Laurent Semanza's Application for Early Release, MICT-13-36-ES.2, 17 September 2020, paras 13, 28.

[42] *Prosecutor v Stakić*, Decision on Sentence Remission and Early Release of Milomir Stakić, MICT-13-60-ES, 31 December 2020, para. 47.

[43] *Prosecutor v Simba*, Public Redacted Version of the President's 7 January 2019 Decision on the Early Release of Aloys Simba, MICT-14-62-ES.1, 7 January 2019, para. 29; *Prosecutor v Brdanin*, Decision on the Application of Radoslav Brdanin for Early Release, MICT-13-48-ES, 28 February 2020, para. 33; *Prosecutor v Bralo*, Decision on the Early Release of Miroslav Bralo, MICT-14-78-ES, 31 December 2019, para. 26; *Prosecutor v Krstić*, Decision on the Early Release of Radislav Krstić, MICT-13-46-ES.1, 10 September 2019, para.

3.1.3 A rebuttable presumption in favour of release

Service of two-thirds of the sentence results in mere eligibility to apply for and be considered for release; it does not entitle a prisoner to release.[44] However, there was a (rebuttable) *presumption in favour of release* at this stage. In *Ćorić*, President Meron noted that the Mechanism 'inherited a long-standing practice of granting requests for early release upon completion of two-thirds of a sentence absent particular circumstances that warrant against it'.[45] President Agius decided that it was in the 'interests of legal certainty and predictability' to follow this practice, and to depart from it 'only for cogent reasons in the interests of justice'.[46] So while service of more than two-thirds will weigh in favour of early release,[47] service of less than two-thirds will result in the application being deemed ineligible and denied unless the applicant can demonstrate that there are compelling or exceptional circumstances to warrant release prior to this.[48] Service of two-thirds of a sentence alone will not result in release where other factors strongly militate against it.[49]

24; *Prosecutor v Semanza*, Decision on Laurent Semanza's Application for Early Release, MICT-13-36-ES.2, 17 September 2020, para. 29.

[44] *Prosecutor v Simba*, Public Redacted Version of the President's 7 January 2019 Decision on the Early Release of Aloys Simba, MICT-14-62-ES.1, 7 January 2019, para. 32; *Prosecutor v Ćorić*, Further Redacted Public Redacted Version of the Decision of the President on the Early Release of Valentin Ćorić and Related Motions, MICT-17-112-ES.4, 16 January 2019, para. 38; *Prosecutor v Bralo*, Decision on the Early Release of Miroslav Bralo, MICT-14-78-ES, 31 December 2019, paras 27, 36; *Prosecutor v Krstić*, Decision on the Early Release of Radislav Krstić, MICT-13-46-ES.1, 10 September 2019, para. 17.

[45] *Prosecutor v Ćorić*, Further Redacted Public Redacted Version of the Decision of the President on the Early Release of Valentin Ćorić and Related Motions, MICT-17-112-ES.4, 16 January 2019, paras 38–9.

[46] Ibid, para. 39.

[47] *Prosecutor v Simba*, Public Redacted Version of the President's 7 January 2019 Decision on the Early Release of Aloys Simba, MICT-14-62-ES.1, 7 January 2019, para. 34; *Prosecutor v Ćorić*, Further Redacted Public Redacted Version of the Decision of the President on the Early Release of Valentin Ćorić and Related Motions, MICT-17-112-ES.4, 16 January 2019, para. 42.

[48] *Prosecutor v Ntawukulilyayo*, Decision on the Application of Dominique Ntawukulilyayo for Early Release, MICT-13-34-ES, 8 January 2020; *Prosecutor v Galić*, Decision on the Early Release of Stanislav Galić, MICT-14-83-ES, 26 June 2019, para. 47; *Prosecutor v Munyakazi*, Decision on the Application of Yussuf Munyakazi for Early Release, MICT-12-18-ES.2, 29 November 2019; *Prosecutor v Krstić*, Decision on the Early Release of Radislav Krstić, MICT-13-46-ES.1, 10 September 2019, paras 19, 25, 28.

[49] *Prosecutor v Bralo*, Decision on the Early Release of Miroslav Bralo, MICT-14-78-ES, 31 December 2019, para. 82.

3.2 Indeterminate Sentences

The availability of release for life-sentenced prisoners has remained subject to strong opposition from Rwanda. The Rwandan Government has argued that the gravity of the crimes committed and the decision by the ICTR to impose the most serious penalty at its disposal should mean that such prisoners are precluded from any consideration for release and should spend the remainder of their lives in prison.[50]

President Agius made it clear that he did not intend to depart from the Mechanism's practice of considering persons sentenced to life imprisonment for release.[51] The threshold established by President Meron was based on a two-thirds calculation of the highest determinate sentence imposed by the ICTY/ICTR or MICT up until that point (45 years).[52] Even though a longer sentence was subsequently imposed by the ICTR (47 years[53]), Agius felt this ICTR case was not relevant for Galić's eligibility as his threshold had 'previously been fixed'[54] and that 'the interests of justice and the principle of legal certainty' led him to consider that Galić would be eligible for release once he had served a minimum of 30 years.[55] However, he was careful to state that this did not prejudice other cases and that 'the consequences of this decision as they may impact future applications for early release of persons serving a sentence of life imprisonment will be discussed if and when required'.[56]

The exact threshold for release eligibility for persons serving indeterminate sentences therefore remains unresolved both generally and for individual prisoners. Decisions to date have not addressed the matter directly as applicants have been deemed ineligible for release.[57] The precise sentence service requirement may vary depending on sentences that are yet to be imposed. It

---

[50] See *Prosecutor v Musema*, Opposition to Application for Commutation of Sentence, MICT-12-15-ES.1, 27 August 2018, 2–3.

[51] *Prosecutor v Galić*, Decision on the Early Release of Stanislav Galić, MICT-14-83-ES, 24 March 2021, para. 22.

[52] *Prosecutor v Galić*, Decision on the Early Release of Stanislav Galić, MICT-14-83-ES, 26 June 2019, para. 17.

[53] *Prosecutor v Nyiramasuhuko et al*, Appeal Judgment, ICTR-98-42-A, 14 December 2015, paras 3538–3539.

[54] *Prosecutor v Galić*, Decision on the Early Release of Stanislav Galić, MICT-14-83-ES, 24 March 2021, para. 23.

[55] *Prosecutor v Galić*, Decision on the Early Release of Stanislav Galić, MICT-14-83-ES, 26 June 2019, paras 6, 33.

[56] Ibid, paras 6, 33.

[57] *Prosecutor v Popović*, Decision on the Early Release of Vujadin Popović, MICT-15-85-ES.2, 30 December 2020.

is clear, however, that until a life-sentenced prisoner has served at least thirty years of their sentence, they will not be eligible for consideration for conditional early release unless there are compelling or extraordinary circumstances warranting release prior to this.[58]

3.3 Provisionally Recognised Sentence Remission

Remission under domestic law can be acknowledged if already granted, or provisionally recognised if its grant is dependent on a Mechanism decision.[59] The provisional recognition of remission granted by enforcing states was designed to prevent inequality between the internationally convicted person and the domestic prison population.[60] The need to ensure equality between persons convicted by international tribunals, however, meant that the two-thirds threshold had to be respected.[61] The compromise solution of provisionally recognising national grants of remission introduced by President Robinson did not change this (or other) eligibility requirement(s).[62]

In *Stakić*, President Agius felt it was necessary to clarify the effect of sentence remission granted by the national authorities of enforcing states due to the ambiguity in ICTY and MICT jurisprudence. This ambiguity, he worried, may have led some convicted persons to expect that remission would reduce the time they had to serve before they were eligible for (early) release.[63] In *Stakić* and later cases, he emphasised that although sentence remission may be provisionally recognised by the Mechanism President, this does not change the calculation of time served for either service of two-thirds of the sentence for eligibility for early release purposes or the end date of the sentence.[64]

In *Jelisić*, Judge de Prada expressed the view that previous recognitions of sentence remission by the ICTY or MICT had created legitimate expectations of a reduction of the sentence as a whole and that this expectation should be

---

58 *Prosecutor v Galić*, Decision on the Early Release of Stanislav Galić, MICT-14-83-ES, 26 June 2019, paras 6–7, 25.

59 *Prosecutor v Stakić*, Decision on Sentence Remission and Early Release of Milomir Stakić, MICT-13-60-ES, 31 December 2020, para. 38.

60 Ibid, para. 27.

61 Ibid, para. 28.

62 Ibid, paras 29–31.

63 Ibid, paras 24, 31–32.

64 Ibid, paras 33, 40, 49; *Prosecutor v Jelisić*, Decision on Sentence Remission and Early Release of Goran Jelisić, MICT-14-63-ES, 11 March 2021, paras 22–36, 39.

protected.[65] President Agius highlighted that none of the previous decisions recognising national grants of remission created an expectation that the end date of the sentence would automatically change, and they unambiguously stated that early release was exclusively within the President's discretion.[66] While 'it will not constitute a commutation of sentence before the Mechanism', grants of remission by national authorities may serve as indicators of good behaviour and rehabilitation.[67]

4. PROCEDURE FOR CONDITIONAL EARLY RELEASE DECISIONS

The President continues to receive both notifications from enforcing states[68] and direct petitions from prisoners serving their sentences in both enforcing states[69] and international detention facilities.[70] The third revision of the Practice Direction notes that the term 'application' refers to both state notifications and direct petitions.[71] The procedure for considering applications has changed in a number of ways since the introduction of a conditional release scheme. A wider range of information is now being sought and considered, an abbreviated procedure for dealing with applications submitted prior to the service of two-thirds of the sentence has been introduced, and a broader consultation process ensures the views of the prosecutor, states and victims play a more prominent role.

4.1 Information

Under the Practice Direction, the President can direct the Registry to collect information required (as listed or any other information considered relevant), request third-party submissions, and transmit the collated information to convicted persons for their views.[72] Release decisions show that Presidents have

---

65 *Prosecutor v Jelisić*, Decision on Sentence Remission and Early Release of Goran Jelisić, MICT-14-63-ES, 11 March 2021, para. 50.

66 Ibid, para. 51.

67 Ibid, para. 52.

68 *Prosecutor v Stakić*, Decision on Sentence Remission and Early Release of Milomir Stakić, MICT-13-60-ES, 31 December 2020, para. 1.

69 *Prosecutor v Nyiramasuhuko*, Decision on the Application for Early Release of Pauline Nyiramasuhuko, MICT-15-90-ES.3, 10 November 2021.

70 *Prosecutor v Lukić*, Decision on the Application for Early Release of Sreten Lukić, MICT-14-67-ES.4, 7 October 2021, para. 5.

71 Para. 2 PDER, MICT/3/Rev.3.

72 Paras 10, 12, 14 PDER, MICT/3/Rev.3.

reviewed a wide range of internal, external and independent expert documentation; submissions from the applicant, a memorandum from the Prosecutor on cooperation, submissions from Rwanda (for ICTR convicted persons), reports from national courts on release eligibility, reports from international detention facilities or enforcing state prison authorities on behaviour and release eligibility, prison reports on conditions of imprisonment, and medical and psychiatric records and reports.[73]

The introduction of the conditional release scheme has resulted in requests for further pertinent information, such as the impact of release on the area of requested residence (feedback from national and local government authorities, information from the MICT Victims and Witnesses Support Unit (WISP) and local victim associations), input from the OTP, and a review of recent media reports.[74] There are also signs that more comprehensive risk assessments and mental health assessments are being requested from national authorities,[75] though these have been treated cautiously as they do not take into account the situation in the relocation area.

4.2 Delays in Decision-making

In some cases, the time from submission of applications to the delivery of decisions can be more than two years. Several factors can lead to delays.

Firstly, the Rules and Practice Direction requires consideration of a number of factors and probative materials. Delays can be experienced due to a delay or failure on the part of enforcing states to provide the requested materials. In *Simba*, the application was delayed for two years, in part due to the delay in receiving materials from the Beninese authorities.[76] In *Ntawukulilyayo*, the Malian authorities failed to provide information on eligibility for release

---

73 *Prosecutor v Simba*, Public Redacted Version of the President's 7 January 2019 Decision on the Early Release of Aloys Simba, MICT-14-62-ES.1, 7 January 2019, paras 7, 15; *Prosecutor v Ćorić*, Further Redacted Public Redacted Version of the Decision of the President on the Early Release of Valentin Ćorić and Related Motions, MICT-17-112-ES.4, 16 January 2019, para. 6; *Prosecutor v Krstić*, Decision on the Early Release of Radislav Krstić, MICT-13-46-ES.1, 10 September 2019, para. 7.

74 *Prosecutor v Brdanin*, Decision on the Application of Radoslav Brdanin for Early Release, MICT-13-48-ES, 28 February 2020, paras 10, 15–17, 22.

75 *Prosecutor v Bralo*, Decision on the Early Release of Miroslav Bralo, MICT-14-78-ES, 31 December 2019, para. 13.

76 *Prosecutor v Simba*, Public Redacted Version of the President's 7 January 2019 Decision on the Early Release of Aloys Simba, MICT-14-62-ES.1, 7 January 2019, para. 1.

under national law despite numerous requests.[77] The lack of information can be particularly significant in conditional release systems if the failure to respond relates to the relocation of the applicant. In *Brdanin*, the views of the Bosnian and Herzegovinian authorities on the applicant's proposed relocation were only received months after the deadline specified in the invitation, meaning the applicant did not have time to offer his comments on these views.[78] Likewise in *Semanza*, the Presidential request for the views of the authorities of the proposed site of relocation were not responded to.[79]

Secondly, intervening events in the enforcement of the sentence may contribute to delay. For example, in *Kunarac*, disciplinary and criminal proceedings initiated by German authorities following a physical altercation involving the applicant and other prisoners in Bochum prison (resulting in his hospitalisation) contributed to the release decision taking over two-and-a-half years.[80]

Thirdly, events beyond the enforcement of the sentences can impact the decision-making process. In *Dordević*, for example, the COVID-19 pandemic contributed to a delayed decision as the President-ordered evaluation and risk assessment by a psychologist able to speak Bosnian/Croatian/Serbian was postponed (for more than a year) due to travel restrictions.[81]

In cases of extreme urgency, however, the Practice Direction permits the President to 'dispense with' the usual procedural steps and to accelerate consultations with other judges to the 'extent required by the urgency' of the case and, if necessary, to issue a decision with reasons to follow.[82]

4.3 Abbreviated Procedure for Applications Submitted before Two-thirds

President Agius previously noted that the MICT's establishment of an eligibility threshold does not preclude notifications from enforcing states when convicted persons become eligible under national law and indeed that he welcomed such notifications due to the importance of the information provided

---

[77] *Prosecutor v Ntawukulilyayo*, Decision on the Application of Dominique Ntawukulilyayo for Early Release, MICT-13-34-ES, 8 January 2020.

[78] *Prosecutor v Brdanin*, Decision on the Application of Radoslav Brdanin for Early Release, MICT-13-48-ES, 28 February 2020, para. 86.

[79] *Prosecutor v Semanza*, Decision on Laurent Semanza's Application for Early Release, MICT-13-36-ES.2, 17 September 2020, para. 17.

[80] *Prosecutor v Kunarac*, Decision on Dragoljub Kunarac's Application for Early Release, MICT-15-88-ES.1, 31 December 2020, paras 1, 6, 21–25.

[81] *Prosecutor v Dordević*, Decision on the Applications for Early Release of Vlastimir Dordevic, MICT-14-76-ES, 30 November 2021, paras 10–11, 15.

[82] Para. 21 PDER, MICT/3/Rev.3.

for the determination of future requests for release[83] and that such decisions let prisoners know what they needed to do to be more successful in future applications once they reached the eligibility threshold.[84] Previously, in cases where the prisoner was not eligible to be considered for release due to a failure to establish the sufficient service of sentence, the President considered the material provided by the national authorities in light of the Rule 151 factors and other considerations. Recent practice, however, has demonstrated that the recognition of the two-thirds threshold as 'an admissibility threshold'[85] has resulted in a new, abbreviated procedure for applications received prior to this time.

Rule 151 assessments are now only required if the application is for 'pardon, commutation of sentence or early release' *after* the applicant has served two-thirds of their sentence or if they have demonstrated exceptional or compelling circumstances warranting a waiver of the two-thirds eligibility threshold.[86] Applications received before service of two-thirds of the sentence will be 'considered promptly and without necessarily triggering the multi-step and resource-intensive process of requesting, receiving, translating, sharing and considering additional information before determining whether the application should be denied as premature'.[87] If compelling or humanitarian grounds for release are claimed prior to two-thirds being served, the President can use their discretion to conduct a full review, but such exceptional circumstances will 'arise only rarely and would need to be duly substantiated'.[88] Since December 2020, there have been a number of abbreviated decisions that did not conduct a Rule 151 assessment because the applicant was not eligible for consideration for release due to a lack of sufficient service of sentence.[89]

---

83 *Prosecutor v Galić*, Decision on the Early Release of Stanislav Galić, MICT-14-83-ES, 26 June 2019, para. 48.

84 *Prosecutor v Krstić*, Decision on the Early Release of Radislav Krstić, MICT-13-46-ES.1, 10 September 2019, para. 25.

85 *Prosecutor v Kunarac*, Decision on Dragoljub Kunarac's Application for Early Release, MICT-15-88-ES.1, 31 December 2020, para. 31.

86 *Prosecutor v Stakić*, Decision on Sentence Remission and Early Release of Milomir Stakić, MICT-13-60-ES, 31 December 2020, para. 37.

87 Ibid, para. 43; *Prosecutor v Jelisić*, Decision on Sentence Remission and Early Release of Goran Jelisić, MICT-14-63-ES, 11 March 2021, para. 42.

88 *Prosecutor v Stakić*, Decision on Sentence Remission and Early Release of Milomir Stakić, MICT-13-60-ES, 31 December 2020, para. 44.

89 Ibid, para. 45; *Prosecutor v Nchamihigo*, Decision on Siméon Nchamihigo's Application for Commutation of Sentence, MICT-12–19.ES.1, 31 December 2020 at 3–4; *Prosecutor v Nyiramasuhuko*, Decision on the Application for Early Release of Pauline Nyiramasuhuko, MICT-15-90-ES.3, 10 November 2021; *Prosecutor v Popović*, Decision on the Early Release of Vujadin Popović, MICT-15-85-ES.2, 30

This abbreviated process makes sense due to the retention of the state notification process. In *Galić,* for example, Germany has submitted numerous notifications to the Mechanism that he was eligible to have his life sentence suspended on probation. Germany was required by domestic law to conduct a review of the possibility of probationary suspension at least every two years (either *proprio motu* or at the convicted person's request) and, pursuant to its bilateral sentence enforcement agreement, to notify the Mechanism of the outcome of this review.[90] In *Prlić*, President Agius tried to address this scenario by informing the enforcing state (UK) that Prlić would only become eligible for early release after service of two-thirds of the sentence in April 2024, without prejudice to any compelling or exceptional circumstances arising in the interim.[91]

A Rule 151 assessment is also no longer required if the application is for the provisional recognition of sentence remission granted under the domestic law of enforcing states.[92]

4.4 Broader Consultations in the Interests of Justice

The President is required to consult with at least two judges when making release decisions.[93] If none of the current judges at the MICT were judges of the sentencing Chamber, the President is required to consult with other judges.[94] Release decisions state which judges were consulted and their roles.[95]

December 2020; *Prosecutor v Galić*, Decision on the Early Release of Stanislav Galić, MICT-14-83-ES, 24 March 2021, paras 11, 24, 30, 34–5; *Prosecutor v Jelisić*, Decision on Sentence Remission and Early Release of Goran Jelisić, MICT-14-63-ES, 11 March 2021, paras 48, 55.

[90] *Prosecutor v Galić*, Decision on the Early Release of Stanislav Galić, MICT-14-83-ES, 24 March 2021, paras 1, 7–8.

[91] *Prosecutor v Prlić*, Decision on the Early Release of Jadranko Prlić, MICT-17-112-ES.2, 23 March 2021.

[92] *Prosecutor v Stakić*, Decision on Sentence Remission and Early Release of Milomir Stakić, MICT-13-60-ES, 31 December 2020, paras 36–37, 40; *Prosecutor v Jelisić*, Decision on Sentence Remission and Early Release of Goran Jelisić, MICT-14-63-ES, 11 March 2021, paras 39, 43.

[93] Para. 16 PDER, Rev 3.

[94] Rule 150 MICT RPE.

[95] *Prosecutor v Ćorić*, Further Redacted Public Redacted Version of the Decision of the President on the Early Release of Valentin Ćorić and Related Motions, MICT-17-112-ES.4, 16 January 2019, para. 9; *Prosecutor v Brdanin*, Decision on the Application of Radoslav Brdanin for Early Release, MICT-13-48-ES, 28 February 2020, para. 23; *Prosecutor v Bralo*, Decision on the Early Release of Miroslav Bralo, MICT-14-78-ES, 31 December 2019, para. 16;

Consultations 'form a meaningful part of the President's assessment' and practice has been to grant early release where a majority of judges (including the President) are in favour of granting it and to deny release where a majority are opposed unless there are compelling considerations to do otherwise.[96]

In some cases, the views of consulted judges on both release and factors involved in the decision-making process are shared. For example, in *Ćorić*, Judge Antonetti stressed the need to show fairness when considering the applicant's role in the events compared to the greater role played by others and the need to reintegrate rather than exclude convicted persons.[97] In *Simba*, Judge Liu Daqun supported early release as Simba's crimes were not the most serious crimes tried at the ICTR, he had served two-thirds of his sentence, and his health constituted an extraordinary circumstance.[98]

In 2019, a new approach of engaging in consultations with other stakeholders was presented by President Agius to the UN Security Council as a means of ensuring 'greater transparency and to more fully consider the broader impact of early release'.[99] The President may now 'decide to seek or accept submissions from third parties'.[100]

4.4.1 Prosecution submissions on sentence enforcement matters

President Meron repeatedly stated that the Prosecution had no standing to make submissions on sentence enforcement matters other than to provide information on the applicant's cooperation.[101] Further, even though the

---

Prosecutor v Galić, Decision on the Early Release of Stanislav Galić, MICT-14-83-ES, 26 June 2019, para. 10.

[96] *Prosecutor v Ćorić*, Further Redacted Public Redacted Version of the Decision of the President on the Early Release of Valentin Ćorić and Related Motions, MICT-17-112-ES.4, 16 January 2019, para. 59.

[97] Ibid, para. 60.

[98] *Prosecutor v Simba*, Public Redacted Version of the President's 7 January 2019 Decision on the Early Release of Aloys Simba, MICT-14-62-ES.1, 7 January 2019, para. 81.

[99] Para 62, Annex I, Assessment and progress report of the President of the International Residual Mechanism for Criminal Tribunals, Judge Carmel Agius, for the period from 16 November 2018 to 15 May 2019, Letter dated 20 May 2019 from the President of the International Residual Mechanism for Criminal Tribunals addressed to the President of the Security Council, S/2019/417, 20 May 2019.

[100] Para. 14 PDER, MICT/3/Rev.3.

[101] *Prosecutor v Simba*, Public Redacted Version of the President's 7 January 2019 Decision on the Early Release of Aloys Simba, MICT-14-62-ES.1, 7 January 2019, para. 20; *Prosecutor v Ćorić*, Further Redacted Public Redacted Version of the Decision of the President on the Early Release of Valentin Ćorić and Related Motions, MICT-17-112-ES.4, 16 January 2019, paras 14, 17.

President had discretion to consider other relevant information, he argued that the Prosecution would have to demonstrate compelling reasons of special circumstances in order to have standing to make such submissions.[102] In *Bralo*, President Agius turned this longstanding practice on its head by allowing the Prosecutor to make submissions on sentence enforcement matters. This does not seem directly linked to the introduction of a CER scheme, as it was justified on the basis of the President's interpretation of the existing legal framework.

Agius had made his interpretative analysis of this framework known during consultations on other cases, noting that he objected to President Meron's approach. In particular, he argued that it was not in the interests of justice to accept information from the UN Detention Unit's Commanding Officer and Medical Officer but not the OTP, who may have information relevant to rehabilitation.[103] Agius had also argued that Meron had received submissions from the Rwandan Government. Meron responded by stating he had considered the Rwandan Government's submissions under Rule 125 of the ICTR RPE and not his discretion to receive further information under the Practice Direction. Meron was very clear that he would, and felt he only could, consider submissions from the Prosecutor if the Rules were formally amended to allow this. Meron was also keen to note that other consulted judges disagreed with Agius's interpretation[104] and indeed were critical of the Prosecutor's submissions. Judge Antonetti, for example, felt that the Prosecutor's position was 'open to criticism' and that the Prosecutor 'relentlessly hounds' convicted persons who are 'entitled to be reintegrated into society and not to be permanently excluded'.[105]

In light of Security Council Resolution 2622, the OTP noted that it would 'continue to make submissions opposing the early release of specific convicted persons and requesting the President to consider imposing conditions for any early release' granted.[106] In *Bralo*, the Prosecutor argued that it was in the

---

[102] *Prosecutor v Simba*, Public Redacted Version of the President's 7 January 2019 Decision on the Early Release of Aloys Simba, MICT-14-62-ES.1, 7 January 2019, para. 21; *Prosecutor v Ćorić*, Further Redacted Public Redacted Version of the Decision of the President on the Early Release of Valentin Ćorić and Related Motions, MICT-17-112-ES.4, 16 January 2019, para. 16.

[103] *Prosecutor v Ćorić*, Further Redacted Public Redacted Version of the Decision of the President on the Early Release of Valentin Ćorić and Related Motions, MICT-17-112-ES.4, 16 January 2019, para. 18.

[104] Ibid, para. 19.

[105] Ibid.

[106] Para. 31, Progress report of the Prosecutor of the International Residual Mechanism for Criminal Tribunals, Serge Brammertz, for the period from 16 November 2018 to 15 May 2019 at 40, Annex II of the Letter dated 20 May 2019

interests of justice and the general principles of law that the President should exercise his discretion to give consideration to his submissions on sentence enforcement matters and also to consult with affected parties (victims, witnesses and States). The Prosecutor argued that the MICT's current practice departed from the overwhelming trend in national and international jurisdictions (ICC and SCSL).[107]

President Agius set out in *Bralo* why he disagreed with his predecessor's position. Firstly, he interpreted the silence of the legal framework on the matter as meaning that the Prosecutor was not barred from making such submissions. Moreover, the President was not prevented from requesting or accepting such submissions given the broad discretion granted to the President under Article 26 of the Statute and the explicit permission to seek any other information the President considers relevant and to have regard to such information when making the release decision.[108] Secondly, he was unconvinced that he was bound in the exercise of this discretion by prior practice of not consulting the Prosecutor. He felt that as the Prosecutor was a party to the legal proceedings and had intimate knowledge of the case, he or she may possess information that is highly relevant to the assessment of the convicted person's rehabilitation, the gravity of crimes and identifying vulnerable witnesses that would be affected by release.[109] Agius also argued that the Prosecutor would be 'well placed to represent the views of the victims and affected communities' which he notes 'ought to be considered in the context of mass atrocity crimes'.[110] The Prosecution's submissions, he argued, were therefore 'part of a broader consultation process to obtain relevant material in the interests of justice'.[111]

In and following *Bralo*, President Agius received and gave consideration to general comments from the Prosecution on release applications.[112] In addition to the applicant's cooperation, Prosecution submissions now include

from the President of the International Residual Mechanism for Criminal Tribunals addressed to the President of the Security Council, S/2019/417, 20 May 2019.

107 *Prosecutor v Bralo*, Decision on the Early Release of Miroslav Bralo, MICT-14-78-ES, 31 December 2019, para. 65.

108 Ibid, para. 67.

109 Ibid, para. 68.

110 Ibid.

111 Ibid.

112 Ibid, paras 69, 76; *Prosecutor v Brdanin*, Decision on the Application of Radoslav Brdanin for Early Release, MICT-13-48-ES, 28 February 2020, para. 83; *Prosecutor v Ćorić*, Decision on Motions Related to Valentin Ćorić's Request for Variation of Early Release Conditions, MICT-17-112-ES.4, 21 February 2020, para. 18; *Prosecutor v Semanza*, Decision on Laurent Semanza's Application for Early Release, MICT-13-36-ES.2, 17 September 2020, para. 15.

information on risks to victims and witnesses and the impact on the community if release is granted, the gravity of the crimes, whether rehabilitation has been demonstrated or substantiated, observations on the sincerity of expressions of remorse or the applicant's acceptance of responsibility for the crimes convicted of, the appropriateness of release, what conditions should be imposed if release is granted, and the appointment of a monitoring authority in the state of relocation.[113]

President Agius clearly viewed the Prosecutor's submission as helpful in conditional early release decisions. Agius was careful to note, however, that 'caution needs to be exercised to avoid any unreasonable imbalance to the detriment of the convicted person' and that he intended to 'carefully assess on a case-by-case basis which submissions are of actual relevance … mindful of the rights of the convicted person'.[114]

4.4.2 Victim standing to make submissions on release

Former President Meron applied the same reasoning to deny victims standing to make submissions on early release: given the longstanding practice of the ICTR, ICTY and MICT not to consult with victims, they could not demonstrate sufficiently compelling reasons to make submissions or for the President to consider them.[115] Agius again noted that the President's broad discretion to consider relevant information should allow for such submissions and their

113 *Prosecutor v Bralo*, Decision on the Early Release of Miroslav Bralo, MICT-14-78-ES, 31 December 2019, paras 74–75; *Prosecutor v Brdanin*, Decision on the Application of Radoslav Brdanin for Early Release, MICT-13-48-ES, 28 February 2020, paras 84–85; *Prosecutor v Semanza*, Decision on Laurent Semanza's Application for Early Release, MICT-13-36-ES.2, 17 September 2020, para. 76; *Prosecutor v Kunarac*, Decision on Dragoljub Kunarac's Application for Early Release, MICT-15-88-ES.1, 31 December 2020, para. 77; *Prosecutor v Lukić*, Decision on the Application for Early Release of Sreten Lukić, MICT-14-67-ES.4, 7 October 2021, paras 79–80; *Prosecutor v Dordević*, Decision on the Applications for Early Release of Vlastimir Dordevic, MICT-14-76-ES, 30 November 2021, para. 83.

114 *Prosecutor v Bralo*, Decision on the Early Release of Miroslav Bralo, MICT-14-78-ES, 31 December 2019, para. 69; *Prosecutor v Brdanin*, Decision on the Application of Radoslav Brdanin for Early Release, MICT-13-48-ES, 28 February 2020, para. 83; *Prosecutor v Semanza*, Decision on Laurent Semanza's Application for Early Release, MICT-13-36-ES.2, 17 September 2020, para. 75; *Prosecutor v Kunarac*, Decision on Dragoljub Kunarac's Application for Early Release, MICT-15-88-ES.1, 31 December 2020, para. 76.

115 *Prosecutor v Simba*, Public Redacted Version of the President's 7 January 2019 Decision on the Early Release of Aloys Simba, MICT-14-62-ES.1, 7 January 2019, paras 72–3; *Prosecutor v Ćorić*, Further Redacted Public Redacted Version

inclusion in decision-making.[116] Meron counter-argued that as there was no basis in the legal framework and no antecedent, the consideration of victims' submissions on release could only take place if 'approved by formal amendment of the Rules'.[117] Again Meron noted that Agius's arguments represented a minority view, with Judges Antonetti and Lui disagreeing with his approach. Judge Antonetti stated that 'our mission goes beyond [the victims'] trauma and involves bringing back into society those who have transgressed while ensuring they do not reoffend'.[118] While Meron did not consider their submissions, he agreed to allow them to be made public following the Prosecutor's request.[119]

During his Presidency, Agius sought information about the number and location of vulnerable witnesses and their perceptions of any risks associated with release from WISP, particularly for those living in the applicant's intended place of residence.[120] WISP repeatedly stated that it was not in a position to assess if applicants would be capable of or would, in fact, harm any witnesses and that a fuller assessment required information that would necessitate contacting each individual witness.[121] Considering the potential negative impact involved in doing so, Agius decided that it was not necessary to 'disturb' them to gain their views on release.[122] An alternative approach

---

of the Decision of the President on the Early Release of Valentin Ćorić and Related Motions, MICT-17-112-ES.4, 16 January 2019, paras 21–23.

116 *Prosecutor v Ćorić*, Further Redacted Public Redacted Version of the Decision of the President on the Early Release of Valentin Ćorić and Related Motions, MICT-17-112-ES.4, 16 January 2019, para. 24.

117 Ibid, para. 25.

118 Ibid, para. 26.

119 Ibid, paras 27, 32.

120 *Prosecutor v Brdanin*, Decision on the Application of Radoslav Brdanin for Early Release, MICT-13-48-ES, 28 February 2020, para. 89; *Prosecutor v Dordević*, Decision on the Applications for Early Release of Vlastimir Dordevic, MICT-14-76-ES, 30 November 2021, para. 10; *Prosecutor v Lukić*, Decision on the Application for Early Release of Sreten Lukić, MICT-14-67-ES.4, 7 October 2021, para. 12.

121 *Prosecutor v Brdanin*, Decision on the Application of Radoslav Brdanin for Early Release, MICT-13-48-ES, 28 February 2020, para. 90; *Prosecutor v Dordević*, Decision on the Applications for Early Release of Vlastimir Dordevic, MICT-14-76-ES, 30 November 2021, paras 87–8; *Prosecutor v Lukić*, Decision on the Application for Early Release of Sreten Lukić, MICT-14-67-ES.4, 7 October 2021, para. 85.

122 *Prosecutor v Brdanin*, Decision on the Application of Radoslav Brdanin for Early Release, MICT-13-48-ES, 28 February 2020, paras 84, 90; *Prosecutor v Dordević*, Decision on the Applications for Early Release of Vlastimir Dordević,

of contacting victims' associations has not proven successful. In *Brdanin*, no response was received and in *Lukić,* the lack of a public or online presence made it difficult to identify a relevant association.[123] Agius has therefore relied instead on the general assessment of vulnerability, and perceived and actual risk provided by WISP (and the Prosecutor).[124]

4.4.3 State of relocation standing to make submissions on release

The introduction of a conditional release scheme, and the resulting dependence on the cooperation of national authorities to oversee compliance with conditions, has resulted in the need to seek the views of the proposed state of relocation. In all cases where release has been granted, the requested state has supported the grant of release and stated that there are no legal obstacles for the applicant's return. Local authorities in the proposed area of residence have also expressed support for release.[125] National authorities in Serbia have provided binding and unequivocal assurances that authorities will monitor the fulfilment of conditions.[126] In *Lukić*, Serbia, following a request to do so, confirmed that the applicant's ICTY conviction had been entered into the national criminal record and agreed to revoke any firearm licences.[127] Such support has been considered by President Agius to be relevant to the applicant's reintegration potential, the overall merit of the application, and the conditions that can be imposed.[128]

MICT-14-76-ES, 30 November 2021, para. 88; *Prosecutor v Lukić*, Decision on the Application for Early Release of Sreten Lukić, MICT-14-67-ES.4, 7 October 2021, para. 85.

[123] *Prosecutor v Brdanin*, Decision on the Application of Radoslav Brdanin for Early Release, MICT-13-48-ES, 28 February 2020, para. 91; *Prosecutor v Lukić*, Decision on the Application for Early Release of Sreten Lukić, MICT-14-67-ES.4, 7 October 2021, para. 86.

[124] *Prosecutor v Dordević*, Decision on the Applications for Early Release of Vlastimir Dordevic, MICT-14-76-ES, 30 November 2021, para. 89.

[125] *Prosecutor v Brdanin*, Decision on the Application of Radoslav Brdanin for Early Release, MICT-13-48-ES, 28 February 2020, para. 86.

[126] *Prosecutor v Lukić*, Decision on the Application for Early Release of Sreten Lukić, MICT-14-67-ES.4, 7 October 2021, para. 82; *Prosecutor v Dordević*, Decision on the Applications for Early Release of Vlastimir Dordevic, MICT-14-76-ES, 30 November 2021, para. 85.

[127] *Prosecutor v Lukić*, Decision on the Application for Early Release of Sreten Lukić, MICT-14-67-ES.4, 7 October 2021, paras 29–31.

[128] Ibid, para. 83; *Prosecutor v Brdanin*, Decision on the Application of Radoslav Brdanin for Early Release, MICT-13-48-ES, 28 February 2020, para. 88.

Challenges in this regard are foreseeable given either the failure of requested states to respond[129] or the inability to identify a state of relocation due to the immigration status of the applicant.[130]

4.5 Appeal and Reapplications

It remains the case that applicants cannot appeal the President's decision to deny release.[131] The President will consider requests to reconsider decisions if there has been a clear error of reasoning, or if particular circumstances or new facts exist to justify reconsidering the order to avoid injustice.[132] Decisions denying release may indicate an appropriate timeframe for a renewed application. This does not preclude applications at an earlier stage if the enforcing state authorities are required by national law to do so or if there has been an important change in circumstances.[133]

5. RULE 151 FACTORS FOR DETERMINING THE APPROPRIATENESS OF CONDITIONAL EARLY RELEASE

The enumerated factors to be considered in release decisions under Rule 151 have not changed with the introduction of a conditional early release scheme. This section will analyse the application of the gravity, treatment of similarly-situated prisoners and cooperation with the Prosecution, while the demonstration of rehabilitation will be dealt with separately in the following section.

---

129 *Prosecutor v Semanza*, Decision on Laurent Semanza's Application for Early Release, MICT-13-36-ES.2, 17 September 2020, para. 17.

130 See Chapter 7, section 5 and Chapter 8, section 4.2.

131 Para. 24 PDER Rev 3 – 'the decision of the President is final and not subject to appeal'.

132 *Prosecutor v Musema*, Decision on the Request for Reconsideration of the Decision Denying Early Release, MICT-12-15-ES.1, 10 January 2020; *Prosecutor v Simba*, Public Redacted Version of the President's 7 January 2019 Decision on the Early Release of Aloys Simba, MICT-14-62-ES.1, 7 January 2019, para. 4; *Prosecutor v Brdanin*, Decision on the Application of Radoslav Brdanin for Early Release, MICT-13-48-ES, 28 February 2020, paras 1, 5–6.

133 *Prosecutor v Bralo*, Decision on the Early Release of Miroslav Bralo, MICT-14-78-ES, 31 December 2019, para. 84.

5.1 Gravity

Conditional early release decisions contain extensive extracts from trial and appeal judgments that demonstrate the factors and facts relevant to gravity, such as the number of victims, the characteristics and vulnerability of victims, the impact of the offence on victims, the number of offences and their discriminatory nature, the time scale and pattern of commission of the crimes, motivations, the manner of commission, the position and level of responsibility of the convicted person, their mode of criminal liability and role in planning and commission.[134]

Presidents have also considered the sentences imposed and whether they were increased or decreased on appeal,[135] though President Agius rejected requests to take account of a lack of judicial unanimity in sentencing.[136] Release decisions have, however, acknowledged mitigating findings in sentencing such as the fact that a convicted person had not been a physical perpetrator and had no particular zeal for the commission of the crimes,[137] the lower gravity of offences, voluntary surrender and compliance with conditions on provisional release.[138]

In all cases, the crimes were considered to have been of high gravity. In some cases, how gravity affected the release decision was not discussed.[139] In most

---

[134] *Prosecutor v Simba*, Public Redacted Version of the President's 7 January 2019 Decision on the Early Release of Aloys Simba, MICT-14-62-ES.1, 7 January 2019, paras 36–38; *Prosecutor v Brdanin*, Decision on the Application of Radoslav Brdanin for Early Release, MICT-13-48-ES, 28 February 2020, paras 36–43; *Prosecutor v Bralo*, Decision on the Early Release of Miroslav Bralo, MICT-14-78-ES, 31 December 2019, paras 28–32; *Prosecutor v Kunarac*, Decision on Dragoljub Kunarac's Application for Early Release, MICT-15-88-ES.1, 31 December 2020, paras 34–36; *Prosecutor v Dordević*, Decision on the Applications for Early Release of Vlastimir Dordevic, MICT-14-76-ES, 30 November 2021, para. 39.

[135] See *Prosecutor v Semanza*, Decision on Laurent Semanza's Application for Early Release, MICT-13-36-ES.2, 17 September 2020, paras 33–37.

[136] *Prosecutor v Galić*, Decision on the Early Release of Stanislav Galić, MICT-14-83-ES, 26 June 2019, paras 29–30.

[137] *Prosecutor v Simba*, Public Redacted Version of the President's 7 January 2019 Decision on the Early Release of Aloys Simba, MICT-14-62-ES.1, 7 January 2019, para. 38.

[138] *Prosecutor v Ćorić*, Further Redacted Public Redacted Version of the Decision of the President on the Early Release of Valentin Ćorić and Related Motions, MICT-17-112-ES.4, 16 January 2019, para. 45.

[139] *Prosecutor v Brdanin*, Decision on the Application of Radoslav Brdanin for Early Release, MICT-13-48-ES, 28 February 2020, para. 44; *Prosecutor v Bralo*,

cases, it was explicitly held to have weighed against granting early release. President Agius dismissed a submission in *Kunarac* that gravity should not be an aggravating factor used to deny release, given that it was already considered in sentencing, but stated that other factors considered in mitigation in sentencing can be taken into account in favour of release (cooperation with the Prosecutor, expressions of remorse or regret).[140] Despite the detailed analysis of gravity and its stated weight against release, release continues to be granted 'notwithstanding' the high gravity of the offences committed.[141]

In *Dordević,* President Agius explained that an assessment of the severity of the convicted person's criminal conduct, the primary consideration in determining the length of the sentence imposed, is considered to be a 'factor of fundamental importance' in early release decisions.[142] For this reason, President Agius emphasised that, 'as a general rule, a sentence should be served in full unless it can be demonstrated that a convicted person should be granted early release'.[143] Gravity of the crimes could therefore 'determine the threshold that the arguments in favour of early release must reach'.[144]

5.2 Treatment of Similarly Situated Persons

Although the analysis of the treatment of similarly situated persons is still discussed separately in decisions – it has remained confined to the application of the eligibility threshold of serving two-thirds (or more than 30 years) of the sentence. Attempts to introduce comparisons to the eligibility of prisoners held in enforcing states have been dismissed on the basis of the need for equality between persons supervised by the Mechanism.[145] Further, eligibility requirements for indeterminate sentences were introduced to ensure persons serving life sentences were not treated more favourably than persons sentenced to

---

Decision on the Early Release of Miroslav Bralo, MICT-14-78-ES, 31 December 2019, para. 34; *Prosecutor v Lukić*, Decision on the Application for Early Release of Sreten Lukić, MICT-14-67-ES.4, 7 October 2021, para. 48.

[140] *Prosecutor v Kunarac*, Decision on Dragoljub Kunarac's Application for Early Release, MICT-15-88-ES.1, 31 December 2020, paras 37–38.

[141] See *Prosecutor v Lukić*, Decision on the Application for Early Release of Sreten Lukić, MICT-14-67-ES.4, 7 October 2021, para. 93.

[142] *Prosecutor v Dordević*, Decision on the Applications for Early Release of Vlastimir Dordevic, MICT-14-76-ES, 30 November 2021, para. 36.

[143] Ibid.

[144] Ibid.

[145] *Prosecutor v Galić*, Decision on the Early Release of Stanislav Galić, MICT-14-83-ES, 26 June 2019, para. 31.

fixed terms of imprisonment.[146] Once an applicant has been found eligible for release, further comparisons to other similarly situated persons are inconsequential as each case presents unique circumstances that the President must consider on merit.[147]

5.3 Substantial Cooperation with the Prosecution

Since the introduction of conditional release, the cooperation with the Prosecutor factor has had little impact on decision-making. In most cases, it was a neutral factor (or had no weight) given that it was not sought or required.[148]

In *Kunarac* and *Lukić*, Agius dismissed the Prosecutor's submission that cooperation was not relevant for release decisions as it was already considered in mitigation, pointing to the Mechanism's legal framework and practice and the fact that an analysis of factors both in the convicted person's favour (cooperation, remorse, regret) and to his detriment (gravity) are required by a Rule 151 assessment.[149] In *Bralo*, the Prosecutor noted that the applicant had received substantial mitigation of sentence (five years) for his cooperation, efforts to atone for crimes, and expressions of remorse. Since then, however, he had denied responsibility for some crimes and indicated that he regrets nothing. Accordingly, the Prosecutor argued, it was not appropriate to attach weight

146 Ibid, para. 32.

147 *Prosecutor v Kunarac*, Decision on Dragoljub Kunarac's Application for Early Release, MICT-15-88-ES.1, 31 December 2020, para. 40; *Prosecutor v Dordević*, Decision on the Applications for Early Release of Vlastimir Dordevic, MICT-14-76-ES, 30 November 2021, paras 43–4; *Prosecutor v Semanza*, Decision on Laurent Semanza's Application for Early Release, MICT-13-36-ES.2, 17 September 2020, para. 43.

148 *Prosecutor v Simba*, Public Redacted Version of the President's 7 January 2019 Decision on the Early Release of Aloys Simba, MICT-14-62-ES.1, 7 January 2019, para. 49; *Prosecutor v Ćorić*, Further Redacted Public Redacted Version of the Decision of the President on the Early Release of Valentin Ćorić and Related Motions, MICT-17-112-ES.4, 16 January 2019, para. 55; *Prosecutor v Brdanin*, Decision on the Application of Radoslav Brdanin for Early Release, MICT-13-48-ES, 28 February 2020, para. 82; *Prosecutor v Semanza*, Decision on Laurent Semanza's Application for Early Release, MICT-13-36-ES.2, 17 September 2020, para. 74.

149 *Prosecutor v Kunarac*, Decision on Dragoljub Kunarac's Application for Early Release, MICT-15-88-ES.1, 31 December 2020, para. 73; *Prosecutor v Lukić*, Decision on the Application for Early Release of Sreten Lukić, MICT-14-67-ES.4, 7 October 2021, para. 75.

to his guilty plea in considering release.[150] President Agius agreed that while a guilty plea constitutes a degree of cooperation (as it beneficially impacted the efficient administration of justice), it will only weigh in favour of early release if there has been substantial cooperation (otherwise it will be a neutral factor).[151] In *Lukić*, however, cooperation with the Prosecutor before the applicant came under the ICTY's jurisdiction was highly commended and given positive weight even though it did not constitute 'substantial' cooperation:[152] 'less-than-substantial cooperation … merits consideration as part of the overall assessment' of the release application.[153] Less than substantial cooperation with national prosecutorial authorities was also deemed to merit some consideration.[154]

6. REHABILITATION

Other than the introduction of conditional release, the biggest change to the MICT release system has been the new approach to the interpretation and application of rehabilitation during Rule 151 assessments by President Agius. Jurisprudential analysis now involves a much deeper examination of a wide range of indicators of rehabilitation progress and the applicant's ability to successfully and peacefully reintegrate into a given society. The applicant must now convince the President that they have made 'sufficient progress' towards rehabilitation so that the grant of release before the full sentence is served would be a 'responsible exercise' of Presidential discretion.[155]

6.1 President Meron's Approach

Under President Meron, rehabilitation continued to be considered on a light-touch basis under the conditional release scheme. Consideration was given to behaviour in prison, the prisoner's relationship with family, mental health,

---

150 *Prosecutor v Bralo*, Decision on the Early Release of Miroslav Bralo, MICT-14-78-ES, 31 December 2019, para. 73.

151 Ibid, para. 72.

152 *Prosecutor v Lukić*, Decision on the Application for Early Release of Sreten Lukić, MICT-14-67-ES.4, 7 October 2021, para. 77.

153 Ibid, para. 76.

154 *Prosecutor v Dordević*, Decision on the Applications for Early Release of Vlastimir Dordevic, MICT-14-76-ES, 30 November 2021, para. 81.

155 *Prosecutor v Kunarac*, Decision on Dragoljub Kunarac's Application for Early Release, MICT-15-88-ES.1, 31 December 2020, para. 43.

and plans for resettlement.[156] On the basis of reports, prisoners were found to have demonstrated rehabilitation to be capable of reintegrating into society and deemed to pose a low risk of recidivism.[157] If any signs of rehabilitation were found, they weighed in favour of release.[158] This was even the case in *Simba* when the applicant continued to proclaim his innocence for the crimes for which he had been convicted and to claim his imprisonment was unjust.[159] Meron contextualised this by highlighting that the applicant had not denied the existence of the genocide and had condemned it.[160] Meron justified this approach by arguing that (in contrast to a small number of cases at the ICTY) remorse is not generally considered to be a primary requirement for commutation of sentence and numerous convicted persons had been granted early release where there was 'no clear indication of remorse' and where prisoners had 'expressly denied the crimes for which they were convicted'.[161] He ruled that based on this case law and the applicable legal framework (which does not require it), remorse should not be 'treated as a determining factor … in determining early release applications'.[162]

It was clear that this approach was not going to be continued by the incoming President. In the *Ćorić* release decision at the end of Meron's Presidency, the tension between Meron's approach and Agius's views on how rehabilitation should be applied in cases of atrocity crimes was made explicit. Meron had consulted with Agius on the appropriateness of release. Unlike the other judges, Agius did not feel that Ćorić had demonstrated an acceptable measure of rehabilitation in the context of war crimes and felt that more information was necessary to establish his readiness and preparedness to reintegrate into society. This should include information on where he intended to live upon

---

156 *Prosecutor v Simba*, Public Redacted Version of the President's 7 January 2019 Decision on the Early Release of Aloys Simba, MICT-14-62-ES.1, 7 January 2019, paras 42–3, 45; *Prosecutor v Ćorić*, Further Redacted Public Redacted Version of the Decision of the President on the Early Release of Valentin Ćorić and Related Motions, MICT-17-112-ES.4, 16 January 2019, para. 49.

157 *Prosecutor v Simba*, Public Redacted Version of the President's 7 January 2019 Decision on the Early Release of Aloys Simba, MICT-14-62-ES.1, 7 January 2019, para. 45; *Prosecutor v Ćorić*, Further Redacted Public Redacted Version of the Decision of the President on the Early Release of Valentin Ćorić and Related Motions, MICT-17-112-ES.4, 16 January 2019, para. 52.

158 Ibid.

159 *Prosecutor v Simba*, Public Redacted Version of the President's 7 January 2019 Decision on the Early Release of Aloys Simba, MICT-14-62-ES.1, 7 January 2019, paras 42, 45.

160 Ibid, para. 45.

161 Ibid, para. 44.

162 Ibid.

release, intelligence on the situation in such areas to assess the appropriateness of releasing him there, a demonstration from the applicant of how he would be successfully reintegrated into that society, and that he deserves release in light of statements made during trial about the Prosecution's methods and view that his trial was fraudulent.[163]

Referring to conduct in detention, while noting this may be a measure of rehabilitation in some countries, Agius argued that 'for the purposes of the crimes for which our prisoners have been convicted and always keeping in mind the context of peace and security, this understanding of rehabilitation is … a disservice to international criminal law and the legacy of the ad hoc tribunals'.[164] Moreover, he stated that he had been critical of this approach to rehabilitation – which he acknowledged may make sense at the domestic level, for normal crimes and normal criminals – for years. He reiterated his strong view that 'it does not make sense in a context of the gravest crimes against humanity, war crimes and genocide'.[165]

As the final decision lay with the President, Meron respectfully disagreed and found that his positive behaviour in detention had been an indicator of rehabilitation.[166] Further, following receipt of additional information, he was satisfied with Ćorić's explanation and apology in relation to his statement during his trial and found sufficient signs of rehabilitation to weigh in favour of release.[167]

6.2 A New President and a New Approach

It was abundantly clear from the *Ćorić* decision that Agius intended to introduce an atrocity crime-specific approach to rehabilitation once he became President. This new approach, and the indicators that would inform future assessments of rehabilitation, were set out and applied in *Bralo* and subsequent decisions.

6.2.1 Rehabilitation indicators for atrocity crimes

In *Bralo*, President Agius explained that while rehabilitation had been referred to as a sentencing goal at the ICTY and ICTR, and referred to in release decisions, it had never been defined. Accordingly, there was 'no settled definition

163 *Prosecutor v Ćorić*, Further Redacted Public Redacted Version of the Decision of the President on the Early Release of Valentin Ćorić and Related Motions, MICT-17-112-ES.4, 16 January 2019, para. 61.

164 Ibid, para. 62.

165 Ibid.

166 Ibid, para. 63.

167 Ibid, paras 64–6.

of the exact contours of the concept of rehabilitation in the context of genocide, crimes against humanity or war crimes'.[168] He stressed that it was not appropriate to look at the rehabilitation of perpetrators of atrocity crimes through 'the exact same paradigm as the rehabilitation of perpetrators of domestic or ordinary crimes'.[169] Assessments of rehabilitation had previously focused mostly on good behaviour in prison; while this could be an indicator of rehabilitation in a general sense, it could not, by itself, demonstrate the rehabilitation of a person convicted of heinous international crimes.[170]

In his conditional release jurisprudence, Agius developed a non-exhaustive list of indicators that can demonstrate rehabilitation. In addition to conduct in detention, these included:

- Acceptance of responsibility for crimes convicted for or actions which enabled the commission of the offences
- Critical reflection upon crimes
- Expressions of genuine remorse or regret
- Actions to foster reconciliation or seek forgiveness
- Evidence of a positive attitude toward other backgrounds
- Participation in rehabilitation programmes in prison
- A person's mental health status.

He noted that, although the burden of proof to demonstrate rehabilitation lay with the convicted person, there was no expectation for applicants to fulfil all of these indicators in order to demonstrate rehabilitation.[171] The President

---

[168] *Prosecutor v Bralo*, Decision on the Early Release of Miroslav Bralo, MICT-14-78-ES, 31 December 2019, para. 37.

[169] *Prosecutor v Miroslav Bralo*, Decision on the Early Release of Miroslav Bralo, MICT-14-78-ES, 31 December 2019, para. 38; *Prosecutor v Brdanin*, Decision on the Application of Radoslav Brdanin for Early Release, MICT-13-48-ES, 28 February 2020, para. 48; *Prosecutor v Semanza*, Decision on Laurent Semanza's Application for Early Release, MICT-13-36-ES.2, 17 September 2020, para. 45; *Prosecutor v Kunarac*, Decision on Dragoljub Kunarac's Application for Early Release, MICT-15-88-ES.1, 31 December 2020, para. 42.

[170] *Prosecutor v Bralo*, Decision on the Early Release of Miroslav Bralo, MICT-14-78-ES, 31 December 2019, paras 37–38; *Prosecutor v Brdanin*, Decision on the Application of Radoslav Brdanin for Early Release, MICT-13-48-ES, 28 February 2020, para. 48; *Prosecutor v Semanza*, Decision on Laurent Semanza's Application for Early Release, MICT-13-36-ES.2, 17 September 2020, para. 45; *Prosecutor v Kunarac*, Decision on Dragoljub Kunarac's Application for Early Release, MICT-15-88-ES.1, 31 December 2020, para. 42.

[171] *Prosecutor v Bralo*, Decision on the Early Release of Miroslav Bralo, MICT-14-78-ES, 31 December 2019, para. 39; *Prosecutor v Brdanin*, Decision

stressed that rehabilitation 'is a process, rather than a definite result' and it remained only one factor to be considered alongside other factors in release decisions.[172] Conditional release could still be granted, despite a lack of sufficient evidence of rehabilitation, due to the prevalence of other factors.[173]

6.2.2 Reintegration

In addition to the assessment of rehabilitation, President Agius also assessed prospects for a convicted person's successful and peaceful reintegration into a given society.[174] The assessment of reintegrative readiness and preparedness included post-release plans and the suitability of the envisaged place of residence.[175] If the indicated place of residence was in the region where the crimes were committed, extra scrutiny was applied due to the fact that the MICT and its predecessor institutions were established under Chapter VII of the UN Charter to contribute to the restoration and maintenance of peace and security.[176] As a general rule, Agius did not feel that it was appropriate 'to enable

---

on the Application of Radoslav Brdanin for Early Release, MICT-13-48-ES, 28 February 2020, para. 49; *Prosecutor v Semanza*, Decision on Laurent Semanza's Application for Early Release, MICT-13-36-ES.2, 17 September 2020, para. 46; *Prosecutor v Kunarac*, Decision on Dragoljub Kunarac's Application for Early Release, MICT-15-88-ES.1, 31 December 2020, para. 43.

172 *Prosecutor v Kunarac*, Decision on Dragoljub Kunarac's Application for Early Release, MICT-15-88-ES.1, 31 December 2020, para. 45.

173 *Prosecutor v Bralo*, Decision on the Early Release of Miroslav Bralo, MICT-14-78-ES, 31 December 2019, para. 41; *Prosecutor v Brdanin*, Decision on the Application of Radoslav Brdanin for Early Release, MICT-13-48-ES, 28 February 2020, para. 51; *Prosecutor v Semanza*, Decision on Laurent Semanza's Application for Early Release, MICT-13-36-ES.2, 17 September 2020, para. 48.

174 *Prosecutor v Brdanin*, Decision on the Application of Radoslav Brdanin for Early Release, MICT-13-48-ES, 28 February 2020, para. 50; *Prosecutor v Bralo*, Decision on the Early Release of Miroslav Bralo, MICT-14-78-ES, 31 December 2019, para. 39; *Prosecutor v Semanza*, Decision on Laurent Semanza's Application for Early Release, MICT-13-36-ES.2, 17 September 2020, para. 47.

175 *Prosecutor v Kunarac*, Decision on Dragoljub Kunarac's Application for Early Release, MICT-15-88-ES.1, 31 December 2020, para. 44.

176 UN Security Council Resolution 1966, 22 December 2010 at 1; UN Security Council Resolution 955, 8 November 1994 at 1; UN Security Council Resolution 808, 22 February 1993 at 2; *Prosecutor v Brdanin*, Decision on the Application of Radoslav Brdanin for Early Release, MICT-13-48-ES, 28 February 2020, para. 50; *Prosecutor v Semanza*, Decision on Laurent Semanza's Application for Early Release, MICT-13-36-ES.2, 17 September 2020, para. 47; *Prosecutor v Kunarac*, Decision on Dragoljub Kunarac's Application for Early Release, MICT-15-88-ES.1, 31 December 2020, para. 44.

convicted persons to return to the affected region before they have served their full sentence, without having demonstrated a certain degree of rehabilitation, including that their release will not endanger peace and security in the envisaged place of residence'.[177]

6.2.3 Information

In addition to the applications/submissions from convicted persons, the President reviewed reports from prisons on behaviour, medical reports (mental and physical), risk assessments (attitude to crime and risk of reoffending, psychiatric reports), and reports from religious advisors.[178] Submissions from the Office of the Prosecutor, evidence provided by applicants in trials, and the views of relevant states and state officials on relocation have also been considered.[179] The Practice Direction now includes a provision stating information should be collated on where the convicted person intends to live if released early.[180]

The *Bralo* decision, however, highlighted the difficulties of gaining an accurate picture of rehabilitation when a prisoner has been transferred numerous times within a foreign prison system and reports from different authorities contain different accounts.[181] Likewise, in *Semanza*, the applicant had served his sentence in different enforcing states, and they disagreed on whether or not release should be granted. The first (and longest) state of enforcement (Mali) supported the application for release, while the second and current state of

---

177 *Prosecutor v Bralo*, Decision on the Early Release of Miroslav Bralo, MICT-14-78-ES, 31 December 2019, para. 39; *Prosecutor v Brdanin*, Decision on the Application of Radoslav Brdanin for Early Release, MICT-13-48-ES, 28 February 2020, para. 50; *Prosecutor v Semanza*, Decision on Laurent Semanza's Application for Early Release, MICT-13-36-ES.2, 17 September 2020, para. 47; *Prosecutor v Kunarac*, Decision on Dragoljub Kunarac's Application for Early Release, MICT-15-88-ES.1, 31 December 2020, para. 44.

178 *Prosecutor v Bralo*, Decision on the Early Release of Miroslav Bralo, MICT-14-78-ES, 31 December 2019, paras 42–45; *Prosecutor v Semanza*, Decision on Laurent Semanza's Application for Early Release, MICT-13-36-ES.2, 17 September 2020, para. 49.

179 *Prosecutor v Brdanin*, Decision on the Application of Radoslav Brdanin for Early Release, MICT-13-48-ES, 28 February 2020, para. 52; *Prosecutor v Semanza*, Decision on Laurent Semanza's Application for Early Release, MICT-13-36-ES.2, 17 September 2020, paras 65–66.

180 Para. 10(d) PDER, MICT/3/Rev.3.

181 *Prosecutor v Bralo*, Decision on the Early Release of Miroslav Bralo, MICT-14-78-ES, 31 December 2019, paras 42–45.

enforcement (Benin) stated that he did not fulfil the conditions for release under national law.[182]

In *Lukić*, Agius rejected the submission from the applicant that a finding that rehabilitation had been demonstrated in two previous release applications should be relied on, stating that while such findings could be taken into account, the receipt of updated and additional information made it necessary to conduct an assessment in light of 'the entirety of information now available'.[183] It is also interesting to note in this case that the President relied on information provided by the Polish prison authorities despite the fact that Lukić had been transferred back to and was currently serving his sentence at the UN Detention Unit.[184]

6.3 The Application of Rehabilitation Indicators

The deeper analysis of rehabilitation demonstration and reintegrative potential has resulted in decisions containing lengthy discussions of applied indicators. Different decisions have used different formats and headings but ultimately assess the same factors depending on the facts in hand.

6.3.1 Mental state and risk of reoffending

The analysis of mental state and the risk of reoffending in decisions has discussed the results of risk assessments, participation in prison programmes and therapy, and the convicted person's acceptance of responsibility for the crimes of which they were convicted.

In *Bralo*, mental state and the risk of reoffending were considered separately. Under the discussion of mental state, it was noted that the prison's risk assessment stated the convicted person had not participated in rehabilitation programmes or psychotherapy.[185] Further, statements that he did not regret anything, denials of (and responsibility for) crimes he had been convicted of, and claims that he had already made amends as he had pointed out the location of graves and apologised during his trial led President Agius to conclude that nothing in the assessment of Bralo's personality inspired 'trust in a successful

[182] *Prosecutor v Semanza*, Decision on Laurent Semanza's Application for Early Release, MICT-13-36-ES.2, 17 September 2020, paras 9–10, 13.

[183] *Prosecutor v Lukić*, Decision on the Application for Early Release of Sreten Lukić, MICT-14-67-ES.4, 7 October 2021, para. 55.

[184] Ibid, para. 56.

[185] *Prosecutor v Bralo*, Decision on the Early Release of Miroslav Bralo, MICT-14-78-ES, 31 December 2019, paras 46–47.

reintegration into society'.[186] In relation to the risk of reoffending, the decision noted that Bralo's risk assessment outlined his intention to bear arms to protect himself in his home, his claim to have hidden weapons, and his willingness to buy new arms if necessary. This was considered concerning given Bralo's history of violence and anti-social behaviour, the sadistic, serious and sexual nature of his offences, and his view that his acts were justifiable.[187] The national authorities concluded that Bralo's treatability was low and that there was a significantly elevated risk of return to serious violent offending.[188] The national authorities recommended that any release should be conditional and subject to monitoring of sobriety, a requirement to continuously contact the local legal system, or electronic monitoring.[189]

In *Brdanin*, the Danish report gave a positive assessment of the applicant's mental state and personality, concluding there was no evidence of dangerousness or risk of recidivism.[190] Agius emphasised that as this assessment was not undertaken with respect to the society to which Brdanin would be released and reintegrated into, this limited the extent to which it could be relied on as a tool to forecast the risk of reoffending.[191] Meron, when consulted on this case, disagreed with this analysis, arguing this psychological report constituted the best evidence of Brdanin's rehabilitation.[192]

In *Semanza*, Agius noted that his mental state appeared to be stable and that he did not suffer from any apparent mental illness.[193]

In *Kunarac*, mental state was considered along with acceptance of responsibility and reflection on the crimes committed. The decision shows that Kunarac had access to psychological services through an interpreter.[194] During these discussions, he had disputed responsibility for or the correctness of the verdict against him for most of the crimes he had been convicted for.[195] Kunarac explained that he could not attend prison programmes due to language barri-

---

186 *Prosecutor v Bralo*, Decision on the Early Release of Miroslav Bralo, MICT-14-78-ES, 31 December 2019, para. 49.

187 Ibid, para. 54.

188 Ibid, paras 55, 57.

189 Ibid, para. 56.

190 *Prosecutor v Brdanin*, Decision on the Application of Radoslav Brdanin for Early Release, MICT-13-48-ES, 28 February 2020, paras 69, 71.

191 Ibid, para. 72.

192 Ibid, para. 94.

193 *Prosecutor v Semanza*, Decision on Laurent Semanza's Application for Early Release, MICT-13-36-ES.2, 17 September 2020, para. 55.

194 *Prosecutor v Kunarac*, Decision on Dragoljub Kunarac's Application for Early Release, MICT-15-88-ES.1, 31 December 2020, paras 53–55.

195 Ibid, para. 56.

ers, the lack of programmes dealing with the 'resocialisation of war criminals' and the fact that he had not admitted liability for all of the crimes he had been convicted of.[196]

Mental state and risk of reoffending were assessed along with prospects for social reintegration in *Dordević* and *Lukić*. In *Dordević*, President Agius noted positive signs of rehabilitation due to an interest in participating in psychological therapy and the fact that a psychiatric risk assessment indicated a very low risk that he would repeat the crimes he was charged with.[197] In *Lukić*, the completion of a programme dealing with aggression and violence prevention, though it did not in and of itself demonstrate rehabilitation, willingness to participate was deemed a positive indicator.[198] Feedback from the prison director that Lukić spoke of his crimes and refused media interviews was also welcomed.[199]

6.3.2 Acceptance of responsibility, signs of critical reflection and genuine expressions of remorse

Although these elements were discussed in *Bralo* under the heading 'personality and mental state', this was a distinct section of analysis for the first time in *Brdanin*. Consideration of the range of probative materials (the application, prison and psychiatric reports, media and trial statements) revealed a continued deflection of responsibility for acts, lack of acceptance of guilt or the credibility of the trial process, a failure to engage in sincere critical reflection or express remorse and therefore revealed no positive indicators of rehabilitation.[200] Though Brdanin made statements expressing regret and empathy for victims and their suffering, this was in reference to 'crimes committed by my people against other peoples'. In addition to continued attempts to distance himself from responsibility, he had failed to support claims that he would take steps to foster reconciliation.[201] He also felt his sentence could and should have been shorter and statements of remorse were not felt to be sincere.[202]

196 Ibid, para. 57.

197 *Prosecutor v Dordević*, Decision on the Applications for Early Release of Vlastimir Dordevic, MICT-14-76-ES, 30 November 2021, paras 72–75.

198 *Prosecutor v Lukić*, Decision on the Application for Early Release of Sreten Lukić, MICT-14-67-ES.4, 7 October 2021, para. 63.

199 Ibid, para. 66.

200 *Prosecutor v Brdanin*, Decision on the Application of Radoslav Brdanin for Early Release, MICT-13-48-ES, 28 February 2020, paras 54–60.

201 Ibid, para. 62.

202 Ibid, para. 63.

Agius concluded that he had not demonstrated critical reflection on his crimes, acceptance of responsibility for them or his actions which enabled them.[203]

In *Brdanin*, Meron questioned whether a convicted person should be legally required to admit or accept responsibility for crimes in order to demonstrate rehabilitation or to use this as a precondition for release.[204] Agius responded that acceptance of responsibility for the crimes for which a person is convicted is only one of several positive indicators that can demonstrate rehabilitation, and Meron and others before him have noted this in the past. Further, as one of many indicators assessed, it is evident that it 'did not constitute a legal requirement to demonstrate rehabilitation, let alone serve as a precondition for early release'.[205]

In *Semanza*, however, this indicator seems to have been an influential ground for finding that the applicant had not been sufficiently rehabilitated. Agius found Semanza's 'choice of vocabulary in describing the events leading to the genocide to be concerning'.[206] Further, Semanza continued to deny the crimes he was convicted of and viewed himself as an innocent victim of injustice.[207] While he did make expressions of remorse in his confidential Personal Statement submitted as part of the application for release, the statements were general in nature (not specific to his crimes or victims), and they were not made publicly.[208] Agius took note of the Prosecutor's observations that Semanza's claim of sympathy for the victims of the genocide was a 'self-serving afterthought' that should be considered against his earlier position on the genocide and portrayal of himself as a victim of events,[209] and the view of the Rwandan authorities that 'it is difficult to see how a man who does not accept responsibility for this crimes has demonstrated any serious degree of rehabilitation'.[210] Agius concluded that Semanza 'shows no sign of critical reflection upon the crimes for which he was convicted' and his views of the genocide demonstrated 'a lack of nuanced understanding of the policies and ideology that allowed for the commission of these crimes'.[211] Overall,

---

203 Ibid, para. 64.

204 Ibid, para. 94.

205 Ibid, para. 95.

206 *Prosecutor v Semanza*, Decision on Laurent Semanza's Application for Early Release, MICT-13-36-ES.2, 17 September 2020, para. 57.

207 Ibid, paras 58–59.

208 Ibid, paras 60, 67.

209 *Prosecutor v Semanza*, Decision on Laurent Semanza's Application for Early Release, MICT-13-36-ES.2, 17 September 2020, para. 65.

210 Ibid, para. 66.

211 Ibid, para. 67.

the demonstration of general regret and compassion for the crimes committed against the Tutsi was insufficient to demonstrate rehabilitation.

In *Dordević*, the applicant had expressed remorse from the outset and throughout his trial, by asking counsel to apologise to testifying victims and expressing remorse publicly in the press.[212] The Prosecutor, while acknowledging and commending these public expressions of sympathy for victims, suggested concrete actions were required to demonstrate rehabilitation.[213] Dordević explained that he had not reached out to victims due to fears that such actions would be misinterpreted.[214] President Agius felt that given the consistency of his statements, and the psychological report from the prison, there was nothing to make him question the sincerity of his public expressions of remorse and they therefore constituted a positive indicator of rehabilitation.[215] He elaborated that remorse required the 'acceptance of some measure of moral blameworthiness for personal wrongdoing' even if it falls short of an admission of criminal responsibility.[216] While general public expressions of remorse would always be positive indicators of rehabilitation, the weight placed on such expressions would be 'linked to the degree to which the convicted person has accepted responsibility for his wrongdoing'.[217] Consequently, statements expressing remorse for the full scope of the convicted person's responsibility will carry greater weight.

In *Dordević*, Agius reiterated that while acceptance of responsibility does not constitute a legal requirement or a precondition for early release, it remains an important factor in assessing rehabilitation.[218] Though partial acceptance of responsibility merits positive weight,[219] notable differences between the role the convicted person 'ascribes to himself and the role he actually played' will suggest that the convicted person has 'not sufficiently engaged in crucial reflection upon his crimes'.[220]

In *Lukić*, the prison report finding that the convicted person presented a critical view of the crimes for which he was convicted was deemed to be a

[212] *Prosecutor v Dordević*, Decision on the Applications for Early Release of Vlastimir Dordevic, MICT-14-76-ES, 30 November 2021, para. 56.
[213] Ibid, para. 58.
[214] Ibid.
[215] Ibid, para. 59.
[216] Ibid, para. 60.
[217] Ibid.
[218] Ibid, para. 70.
[219] Ibid, paras 65, 67.
[220] Ibid, para. 70.

positive indicator of rehabilitation, as was his public (and perceived to be genuine) apology to victims during his appeal hearing.[221]

6.3.3 Prospects of successful reintegration

The analysis of rehabilitation has also included an assessment of the likelihood of reintegration being successful and peaceful. This discussion has been influenced by where the person wishes to relocate and the state, local, family and financial support for resettlement plans. A recurring theme has been the uncertainty surrounding future residence plans.

There was a lack of clarity/confusion about Bralo's intended place of residence post-release, though one proposed location was close to the site of the commission of the crimes for which he had been convicted.[222] Further, after many years on the run and in prison, Bralo had very little social support or contact with family, work experience or education.[223] He therefore had no concrete plans for supporting himself should he be released.[224]

Brdanin, in contrast, wanted to return to Banja Luka in Bosnia-Herzegovina, where he would have a regular income from a pension or work as an engineer and had support from his wife and children with whom he had maintained a close relationship.[225] This plan was supported by the authorities in Republika Srpska and Banja Luka.[226] However, Agius was dismissive of references to cordial relationships with all inmates in a multi-ethnic prison (and letters from fellow prisoners) as evidence of his ability to reconcile with other people in the community.[227] Overall, he felt the circumstances of the case meant this information was 'insufficient to convince me that Brdanin would reintegrate successfully into the society in which he wishes to return'.[228]

Semanza indicated that he would be a retiree upon release and would be supported financially by his son.[229] He referred to reports supplied by Mali to demonstrate he would not pose any threat to the community upon release

---

[221] *Prosecutor v Lukić*, Decision on the Application for Early Release of Sreten Lukić, MICT-14-67-ES.4, 7 October 2021, paras 60–61.

[222] *Prosecutor v Bralo*, Decision on the Early Release of Miroslav Bralo, MICT-14-78-ES, 31 December 2019, para. 59.

[223] Ibid, para. 60.

[224] Ibid.

[225] *Prosecutor v Brdanin*, Decision on the Application of Radoslav Brdanin for Early Release, MICT-13-48-ES, 28 February 2020, paras 73–74.

[226] Ibid, para. 78.

[227] Ibid, paras 75–77.

[228] Ibid, para. 78.

[229] *Prosecutor v Semanza*, Decision on Laurent Semanza's Application for Early Release, MICT-13-36-ES.2, 17 September 2020, para. 69.

and was capable of reintegration.[230] He also declared that he was willing to abide by conditions on his release.[231] The main issue in this case seems to have revolved around the lack of clarity about where the applicant intended to live if released: even though one location had been mentioned, there was no evidence to show that any effort had been made to acquire a legal right to reside there.[232] Moreover, the authorities of this identified location had failed to respond to a request for views on this relocation proposal.[233] Overall, Agius felt the lack of information about his post-release plans meant he could not establish whether Semanza could successfully reintegrate into society.

Kunarac had maintained contact with his children throughout his imprisonment and saved money from his work in the prison library to support himself upon release, where he could request housing from the state or live with family members.[234] The difficulty again lay in the fact that Kunarac was unclear about where he would relocate to if release was granted.[235] He had expressed fears for his life if he returned to Bosnia Herzegovina and a desire to resettle in a number of undisclosed locations. The decision noted, however, that Germany had previously declined to grant asylum and other national authorities had not granted residency rights. Accordingly, he claimed that the unresolved nature of his citizenship meant that he was 'a person without a state'.[236]

Dordević had declared his wish to reside in Serbia if release was granted, his intention to dedicate himself to his family, and his willingness to obey all conditions imposed on release.[237] The prison authorities confirmed that he had maintained contact with his family and had received regular visits.[238] Agius noted the positive weight ascribed to the maintenance of family connections, the psychological report's conclusion that his reintegration was likely to be peaceful, and the Serbian authorities' willingness to monitor conditions in the assessment of reintegration potential.[239] However, the fact that he had evaded arrest by Serbian authorities for years by disguising himself (even from his own family) to avoid trial, and that the President of Serbia had informed

230 Ibid, para. 70.
231 Ibid.
232 Ibid, para. 71.
233 Ibid, para. 68.
234 *Prosecutor v Kunarac*, Decision on Dragoljub Kunarac's Application for Early Release, MICT-15-88-ES.1, 31 December 2020, paras 60, 63.
235 Ibid, para. 58.
236 Ibid, para. 61.
237 *Prosecutor v Dordević*, Decision on the Applications for Early Release of Vlastimir Dordević, MICT-14-76-ES, 30 November 2021, paras 6–7, 71.
238 Ibid, para. 72.
239 Ibid, para. 75.

the Security Council of attempts to extradite Dordević to face a new trial (in Kosovo), made Agius question if Dordević could be trusted to comply with the conditions of release.[240]

The Dordević decision also highlights the implications of pre-trial behaviour for conditional release decisions. Agius noted that Dordević had been in hiding for several years to avoid trial. This caused his trial to be held separately from persons charged in respect of the same matters, causing delay and an unnecessary waste of resources, and prolonged distress for victims. This background, coupled with the fact that he contacted an organised crime figure while serving his sentence in Germany, 'gives me serious concern about whether Dordević could be trusted to comply with conditions of early release'.[241]

In *Lukić*, Agius placed significant weight on the applicant's statements that he disowned any interest in politics in the region and would not support the use of his name or image for political purposes.[242] In particular, Lukić volunteered in his application to refrain from interfering in administrative justice cases before the MICT, contacting victims or prosecution witnesses from his ICTY trial, visiting Kosovo or Metohija, engaging in public appearances or with the media in relation to his conviction, engaging with politics or advocating for or promoting any political party, and promised to adhere to all orders on protective measures and confidentiality in his case.[243] The Serbian Ministry of Justice's support for Lukić's return to his indicated area of residence and willingness to monitor conditions were also seen to support his ability to reintegrate successfully and peacefully into society.[244] Weight was also placed on the prison director's confirmation of his close family ties and recommendation that no post-release assistance would be required.[245]

6.3.4 Behaviour in prison

Relying on reports from detaining authorities, assessments of behaviour in prison have provided insights into rehabilitation progress, reintegrative potential and risk of re-offending.

---

240 Ibid, para. 76.

241 Ibid, para. 55.

242 *Prosecutor v Lukić*, Decision on the Application for Early Release of Sreten Lukić, MICT-14-67-ES.4, 7 October 2021, para. 65.

243 Ibid, para. 67.

244 *Prosecutor v Lukić*, Decision on the Application for Early Release of Sreten Lukić, MICT-14-67-ES.4, 7 October 2021, para. 68.

245 Ibid, paras 69–70.

In *Brdanin*, prison records and psychological reports revealed no issues or disciplinary procedures:[246] he was 'in every way unproblematic'.[247] The reports also testified that *Bralo* had been a 'conscientious inmate' without any misconduct, inappropriate behaviour, disobedience, or violence.[248] This changed, however, in 2015 following a transfer to a prison for persons convicted of sexual offences (which he had been). He threatened to physically attack another inmate in order to have his request for transfer fulfilled.[249] The situation declined further after 2017, when Bralo stopped cooperating with prison authorities as he felt he had served the requisite amount of his sentence (when he passed the date for conditional release eligibility in Sweden).[250] This included daily instances of disobedience (refusal to work or provide samples for drug testing), misconduct (being naked during roll-call), refusal to communicate, and undertaking protest hunger-strikes.[251] Agius felt this lack of cooperation undermined any positive assessment that could have been given for many years of good behaviour.[252]

In *Semanza*, the prison report from Benin noted that he was a calm prisoner and there were no complaints about his conduct, while the psychiatric evaluation concluded that he 'displayed appropriate and cooperative behaviour'.[253] The reports from Mali also indicated that other than a few minor incidents, he had not caused any significant problems, although he was not very cooperative or socially integrated.[254] President Agius accepted that these reports showed that his conduct had generally conformed to the authorities' expectations.[255]

The prison reports in *Kunarac* stated that he had not adjusted well to prison life, was verbally aggressive, and unable to handle decisions that countered his wishes.[256] They detailed his involvement in physical and verbal confrontations with both prisoners and staff, as well as disciplinary proceedings for the

[246] *Prosecutor v Brdanin*, Decision on the Application of Radoslav Brdanin for Early Release, MICT-13-48-ES, 28 February 2020, paras 66–68.

[247] Ibid, para. 65.

[248] *Prosecutor v Bralo*, Decision on the Early Release of Miroslav Bralo, MICT-14-78-ES, 31 December 2019, para. 50.

[249] Ibid.

[250] Ibid, para. 52.

[251] Ibid, para. 51.

[252] Ibid, para. 53.

[253] *Prosecutor v Semanza*, Decision on Laurent Semanza's Application for Early Release, MICT-13-36-ES.2, 17 September 2020, para. 50.

[254] Ibid, para. 51.

[255] Ibid, para. 53.

[256] *Prosecutor v Kunarac*, Decision on Dragoljub Kunarac's Application for Early Release, MICT-15-88-ES.1, 31 December 2020, para. 47.

possession of narcotics.[257] His work in the library, however, was considered exemplary.[258]

In *Dordević*, the German prison authorities revealed a radical change in conduct a year prior to the application, when due to concerns about an attempt to make contact with another prisoner with a known association with organised crime, Dordević was transferred to a high security prison.[259] Agius felt that as the enforcing state authorities had 'deemed his behaviour so alarming as to warrant his transfer to another prison, with a high security classification on a permanent basis', this had to weigh against a conclusion that he had been rehabilitated.[260] This behaviour, coupled with the fact that he had been in hiding for years before this trial, gave Agius 'serious concern about whether Dordević could be trusted to comply with conditions of early release'.[261]

In *Lukić*, the prison authorities reported no breaches of the rules, disciplinary issues or punishments, but rather the grant of awards for employment performance and concessions for good behaviour.[262] Agius only attached minimal weight to these rewards, but he did emphasise the description of Lukić's outstanding behaviour by the prison directors. Despite the limitations of the consideration of behaviour in prison for rehabilitation analysis, he felt these observations were pertinent to the consideration of his mental state, personality and risk of reoffending.[263]

6.4 Overall Assessment of Rehabilitation

Following the separate analysis of the indicators based on the information at hand in each case, President Agius then made an overall assessment of the applicant's demonstration of rehabilitation and a decision as to whether or not this Rule 151 factor should weigh in favour of release. These decisions go beyond individualised rehabilitation to look at reintegrative potential, an ability to comply with conditions and the implications of release for peace and security.

---

257 *Prosecutor v Kunarac*, Decision on Dragoljub Kunarac's Application for Early Release, MICT-15-88-ES.1, 31 December 2020, paras 48–49.

258 Ibid, para. 50.

259 *Prosecutor v Dordević*, Decision on the Applications for Early Release of Vlastimir Dordevic, MICT-14-76-ES, 30 November 2021, para. 52.

260 Ibid, para. 54.

261 Ibid, para. 55.

262 *Prosecutor v Lukić*, Decision on the Application for Early Release of Sreten Lukić, MICT-14-67-ES.4, 7 October 2021, paras 57–58.

263 Ibid, para. 59.

In *Bralo*, Agius noted that as a 'perpetrator of violent crimes … [who had] lived an adult life dominated by experiences of war, hiding from prosecution and long-term imprisonment' Agius felt it would be dangerous to release Bralo unconditionally without adequate preparations for his release. Further, in light of his violent tendencies, elevated risk of reoffending, lack of cooperation with prison authorities, lack of remorse and denial of serious crimes for which he entered a guilty plea, and a failure to critically reflect on his actions, Agius felt there was nothing that would result in a conclusion that Bralo had demonstrated any signs of rehabilitation.[264] Denying release, Agius set out the steps the applicant could and should take to increase a finding of rehabilitation in future release applications: participation in programmes (anti-violence or psychotherapy), critical reflection on his attitude to violence, actions and motivations that led to the crimes, a return to good behaviour in prison, and preparation for release.[265]

In *Brdanin*, Agius recognised that while there were some promising aspects that demonstrated signs of rehabilitation (no risk of reoffending, good behaviour, strong family relationships and post-release support), these must be seen in light of a bigger reintegration context in which the lack of critical reflection on crimes and the extent to which he had distanced himself from or justified his crimes showed that rehabilitation remained 'a work in progress'.[266] The deflection of responsibility was seen by Agius as having both a negative impact on his reintegration and a potentially damaging factor for the restoration and maintenance of peace and security in Banja Luka and surrounding areas.[267] Overall, Brdanin was considered to have failed to sufficiently demonstrate rehabilitation.[268]

In *Semanza*, good behaviour in prison and confidential expressions of sympathy for victims were taken to demonstrate some degree of rehabilitation. However, the general nature of expressions of sympathy did not constitute acceptance of responsibility for the crimes for which he had been convicted or sympathy for the victims of his crimes and therefore proper critical reflection on his crimes. A failure to act on claims to wish to contribute to reconciliation,

---

264 *Prosecutor v Bralo*, Decision on the Early Release of Miroslav Bralo, MICT-14-78-ES, 31 December 2019, paras 62–64.

265 *Prosecutor v Bralo*, Decision on the Early Release of Miroslav Bralo, MICT-14-78-ES, 31 December 2019, paras 49, 53, 61–62, 64, 83.

266 *Prosecutor v Brdanin*, Decision on the Application of Radoslav Brdanin for Early Release, MICT-13-48-ES, 28 February 2020, para. 79.

267 Ibid, para. 80.

268 Ibid, para. 81.

a lack of a public expression of remorse, and vague post-release plans resulted in an overall finding of a failure to sufficiently demonstrate rehabilitation.[269]

Kunarac was previously denied early release by President Meron due to, inter alia, a failure to demonstrate sufficient rehabilitation.[270] Agius reached the same conclusion.[271] Though he welcomed his desire to participate in prison programmes, he was concerned about the confrontations with female prison officers (given the gender and ethnicity-based nature of his criminal offences). His stated inability to avoid conflict, his continued denial of involvement or role in his offences or responsibility for them, his view of himself as a victim and the fact that the German prison authorities were not in favour of granting conditional release seem to have been influential factors.[272] Further, his post-release plans remained uncertain, as it was unclear where he would reside if released, and there was an indictment filed against him in Bosnia-Herzegovina for crimes committed during the war.[273] Against this background, positive behaviour in the library and limited expressions of regret were not sufficient to justify release. Agius encouraged Kunarac to continue to develop the skills and make preparations for reintegration when he is eventually released.[274]

In *Dordević*, a holistic assessment of the public expressions of remorse and a minimal risk of reoffending was balanced against the gravity of the crimes and the only partial acceptance of responsibility for them to find that there was some level of rehabilitation.[275] Despite this finding, the transfer to a high-security prison in the enforcing state, 'previous successful attempts to abscond from justice and hid from national authorities' for a number of years, and the public announcement of the possibility of new criminal proceedings against Dordević meant Aguis simply could not conclude that he could be trusted to comply with the conditions of early release.[276]

In *Lukić*, Agius held that both 'individually and cumulatively' the indicators and information demonstrated a 'fair level of rehabilitation'.[277] Independently

---

269 *Prosecutor v Semanza*, Decision on Laurent Semanza's Application for Early Release, MICT-13-36-ES.2, 17 September 2020, paras 72–73.

270 *Prosecutor v Kunarac*, Decision on Dragoljub Kunarac's Application for Early Release, MICT-15-88-ES.1, 31 December 2020, para. 5.

271 Ibid, para. 69.

272 Ibid, paras 59, 64–66.

273 Ibid, para. 68.

274 Ibid, para. 69.

275 *Prosecutor v Dordević*, Decision on the Applications for Early Release of Vlastimir Dordevic, MICT-14-76-ES, 30 November 2021, para. 77.

276 Ibid, para. 78.

277 *Prosecutor v Lukić*, Decision on the Application for Early Release of Sreten Lukić, MICT-14-67-ES.4, 7 October 2021, para. 72.

verified and mutually reinforcing positive indicators of rehabilitation included critical reflection, public apologies during trial, praise from prison directors, the denouncement of political parties glorifying persons convicted by the ICTY, a refusal to discuss the case with the media, the voluntary enrolment and completion of a rehabilitation programme in prison, and the maintenance of close ties with his family.[278] These positive indicators generated an expectation that he could successfully and peacefully reintegrate into society, comply with the conditions of his release, and uphold the administration of justice.

7. OTHER CONSIDERATIONS: NON-RULE 151 FACTORS

Rule 151 provides a non-exhaustive list of factors to be considered by the President. Under the Practice Direction, the President can also consider any other information that he or she considers relevant to supplement the Rule 151 assessment.[279] President Agius has considered this information under the heading 'other considerations'.

7.1 Humanitarian Grounds

The consideration of humanitarian grounds is particularly important as they can constitute compelling or exceptional circumstances warranting release prior to the service of two-thirds of the sentence.[280] Humanitarian grounds can include illness and advanced age. The 2020 revision of the Practice Direction not only requires medical reports on the convicted person's physical condition but also information on whether 'the convicted person is capable of serving his sentence in the enforcement state'.[281] Decisions since the introduction of conditional release at the MICT continue to adopt the position (in line with human rights law) that 'the condition of a convicted persons' health may be taken into account in the context of an application for early release especially when the

[278] Ibid, para. 71.

[279] Para. 10(f) PDER, Rev 3.

[280] *Prosecutor v Galić*, Decision on the Early Release of Stanislav Galić, MICT-14-83-ES, 26 June 2019, para. 46; *Prosecutor v Munyakazi*, Decision on the Application of Yussuf Munyakazi for Early Release, MICT-12-18-ES.2, 29 November 2019; *Prosecutor v Bralo*, Decision on the Early Release of Miroslav Bralo, MICT-14-78-ES, 31 December 2019, para. 82.

[281] Para. 10(c) PDER, Rev 3.

seriousness of the condition makes it inappropriate for the person to remain in prison any longer'.[282] Health includes mental health.[283]

The *Simba* case demonstrated the issues the current system of sentence enforcement can create for release decision-making. The MICT experienced difficulties in accessing the prisoner's medical records as it needed to obtain the prisoner's consent to access them and also to share them with consulted judges. In addition, the MICT had to engage an independent medical officer based in the enforcing state (Chief Medical Officer of the UN Development Programme, Benin) to obtain and assess medical records and appoint an independent medical consultant to examine the applicant.[284] In *Munyakazi*, despite numerous requests for information about the applicant's health, and promises to furnish it, no response was received from Mali.[285]

Health and age have not weighed in favour of release since conditional release was introduced in any case in which it has been raised by the applicant.[286] This is often because the medical condition or illness could be adequately managed in prison through access to medical treatment and appropriate detention conditions.[287] President Agius now routinely assesses the appropriateness of continued detention on health grounds even where it has not been raised by

---

282 *Prosecutor v Simba*, Public Redacted Version of the President's 7 January 2019 Decision on the Early Release of Aloys Simba, MICT-14-62-ES.1, 7 January 2019, para. 51; *Prosecutor v Ćorić*, Further Redacted Public Redacted Version of the Decision of the President on the Early Release of Valentin Ćorić and Related Motions, MICT-17-112-ES.4, 16 January 2019, para. 56; *Prosecutor v Kunarac*, Decision on Dragoljub Kunarac's Application for Early Release, MICT-15-88-ES.1, 31 December 2020, para. 79.

283 *Prosecutor v Ćorić*, Further Redacted Public Redacted Version of the Decision of the President on the Early Release of Valentin Ćorić and Related Motions, MICT-17-112-ES.4, 16 January 2019, para. 58.

284 *Prosecutor v Simba*, Public Redacted Version of the President's 7 January 2019 Decision on the Early Release of Aloys Simba, MICT-14-62-ES.1, 7 January 2019, paras 5, 9–11.

285 *Prosecutor v Munyakazi*, Decision on the Application of Yussuf Munyakazi for Early Release, MICT-12-18-ES.2, 29 November 2019.

286 *Prosecutor v Kunarac*, Decision on Dragoljub Kunarac's Application for Early Release, MICT-15-88-ES.1, 31 December 2020, para. 84; *Prosecutor v Dordević*, Decision on the Applications for Early Release of Vlastimir Dordevic, MICT-14-76-ES, 30 November 2021, para. 93.

287 *Prosecutor v Kunarac*, Decision on Dragoljub Kunarac's Application for Early Release, MICT-15-88-ES.1, 31 December 2020, paras 80–83.

the applicant, confirming when there is 'no indication that health is an impediment to continued detention'.[288]

In terms of other possible humanitarian grounds, Agius noted in *Dordević* that he was willing to give limited consideration to the stress experienced by family members coping with a convicted person serving a sentence in an enforcing state under this factor, in this particular case, in the interests of justice.[289]

7.2 Relocation

The introduction of conditional release resulted in the examination of the suitability of the proposed country and place of relocation for reintegration purposes, on security grounds (the applicant's safety and the impact of release for the state) and for the protection of victims and witnesses ((any) risks posed by the applicant if released).[290] Both the Registrar and the applicant have been asked for information on these grounds.[291] Media reports have also been analysed to ascertain if there are any credible threats towards the convicted person, or if the convicted person has been engaging with the media in a way that creates risks for victims and witnesses.[292]

A requested state's willingness to accept an individual's return on conditional release and their longer-term resettlement is a crucial element required to facilitate the community implementation of an internationally imposed sanction.[293] This is particularly true for persons not returning to their country of origin: a grant of residency by a third country is likely to be critical for the grant of release.[294]

---

288 *Prosecutor v Brdanin*, Decision on the Application of Radoslav Brdanin for Early Release, MICT-13-48-ES, 28 February 2020, para. 93; *Prosecutor v Bralo*, Decision on the Early Release of Miroslav Bralo, MICT-14-78-ES, 31 December 2019, paras 78–9; *Prosecutor v Semanza*, Decision on Laurent Semanza's Application for Early Release, MICT-13-36-ES.2, 17 September 2020, para. 93.

289 *Prosecutor v Dordević*, Decision on the Applications for Early Release of Vlastimir Dordević, MICT-14-76-ES, 30 November 2021, para. 94.

290 *Prosecutor v Ćorić*, Further Redacted Public Redacted Version of the Decision of the President on the Early Release of Valentin Ćorić and Related Motions, MICT-17-112-ES.4, 16 January 2019, paras 69–70.

291 Ibid, para. 67.

292 Ibid, para. 72.

293 *Prosecutor v Lukić*, Decision on the Application for Early Release of Sreten Lukić, MICT-14-67-ES.4, 7 October 2021, para. 83.

294 *Prosecutor v Simba*, Public Redacted Version of the President's 7 January 2019 Decision on the Early Release of Aloys Simba, MICT-14-62-ES.1, 7 January 2019, paras 75–77.

Relocation plans have also been assessed in light of potential trials following release: decisions have focused on the implications of the threat of prosecution for the convicted person's willingness to comply with release conditions handed down by the MICT.[295] Relocation analysis also centres on the impact of any possible release on victims and witnesses. The broader consultation process (outlined above) has focused on establishing the risk to victims and witnesses who testified at the convicted person's trial, particularly those who live near to the requested area of residence.[296]

8. WEIGHING OF FACTORS

The decision whether or not to grant release should be based on the interests of justice and the general principles of law (Article 26), an assessment of the criteria set out in Rule 151 and any other relevant information, and the views of the consulted judges (Rule 150).[297] Presidential discretion to grant or deny release is informed by the 'totality of the circumstances in each case'.[298] An individualised approach has been adopted as 'each case presents unique circumstances that must be considered on their own merits'.[299]

The introduction of conditional release did not seem to alter Meron's approach to release decision-making: other than the new possibility to include conditions, release would be granted 'despite' or 'notwithstanding' the gravity of the crimes so long as the convicted person had served two-thirds of the sentences and there were some signs of rehabilitation.[300]

Since the adoption of a deeper approach to the analysis of rehabilitation and reintegration, there has been an increased rate of denial of applications. Of the

[295] *Prosecutor v Dordević*, Decision on the Applications for Early Release of Vlastimir Dordevic, MICT-14-76-ES, 30 November 2021, para. 78.

[296] See *Prosecutor v Dordević*, Decision on the Applications for Early Release of Vlastimir Dordevic, MICT-14-76-ES, 30 November 2021, para. 89; *Prosecutor v Lukić*, Decision on the Application for Early Release of Sreten Lukić, MICT-14-67-ES.4, 7 October 2021, para. 84.

[297] Para. 19 PDER, Rev 3.

[298] *Prosecutor v Ćorić*, Further Redacted Public Redacted Version of the Decision of the President on the Early Release of Valentin Ćorić and Related Motions, MICT-17-112-ES.4, 16 January 2019, para. 38.

[299] *Prosecutor v Brdanin*, Decision on the Application of Radoslav Brdanin for Early Release, MICT-13-48-ES, 28 February 2020, para. 46.

[300] See *Prosecutor v Simba*, Public Redacted Version of the President's 7 January 2019 Decision on the Early Release of Aloys Simba, MICT-14-62-ES.1, 7 January 2019, para. 79; *Prosecutor v Ćorić*, Further Redacted Public Redacted Version of the Decision of the President on the Early Release of Valentin Ćorić and Related Motions, MICT-17-112-ES.4, 16 January 2019, para. 74.

decisions handed down by President Agius, only one applicant was granted conditional release. In *Lukić*, conditional release was granted 'notwithstanding' the high gravity of the crimes due to cooperation with the Prosecution, positive indicators of rehabilitation and reintegration potential, no identified risks for witnesses, and the willingness of the requested state to monitor compliance.[301]

In all other cases where the applicant had served two-thirds of their sentence, release was denied primarily on the basis that the applicant had failed to demonstrate sufficient rehabilitation or ability to peacefully reintegrate into society.[302] In *Bralo*, not only were there no signs of rehabilitation, but there was also a 'significantly elevated risk' of a return to violent offending.[303] In *Dordević*, despite findings of some level of rehabilitation and cooperation with the Prosecution, release was denied due to concerns that he could not be trusted to abide by conditions if released and concerns about risks to witnesses.[304] At first glance, it may appear that these outcomes are the result of a deeper examination of rehabilitation and reintegration potential. It should be noted, however, that former President Meron was consulted in some of these cases and he agreed that release should be denied.[305] In fact, in all cases, the decision to deny release was unanimously supported by consulted judges.[306]

9. CONDITIONS OF RELEASE

There is no formal or explicit procedure for determining which conditions should apply to the release of any individual. The Statute and Rules do not discuss conditional release, and the Practice Direction simply states that release may be subject to conditions. The types of conditions that can or should be

---

[301] *Prosecutor v Lukić*, Decision on the Application for Early Release of Sreten Lukić, MICT-14-67-ES.4, 7 October 2021, paras 93–4.

[302] *Prosecutor v Kunarac*, Decision on Dragoljub Kunarac's Application for Early Release, MICT-15-88-ES.1, 31 December 2020, para. 86; *Prosecutor v Brdanin*, Decision on the Application of Radoslav Brdanin for Early Release, MICT-13-48-ES, 28 February 2020, paras 96–97.

[303] *Prosecutor v Bralo*, Decision on the Early Release of Miroslav Bralo, MICT-14-78-ES, 31 December 2019, para. 81.

[304] *Prosecutor v Dordević*, Decision on the Applications for Early Release of Vlastimir Dordević, MICT-14-76-ES, 30 November 2021, paras 97–8.

[305] *Prosecutor v Bralo*, Decision on the Early Release of Miroslav Bralo, MICT-14-78-ES, 31 December 2019, para. 16; *Prosecutor v Kunarac*, Decision on Dragoljub Kunarac's Application for Early Release, MICT-15-88-ES.1, 31 December 2020, para. 85.

[306] See *Prosecutor v Dordević*, Decision on the Applications for Early Release of Vlastimir Dordević, MICT-14-76-ES, 30 November 2021, para. 95.

imposed and the process for supervising compliance with such conditions can only be deduced from the decisions granting release.

9.1 The Procedure for Imposing Conditions

In earlier cases, the process of outlining the conditions that would apply and seeking the applicant's agreement to be bound by them began before the final decision on release had been handed down.

In October 2018, Meron felt it was 'necessary and appropriate, in the interests of justice, to ascertain whether Simba would be prepared to sign an undertaking to abide by the following applicable conditions on his early release, to be attached to the decision on his Application and to be filed on the record'.[307] Simba confirmed that he was willing to abide by the explicit conditions and sign an undertaking in this regard.[308] President Meron also sought proof from the convicted person that his family would accept responsibility for him and his medical care if released and that the state of the proposed relocation would be willing to accept him on its territory for the purpose of family reunification.[309] This process of issuing an interim order for submissions on conditions and assurances was repeated in *Ćorić*.[310]

In *Simba*, the conditions applicable to release were contained in a Conditional Early Release Agreement (CERA) annexed to the decision granting release. The applicant had to sign and file it on record within a specified period of time after the release decision was issued in order for release to be granted.[311] The agreement had to be signed by witnesses attesting to the fact that it was signed by the released person and that the released person confirmed that he had been 'fully advised of its conditions and the consequences of any breach of this Agreement, understands the terms and conditions of this Agreement, and freely and voluntarily signs it with the knowledge of the binding nature of this Agreement and its terms and conditions'.

---

[307] *Prosecutor v Simba*, Interim Order for Further Submissions, MICT-14-62-ES.1, 23 October 2018.

[308] *Prosecutor v Simba*, Public Redacted Version of the President's 7 January 2019 Decision on the Early Release of Aloys Simba, MICT-14-62-ES.1, 7 January 2019, paras 71, 78.

[309] Ibid, para. 16.

[310] *Prosecutor v Ćorić*, Further Redacted Public Redacted Version of the Decision of the President on the Early Release of Valentin Ćorić and Related Motions, MICT-17-112-ES.4, 16 January 2019, para. 8.

[311] *Prosecutor v Simba*, Public Redacted Version of the President's 7 January 2019 Decision on the Early Release of Aloys Simba, MICT-14-62-ES.1, 7 January 2019, paras 78, 81–2.

In *Ćorić*, in contrast, the applicable conditions were listed in the disposition of the early release decision. There is no mention of a conditional early release agreement or any requirement to sign or file one in the decision. The disposition simply states that Ćorić shall 'be subject to the terms of the conditions as stated herein'.[312]

In *Lukić*, where conditional release was granted by President Agius, the conditions of release were contained in a CERA annexed to the decision.[313] Agius noted that Lukić's agreement to abide by the conditions was a prerequisite for his release.[314] Once he signed and submitted the annexed agreement (both the authoritative English and BCS versions), the Registrar was responsible for ensuring he was transferred as expeditiously as possible to Serbia.[315] The agreement required Lukić to verify that he had received both translations, been advised by Counsel in relation to the agreement's contents and individual conditions, and that he understood and agreed to comply fully with all conditions.[316] Further, he understood that he was bound by these conditions until the completion of his sentence unless they were revoked or modified by the President.[317] The agreement was signed by a witness for Lukić and a witness for the Mechanism.

9.2 Conditions Imposed

In both cases in which conditional release was granted by President Meron, the conditions imposed were virtually identical. The conditions included obligations

- to have no contact whatsoever or to try to harm, intimidate, or interfere with victims or witnesses who testified against them at trial or other UN

---

312 *Prosecutor v Ćorić*, Further Redacted Public Redacted Version of the Decision of the President on the Early Release of Valentin Ćorić and Related Motions, MICT-17-112-ES.4, 16 January 2019, para. 78(h).

313 *Prosecutor v Lukić*, Decision on the Application for Early Release of Sreten Lukić, MICT-14-67-ES.4, 7 October 2021, para. 96.

314 Ibid, para. 95.

315 Ibid, para. 97.

316 Conditional Early Release Agreement, Annex to the Decision on the Application for Early Release of Sreten Lukić, MICT-14-67-ES.4, 7 October 2021, paras 1–3.

317 Ibid, paras 4–5.

Tribunal trials or otherwise interfere in the proceedings of the Mechanism or the administration of justice;[318]

- to conduct themselves honourably and peacefully in the communities to which they were released, and not engage in secret meetings intended to plan civil unrest or engage in any political activities;[319]
- to refrain from discussing any aspects of the events in FRY that were the subject of trial (*Ćorić*[320]) or any aspect of the Genocide (*Simba*[321]) with anyone including the media or pro bono counsel;
- not to purchase, possess, use or handle any weapons;[322]
- not to commit any offence;[323] or
- pose a risk of harm to any person[324] (in *Simba* this was not listed as a condition but as a ground for detention and transfer back to the MICT).

---

318 *Prosecutor v Simba*, Public Redacted Version of the President's 7 January 2019 Decision on the Early Release of Aloys Simba, MICT-14-62-ES.1, 7 January 2019, Annex A, para. II (a); *Prosecutor v Ćorić*, Further Redacted Public Redacted Version of the Decision of the President on the Early Release of Valentin Ćorić and Related Motions, MICT-17-112-ES.4, 16 January 2019, para. 78(a).

319 *Prosecutor v Simba*, Public Redacted Version of the President's 7 January 2019 Decision on the Early Release of Aloys Simba, MICT-14-62-ES.1, 7 January 2019, Annex A, para. II (B); *Prosecutor v Ćorić*, Further Redacted Public Redacted Version of the Decision of the President on the Early Release of Valentin Ćorić and Related Motions, MICT-17-112-ES.4, 16 January 2019, para. 78(b).

320 *Prosecutor v Ćorić*, Further Redacted Public Redacted Version of the Decision of the President on the Early Release of Valentin Ćorić and Related Motions, MICT 17 112 ES.4, 16 January 2019, para. 78(c).

321 *Prosecutor v Simba*, Public Redacted Version of the President's 7 January 2019 Decision on the Early Release of Aloys Simba, MICT-14-62-ES.1, 7 January 2019, Annex A, para. II (c); *Prosecutor v Ćorić*, Further Redacted Public Redacted Version of the Decision of the President on the Early Release of Valentin Ćorić and Related Motions, MICT-17-112-ES.4, 16 January 2019, para. 78(c).

322 *Prosecutor v Simba*, Public Redacted Version of the President's 7 January 2019 Decision on the Early Release of Aloys Simba, MICT-14-62-ES.1, 7 January 2019, Annex A, para. II(d); *Prosecutor v Ćorić*, Further Redacted Public Redacted Version of the Decision of the President on the Early Release of Valentin Ćorić and Related Motions, MICT-17-112-ES.4, 16 January 2019, para. 78(d).

323 *Prosecutor v Simba*, Public Redacted Version of the President's 7 January 2019 Decision on the Early Release of Aloys Simba, MICT-14-62-ES.1, 7 January 2019, Annex A, para. II (e); *Prosecutor v Ćorić*, Further Redacted Public Redacted Version of the Decision of the President on the Early Release of Valentin Ćorić and Related Motions, MICT-17-112-ES.4, 16 January 2019, para. 78(e).

324 *Prosecutor v Simba*, Public Redacted Version of the President's 7 January 2019 Decision on the Early Release of Aloys Simba, MICT-14-62-ES.1, 7 January 2019, Annex A, para. IV.

Simba was also obliged not to 'make any statement denying the 1994 Genocide against the Tutsi in Rwanda'.[325]

In *Lukić*, more numerous and detailed conditions were listed in the CERA. They were as follows:

- to have no contact with or directly or indirectly try to harm, intimidate, or interfere with victims or witnesses in his case or other cases before the ICTY or MICT (or members of their families), with the sole exception of witnesses that testified in his defence;[326]
- not to interfere with any proceedings of the MICT or the administration of justice;[327]
- not to violate any ICTY/MICT orders or reveal the identity of (potential) witnesses;[328]
- not to discuss his case (or any aspect of events in FRY that were the subject of his case) with the media, through social media, or anyone other than legal counsel recognised by MICT unless authorised by the President in advance;[329]
- not to make any statement denying crimes over which ICTY/MICT had/has jurisdiction that were committed during the conflict in FRY;[330]
- under no circumstances, express publicly any agreement with or contribute in any way to the glorification of persons convicted by ICTY/MICT;[331]
- if he intends to travel outside Serbia, to notify the monitoring authority and seek approval from the President; [332]
- not to visit Kosovo under any circumstance;[333]
- to conduct himself honourably and peacefully in the community and not engage in meetings or associations intended to plan civil unrest or actively engage in any political activities except for voting;[334]

---

325 *Prosecutor v Simba*, Public Redacted Version of the President's 7 January 2019 Decision on the Early Release of Aloys Simba, MICT-14-62-ES.1, 7 January 2019, Annex A, para. II (c).

326 Conditional Early Release Agreement, Annex to the Decision on the Application for Early Release of Sreten Lukić, MICT-14-67-ES.4, 7 October 2021, para. 3(E).

327 Ibid, para. 3(F).

328 Ibid, para. 3(G).

329 Ibid, para. 3(H).

330 Ibid, para. 3(I).

331 Ibid, para. 3(J).

332 Ibid, para. 3(K).

333 Ibid, para. 3(L).

334 Ibid, para. 3(M).

- deposit any firearms or weapons that require a licence with Serbian authorities and refrain from purchasing, possessing, using or handling any firearms or other weapons requiring a licence;[335]
- not to commit any offence punishable by a term of imprisonment or publicly or privately incite or promote such an offence;[336]
- to notify the monitoring authority of any arrest, summons, or questioning by a law enforcement officers;[337] and
- to continue to make efforts to contribute to rehabilitation and resocialisation.[338]

Lukić's CERA also set out other conditions discussed within the release decision – the requirement for Serbia to register his final conviction on his national criminal record and revoke any firearm licences in his name.[339] Lukić also had to accept the obligation on Serbia to immediately transfer him back to the custody of the MICT following a request from the Mechanism.[340]

The lengthier list of conditions in Lukić's case is due in part to the voluntary undertakings made by the convicted person in his application for release.[341] The added detail to typical conditions provides clarity that will assist both compliance and the monitoring of compliance. For example, the ban on contact with witnesses does not include defence witnesses, and the ban on political activity does not include voting. The ban on committing offences is explicitly limited to offences that are punishable by a term of imprisonment, and the obligation not to have or use weapons is specified as applying only to weapons that require a licence. On the other hand, the breadth and vagueness of a new condition – to continue to make efforts to contribute to rehabilitation and resocialization – will make compliance and its monitoring challenging.

335 Ibid, para. 3(N).
336 Ibid, para. 3(O).
337 Ibid, para. 3(P).
338 Ibid, para. 3(Q).
339 Ibid, para. 7(a)–(b).
340 Ibid, para. 7(c).
341 *Prosecutor v Lukić*, Decision on the Application for Early Release of Sreten Lukić, MICT-14-67-ES.4, 7 October 2021, para. 67.

9.3 The Revocation or Modification of Conditions

Release decisions and CERAs state that released persons are bound by the conditions imposed until the completion of the sentence unless they are revoked or modified by the President.[342]

9.3.1 Variation or removal of conditions

In April 2019, Ćorić requested the variation or removal of one of his conditions of release so that he could continue with legal proceedings he had initiated in Croatia prior to release being granted.[343] The proceedings were against a former witness against Ćorić at the ICTY and had been on hold until release was granted. A judge of the Zagreb Criminal Municipal Court ordered Ćorić to clarify the conditions of his release with the MICT.[344] Agius felt it was necessary 'in the interests of justice' to issue an interim order on the matter in which he ordered Ćorić to comply strictly with the first condition of his release and refrain from participating in proceedings against a former witness while the motion on the variation of conditions was pending.[345] In response, Ćorić notified the President that he had complied with the condition by sending the interim order to the Zagreb court and obtaining a continuance.[346] Ultimately Agius denied the motion ruling that Ćorić had failed to demonstrate that any restrictions on his ability to exercise his rights, duties or obligations warranted the clarification, variation or removal of his release conditions and expressed concern at his attempts to continue litigation against a witness who testified

---

342 *Prosecutor v Simba*, Public Redacted Version of the President's 7 January 2019 Decision on the Early Release of Aloys Simba, MICT-14-62-ES.1, 7 January 2019, Annex A, paras V-VI; *Prosecutor v Ćorić*, Further Redacted Public Redacted Version of the Decision of the President on the Early Release of Valentin Ćorić and Related Motions, MICT-17-112-ES.4, 16 January 2019, para. 78(h)–(i); *Prosecutor v Ćorić*, Decision on Motions Related to Valentin Ćorić's Request for Variation of Early Release Conditions, MICT-17-112-ES.4, 21 February 2020, para. 40; Conditional Early Release Agreement, Annex to the Decision on the Application for Early Release of Sreten Lukić, MICT-14-67-ES.4, 7 October 2021, paras 4–5.

343 *Prosecutor v Ćorić*, Decision on Motions Related to Valentin Ćorić's Request for Variation of Early Release Conditions, MICT-17-112-ES.4, 21 February 2020, paras 5–6.

344 Ibid, para. 6.

345 *Prosecutor v Ćorić*, Interim order on Valentin Ćorić's Urgent Motion Seeking Variation of Conditions of Early Release, MICT-17-112-ES.4, 25 April 2019.

346 *Prosecutor v Ćorić*, Decision on Motions Related to Valentin Ćorić's Request for Variation of Early Release Conditions, MICT-17-112-ES.4, 21 February 2020, para. 8.

against him given that this would clearly result in a breach of his conditions of release.[347]

Ćoric had argued that the conditions imposed on his release affected his ability to exercise his rights, duties and obligations as an ordinary Croatian citizen, in particular, his right to participate in legal proceedings.[348] Agius, rightfully, responded with a reminder that 'he has not returned to the life of an ordinary citizen … [he was] released early from serving his sentence in confinement, subject to the strict fulfilment of specific conditions, including certain restrictions on the rights that ordinary citizens may exercise'.[349]

9.3.2 Legal aid

Ćorić requested remuneration for Counsel for their work in applying for the variation of conditions. While he admitted there was no right to legal aid, and that it was a matter of judicial discretion, he argued 'as a matter of first instance … it required considerable research by the Counsel to prepare the Motion'.[350] Agius declined the request, stating that that the Statute, Rules and Practice Direction do not provide for the assignment of counsel to convicted persons following the issuance of final judgments, and this included proceedings related to early release.[351] While the Appeals Chamber had determined that legal aid may be granted pursuant to a judicial order 'in exceptional circumstances' and that this meant to ensure the fairness of proceedings in the release context, Agius stated that Ćorić had failed to demonstrate that Counsel's assistance was necessary to ensure the fairness of proceedings.[352]

9.4 Supervision

Neither the *Simba* nor *Ćorić* decisions set out the applicable supervision regime. The conditions imposed in *Lukić* shed some light on the monitoring system envisaged to ensure compliance with the conditions imposed. Lukić is obliged to remain under the supervision of a monitoring authority (MA)

---

[347] Ibid, paras 41–42.

[348] *Prosecutor v Ćorić*, Decision on Motions Related to Valentin Ćorić's Request for Variation of Early Release Conditions, MICT-17-112-ES.4, 21 February 2020, para. 31.

[349] Ibid, para. 41.

[350] Ibid, para. 10.

[351] Article 19(4) MICTSt refers to the 'determination of any charge against [the] accused'. See ibid, para. 11.

[352] Ibid, paras 12–13.

designated by Serbia until the completion of his sentence.[353] During this time, he has to comply with any requirement made by the MA, including a request to contact an agent of the MA.[354] Lukić is required to report to the MA, a police station, or any other designated location if and when directed to do so by either the MA or the MICT President.[355] During the community service of his sentence, he must notify the MICT and the MA of his address and give at least 14 days of notice of any proposed change to this address.[356] Further, any plans to travel outside of Serbia must be notified to the MA and approval sought in advance from the MICT President.[357] Oddly, the CERA also frames the duties of Serbia in relation to supervision as a condition of Lukić's release.[358] These include the requirement to submit a quarterly report on Lukić's compliance with the conditions of his release to the MICT.[359]

10. DEALING WITH ALLEGED VIOLATION(S)

One of the most controversial aspects of the conditional release scheme introduced at the MICT has been the lack of detail (or sound legal basis) for dealing with breaches. Agius appears to have distanced himself from Meron's threat of contempt of court proceedings to deal with violations of release conditions. Yet no process or penalties have been established other than warnings of the possible revocation of release.

10.1 Procedure for Dealing with Alleged Violations

It is only possible to deduce a skeletal procedure for dealing with alleged violations from the CER decisions and agreements. In *Simba* and *Ćorić*, the following steps will be followed in the event of a suspected violation of release conditions:[360]

---

353 Conditional Early Release Agreement, Annex to the Decision on the Application for Early Release of Sreten Lukić, MICT-14-67-ES.4, 7 October 2021, para. 3(A).

354 Ibid, para. 3(B).

355 Ibid, para. 3(C).

356 Ibid., para. 3(D).

357 Ibid, para. 3(K).

358 Ibid, para. 8.

359 Ibid, para. 8(e).

360 *Prosecutor v Simba*, Public Redacted Version of the President's 7 January 2019 Decision on the Early Release of Aloys Simba, MICT-14-62-ES.1, 7 January 2019, Annex A, paras III–IV; *Prosecutor v Ćorić*, Further Redacted Public

- The convicted person will be detained by the national authorities of the State of relocation if they have reason to believe the convicted person has failed to comply with any release condition (and, in Simba's case, if he poses a risk of harm to any person).
- The convicted person will be transferred by the State of relocation to the MICT (with no need for any order from the MICT).
- The MICT President will consider the alleged violation(s).

The outlined procedure is spectacularly basic and void of any real insight into how the system will operate in practice. There do not appear to be any procedural safeguards for the convicted person or any scope for the MA to deal with minor infringements.

Under the *Lukić* CERA, any failure to comply with the conditions must be reported to the Mechanism within 24 hours.[361] Further, the Serbian authorities are obligated to arrest and transfer *Lukić* back to MICT custody following a request to do so from the Mechanism.[362] However, the MA must also arrest Lukić immediately (without the need for a request from the Mechanism) if he poses a threat to victims or witnesses, commits any crime punishable by a term of imprisonment, seeks to leave Serbia without permission, or if Serbia or the monitoring authority feel arrest is necessary to ensure compliance.[363]

10.2 Consequences of Violating the Conditions of Release

In *Simba* and *Ćorić*, Meron stated that if the convicted person was found by the President to be guilty of breaching the conditions of his release, the convicted person would be held in *contempt of court* pursuant to Rule 90 and conditional release would be revoked.[364] The invocation of Rule 90 to deal with sentence

---

Redacted Version of the Decision of the President on the Early Release of Valentin Ćorić and Related Motions, MICT-17-112-ES.4, 16 January 2019, para. 78(f)–(g).

361 Conditional Early Release Agreement, Annex to the Decision on the Application for Early Release of Sreten Lukić, MICT-14-67-ES.4, 7 October 2021, para. 8(b).

362 Ibid, paras 6, 7, 8(c).

363 Ibid, para. 8(d).

364 *Prosecutor v Simba*, Interim Order for Further Submissions, MICT-14-62-ES.1, 23 October 2018; *Prosecutor v Simba*, Public Redacted Version of the President's 7 January 2019 Decision on the Early Release of Aloys Simba, MICT-14-62-ES.1, 7 January 2019, para. 84(c) and Annex A, paras III–IV; *Prosecutor v Ćorić*, Further Redacted Public Redacted Version of the Decision of the President on the Early Release of Valentin Ćorić and Related Motions, MICT-17-112-ES.4, 16 January 2019, para. 78(f)–(g).

enforcement matters was seriously problematic. Rule 90 refers to proceedings before the Tribunals,[365] not the supervision of sentence enforcement. Rule 90 also refers to a failure to comply with orders issued by Chambers or a Single Judge, not conditions imposed by the President in a release decision.[366] Further, persons found guilty of contempt can be sentenced to up to seven years in prison, a fine up to €50,000, or both.[367] Rule 90 does not refer to revocation and return to custody but rather the imposition of a (new) custodial term, a fine, or the combination of custodial and pecuniary penalties. What would happen if the remaining term of the sentence was longer than seven years (as is likely in lengthy determinate and life sentence cases)? Could a fine be imposed instead of a return to custodial service of the sentence? Rule 90 is an unsuitable legal basis for the operation of the new conditional release system.

In *Lukić*, in sharp contrast, President Agius does not mention Rule 90 or contempt of court. He simply states that 'any failure to strictly adhere to these conditions would immediately jeopardise his conditional early release'.[368] The CERA further states that violations or a failure to comply fully with any conditions *may result in the revocation* of early release at the sole discretion of the President.[369]

These cases illustrate the complete lack of clarity surrounding the legal basis, process and consequences that will apply to (alleged) violations of conditions of early release.[370]

11. CONCLUSION

Criticisms for adopting a conditional release system following years of operating an unconditional release system have been dismissed on the basis of the need to prioritise harmony between the branches of the Mechanism and equality of treatment of supervised prisoners. The political catalyst for its adoption was quietly side-lined. Conditional early release, once rejected by the plenary of Judges, is now the system in place and has been used by MICT Presidents to

---

365 Rule 90(A) MICT RPE.

366 Rule 90(A)(iii) MICT RPE.

367 Rule 90(G) MICT RPE.

368 *Prosecutor v Lukić*, Decision on the Application for Early Release of Sreten Lukić, MICT-14-67-ES.4, October 2021, para. 95.

369 Conditional Early Release Agreement, Annex to the Decision on the Application for Early Release of Sreten Lukić, MICT-14-67-ES.4, 7 October 2021, para. 6.

370 For further discussion, see Chapter 6, section 5.1.

prepare convicted persons for release and enable local authorities to take part in the reintegration of released persons.[371]

The conditional system remains in its infancy, however, and many crucial elements remain underdeveloped. It is unclear what procedure or consequences will apply in instances of allegations of breaches of conditions. Further, it is highly dependent on state cooperation for the relocation of released persons and the monitoring of compliance. In fact, in some cases, it relies on countries that are banned from enforcing custodial sentences of imprisonment to ensure the implementation of conditions of community sanctions. Issues surrounding the legal basis for state cooperation have not been adequately addressed.

In addition to the adoption of a conditional system, the release decision-making procedure has also transformed under President Agius to include broader consultations with the Prosecution, states, and the consideration of the impact of release on victims and witnesses. Furthermore, release decisions now include a deeper analysis of rehabilitative progress and reintegrative potential based on a number of enumerated indicators.

At the UN Security Council, the Rwandan government urged the MICT to amend its release system on the basis of best practices of the SCSL. But the legal framework and operation of these systems differ in numerous ways. Chapter 6 compares and contrasts all release systems operating in the international criminal justice system and seeks to understand trends and influences on release in international criminal justice.

---

371 *Prosecutor v Bralo*, Decision on the Early Release of Miroslav Bralo, MICT-14-78-ES, 31 December 2019, para. 58.

6. The evolution of conditional early release in international criminal law

1. THE EVOLVING NATURE OF RELEASE IN INTERNATIONAL CRIMINAL LAW

It is clear that the form of release has evolved in international criminal law in a way that was not originally foreseen. The UN Tribunals' original statutory system granted the President the power to issue pardons and order a commutation of sentence. Despite the clear terms used in the statutes, this Presidential power was consistently interpreted and applied as facilitating early release.[1] Until 2018, therefore, Presidents would routinely grant unconditional release once the prisoner had served two-thirds of their sentence.[2] While automatic release systems may provide predictability and align with a truth-in-sentencing perspective, they do not reflect a convicted person's readiness for release into society.[3] This is a particularly salient point in (post-)conflict contexts. Following political discussions and recommendations from the UN Security Council, a new practice of granting release on a conditional basis was introduced at the MICT.[4] The SCSL statute replicated the provisions of the UN Tribunals' statutes, granting the President the power to grant pardon and commutation of sentence. Prior to the first application for release, however, it was decided that it was important to develop a detailed release scheme that only permitted conditional early release.[5]

Conditional release facilitates the enforcement of sentences of imprisonment outside of the prison by placing offenders in the community and restricting their liberty through the imposition of conditions. It is important to note

---

1 Theodore Meron, *Standing Up for Justice: The Challenges of Trying Atrocity Crimes* (OUP 2021) 264, 266.

2 See Chapter 2, section 3.

3 Martine Herzog-Evans, 'Setting the Stage: Defining the Concepts' in Herzog-Evans (ed) *Offender Release and Supervision: The Role of Courts and the Use of Discretion* (Wolf Legal Publishers 2014) 13.

4 See Chapter 5, section 1.

5 See Chapter 4, section 1.

that conditional release constitutes a community sanction and measure.[6] Community sanctions and measures, implemented post-sentencing in the form of conditional release, can help avoid institutionalisation, assist with reintegration, protect society and maintain legal order.[7] Contemporary international and regional standards regulate the use of community measures, including the 1990 UN Standard Minimum Rules for Non-custodial Measures[8] and the Council of Europe's recommendations on conditional release,[9] probation,[10] and community sanctions and measures.[11]

In contrast to the temporary courts, the Rome Statute only enables judges to grant sentence reductions. This involves unconditional release at the end of service of a (revised) sentence. However, the ICC rules refer to early release,[12] as does a recent ICC sentence review decision. Early release occurs prior to the completion of the original sentence.[13] Despite the inconsistent use of terminology, the form of release at the ICC has remained unchanged since the adoption of the Rome Statute. However, it is important for the ICC to pay attention to the operation of conditional release systems at other international courts, as victims are increasingly calling for post-release supervision of persons granted sentence reductions[14] and there is a clear need for the ICC to introduce a form of conditional early release for urgent humanitarian situations.[15]

This chapter compares and critiques the motivations and mechanisms for introducing conditional release in international criminal law, the extent and scope of conditions imposed on released persons, the challenges of operationalising conditional release systems (cooperation and laconic legal frameworks), and the consequences for breaching the conditions of release (recall). Further, the expanding penal reach and impact of international criminal sanctions will be explored, as will the fact that conditional early release will not be available

---

6 Rule 9.2(c) UN Standard Minimum Rules on Non-Custodial Measures 1990 (Tokyo Rules); Recommendation CM/Rec(2017)3 on the European Rules on Community Sanctions and measures (hereafter ERCSM), Definitions.

7 Rules 9.1 and 9.2(c) Tokyo Rules; ERCSM, Scope and Purpose A.

8 Tokyo Rules.

9 Recommendation Rec(2003)22 of the Committee of Ministers to member states on conditional release (parole) (hereafter RCR).

10 Recommendation CM/Rec(2010)1 of the Committee of Ministers to member states on the Council of Europe Probation Rules (hereafter PR).

11 ERCSM.

12 Rule 223(c)–(d) ICC RPE.

13 See *Prosecutor v Ahmad Al Faqi Al Mahdi*, Public Redacted Version of the Decision on the Review concerning reduction of sentence of Mr Ahmad Al Faqi Al Mahdi, ICC-01/12-01/15, 25 November 2021, paras 52, 59.

14 See Chapter 8, section 3.3.

15 See Chapter 9.

for some internationally convicted persons on account of a lack of cooperation from States or the suitability of States offering to cooperate.

2. THE INTRODUCTION OF CONDITIONAL RELEASE IN INTERNATIONAL CRIMINAL LAW

At the ICC, the sentence reduction review system can result in *de jure* changes to the original sentence. The unconditional release system used by the UN Tribunals until 2018 *de facto* altered the original sentence. The conditional release systems operated by the RSCSL and the MICT since 2018 prioritise the maintenance of the original sentence imposed. However, the motivations and procedures for introducing the systems at the MICT and the RSCSL can be distinguished on numerous grounds.

2.1 Conditional Early Release at the RSCSL

The process of creating a release system for the RSCSL was both a principled and pragmatic exercise that followed the recommendations of an internal judicial committee on how to operationalise the rules on release. While the ordinary meaning of pardon and commutation were indisputable (a sentence being set aside or reduced), the Sub-Committee felt that as neither had been applied by international courts, the terms had a special meaning in international criminal law that included early release (as demonstrated by the practice of the UN Tribunals).[16] The statutory provisions were interpreted as requiring the continued importance of sentencing priorities and ensuring public safety (interests of justice) and the equal treatment and individualised rehabilitation of convicted persons (general principles of law). Although there was recognition that distinct goals informed sentence determination and sentence enforcement, the Sub-Committee felt that paramount sentencing and sentence determination objectives (gravity and deterrence) dictated a need to preserve the integrity of the sentence imposed.[17] It was also considered important to enhance public safety by reducing opportunities for re-engagement in atrocity crime or risks that released persons would threaten those involved in their prosecution or societal peace.[18] Ensuring equality of treatment, it was argued, would require the development of objective criteria for release decision-making that

---

[16] Teresa Anne Doherty and Shireen Avis Fisher, 'Enforcement of sentences and oversight of prisoners convicted by the SCSL' in R Mulgrew and D Abels (eds) *Research Handbook on the International Penal System* (Edward Elgar Publishing, 2016) 355–380 at 361.

[17] Ibid at 364, 366.

[18] Ibid at 365.

would apply irrespective of the jurisdiction in which the sentence was being served.[19] Further, the international penal goal of rehabilitation, important for philosophical (upholding human dignity and reinforcing the rule of law) and practical reasons (as the statute precludes life imprisonment, every prisoner has the theoretical possibility of release), should be incorporated through the inclusion of 'consistent transparent subjective criteria'.[20]

The Sub-Committee rejected unconditional forms of early release found in domestic practice, such as remission and amnesty but also, surprisingly, the form practised by the ICTY and ICTR – judicial discretionary unconditional release.[21] The basic premise for the (R)SCSL release scheme was that it would operate in a way that did not change the original sentence: 'an early release programme that reduces the sentence is not acceptable'.[22] The Sub-Committee determined that early release should involve the service of the remainder of the sentence in the community under restrictions and Court supervision, with the possibility of return to prison in the case of a breach of the conditions of release.[23] Such a system of judicial discretionary conditional release was possible in the (R)SCSL context given the willingness of both the court's host State, Sierra Leone, and its main enforcing State, Rwanda, to cooperate with the creation and implementation of this scheme. The Sierra Leone Government agreed to 'supervise the conditions … [and] cooperate in any way necessary with reporting and violation provisions' while the Rwandan authorities 'agreed to work with the Court to provide rehabilitation programmes within the prison individualised according to the needs of the individual prisoners and furnish reports to the Court to make decisions on early release'. [24]

The system was designed on the basis of European penal policy, national practice (particularly Commonwealth countries) and consultations with external experts.[25] The RSCSL's conditional early release scheme was formalised in the 2013 Practice Direction on the Conditional Early Release of Persons Convicted by the Special Court for Sierra Leone, which includes application forms and draft orders. This was revised in December 2016 to reflect lessons learnt following two applications and a breach of conditions proceeding in the *Fofana* case.[26] The 2013 Practice Direction created a conditional early

---

[19] Ibid at 366.
[20] Ibid at 366, 368.
[21] Ibid at 368–369.
[22] Ibid at 355, 361, 364.
[23] Ibid at 365.
[24] Ibid at 370–371.
[25] Ibid at 370.
[26] First Annual Report of the President of the RSCSL, January 2014–December 2014 at 26; Second Annual Report of the President of the RSCSL,

release scheme for the first time in international criminal law. This policy, and the annexed documentation, established a comprehensive system for determining eligibility for conditional release, imposing conditions, executing release, supervising releasees, dealing with breaches and terminating conditional release.

2.2 Conditional Early Release at the MICT

Neither the Statutes nor the Rules of the ICTY nor ICTR referred to early release. They spoke only of pardon and commutation of sentence.[27] The concept of 'early release' was introduced at the UN Tribunals through a presidential Practice Direction in 1999.[28] No pardon or commutation of sentence has been granted by a UN Tribunal to date. Despite this reality, the MICT Statute also **only** refers to pardon and commutation.[29] This successor institution did, however, refer to early release in its rules.[30] More reflective of both earlier procedure and practice, President Meron's Practice Direction set out the procedure for determining applications for 'pardon, commutation of sentence and early release'.[31]

Until 2018 virtually all persons convicted by the ICTY, ICTR and MICT were released on an unconditional basis. However, a Security Council debate in June 2018 created the political catalyst that ushered in significant change. Numerous countries, led by a strong Rwandan voice, expressed serious concerns about the lack of remorse and the denial of the genocide by ICTR convicted persons released on an unconditional basis.[32] This state of affairs, they argued, was having a detrimental impact on the Tribunals' legacies and the

---

January 2015–December 2015 at 23; Third Annual Report of the President of the RSCSL, January 2016–December 2016 at 6, 7, 12, 17, 23.

[27] Art. 28 ICTYSt; Art. 27 ICTRSt; Part Nine, Rules of Procedure and Evidence.

[28] Practice Direction on the Procedure for the Determination of Applications for Pardon, Commutation of Sentence, and Early Release of Persons Convicted by the International Tribunal Practice Direction (hereafter ICTY PDER). The ICTR did not publish its practice direction, but the same terms were used – see para. 1 MICT PDER.

[29] Art. 26 MICTSt.

[30] See Rules 149–151 MICT RPE, MICT/1, 8 June 2012.

[31] Practice Direction on the Procedure for the Determination of Applications for Pardon, Commutation of Sentence, and Early Release of Persons Convicted by the ICTR, the ICTY or the Mechanism, MICT/3, 5 July 2012.

[32] Statements of the representatives of Peru, Bolivia, and the USA, UN Security Council, 8278th Meeting, S/PV.8278, 6 June 2018 at 6, 14, 16.

fight against impunity.[33] The solution, it was argued, was to introduce a conditional early release system akin to that adopted by the SCSL that would prevent released persons from participating in activities that promoted genocide ideology and denial.[34] The Security Council adopted a resolution that encouraged the MICT to consider adding conditions to early release in appropriate cases.[35] Despite the non-obligatory nature of this recommendation, and the fact that it only referred to ICTR convicted persons, the MICT has only granted release on a conditional basis to persons under its supervision since then, irrespective of the sentencing Tribunal, citing the need to harmonise practice.

2.3 Implications of the Varying Motivations for Introducing Conditional Release

The MICT decision to transform its release system from a quasi-automatic unconditional system of release to a conditional system of release based on a presumption against release can be distinguished from the RSCSL approach on numerous grounds.

The RSCSL system was created in recognition of the need to have a consistent and principled scheme in place prior to the first applications for release. In sharp contrast, the MICT system of conditional release was introduced years after the establishment of the MICT and decades of unconditional release policy and practice. The RSCSL system was based on changes to the regulatory framework and the creation of a detailed and comprehensive schema (with tailored documentation) inspired by legal, penological, rights, public safety, victimological and transitional justice goals. The MICT system was introduced following a political debate, a recommendation and the introduction of eight words into the Practice Direction.[36] The unilateral decision to introduce and extend a conditional release system to all persons supervised by the MICT by the President,[37] flew in the face of the decision by the plenary of judges not to amend the rules to include a conditional release system when

[33] Statement of the representatives of Bolivia and the USA, UN Security Council, 8278th Meeting, S/PV.8278, 6 June 2018 at 6, 16.

[34] Statement of the representatives of France, Kuwait and Rwanda, UN Security Council, 8278th Meeting, S/PV.8278, 6 June 2018 at 9, 11, 24–25.

[35] UN Security Council Resolution 2622, para. 10.

[36] MICT/3/Rev. 3, 15 May 2020.

[37] *Prosecutor v Ćorić*, Further Redacted Public Redacted Version of the Decision of the President on the Early Release of Valentin Ćorić and Related Motions, MICT-17-112-ES.4, 16 January 2019, para. 73.

they were requested to do so by the Office of the Prosecutor.[38] It is difficult to categorise the creation of conditional release at the MICT as anything other than a unilateral act of judicial legislation, particularly given that the change introduced penal consequences not foreseen or facilitated by the Statute or Rules. The new 'practice of conditional early release'[39] was introduced without judicial support, procedure, policies or cooperation agreements, and no plan for the budgetary implications of requiring judicial oversight and potential detention capacity until the final day of the final sentence imposed by the ICTY, ICTR and MICT has been served.

The internal judicial decision to create a system of release that would apply equally to all SCSL convicted persons stands in stark contrast to the externally and politically imposed system of conditional release, introduced by the MICT President after an unconditional system had been in operation for years and contrary to the decision of a majority of judges.

3. CONDITIONS GOVERNING RELEASE IN INTERNATIONAL CRIMINAL LAW

3.1 Procedures for Imposing Conditions

Conditional early release cannot be granted unless the convicted person agrees to enter into and comply fully with the conditions of their release. At the RSCSL, these conditions are specified in a conditional early release agreement.[40] At the MICT, practice has varied. Presidents have issued an interim order seeking submissions on undertakings to accept and abide by conditions prior to the release decision being finalised,[41] or included conditions in a con-

---

[38] See Progress Report of the Prosecutor of the International Residual Mechanism for Criminal Tribunals, Serge Brammertz (16 November 2018 to 15 May 2019) at 39, Annex II of the Letter dated 20 May 2019 from the President of the MICT addressed to the President of the Security Council, S/2019/417, 20 May 2019, para. 30; *Prosecutor v Ćorić*, Urgent Motion Seeking Variation of Conditions of Early Release of 15 January 2019 and Request for Legal Aid, MICT-17-112-ES.4, 2 April 2019, paras 15, 17–19.

[39] *Prosecutor v Bralo*, Decision on the Early Release of Miroslav Bralo, MICT-14-78-ES, 31 December 2019, para. 83.

[40] See Art. 8(C)(i) PDCER.

[41] *Prosecutor v Simba*, Interim Order for Further Submissions, MICT-14-62-ES.1, 23 October 2018; *Prosecutor v Simba*, Public Redacted Version of the President's 7 January 2019 Decision on the Early Release of Aloys Simba, MICT-14-62-ES.1, 7 January 2019, paras 71, 78; *Prosecutor v Ćorić*, Further Redacted Public Redacted Version of the Decision of the President on the Early Release of Valentin Ćorić and Related Motions, MICT-17-112-ES.4, 16 January 2019, para. 8.

ditional early release agreement annexed to the release decision, which convicted persons were required to sign and file on the record as a prerequisite for release being effected.[42] In another case, the conditions attaching to release were listed in the release decision's disposition without reference to a separate conditional release agreement (or any requirement to sign one).[43]

Persons granted conditional early release by the RSCSL President are informed at several stages of the process about the controls they will be subject to. The Practice Direction makes it clear that in order to be considered eligible for consideration for release (the first stage of a two-stage process), convicted persons must confirm in writing that they understand release is subject to agreeing to conditions, and its continuation is subject to compliance with them.[44] The convicted person must also affirm willingness to the prison authorities to submit to supervision in the community.[45] Further, the applicant is provided with advice from the Principal Defender on the conditions and consequences of their breach, and the applicant must testify that they understand these aspects and the possibility for arrest and recall before release will be affected.[46] To prevent the transfer of convicted persons back to Sierra Leone without complete acceptance of the terms of their release, applicants are now required to reaffirm their understanding and voluntary acceptance of conditions to the RSCSL Registrar while still in custody in the enforcement State and for the Registrar to be satisfied that the convicted person freely entered, understood and intends to comply with the CERA.[47] The process for ensuring applicants fully understand the extent of conditions that govern the service of the sanction in the community and the consequences for any breach thereof remains under-developed at the MICT.

---

42 *Prosecutor v Lukić*, Decision on the Application for Early Release of Sreten Lukić, MICT-14-67-ES.4, 7 October 2021, paras 95–96; *Prosecutor v Simba*, Public Redacted Version of the President's 7 January 2019 Decision on the Early Release of Aloys Simba, MICT-14-62-ES.1, 7 January 2019, paras 78, 81–82.

43 *Prosecutor v Ćorić*, Further Redacted Public Redacted Version of the Decision of the President on the Early Release of Valentin Ćorić and Related Motions, MICT-17-112-ES.4, 16 January 2019, para. 78(h).

44 Art. 2(D) PDCER.

45 Art. 5(D)(iii)(iv) PDCER.

46 Art. 10(A) PDCER; Paras 1–2, 4, 8 Pro Forma CERA, Annex C PDCER.

47 Art. 10(C)–(E) PDCER. See Róisín Mulgrew 'Projet sur vingt-cinq ans: une analyse du système de liberation conditionnelle du Tribunal special pour la Sierra Leone', (2014) 27 *Cahiers de la Sécurité et de la Justice* 142–153 at 148. Previously, additional advice was given on return to Freetown, but fears of rejection of the terms before release into the community after the *Senessie* case prompted this change in procedure.

To ensure that the process accords with contemporary recommendations to ensure consent is informed and explicit, conditional release decisions and conditions should be explained to applicants in a language they understand.[48] Evidence of this is apparent in efforts to engage staff that speak a local language and interpreters (RSCSL), and the written translation of conditional early release agreements (MICT).[49] For both courts, witnesses (if applicable) must attest that the convicted person signed the agreement voluntarily.[50]

While these steps are designed to provide procedural safeguards for convicted persons by ensuring informed consent to conditional release and community supervision, this goal is undermined by the lack of knowledge about the number and scope of conditions that will ultimately attach should release be granted. Contemporary standards require that consent should be based on *full* knowledge of the extent of conditions.[51] The lack of knowledge about the true scope of the control that will be exerted through the conditions of release is explicitly recognised in the RSCSL process, with the inclusion of a direction that the prisoner must acknowledge and accept that the President may impose further Special Conditions of Release'.[52] Perhaps more significantly, complete uncertainty remains in both systems about the consequences that will attach to the breach of particular conditions.

3.2 Substantive Conditions

The Tokyo Rules state that conditions must be 'precise and as few as possible, and be aimed at reducing the likelihood of an offender relapsing into criminal behaviour and of increasing the offender's chances of social integration', taking into account the needs of victims.[53] It is questionable if the approach currently adopted by the RSCSL or the MICT aligns with these requirements.

3.2.1 Conditions of release at the RSCSL

All persons granted conditional release are subject to the same list of general conditions (listed in an annex to the Practice Direction). In addition, they

48 Rules 30, 61 ERCSM; Rule 12.3 Tokyo Rules.

49 See Conditional Early Release Agreement, Annex to the Decision on the Application for Early Release of Sreten Lukić, MICT-14-67-ES.4, 7 October 2021, paras 1–3.

50 See Art. 10(B) PDCER.

51 Commentary on Rule 57 ERCSM.

52 Form A(1) PDCER.

53 Rule 12.2 Tokyo Rules.

may be subject to further special conditions imposed by the President.[54] The general conditions relate to the role of the monitoring authority and refer to a range of issues such as the use of substances, weapons, association with others, involvement in crime and the intimidation of witnesses.[55]

Contemporary standards, based on the legality principle, demand that conditions are clear, concise and explicit: precision and comprehensibility are important to ensure the person subject to them knows how to comply with them.[56] Yet, it is unclear what acts or omissions will constitute a breach of particular conditions. What exactly does the purchase or possession of a weapon involve? Does this prohibit the purchase of an axe or a kitchen knife? At what point does a convicted person have to notify the monitoring authority of an arrest or drugs tests? Does the requirement begin immediately, as soon as possible, or a week later? Without a timeframe, it is unclear how to comply with this condition. What is required by the demand that convicted persons conduct themselves 'honourably and peacefully'? The scope of many of the RSCSL's general conditions is vague. Does the prohibition on association with named persons involve direct and deliberate communication, or can it be breached by unintentional presence at a church service or at the doctor's office? All released persons are liable to recall if they commit 'any' offence. Does this include administrative offences? Can the procedure for dealing with breaches be initiated by a speeding ticket? If so, and if conditions cover minor and administrative law infringements, what relevance does this have to the jurisdiction and objectives of the Special Court? Following the same logic, the blanket ban on the consumption of alcohol and drugs for all persons granted conditional release to date is questionable if the use or abuse of alcohol or drugs was not 'manifestly associated with the commission of the crime'.[57] Further, from a compliance perspective, Mujuzi notes that alcohol can be used in non-crime related instances such as for medicinal purposes or during cultural or religious rituals or practices.[58]

---

[54] Arts 8(F) and 9(C)(i) PDCER. See also Annex D (Pro Forma Draft SCSL Supervision and Transfer Order).

[55] See paras 5 and 6 Pro Forma CERA, Annex C PDCER. See Chapter 4, sections 7.2 and 7.3 for further details.

[56] Rules 15, 30 ERCSM; Commentary to Rule 15 ERCSM.

[57] Para. 8 RCR.

[58] Jamil Ddamulira Mujuzi, 'The Conditional Early Release of Offenders Transferred from the Special Court of Sierra Leone to Serve Their Sentences in Designated States: Some Observations and Recommendations' (2014) *African Yearbook of International Humanitarian Law* 154–170 at 164.

The use of broad and vague conditions creates space for 'quick revocations' as it is easier to conclude that an ambiguous condition has been breached.[59] As Van Zyl Smit and Snacken argue, the imposition of overly strict conditions can be counterproductive as it is likely to result in infringements and recall.[60] The current approach may do what Boone and Herzog-Evans warn against – overburdening offenders with too many obligations and imposing conditions that impose too high a level of constraint.[61] Or, as occurred in *Senessie*, result in offenders preferring to serve their full sentence in custody rather than submitting to 'the terms imposed by the Court' if released.[62] Moreover, the 'predictive validity' of conditions imposed on release has not been demonstrated by research in national contexts: in other words, compliance with a long list of general conditions does not necessarily predict a reduced risk of re-offending or successful reintegration.[63] On this basis, it may be argued that specially tailored conditions are more appropriate.

At the RSCSL, special conditions can be imposed *in addition* to these predetermined general conditions. Though the documentation indicates that five special conditions may be added,[64] there is no specific or explicit limit on the number that can be included. In *Gbao*, nine special conditions were imposed.[65] A clear link has emerged in RSCSL jurisprudence between the recommendations made by the Prosecutor, and witnesses and community members consulted in relation to the potential release, and the special conditions added.[66] While this approach has clear merit in enhancing the acceptability of the release to victims and communities, the conditions imposed often repeated or overlapped with requirements already contained in the general conditions in relation to witness interference, association, political activity and monitoring.

59 Kristel Beyens, Lars Breuls, Lana De Pelecijn, Marijke Roosen and Veerle Scheirs, 'Recall to prison in Belgium: Back-end sentencing in search of reintegration' (2020) 67(1) *Probation Journal* 6–25 at 14.

60 See Dirk Van Zyl Smit and Sonja Snacken, *Principles of European Prison Law and Policy* (OUP, 2009) at 326.

61 Miranda Boone and Martine Herzog-Evans, 'Decision-Making and Offender Supervision' in F. McNeill and K. Beyens (eds), *Offender Supervision in Europe* (Palgrave Macmillan: London, 2013), 51–96 at 56.

62 See RSCSL press release, 'Moinina Fofana granted conditional early release, after six more months in prison'.

63 Christopher M. Campbell 'Rethinking Conditional Release as an Assumption-Based Test of Offender Readiness' (2018) 43(2) *Criminal Justice Review* 216–235 at 218.

64 Art. 9(C)(ii) PDCER; para. 1 Pro Forma CERA, Annex C PDCER.

65 *Prosecutor v Gbao*, Decision of the President on Application for Conditional Early Release, RSCSL-04-15-ES, 8 September 2020, para. 83.

66 See Chapter 4, section 7.3.

This act of imposing additional conditions may serve a communicative or performative function that seeks to demonstrate judicial responsiveness to concerns about an individual's release. However, in some instances, this approach confusingly frames requirements that have already been complied with to gain release (to apologise, acknowledge guilt, renounce ideologies and show remorse[67]) as post-release supervision requirements (a breach of which could result in recall to detention).

It is particularly notable in the *Gbao* decision that consultations with the community resulted in special conditions being used to increase the penal depth and reach of the initial sanction by requiring him to undertake community service while on conditional release.[68] This would not have been an apparent element of conditional release when he was initially asked to agree to it. Perhaps this unprecedented requirement was an attempt to avoid cynical views in relation to offenders promising to commit acts in order to regain liberty and then reneging on such promises? In a further unexpected use of special conditions, Gbao had to promise to pay his own medical bills and allow the RSCSL to monitor his medical conditions. How a lack of money or a refusal of consent to access private medical records could constitute grounds for recall to prison is highly questionable on legal, penal and ethical grounds. Another striking and odd aspect of the implementation of special conditions at the RSCSL is their use to impose obligations on the RSCSL Registrar.[69] The conditions of release contained in an agreement signed by the releasee should only relate to the obligations of that individual.

3.2.2 Conditions of release at the MICT

MICT conditions are not labelled or distinguished as general or special. The conditions imposed on those granted conditional early release have covered a broad range of grounds including witness intimidation, public behaviour, involvement in political activity, discussion of the offences (or their context)

---

[67] *Prosecutor v Fofana and Kondewa*, Decision of the President on Application for Conditional Early Release, SCSL-04-14-ES (1270–1291) 11 August 2014, para. 33; *Prosecutor v Kondewa*, Decision of the President on Application for Conditional Early Release, RSCSL-04-14-ES (1581–1604), The Hague, 29 May 2017, para. 61(i); *Prosecutor v Gbao*, Decision of the President on Application for Conditional Early Release, RSCSL-04-15-ES, 8 September 2020, para. 83(i).

[68] *Prosecutor v Gbao*, Decision of the President on Application for Conditional Early Release, RSCSL-04-15-ES, 8 September 2020, paras 78, 83(viii).

[69] See *Prosecutor v Fofana and Kondewa*, Decision of the President on Application for Conditional Early Release, SCSL-04-14-ES (1270–1291) 11 August 2014, para. 49(v); *Prosecutor v Gbao*, Decision of the President on Application for Conditional Early Release, RSCSL-04-15-ES, 8 September 2020, para. 83(x).

and in some cases atrocity/genocide denial. The number and detail of conditions have increased over time, with a heightened focus on requirements to engage with the appointed monitoring authority and protect the administration of justice at the tribunal (and witnesses) and the inclusion of specific travel restrictions.[70]

The earlier conditions at the MICT were susceptible to the same criticisms outlined above in relation to RSCSL conditions in terms of vagueness and a lack of nexus to both the original sentence and the mandate of the court. However, under President Agius, much-needed clarity was added. Under previous decisions, releasees could have no contact whatsoever with victims and witnesses that had testified against them at any UN Tribunal. In *Lukić*, though the prohibition on contacting victims and witnesses who testified at the Tribunals was extended to include members of victims' and witnesses' families,[71] it was made clear that he was permitted to have contact with witnesses that testified in his defence.[72] It was further clarified that the prohibition against engaging in any political activity[73] did not extend to voting.[74]

Previous release conditions had contained broad controls over the freedom of expression, which included refraining from discussing any aspects of the events that were the subject of trial (*Ćorić*[75]) or any aspect of the Genocide

---

70 See Conditional Early Release Agreement, Annex to the Decision on the Application for Early Release of Sreten Lukić, MICT-14-67-ES.4, 7 October 2021, para. 3(B)–(G), (K)–(L).

71 See *Prosecutor v Simba*, Public Redacted Version of the President's 7 January 2019 Decision on the Early Release of Aloys Simba, MICT-14-62-ES.1, 7 January 2019, Annex A, para. II(a); *Prosecutor v Ćorić*, Further Redacted Public Redacted Version of the Decision of the President on the Early Release of Valentin Ćorić and Related Motions, MICT-17-112-ES.4, 16 January 2019, para. 78(a).

72 Conditional Early Release Agreement, Annex to the Decision on the Application for Early Release of Sreten Lukić, MICT-14-67-ES.4, 7 October 2021, para. 3(E).

73 See *Prosecutor v Simba*, Public Redacted Version of the President's 7 January 2019 Decision on the Early Release of Aloys Simba, MICT-14-62-ES.1, 7 January 2019, Annex A, para. II(b); *Prosecutor v Ćorić*, Further Redacted Public Redacted Version of the Decision of the President on the Early Release of Valentin Ćorić and Related Motions, MICT-17-112-ES.4, 16 January 2019, para. 78(b).

74 Conditional Early Release Agreement, Annex to the Decision on the Application for Early Release of Sreten Lukić, MICT-14-67-ES.4, 7 October 2021, para. 3(M).

75 *Prosecutor v Ćorić*, Further Redacted Public Redacted Version of the Decision of the President on the Early Release of Valentin Ćorić and Related Motion*s*, MICT-17-112-ES.4, 16 January 2019, para. 78(c).

(*Simba*[76]) with *anyone,* including the media (except for pro bono counsel). This also applied to *Lukić*,[77] as did an absolute prohibition on glorifying persons convicted by the ICTY or MICT.[78] In *Lukić*, however, this restriction was limited to aspects that related to the case, and the condition created an opportunity to do so, as the President could grant prior authorisation.[79] The scope of the ban on purchasing, possessing, using or handling any weapon (seen in previous cases[80]) was clarified to extend only to those weapons or firearms that required a licence.[81]

In a similar vein, the overly broad condition that referred to the commission of *any* offence,[82] was narrowed to only allow recall for offences punishable by imprisonment.[83] The conditions imposed in *Lukić* also provided more detailed provisions that outlined the supervision process and requirements to submit to monitoring, respect requests, and requirements to report and to notify of change of address or intention to travel. Despite these numerous attempts to bring clarity, it is perhaps surprising that one condition in *Lukić* seems to be one of the broadest and vaguest conditions imposed to date in international

[76] *Prosecutor v Simba*, Public Redacted Version of the President's 7 January 2019 Decision on the Early Release of Aloys Simba, MICT-14-62-ES.1, 7 January 2019, Annex A, para. II (c); *Prosecutor v Ćorić*, Further Redacted Public Redacted Version of the Decision of the President on the Early Release of Valentin Ćorić and Related Motions, MICT-17-112-ES.4, 16 January 2019, para. 78(c).

[77] Conditional Early Release Agreement, Annex to the Decision on the Application for Early Release of Sreten Lukić, MICT-14-67-ES.4, 7 October 2021, para. 3(I).

[78] Ibid, para. 3(J).

[79] Ibid, para. 3(H).

[80] *Prosecutor v Simba*, Public Redacted Version of the President's 7 January 2019 Decision on the Early Release of Aloys Simba, MICT-14-62-ES.1, 7 January 2019, Annex A, para. II (d); *Prosecutor v Ćorić*, Further Redacted Public Redacted Version of the Decision of the President on the Early Release of Valentin Ćorić and Related Motions, MICT-17-112-ES.4, 16 January 2019, para. 78(d).

[81] Conditional Early Release Agreement, Annex to the Decision on the Application for Early Release of Sreten Lukić, MICT-14-67-ES.4, 7 October 2021, para. 3(N).

[82] *Prosecutor v Simba*, Public Redacted Version of the President's 7 January 2019 Decision on the Early Release of Aloys Simba, MICT-14-62-ES.1, 7 January 2019, Annex A, para. II(e); *Prosecutor v Ćorić*, Further Redacted Public Redacted Version of the Decision of the President on the Early Release of Valentin Ćorić and Related Motions, MICT-17-112-ES.4, 16 January 2019, para. 78(e).

[83] Conditional Early Release Agreement, Annex to the Decision on the Application for Early Release of Sreten Lukić, MICT-14-67-ES.4, 7 October 2021, para. 3(A)-(D), (K), (O).

criminal law: a duty to 'continue to make efforts to contribute to rehabilitation and resocialisation'. It is extremely unclear what constitutes 'effort', and therefore what the threshold for breaching this condition will be.

3.3 The Expanding Penal Reach of International Sentences

Carr and Blay draw attention to the fact that as conditional release is a penal measure, it is important to pay attention to the 'varying content of the conditions imposed as well as the degree of control and/or support provided' to released persons.[84] Post-release supervision, they argue, is part of the 'widening of the nets of penal control' witnessed in domestic criminal justice systems.[85] Contemporary standards also warn that the total 'package' of sanctions must be 'proportionate and feasible for the individual in their own particular circumstances'.[86] The UN recommends that the conditions imposed be 'as few as possible'.[87] It is therefore important to appreciate the impact of community measures from a qualitative perspective, taking into consideration the lived experience of supervision and the 'weight, breadth and tightness of conditional release and post-custodial supervision'.[88]

Although conditions should be individualised, they are often imposed in a standardised manner in domestic systems.[89] International criminal courts also automatically apply an extensive list of conditions to all offenders granted CER.[90] In addition to the vagueness of many conditions, the rigidity of the range of (general) conditions imposed may undermine the obligation to individualise conditions in light of the particular circumstances and rights of the offender and (any) *specific risk* they pose.[91] It is not apparent that all of these conditions are necessary or appropriate for all convicted persons. This approach may in fact be counter-productive. Campbell argues that reliance on a large number of general conditions indicates a crime control approach to supervision that may result in higher levels of violations and act as an obstacle to re-entry.[92]

---

84 Nicola Carr and Ester Blay, 'Parole and prisoner release: Exploring rationalities across time and place' (2019) 11(3) *European Journal of Probation* 119–123 at 120.

85 Ibid.

86 Commentary to Rule 60 ERCSM.

87 Rule 12.2 Tokyo Rules. See also Rule 4 ERCSM.

88 Carr and Blay, note 84 at 120.

89 Beyens et al., note 59 at 14.

90 Art. 9(C)(i) PDCER.

91 Rule 60 ERCSM; Rule 12.4 Tokyo Rules.

92 Campbell, note 63 at 223.

Rather than being used to individualise post-release control, special conditions imposed by the RSCSL have been used to require the re-enactment of already performed pre-requisites for release, enable the monitoring of a releasee's health, create obligations for Court officials, and impose new and unprecedented sanctions or measures. At the MICT, though not labelled as special conditions, President Meron also sought proof from a convicted person that his family would accept responsibility for him and his medical care if released.[93]

Core elements crucial for conditional release are included in the conditions imposed on released persons by both Courts – monitoring systems, public safety in both general and post-conflict terms and risk factors for recidivism (preventing atrocity denial and glorification). There are also conditions that seek to protect the administration and legacies of international criminal justice institutions. However, the vagueness, broad scope and penal impact of some conditions are indicative of the growing penal reach and evolving control exercised by international criminal courts and tribunals through the implementation of sanctions.

4 OVERSEEING CONDITIONAL EARLY RELEASE IN INTERNATIONAL CRIMINAL LAW

4.1 Overseeing Conditional Release at the RSCSL

Geo-political connections between the Special Court and the country of residence of the majority of convicted persons, and an underpinning legal framework which facilitated Government cooperation with requests to arrest and transfer persons into RSCSL custody, clearly helped to create an operational monitoring system. The RSCSL model provides a frame for analysing how conditional release can be assisted by community participation on the one hand, and why control-orientated monitoring powers need to be constrained and overseen to ensure respect for the dignity of released persons on the other. RSCSL practice also highlights the direct responsibility international courts may have to assume to monitor conditional release when reliance on national authorities is problematic.

---

93 *Prosecutor v Simba*, Public Redacted Version of the President's 7 January 2019 Decision on the Early Release of Aloys Simba, MICT-14-62-ES.1, 7 January 2019, para. 16.

4.1.1 Reintegrative support and community participation

Conditional release should aim not only to reduce re-offending but also to support social rehabilitation and reintegration.[94] A failure to provide reintegration preparation and support may mean that the release system is dictated by simple managerialist capacity concerns.[95] Supervision should involve control *and* support. Support encompasses advice, assistance with material resettlement needs (employment, housing and education), psychological and social support to enhance successful reintegration, and motivation with compliance.[96] The general conditions listed in the RSCSL CER scheme reveal a control-orientated system. Unsurprisingly, the monitoring authority has been assigned a control-focused role. Moreover, some criteria for release use a lack of available support as grounds for denying CER.[97]

One potential source of support that the RSCSL scheme does promote is community participation. The monitoring authority's mandate to implement release decisions is stated to be 'supported' by local paramount chiefs and members of the community.[98] In addition, members of civil society, Chiefdom speakers and community leaders have pledged their willingness to take part in monitoring CER and to ensure released individuals abide by the terms of their release.[99] It is unclear, however, what this support or collaboration means in practice. Contemporary standards recognise the importance of including public and private community organisations and individuals in the implementation of community sanctions.[100] The creation of a complementary working relationship with the community is a 'major resource' that provides 'an opportunity for members of the community to contribute to the protection of

---

94 ERCSM, Scope and Purpose A; Rules 10.1, 12.2 Tokyo Rules.

95 Martine Herzog-Evans, 'Setting the Stage: Defining the Concepts' in Herzog-Evans (ed) *Offender Release and Supervision: The Role of Courts and the Use of Discretion* (Wolf Legal Publishers, 2014) at 13.

96 Paras 9, 15 RCR; paras 55, 61 PR; Rule 10.4 Tokyo Rules.

97 See for example Chapter 4, section 4.3.

98 RSCSL Press Release, 'CDF Convict Moinina Fofana Returned to Bo' Freetown, Sierra Leone, 16 March 2015; Second Annual Report of the President of the RSCSL, January 2015 – December 2015 at 20.

99 *Prosecutor v Fofana and Kondewa*, Decision of the President on Application for Conditional Early Release, SCSL-04-14-ES (1270–1291) 11 August 2014, para. 24; *Prosecutor v Kondewa*, Decision of the President on Application for Conditional Early Release, RSCSL-04-14-ES (1581–1604), The Hague, 29 May 2017, para. 21; *Prosecutor v Gbao*, Decision of the President on Application for Conditional Early Release, RSCSL-04-15-ES, 8 September 2020, paras 41–43, 45–46, 48, 50, 52, 53–54.

100 Rule 31 ERCSM.

their society'.[101] Accordingly, the need for public participation and the importance of the role of the community in the implementation of CER should be highlighted.[102] This form of collaboration can help to meet the reintegrative needs of offenders by helping them develop meaningful social ties and promoting their social inclusion while also enhancing community safety.[103] Conversely, the lack of such engagement can result in an 'insular' system that fails to 'achieve full potential in narrowing the gap between offenders and the community'.[104] It is particularly important in a post-atrocity crime context that justice is not 'administered in isolation from the community it seeks to serve'.[105] However, it must be clear what role these community-based groups or individuals can undertake.[106] Moreover, the imposing or implementing authorities cannot delegate their overall responsibility and must ensure that such bodies are 'responsible and reliable' and show respect for the rights of offenders and the requirements of confidentiality.[107]

4.1.2 Reducing potential for abuse of power

It is a fundamental principle that conditions imposed on a conditionally released individual should not be interpreted and/or implemented in a manner that 'aggravate[s] their afflictive nature' and affected rights should not be restricted to a greater extent than necessary.[108] Failure to do so would create not only injustice but also resistance and unwillingness to comply.[109] The difficulty facing the monitoring authority is the vagueness of the conditions imposed. For example, a convicted person may be detained if they 'pose a risk of harm to any person'. What constitutes 'risk' or 'harm' in this context? The current lack of clarity may leave the system prone to abuse. For example, the supervisee must agree to submit to searches of his person, property and possessions. There is no discussion of any need to have reasonable cause or to exercise care to respect the individual's dignity and property during such searches. Nor does it provide any system to complain about the frequency or potentially unwarranted nature of such use of power. Under human rights law, interference with private and family life should be strictly limited and proportionate.[110]

101 Rule 17 Tokyo Rules.
102 Rule 18.2, 18.4, Tokyo Rules.
103 Rules 50–51 ERCSM.
104 Commentary to Rule 50 ERCSM.
105 Commentary to Rule 51 ERCSM.
106 Commentary on Rule 31 ERCSM.
107 Rules 53–54 ERCSM.
108 Rule 11 ERCSM; Rule 3.10 Tokyo Rules.
109 Commentary on Rule 11 ERCSM.
110 Commentary on Rule 8 ERCSM.

An overly zealous application of supervisory powers can prevent successful reintegration, facilitate a legitimised form of harassment and ultimately lead to the deprivation of liberty of an individual without real cause. Harassment, defined as 'the vexing, troubling or worrying of … offenders through unduly frequent controlling or checking activities' should be prohibited and safeguards should be put in place to avoid 'jeopardising the offender's sense of self respect, family and other intimate relationships, community links and ability to function in the community [and] … to protect them from insult or improper curiosity or publicity'.[111] The PDCER should highlight the duty to respect and protect the rights, privacy and dignity of offenders, their families and others and to ensure that supervision does not aggravate the conditions imposed or become a form of harassment.[112] Codes of conduct for implementing staff can help to confer legitimacy and credibility upon community measures.[113]

Violations of offenders' rights during the monitoring process can undermine the offenders' cooperation with CER and detract from its legitimacy.[114] A complaints procedure and oversight system should be put in place. Supervisees should be able to access a fair, impartial and effective procedure that can investigate and respond to complaints regarding their supervision.[115] UN standards state that an offender should be entitled to make a 'complaint to a judicial or other competent independent authority on matters affecting his or her individual rights in the implementation of noncustodial measures'[116] and that 'appropriate machinery shall be provided for the recourse and, if possible, redress of any grievance related to non-compliance with internationally recognized human rights'.[117] Moreover, the work of the monitoring authority should be regularly reviewed by an external and independent body.[118]

4.1.3 Increased international involvement due to efficacy concerns

The concerns that transpired in practice at the RSCL, however, were not in relation to the abuse of monitoring powers to the detriment of releasees but rather to the abuse of the monitoring powers to the detriment of the RSCSL's legitimacy. The first breach dealt with by the RSCL resulted from the police assisting a released person to doctor the reporting register so that he could

111 Commentary on Rule 8 ERCSM.
112 Rules 3.9, 3.11 Tokyo Rules; Para. 2 PR; Rule 8 ERCSM.
113 Rule 4 ERCSM.
114 Commentary on Rule 8 ERCSM.
115 Para. 34 RCR; Paras 14, 99, 100 PR; Rule 3.6 Tokyo Rules.
116 Rule 3.6 Tokyo Rules.
117 Rule 3.7 Tokyo Rules.
118 Paras 15, 102–103 PR; Rule 13 ERCSM.

attend a political meeting.[119] This police complicity, which led directly to the violation of the terms of release, resulted in public admonishments from the RSCSL, and the Registrar being tasked with working with the police to ensure strict performance of their duty to enforce release conditions in the future. Numerous meetings with senior police officials ensued, and training sessions were provided for officers on the CER system as part of a re-engagement process. Significantly, the challenges identified in *Fofana* resulted in the RSCSL having to play a more direct role in the operation of the system for supervising releasees through outreach, training, conducting spot checks, authorisation of travel, and designing monitoring regimes.[120]

4.2 Overseeing Conditional Release at the MICT

The Statute, Rules, Practice Direction, UN Security Council Resolution 2622, and MICT release jurisprudence do not refer to any supervising authority or set out any requirements for selecting one. The lack of an identifiable legal basis for the obligation on States to enforce community sanctions imposed by an international tribunal remains. In contrast to the negotiated cooperation between the RSCSL and the Sierra Leone Government,[121] the MICT jurisprudence refers to the duty of UN member States to cooperate with the Mechanism under Article 28 of the Statute entitled 'Cooperation and Judicial Assistance'.[122] This provision was interpreted as obliging all states willing to accept a released prisoner onto their territory for the purpose of relocation to abide by the conditions imposed on early release.[123] The vague obligation

---

[119] See Chapter 4, section 8.1.

[120] See Fourth Annual Report of the President of the RSCSL, January 2017 to December 2017 at 20, 29.

[121] An Agreement to Perform the Duties of the Monitoring Authority, signed 27 September 2015 and 2 March 2015. See *Prosecutor v Fofana*, Disposition of the Matter of Moninia Fofana's Violations of the Terms of his Conditional Early Release, RSCLS-04-14-ES (1416–1440) 25 April 2016, para. 73.

[122] Article 28 MICTSt; *Prosecutor v Ćorić,* Further Redacted Public Redacted Version of the Decision of the President on the Early Release of Valentin Ćorić and Related Motions, MICT-17-112-ES.4, 16 January 2019, para. 79; *Prosecutor v Simba*, Public Redacted Version of the President's 7 January 2019 Decision on the Early Release of Aloys Simba, MICT-14-62-ES.1, 7 January 2019, para. 84(a).

[123] *Prosecutor v Ćorić*, Further Redacted Public Redacted Version of the Decision of the President on the Early Release of Valentin Ćorić and Related Motions, MICT-17-112-ES.4, 16 January 2019, para. 79; *Prosecutor v Simba*, Public Redacted Version of the President's 7 January 2019 Decision on the Early Release of Aloys Simba, MICT-14-62-ES.1, 7 January 2019, para. 84(b) and Annex A, para. IV.

also apparently meant that no order would be required from the MICT for the detention and transfer of releasees if there was a suspected breach of conditions or the individual posed a risk of harm.[124]

However, this and similar cooperation obligations under the ICTY and ICTR statutes have consistently been interpreted to apply to pre-trial and trial-related processes. This is not surprising given that the relevant statutory provisions directly and explicitly refer only to the investigation and prosecution stages of the international criminal justice process. For example, Article 28(1) of the MICT Statute directs that states are obliged to 'cooperate with the Mechanism in the *investigation and prosecution* of persons covered by Article 1 of this Statute'. It is quite astonishing that the same provision has been interpreted and applied in precisely the opposite manner in relation to conditional early release for ICTY convicted prisoners. The bizarre result is that the very states that cannot accept ICTY convicted persons for sentence enforcement purposes are now, by virtue of the same statutory provision, supposedly obliged to supervise the conditions of their release in the community. In other words, the states now relied upon to enforce the non-custodial element of international sentences were, and continue to be, barred from enforcing custodial sanctions imposed by the ICTY.[125] This legal bar to sentence enforcement was completely side-stepped in the acceptance of these barred states to enforce community supervision.

Perhaps the reference to Article 28 was intended to allude to the duty to comply without undue delay with any request for assistance or an order issued by a Single Judge or Trial Chamber to identify or locate persons, take testimony and produce evidence, arrest or detain persons and surrender or transfer them to the Mechanism. However, Article 28(2) specifically states that this duty relates to cases involving persons covered by Article 1 of the Statute. Article 1 sets out the competence of the Mechanism, which includes the continuation of the jurisdiction, rights and obligations of the ICTY and ICTR.[126] The ICTY and ICTR did not operate a conditional early release system and sentence enforcement was a voluntary cooperation act.

This current jurisprudential approach therefore goes against the consistently reaffirmed understanding that this obligation does NOT extend to sentence enforcement matters.[127] Sentence enforcement depends on the two-stage, double opt-in process whereby enforcing states first typically accept to be

---

124 *Prosecutor v Simba*, Interim Order for Further Submissions, MICT-14-62-ES.1, 23 October 2018.

125 See Mulgrew, *Towards the Development of the International Penal System* (CUP, 2013) at 35.

126 Art. 1(1) MICTSt.

127 Mulgrew, note 125 at 33.

considered as potential enforcers of international sentences generally, with actual enforcement depending on the State's specific agreement to enforce the sentence of a particular convicted person. States willing to enforce custodial sentences enter into agreements with the respective court or tribunal. These bilateral enforcement agreements do not extend to the enforcement of non-custodial sanctions or measures. Considering that sentence enforcement is not compulsory (the primary penalty), it is unclear how community sanction enforcement could become compulsory. MICT Presidents have attempted to underpin the reference to the Chapter VII 'obligation' (that does not extend to the enforcement of non-custodial sanctions) with reference to political assurances or guarantees made by the approached State of relocation.

Other obvious issues arise for the model relied upon. No practical arrangements have been put in place, and no specific authority has been appointed to monitor conditions. A state may not (yet) have been identified to accept a released person. There is no discussion in any legal or policy documents about the type of body the monitoring authority should be, what role it should play, how regular monitoring should be … The details have been consigned instead to the conditions attached to individual release decisions or agreements.

5. DEALING WITH BREACH OF CONDITIONS

Despite the clear differences in terms of a legal base for conditional release at the two international courts, even sharper distinctions can be drawn when the process for recalling persons to custody is examined. The MICT's wholly inappropriate original model of relying on contempt law is examined below, as are the consequences of the current laconic system for dealing with breaches of conditions. Ways to improve the RSCSL model are also discussed, including the pros and possibilities for delegating responsibility to monitoring authorities to deal with minor or technical violations, and the need to include greater specificity in relation to the implementation of the most severe consequences for a breach of conditions: recall to prison to serve the original sentence.

5.1 Recall and Consequences for Breach of Conditions at the MICT

The RSCL established a detailed procedure for dealing with alleged or admitted breaches of the terms of conditional early release agreements. This procedure sets out the terms for arrest and transfer, time limits for processes and nominates personnel responsible for critical decisions and actions. The Practice Direction provides a coherent legal framework to govern the determination of probable cause in the event of an alleged breach, a process to consider granting release pending hearings, and stipulations on the hearing on the merits or proceeding with disposition. When the procedure didn't work as planned, it was reviewed and amended.[128]

When the MICT conditional early release system was introduced by the inclusion of a simple sentence in the 2019 Practice Direction, no procedure for dealing with the breach of conditions was outlined. In stark contrast to the RSCSL, it is very difficult to deduce the procedure for dealing with violations of the terms of conditional release in MICT jurisprudence. President Meron simply indicated, in decisions granting conditional release, that the authorities of the State of relocation would arrest the person and transfer them back to the MICT (without the need for a specific legal order) for consideration of the allegations by the President.[129] In a further departure from RSCSL policy, which clearly outlines the range of possible consequences that can result should a breach of conditions be established, early CER jurisprudence stated that this would result in the convicted person being held in contempt of court pursuant to Rule 90 of the Rules of Procedure and Evidence and conditional release being revoked.[130]

Benefits could arise from adopting a contempt frame for recall. As an inherent power, judges can decide whether or not to initiate proceedings for contempt, even if a prima facie case is established, based on considerations of the gravity of the conduct, motivations and the penal goals that would be served by doing so.[131] Legal aid is available to indigent persons indicted or charged with contempt (although Rule 43 restricts the assignment of defence counsel

---

128 Fourth Annual Report of the President of the RSCSL, January 2017 to December 2017, at 6.

129 *Prosecutor v Simba*, Public Redacted Version of the President's 7 January 2019 Decision on the Early Release of Aloys Simba, MICT-14-62-ES.1, 7 January 2019, Annex A, paras III-IV; *Prosecutor v Ćorić*, Further Redacted Public Redacted Version of the Decision of the President on the Early Release of Valentin Ćorić and Related Motions, MICT-17-112-ES.4, 16 January 2019, para. 78(f)–(g).

130 *Prosecutor v Ćorić*, Further Redacted Public Redacted Version of the Decision of the President on the Early Release of Valentin Ćorić and Related Motions, MICT-17-112-ES.4, 16 January 2019, para. 78(f)–(g); *Prosecutor v Simba*, Interim Order for Further Submissions, MICT-14-62-ES.1, 23 October 2018; *Prosecutor v Simba*, Public Redacted Version of the President's 7 January 2019 Decision on the Early Release of Aloys Simba, MICT-14-62-ES.1, 7 January 2019, para. 84(c) and Annex A, paras III–IV.

131 *Prosecutor v Bagosora et al*, Decision on Reconsideration of Order to Reduce Witness List and on Motion for Contempt for Violation of that Order, ICTR-98-41-T, 1 March 2004, para. 9; *Prosecutor v Nsengimana*, Decision on Prosecution Appeal of Decision Concerning Improper Contact with Prosecution Witnesses, ICTR-01-69-A, 16 December 2010, para. 17; *Prosecutor v Nshogoza*, Judgment, ICTR-2007-91-A, 15 March 2010, para. 57; *In the Matter of Deogratius*

to suspects or accused persons, not convicted persons). Further, reliance on Rule 90 would reduce the scope of the recall power, as it requires the breach to have occurred 'knowingly and wilfully' – meaning accidental or negligent breaches would not be punishable.[132] In other words, the violator would need to have had actual knowledge of the order and intended to consciously disregard or violate the order.[133] Moreover, contempt decisions are subject to appeal (both the finding and the penalty imposed),[134] a right not typically available for sentence enforcement decisions.[135] Finally, persons subjected to a custodial sanction following a finding of contempt can apply for early release.[136]

5.1.1 Problems with relying on contempt as the legal basis for recall

However, the law on contempt is designed to prevent the frustration of the administration of justice, not to deal with sentence enforcement matters. Rule 90 governs the procedure for prosecuting and sanctioning contempt of court. Its invocation as a means to operationalise conditional early release is problematic due to its inappropriateness for the task in legal, procedural and penological terms.

Under Rule 90, if a Chamber or Single Judge (not an unknown monitoring authority in an unknown state) 'has reason to believe' that a person may be in contempt of the ICTY, ICTR or the MICT, it will refer the matter to the President. The President must then designate a Single Judge to deal with the matter. The Single Judge can refer the investigation to the Prosecutor, request the Registrar to appoint an amicus curiae to do so, or initiate proceedings themselves.[137] Further, the Single Judge must determine whether there are

---

Sebureze and Maximilian Turinabo, Decisions on Allegations of Contempt of the ICTR, MICT-13-40-R9017, July 2013, paras 14, 18.

132 Rule 90(A) MICT RPE.

133 *Prosecutor v Rukundo*, Decision on the Haguma Report, ICTR-2001-70-T, 14 December 2007, para. 14; *Prosecutor v Kajelijeli*, Decision on Kajelijeli's Motion to Hold Members of the Office of the Prosecutor in Contempt of the Tribunal (Rule 77(C)), ICTR-98-44A-T, 15 November 2002, para. 10; *Prosecutor v Karemera et al*, Decision on Defence Motions for Appointment of Amicus Curiae, ICTR-98-44-T, 26 September 2007, para. 8; *Prosecutor v Nchamihigo*, Decision on Defence Motion on Contempt of Court and Reconsideration of Protective Measures for Defence Witnesses, ICTR-2001-63-T, 9 August 2007, para. 9; *Prosecutor v Nshogoza*, Judgment, ICTR-07-91-T, 7 July 2009, para. 179; *Prosecutor v Mladić*, Decision on Renewed Motion for Contempt, MICT-13-56-A, 15 May 2018 at 3.

134 Rules 90(J) and 91(J) MICT RPE.

135 See PDER Rev 3, para. 24.

136 Decision of the President on the Early Release of Florence Hartmann, MICT-15–57, 29 March 2016.

137 Rule 90(C)(i)–(iii) MICT RPE.

sufficient grounds to proceed before pursuing prosecution.[138] The Rule *does not* empower the President to investigate or decide whether to proceed (as Meron claimed he would have power to do).[139]

In addition to the fact that Rule 90 does not grant the President the power, the offence contemplated under the Rule relates to persons 'who knowingly and wilfully interfere with the administration of justice'.[140] The focus is on proceedings before the tribunal,[141] with no reference made to a potential use to deal with violations of post-conviction conditions of release. The creation of the offence of contempt has already been the subject of criticism on account of the fact that rules should not be used to create (new) criminal offences. This critique was rejected on the ground that it falls within the inherent jurisdiction of a tribunal to ensure its jurisdiction is not frustrated and to safeguard its basic *judicial* functions.[142] Does this inherent power to protect judicial functions (such as the intimidation or interference with witnesses),[143] extend to the (not inherent) power of the MICT to supervise the enforcement of custodial or community sanctions? The closest explicit ground would be the failure to comply with the order of a Chamber or Single Judge, 'without just excuse'.[144] However, Rule 90 refers to failures to attend trial or produce documents – not a failure to attend for reporting duties at national police stations. Moreover, Rule 90 refers to a failure to comply with orders issued by Chamber or a Single Judge – not a Presidential Decision on early release.[145] While some argue that the conduct punishable as contempt is non-exhaustive, using contempt to punish the breach of conditions while serving a sentence in the community (such as drinking alcohol) seems hard to justify in relation to either the letter or spirit of Rule 90.

138 Rule 90(D) MICT RPE.

139 Another possibility is for the case to be referred to national jurisdictions – see Art 6 MICTSt and Rule 90(D) MICT RPE; Case against *Petar Jojić and Vjerica Radeta*, Decision Re-examining the Referral of a Case to the Republic of Serbia, MICT-17-111-R90, 13 May 2019.

140 Art. 1(4) MICTSt.

141 Rule 90(A) MICT RPE.

142 Silvia D'Ascoli, 'Sentencing Contempt of Court in International Criminal Justice: An Unforeseen Problem Concerning Sentencing and Penalties' (2007) 5 *Journal of International Criminal Justice* 735–756 at 737–739.

143 See Rule 90(A) MICT RPE.

144 Rule 90(A)(iii) MICT RPE.

145 Rule 90(A)(iii) MICT RPE.

5.1.2 Penalties for contempt v consequences for violating release conditions

Reliance on a contempt frame would also necessitate reliance on the *penalties* permitted for contempt of court.[146] For RSCSL convicted persons, the consequences for a breach of conditions can include the modification of conditions or revocation of release and return to prison to serve (up to) the remaining term. The regulatory penalty range for contempt of court at the MICT, in contrast, includes the possibility of imposing a custodial term of *up to seven years* in prison or a *fine* of up to €50,000, or both penalties.[147] This would introduce a pecuniary penalty for the first time with respect to sentence enforcement at the UN Tribunals. If a fine is imposed, the Rules also permit a Single Judge (not the President) to convert the fine to a term of imprisonment of up to seven months for a failure to pay the sum within a specified period or to impose an additional penalty for wilful failure to pay.[148] More fundamentally, serious questions about the legality of these penal consequences must be raised. These penalties do not provide for international transfers and recall to imprisonment for a term in excess of seven years. In practice, sentences for contempt have often been short to moderate.[149] Examples of sentence lengths imposed by the ICTY for contempt (under Rule 77) include two to four months for a refusal to testify[150] and two years for a refusal to remove material from a website.[151]

It is interesting to note, however, that international judges have stated that they have the power to (partially) suspend sentences for contempt: given their

146 Rule 90(B) MICT RPE.

147 Rule 90(G) MICT RPE. This differs from previous possible penalties at the ICTY – up to seven years' imprisonment and a fine of up to €100,000 or both (Rule 77(G)) and at the ICTR – up to five years' imprisonment or a fine of up to USD10,000 or both (Rule 77(G)). At the RSCSL, the maximum penalty that can be imposed for contempt is seven years' imprisonment or 20 million leones or both (Rule 77(G)). At the ICC, the Court may impose a term of imprisonment not exceeding five years, a fine or both (Art. 70(3) ICCSt.). Fines can be imposed for each conviction and applied cumulatively up to a maximum value of 50% of the convicted person's identifiable assets and property (following a deduction for the financial needs of the convicted person and their dependents) (Rule 166(3) ICC RPE).

148 Rule 91(C)(iv), (D) MICT RPE.

149 D'Ascoli, note 142 at 754.

150 In the Contempt Case of Milan Tupajić, Judgment on Allegations of Contempt, IT-95-5/18-R77.2, 24 February 2012, para. 35; Contempt Proceedings Against Dragan Jokić, Judgment on Allegations of Contempt, IT-05-88-R77.1, 27 March 2009, para. 42.

151 In the matter of Vojislav Šešelj, Judgment, IT-03-67-R77.42, 8 June 2012, paras 57–58.

inherent power to impose them, the power to suspend sentences represents an integral part of their discretion in sentence determination.[152] At the SCSL, a decision to grant a conditional discharge was based on the fact that the rules only stipulated maximum penalties, not minimum ones.[153] The contempt penalty range could therefore provide a flexible approach to dealing with conditional release issues.

Flexibility aside, it is clear that reliance on contempt penalties to deal with recall risks violating the principle of *nulla poena sine lege*. Even within the contempt context, it has been questioned whether the creation of criminal penalties and the numerous amendments to the rules align with the 'principle that there must be no punishment except in accordance with fixed and predetermined penalties provided for by the law … [that] resides at the very heart of criminal law as one of the basic rights of the accused and as a self-evident principle of justice'.[154] The *nulla poena* principle 'prescribes that penalties to be applied shall not be heavier than the ones applicable at the time when the criminal offence was committed' and should be precisely outlined as to their duration. President Meron seemed to indicate that Rule 90 could be used to exceed the maximum duration established by Rule 90(G) – the period remaining to be served on the sentence could be longer than the maximum permitted custodial penalty of seven years.

The jurisprudence of the SCSL is also instructive on the matter. At the SCSL, an increase to the potential penalty range for contempt of court introduced after the date when the offences were committed could not be applied retrospectively.[155] Further, it has been held that fines are not appropriate sanctions if family members will ultimately be responsible for paying them.[156] Further, where convictions resulted in custodial sentences being imposed for contempt

---

152 See *Prosecutor v Milosević*, Contempt Proceedings Against Kosta Bulatović, Decision on Contempt of the Tribunal, IT-02-54-R77.4 13 May 2005, paras 18–19; *Prosecutor v Jelena Rašić*, Contempt Appeal Judgment, IT-98-32/1-R77.2.A, 16 November 2012, paras 17–18, 28–29. See also *Independent Counsel v H.P. Bangura, S. Kargbo, S.B. Kanu and B.B. Kamara*, Sentencing Judgement in Contempt Proceedings, SCSL-11-02-T, 11 October 2012, para. 92.

153 *Independent Counsel v M.F. Brima, N.B. Bah Jalloh, E. Kamara and A. Kamara,* Sentencing Judgment in Contempt Proceedings, SCSL-2005-02/SCSL-2005–03, 21 September 2005, paras 15, 17–19, 35–40.

154 D'Ascoli, note 142 at 752.

155 *Prosecutor v Senessie*, Sentencing Judgement, SCSL-2011-01-T, 12 July 2012, para. 2; *Independent Counsel v H.P. Bangura, S. Kargbo, S.B. Kanu and B.B. Kamara*, Sentencing Judgement in Contempt Proceedings, SCSL-11-02-T, 11 October 2012, para. 61.

156 *Independent Counsel v H.P. Bangura, S. Kargbo, S.B. Kanu and B.B. Kamara*, Sentencing Judgement in Contempt Proceedings, SCSL-11-02-T,

on persons already in prison for the commission of core crimes (Kamara and Kanu), it was ordered that the term must be served consecutively to this sentence and not concurrently.[157] This further casts doubt on the suitability of contempt penalties as a basis for recall.

5.1.3 The consequences of a laconic scheme

Despite the broad discretion of judges to decide which penalty or combination thereof to impose in typical contempt cases, these penalty options do not correlate to the purpose and usual options for recall from conditional early release, nor indeed grant the President the power to impose them. More seriously, a finding of guilt for contempt would typically constitute a new criminal offence, and result in the imposition of penalties not permissible for the commission of core crimes. The lack of a legal basis and the aggravating potential of these penalties would raise serious questions about the legality of reliance on Rule 90 as a means to impose consequences for the violation of release conditions. The extent of the gap between its intended and proposed use, and the aggravating impact on the original custodial sentence could even trigger debate as to whether its use would violate the fundamental principle of *nulla poena sine lege.*

The *nulla poena* principle requires specificity in punishment: the explicit legal definition of the content and extent of the punishment to be imposed in particular cases.[158] The need to uphold the right to liberty and the legality of penalties should be realised, according to Dana, by applying a progressive interpretation and application of this principle in the international criminal justice context to ensure not only consistency but also the realisation of justice in the distribution of punishment.[159] In other words, sanctions should be explicit, be provided for by law, and individuals should be given fair notice of the specific consequences of violating a particular law.[160]

While a distinction can be drawn between measures that constitute a penalty and measures that concern the execution or enforcement of a penalty, this

---

11 October 2012, para. 89; *Independent Counsel v Prince Taylor,* Sentencing Judgement, SCSL-12-02-T, 14 February 2013, para. 55.

157 *Independent Counsel v H.P. Bangura, S. Kargbo, S.B. Kanu and B.B. Kamara*, Sentencing Judgement in Contempt Proceedings, SCSL-11-02-T, 11 October 2012, paras 93–94.

158 Franz von Liszt, 'The Rationale for the *Nullum Crimen* Principle' (2007) 5 *Journal of International Criminal Justice* 1009–1013.

159 Shahram Dana, 'Beyond Retroactivity to Realising Justice: A Theory on the Principle of Legality in International Criminal Law Sentencing' (2009) 99 *Journal of Criminal Law and Criminology* 857–928 at 859–863.

160 Ibid at 862.

distinction is not always 'clear-cut'. Broader understandings of what constitutes a penalty (in favour of the accused or convicted person) are emerging under human rights law, particularly where a new approach or measure will lead to the redefinition of the scope of the penalty imposed to the accused or convicted person's detriment.[161] In the recall context, it is unclear how a penalty can be imposed without a finding of guilt for contempt and the determination of an additional criminal conviction (not alluded to and certainly not made explicit in the agreed or imposed CERA) and punishment, which may have to be served consecutively.

Violations of the *nulla poena* principle (that seeks to constrain arbitrary judicial decision-making) are often concealed through 'creative legal fiction' or 'camouflaged behind a veil of legal application that gives an impression, albeit a false one, that a court has come to a legally justifiable decision'.[162] Reference to Rule 90, in the absence of a bespoke or specific legal or policy frame for recall, feels like an attempt to create such an impression.

Perhaps in cognisance of these numerous issues, President Agius did not refer to Rule 90 or contempt of court in the *Lukić* conditional release decision. Rather, he simply stated that 'any failure to strictly adhere to these conditions would immediately jeopardise his conditional early release'.[163] The CERA further states that violations or a failure to comply fully with any conditions *may result in the revocation* of early release at the sole discretion of the President.[164] This decision moved away from the problematic invocation of the contempt framework by Meron. Agius failed however to articulate any legal basis to underpin the power to recall a person to custody or to justify an international prisoner transfer. He also failed to explain the process that would be used to determine if allegations are founded and the consequences that could be imposed following a finding of a breach. Agius referred simply to the broad statutory discretion of Presidents of the MICT to grant release

---

161 Susana Sanz-Caballero, 'The Principle of *Nulla Poena Sine Lege* Revisited: The Retrospective Application of Criminal Law in the Eyes of the European Court of Human Rights' (2017) 28(3) *European Journal of International Law* 787–817 at 791, 810.

162 Evgeny Tikhonravov, '*Nulla Poena Sine Lege* in Continental Criminal Law: Historical and Theoretical Analysis' (2019) 13 *Criminal Law and Philosophy* 215–224 at 217, 222–223.

163 *Prosecutor v Lukić*, Decision on the Application for Early Release of Sreten Lukić, MICT-14-67-ES.4, 7 October 2021, para. 95.

164 Conditional Early Release Agreement, Annex to the Decision on the Application for Early Release of Sreten Lukić, MICT-14-67-ES.4, 7 October 2021, para. 6.

as the legal basis for recalling such individuals.[165] The only additional detail appears to be that a request from the MICT may be required prior to arrest in some instances.[166]

5.2 Recall and Consequences for Breach of Conditions at the RSCSL

The RSCSL CER system, in stark contrast, makes the potential consequences for violating conditions of release explicit. The Practice Direction states that if a breach of conditions has been established, release can be revoked and the convicted person sent back to prison, or release can be granted on modified conditions, or the convicted person can be released on the same conditions.[167] Judicial decisions as to the appropriateness of a particular consequence are to be made on a case-by-case basis in light of the circumstances of the particular case.[168] This individualised approach aligns with contemporary standards which advocate for a detailed examination of the facts before imposing a consequence and that a determination that a condition has been breached should not 'automatically lead to the imposition of a custodial measure'.[169] However, the RSCSL system (and others) could further support reintegration by permitting (effective) monitoring authority officials to deal with minor, technical and once-off transgressions, without the need to automatically deprive an individual of their liberty. Further, increased clarity about the scope of the option to re-imprison persons that have breached conditions should be clarified, and its imposition guided by the principles of necessity and proportionality.

5.2.1 Dealing with minor transgressions

While the RSCSL scheme does comply with contemporary standards in so far as convicted persons are aware of the range of potential consequences for non-compliance,[170] it is unclear which consequence will apply for which type of breach. Many conditions are very general in nature, and the breach of particular conditions may be of a trivial nature. Contemporary standards state that controlling activities should only be undertaken to the extent that they are necessary for the proper implementation of CER and must be in proportion

---

165 Ibid.

166 Ibid, paras 6–8.

167 Art. 12(J) PDCER.

168 *Prosecutor v Fofana*, Disposition of the Matter of Moninia Fofana's Violations of the Terms of his Conditional Early Release, RSCSL-04-14-ES, (1416–1440) Freetown, 25 April 2016, para. 24.

169 Rule 14.1–3 Tokyo Rules; Rule 67 ERCSM.

170 Rules 15, 62 ERCSM.

to the offence committed.[171] While 'significant failures to comply' should rightly be reported to the deciding authority (RSCSL),[172] the implementing authority (MA) should be in a position to deal with minor transgressions using discretionary or administrative procedures.[173] Moreover, the MA should be in a position to determine whether a violation is a minor transgression or a significant failure to comply.[174] Instead, the only option currently available under the RSCSL scheme for any violation is for the convicted person to be arrested, transferred to RSCSL custody (which may require recalling custodial capacity from the Home State), and for the RSCSL to issue both a Presidential determination and organise a hearing on the merits/disposition.[175]

While granting both authorities power to deal with breaches may raise 'turf' issues,[176] to avoid unnecessary detention and hearings, thought should be given to enabling the MA to deal with the violation of minor general conditions that are unconnected with the criminal conduct underlying the original conviction. This would not involve the removal of RSCSL oversight over such actions but simply enable swifter, less severe reactions to minor transgressions. National systems often have 'considerable latitude' to make decisions and can draw on 'a large range of intermediate options rather than order recall'.[177]

The current approach is also problematic as contemporary standards posit that supervision should not be based solely on sanctioning for non-compliance.[178] Supervision should not be 'rigid or formalistic' but based on 'constant regard for individualisation' to ensure the sanction corresponds with not only the offence but also the characteristics of the offender.[179] In order to achieve this goal, monitoring staff should 'enjoy a sufficient degree of discretion'.[180] Contemporary standards therefore highlight the 'importance of discretion and principled professional judgement' to 'reconcile the demands of consistency

---

171 Rule 34 ERCSM.

172 Rule 65 ERCSM.

173 Rule 64 ERCSM.

174 Commentary on Rule 65 ERCSM.

175 See Pro Forma Draft SCSL Supervision and Transfer Order (Annex D), paras A, D at 4; *Prosecutor v Fofana and Kondewa*, Presidential Order for Detention and Transfer and for Hearing Pursuant to Article 12(F) of the Practice Direction on Conditional Early Release of Persons Convicted by the SCSL, RSCSL-04-14-ES (1297–1300), The Hague, 9 March 2015 at 3.

176 See Boone and Herzog-Evans, note 61 at 85.

177 Martine Herzog-Evans, 'French early release: McProcedures and McRe-entry' (2019) 11(3) *European Journal of Probation* 188–201 at 189.

178 Para. 85 PR.

179 ERCSM, Scope and Purpose C.

180 Rule 32 ERCSM.

and justice with those of individualisation'.[181] The RSCSL CER system does not permit the MA to deal with minor infringements or to modify conditions in light of positive progress by the convicted person.[182] All supervisory responsibilities are retained by the RSCSL.

5.2.2 Re-imprisonment for the remaining term?

Sociological and criminological insights into prisoner recall practice highlight the risk-orientated sensitivity of recall systems that results in technical violations of conditions of release, *not* reoffending, being the most common reason for the return of releasees to custody.[183] Further, as Campbell warns, a heavy-handed response to minor or vague conditions may create a conflict between control and reintegration.[184] As Beyens et al. argue, recall systems should focus on assisting with (rather than disrupting) the ongoing 'reintegration trajectory' and re-entry process that occurs at the end of a sentence: minor or technical breaches should not result in (quasi) automatic return to custody.[185] Further recall should not be considered an irrevocable incapacitating measure but a 'time-out' tool to allow for reflection and the revision of reintegration and re-entry plans.[186] Accordingly, the time spent in custody following recall should be determined in relation to reintegrative potential, with possibilities for release provided.[187]

Against this background, it is clear that when the power to revoke release and order re-imprisonment in international criminal law is analysed, issues of disproportionality may arise. Without a power to grant indeterminate sentences, the RSCSL is supervising lengthy determinate sentences.[188] The remaining term on the sentence could be as long as 16 years. Greater clarity should be introduced to ensure that a return to custody (potentially in another country) is only permissible for serious or continuing breaches that have a sufficient nexus to the original conviction. Further, this option should not only be restricted to

---

181 Commentary on Rule 32 ERCSM.

182 Only the President can make these changes. Para. 7 Pro Forma CERA, Annex C PDCER. See Mujuzi, note 58 at 169.

183 Nicola Padfield, 'Recalling conditionally released prisoners in England and Wales' (2012) 4(1) *European Journal of Probation* 34–45 at 37; Beyens et al., note 59 at 7.

184 Campbell, note 63 at 217.

185 Beyens et al., note 59 at 8, 11, 16–17, 19.

186 Ibid at 19–20.

187 Ibid at 20.

188 See Art. 20(1) RSCSLSt. In terms of sentence length, for example, Sesay is serving a 52-year sentence, Kanu is serving a 50-year sentence, and Kallon is serving a 40-year sentence.

re-imprisonment for the remaining term; specified periods should be possible. Further, convicted persons that are re-imprisoned should be able to re-apply for CER. Given the lengthy sentences and life sentences imposed by the UN Tribunals, these recommendations are equally applicable for the MICT.

6. IS CONDITIONAL EARLY RELEASE POSSIBLE FOR ALL CONVICTED PERSONS?

It is evident that the conditional early release schemes introduced at the MICT and RSCSL have flaws. Despite these problems, they are operational in the sense that convicted persons have been granted early release on the basis that they serve the remainder of their sentences in their country of origin. The system will also operate if a third country grants the person reunification, residency or citizenship rights. The fundamental challenge facing international courts lies in the fact that state cooperation to oversee obligations is voluntary and is typically dependent on political assurances. It is entirely foreseeable, therefore, that this model will not be accessible for persons convicted by the ICTR or the MICT for crimes committed in Rwanda. In sharp contrast to ICTY released persons, who can usually return home or be released on conditions without obstacle,[189] ICTR released persons ‘cannot return home, nor have they been able to find countries willing to grant them asylum and safety’.[190] As a result, persons released following the completion of sentences imposed by the ICTR often experience a crisis of constructive statelessness and a situation of indefinite and arbitrary liberty deprivation.[191] ICTR released persons often become trapped in custodial-like environments in Host States and states of relocation, with ‘no jobs, no source of income, no identification documents, no adequate immigration status, or means of survival independent’ of the MICT.[192] To overcome the problem of their de facto statelessness in Tanzania (the ICTR’s host state), ICTR acquitted and released persons were transferred to Niger in December 2021 with promises of resettlement and residency rights.

---

[189] Lina Strupinskiene, ‘Life after Conviction at the International Criminal Tribunal for the former Yugoslavia’ (2023) 21 *JICJ* 113–135.

[190] Cécille Lecolle, ‘Relocation Issues of Released and Acquitted at International Criminal Courts and Tribunals – a Defence Perspective’ (2023) 21(1) *JICJ* 167–184 at 169, 172. Countries that previously accepted released persons onto their territory (France, Belgium, Italy) have refused to do so again.

[191] See Kate Gibson and Bonnie Johnston, ‘Acquitted, released and homeless: The crisis of stateless former defendants’ in R Mulgrew and MJ Christensen (eds) *Research Handbook on the Punishment of Atrocity Crimes* (Edward Elgar Publishing, forthcoming 2024).

[192] Lecolle, note 190 at 169.

In direct violation of the terms of its agreement with the MICT,[193] Niger quickly confiscated the transferees' travel documents and served the men with expulsion orders. Without any offer of resettlement from other countries, they have remained there under armed guard with no solution in sight.

The Niger situation has been lauded as 'one of the worst failures of the international community to demonstrate its stated commitment to international justice' and a 'major challenge for the credibility of the execution of the decisions of international criminal tribunals'.[194] This global stalemate and ongoing crisis, in the context of the jurisprudential adoption of a presumption against release, is going to have the foreseeable effect of prolonging the custodial element of the sentence for ICTR and some MICT convicted persons. The deep irony is that the conditional release practice introduced at the MICT in response to a UN Security Council Resolution recommendation to adopt such a system for persons convicted by the ICTR is likely to be entirely unsuitable for the vast majority of this group. Further, the extension of the system to ICTY convicted persons in order to harmonise the treatment of all persons under the MICT's supervision will in fact create a profound inequality of treatment in terms of sentence enforcement and release practice.

It is also foreseeable that the RSCSL system may not be easily extended to all convicted persons. Mr Taylor, a Liberian national, is currently serving his sentence in the UK.[195] The UK will likely seek to deport him at the end of his custodial sentence. The RSCSL conditional release system relies on the cooperation of the Sierra Leone Government and Police. Will the RSCSL seek to negotiate a similar cooperation agreement with the Liberian Police or the police in a third country willing to accept him? If this is not possible, what impact will this have on the early release possibilities for Mr Taylor? Confidence in the cooperation of monitoring authorities is a very significant issue under the RSCSL system: the Practice Direction explicitly states the President *cannot* grant conditional release if a suitable programme of supervision is not available.[196] As this rule demonstrates, the issue is not solely one of cooperation. It is also a question of suitability. The state of origin may be willing to accept the person, and the convicted person may be willing to go, but ongoing political and security instability may prevent the grant of conditional

[193] See Agreement Between the Government of the Republic of Niger and the United Nations on the Relocation of Persons Released or Acquitted by the International Criminal Tribunal for Rwanda or the International Residual Mechanism for Criminal Tribunals, 15 November 2021.

[194] Lecolle, note 190 at 168–169.

[195] Order Designating the State in which Charles Ghankay Taylor is to Serve his Sentence, SCSL-03-01-ES, 4 October 2013.

[196] Art. 8(C)(ii) PDCER.

release. These factors have featured in both interim release[197] and sentence reduction decisions[198] with respect to Mali at the ICC.

7. CONCLUSION

From their statutory mandates to grant pardon and commutation of sentence (neither of which has ever been granted), the UN and SCSL developed systems of conditional early release. Though the MICT and RSCSL both now grant the same form of release, the motivations for the development of these systems, the mechanisms of their creation, and their modus operandi can all be clearly distinguished. Further, there are signs that conditional release is still evolving in international criminal law. At the MICT, it has been suggested that conditional release is not suitable for persons considered to pose a flight risk, determined by attempts to evade capture pre-trial and the threat of domestic prosecution in the proposed state of relocation after release.[199] Further, community service has been introduced at the RSCSL during conditional release.

Conditional release systems also evolve within domestic criminal justice systems, to reflect and achieve penal goals (rehabilitation, reintegration), pragmatic goals (alleviate overcrowding or reduce populations) and control risk.[200] Conditional release systems should, however, aim to achieve a balance between risk management and public safety and the rights and social readjustment of the offender.[201] While conditional release can enhance prospects of social inclusion and therefore desistance from re-offending,[202] it can also be experienced as a coercive and intrusive measure that extends the penal reach of the initial sentence. At present, international conditional release systems seem to be risk-centred and control-focused. Desistance and reintegration support seem to be completely lacking. Carr and Blay warn that a lack of resettlement support can result in the use of conditional release as an administrative or political tool of prison management.[203]

---

197 See *Prosecutor v Al Hassan Ag Abdoul Aziz Mohamed Ag Mahmoud*, Public Redacted version of 'Urgent Defence request for interim release' ICC-01/12/01/18, 23 March 2020, paras 65, 5–75, 78–79.

198 *Prosecutor v Ahmad Al Fazi Al Mahdi,* Public Redacted Version of the Decision on the review concerning reduction of sentence of Mr Ahmad Al Faqi Al Mahdi, ICC-01/12-01/15-434-Red3, 25 November 2021, paras 54–59.

199 *Prosecutor v Dordević*, Decision on the Applications for Early Release of Vlastimir Dordevic, MICT-14-76-ES, 30 November 2021, paras 55, 76, 78, 97–98.

200 Carr and Blay, note 84 at 121; Herzog-Evans, note 177 at 189.

201 Preamble ERCSM; Rule 1.4 Tokyo Rules.

202 Rule 1 ERCSM.

203 Carr and Blay, note 84 at 121.

Further, conditional release schemes should be implemented in light of the aims and objectives of the particular criminal justice system it serves.[204] In addition to maintaining international control over the sanction and prisoners, international punishment should be implemented in a manner that seeks to achieve penological, victimological and transitional justice goals. These factors do seem to have been considered in the creation and operationalisation of conditional early release in international criminal law. That being said, this chapter has highlighted the controversies with, and gaps in, the legal and policy frameworks governing conditional early release systems. These range from the political pressure to adopt this form of release, the unilateral judicial decisions used to introduce them (MICT), and reliance on questionable legal grounds and political guarantees to operationalise them. Issues surrounding the efficacy of monitoring bodies and the efficiency and focus of the monitoring role were also evident. Questions of clarity, equality, necessity and proportionality were raised in relation to several elements of the systems. The changes to the form of release used, and the mode of its implementation, have the potential to increase the penal reach and depth of international penalties, and alter the predictability of international penality. Yet, it is foreseeable that this form of release will not be extendable to all internationally convicted persons due to either a lack of cooperation or unstable security conditions in the proposed state of relocation, creating another level of disparity of treatment among persons supervised by the same international court or tribunal. It is important to bear in mind that the majority of persons convicted by international criminal courts and tribunals will live in society again without conditions (following completion of sentence or a sentence reduction). The re-entry of international prisoners back into society must therefore be assessed not only with regard to the form of the release but also in light of the myriad factors considered in reaching release and sentence reduction decisions.

---

204 Rule 1.3 Tokyo Rules.

7. Factors in release decision-making and the reconceptualisation of rehabilitation

1. FACTORS IN RELEASE DECISION-MAKING

The factors considered in release and sentence reduction decisions can be found, to varying degrees, in the statutes, rules and practice directions of the respective international criminal courts and tribunals. The scope and impact of these factors are determined, however, by their interpretation and application by the international judges responsible for making release decisions. As these decision-making positions are held by different judges over time (MICT and RSCSL) and in particular cases (ICC), it is unsurprising that interpretative approaches may vary. The majority of international release decisions issued to date have emanated from the UN Tribunals and the Mechanism. For this reason, the framework provided by the regulatory factors considered in release decisions at these institutions provides the structure for the initial discussions of release factors in this chapter. The priority given to particular factors changed dramatically at the MICT, however, with the appointment of President Agius in 2019. From this point on, the weight attributed to gravity and rehabilitation, in particular, acquired new significance.

This chapter starts by comparing and critiquing the approach taken by the UN Tribunals, the Mechanism, the RSCSL and the ICC in relation to core factors in release and sentence reduction decisions, focusing on eligibility for release, cooperation with the prosecution, and gravity. The primary focus of the chapter, however, is on how rehabilitation is conceptualised in international criminal law. This analysis begins with the paradigmatic shift in the interpretation and application of this factor at the MICT, and a comparison of this new approach with that of other international courts. The chapter also explores issues related to the operationalisation of rehabilitation within the international penal system, looking at how international criminal behaviour can be addressed, problems with delaying release to provide rehabilitative training at the RSCSL, and the deflection of responsibility to provide rehabilitation programmes by international courts and tribunals. The important question of reintegration post-sentence, particularly in post-conflict contexts, is also examined with regard to the practice of the various international courts. The chapter concludes with a critical analysis of contemporary approaches to rehabilitation in international criminal law and policy.

2. ELIGIBILITY, COOPERATION AND GRAVITY

The rules of the UN Tribunals and the MICT focused release decision-making on four enumerated factors: the treatment of similarly situated persons, gravity, rehabilitation, and cooperation with the prosecutor.[1] The cooperation factor typically carried very little weight at the UN Tribunals. The 'treatment of similarly situated persons' factor has essentially become redundant as a stand-alone substantive consideration and has evolved into a temporal eligibility threshold for these institutions.[2] Yet for a long time, the time served on the sentence was the dominant consideration. An increased focus on gravity has transpired over time. This section explores and compares how these factors have been applied in release decisions in international criminal justice institutions.

2.1 Eligibility for Release

There has been a significant degree of consistency in the practice of the international courts in relation to eligibility for release for persons serving determinate sentences. Since 2012, all of the UN Tribunals, the (R)SCSL and the ICC require that applicants will have served two-thirds of their sentence before they are eligible for (consideration for) release.[3] There is less consistency (and clarity) in relation to practice on the determination of eligibility for those serving indeterminate sentences.

2.1.1 Determinate sentences

As with the UN Tribunals, the MICT President is required by the rules to consider the situation of similarly situated prisoners when making release decisions.[4] Meron justified his introduction of the two-thirds threshold on this ground (given the ICTR practice of requiring service of three quarters of

---

1 Rule 125 ICTY RPE; Rule 126 ICTR RPE; Rule 151 MICT RPE. Presidents can consider any other information deemed relevant (see para. 8 ICTY PDER; para. 9 MICT PDER). This usually involves consideration of humanitarian considerations. The impact of this factor on release is discussed in Chapter 9.

2 See Chapter 2, section 2 and Chapter 5, section 3.

3 See MICT PDER, para. 8; Art. 110(3) ICCSt; Rule 124 SCSL RPE; Art 2(A) SCSL PDCER.

4 See Rule 151 MICT RPE.

the sentence) on the basis of 'fundamental fairness and justice and the need to apply a uniform eligibility threshold' for all convicted persons under the MICT's supervision.[5] Presidents have consistently rejected requests from convicted persons to compare their situation to the treatment of other convicted persons: 'each case presents unique circumstances that must be considered on their own merit' and therefore comparisons to other cases were deemed to be inconsequential to the President's decision on release.[6] Judicial decisions at the MICT have therefore crystallised the operational function of this factor. It acts solely as a harmonising temporal eligibility threshold, to be applied to all persons being supervised by the Mechanism, irrespective of the sentencing body or where the sentence is being served.[7]

Procedural changes, reflecting this threshold, were introduced into MICT release practice from 2020 onwards. Applications for release from or on behalf of applicants who have not yet served two-thirds of their sentence have not been subjected to a full Rule 151 assessment. A new abbreviated procedure has been adopted that results in shorter decisions that deny release due to the lack of sufficient service of sentence (in the absence of compelling or humanitarian circumstances).[8] This enables the consideration of applications without 'triggering the multi-step and resource-intensive process of requesting, receiving, translating, sharing and considering additional information'.[9]

In contrast to how the threshold evolved at the MICT, there is no room for judicial interpretation of temporal eligibility at the ICC. The Rome Statute states explicitly that convicted persons can only be considered for a sentence reduction *after* two-thirds of a determinate sentence has been served.[10] In other words, the Rome Statute bars sentence reviews prior to this point. Furthermore, convicted persons cannot make a direct application for this initial sentence review.

The RSCSL aligned with the ICC's statutory approach of adopting an explicit standard by amending the rules in 2011 to add a fixed temporal threshold for

---

5 Theodore Meron, *Standing Up for Justice: The Challenges of Trying Atrocity Crimes* (OUP 2021), 267.

6 See *Prosecutor v Krstić,* Decision on the Application for Early Release of Radislav Krstić, MICT-13-46-ES.1, 15 November 2022, paras 43–44, 91–92.

7 *Prosecutor v Krstić,* Decision on the Application for Early Release of Radislav Krstić, MICT-13-46-ES.1, 15 November 2022, paras 28–29, 42; *Prosecutor v Popović,* Decision on the Application for Early Release of Vujadin Popović, MICT-15-85-ES.2, 30 January 2023, at 4.

8 See Chapter 5, section 4.3.

9 See *Prosecutor v Popović,* Decision on the Application for Early Release of Vujadin Popović, MICT-15-85-ES.2, 30 January 2023, at 4.

10 Art. 110(3) ICCSt.

consideration for conditional release after a 'minimum of' two-thirds of the sentence had been served.[11] This approach can be distinguished from that of the other courts, however, as eligibility for consideration for release requires the mandatory judicial consideration of a number of enumerated and cumulative factors: not just the amount of time served.[12] Further, the determination of eligibility for consideration for conditional release requires a distinct and separate procedure and Presidential decision.

2.1.2 Life sentences

The Rome Statute establishes an explicit requirement for persons sentenced to life imprisonment to serve 25 years before they will be deemed eligible for consideration for a sentence reduction.[13] Further, at the ICC, convicted persons sentenced to life imprisonment **must** have their sentence reviewed, *proprio motu*, after service of 25 years.[14] The MICT, on the other hand, has failed to conclusively determine the temporal eligibility point for indeterminate sentences. The eligibility for release for those serving indeterminate sentences, President Meron decided, should be fixed in relation to a hypothetical term equivalent to the highest determinate sentence imposed. Consequently, Meron and his successors have all accepted that a convicted person sentenced to life imprisonment must serve, at a minimum, *more than 30 years* of their sentence.[15]

In Meron's view, the 'more than' 30-year threshold was 'broadly in line with the threshold approved by other international and regional courts even those considering or applying different legal frameworks'.[16] Yet, this threshold for consideration for early release for persons serving life sentences is at least five years longer than the threshold for mandatory sentence reduction reviews at the ICC. Van Zyl Smit argues that while the MICT approach has the advantage of clarity and consistency in the treatment of prisoners and makes clear that all life prisoners have the prospect of release (bringing practice in line with the ECtHR ruling in *Vinter*), he stresses that given the lack of any reference to a temporal threshold in the statute, rules or practice direction, the decision

---

11 Rule 124 SCSL RPE.

12 See Chapter 4, section 2.

13 Art. 110(3) ICCSt.

14 Ibid.

15 See *Prosecutor v Galić*, Public Redacted, Reasons for the President's Decision to Deny the Early Release of Stanislav Galić and Decision on Prosecution Motion, MICT-14-83-ES, 23 June 2015, para. 36.

16 Ibid, para. 38.

represents 'an extraordinary example of judicial legislation'.[17] Moreover, he notes that the fact that the 'more than' 30-year minimum term is higher than the term applied or recommended by 'persuasive, if not authoritative' sources (ICC, ECtHR, domestic law) illustrates 'just how wide this discretion is and how inadequate the provisions of the original statute'.[18] For Szydło, the MICT model represents 'an important step towards a more general recognition of the human rights implications of life sentences' and reflects the growing movement towards outlawing irreducible sentences.[19] However, he draws attention to problematic aspects of the model, including the fact that eligibility remains to be determined on a case-by-case basis and that it is unclear at which point in time individual eligibility thresholds will be determined (during service or after 30 years has been served?).[20]

These uncertainties remain. In *Popović* in 2023, President Santana accepted that the temporal point for release eligibility for life prisoners was to be calculated in relation to a hypothetical sentence of between 45–47 years. She declined, however, to fix the exact term of years of either the hypothetical sentence or the exact term of service required, stating this issue would be 'addressed if and when required'.[21] The position of life prisoners under MICT supervision remains uncertain. Presidential decisions to avoid setting an exact point at which persons serving indeterminate sentences become eligible for consideration for release have resulted in a lack of predictability and created a risk of unequal or arbitrary treatment.

2.2 Cooperation with the Prosecution

The cooperation with the prosecutor factor did not have a significant impact on most release decisions at the UN Tribunals.[22] Significant cooperation has

---

17 Dirk van Zyl Smit, 'Determinate and indeterminate sentences of imprisonment in international criminal justice' in R. Mulgrew and D. Abels (eds) *Research Handbook on the International Penal System* (Edward Elgar Publishing, 2016) 80–101 at 95.

18 Ibid.

19 Marek Szydło, 'Reduction of Life Sentences Imposed by International Criminal Tribunals after the Galić Decision: Is There Need for Further Improvement?' (2015) 13 *Journal of International Criminal Justice* 1099–1120 at 1101, 1104.

20 Ibid, at 1111–1112, 1116.

21 See *Prosecutor v Popović*, Decision on the Application for Early Release of Vujadin Popović, MICT-15-85-ES.2, 30 January 2023 at 3.

22 Filip Votja, 'Punishment and Sentence Enforcement for Serious Violations of International Humanitarian Law Committed in the Former Yugoslavia' in

featured as a decisive factor in some decisions granting release.[23] In the majority of cases, however, as cooperation had not been sought (and as there is no obligation to provide it), this factor often carried no weight and tended to act as a neutral factor.[24] In the cases in which cooperation was considered to be a positive factor, all cooperation was counted, even if the cooperation had also been considered in mitigation of sentence. In particular, the entry of a guilty plea and subsequent cooperation favoured release due to the positive impact on the efficient administration of justice.[25] Presidents Meron and Agius defended this approach (following the expression of Prosecutorial concerns) noting that another significant factor that (negatively) influences sentencing, the gravity of offences, is also considered in release decisions.[26]

This approach can be contrasted with that of the RSCSL. The Practice Direction does not foreground cooperation as a crucial component of release decision-making, and the President is only provided with information about cooperation from convicted persons that *was not* taken into account during sentencing.[27]

At the ICC, the cooperation factor, delineated in the Rome Statute, is both broader and, it would seem, more difficult to demonstrate. Firstly, sentence review panels must consider two enumerated categories: (a) cooperation in prosecutions and investigations, and (b) cooperation in the enforcement of the

Kalac, Albrecht and Kilching (eds) *Mapping the Criminological Landscape of the Balkans* (Duncker and Humblot, Berlin, 2014) 401–428 at 418.

[23] See *Prosecutor v Bagaragaza*, Decision on the Early Release of Michel Bagaragaza, ICTR-05-86-S, 24 October 2011, paras 13, 15; *Prosecutor v Rugambarara*, Decision on the Early Release Request of Juvénal Rugambarara, ICTR-00-59, 8 February 2012, paras 10, 13, 16.

[24] See Chapter 2, section 3 and Chapter 5, section 5.3.

[25] See *Prosecutor v Češić*, Public Redacted version of the 30 April 2014 Decision of the President on the Early Release of Ranko Češić, MICT-14-66-ES, 28 May 2014, para. 24; *Prosecutor v M. Nikolić*, Public Redacted Version of the 14 March 2014 Decision on the Early Release of Momir Nikolić, MICT-14-65-ES, 12 October 2015, para. 28; *Prosecutor v Zelenović*, Public Redacted Version of the 28 August 2015 Decision of the President on the Early Release of Dragan Zelenović, MICT-15-89-ES, 18 September 2015, para. 21.

[26] *Prosecutor v Šainović*, Public Redacted Version of the 10 July 2015 Decision of the President on the Early Release of Nikola Šainović, MICT-14-67-ES.1, 27 August 2015, para. 25; *Prosecutor v Kunarac*, Decision on Dragoljub Kunarac's Application for Early Release, MICT-15-88.ES.1, 31 December 2020, para. 73; *Prosecutor v Lukić*, Decision on the Application for Early Release of Sreten Lukić, MICT-14-67-ES.4, 7 October 2021, para. 75.

[27] Art. 5(G) PDCER.

Court's judgments and orders.[28] This latter category relates to the voluntary assistance provided by convicted persons that facilitates the enforcement of ICC judgments and orders, particularly those directed at locating assets subject to fines, forfeiture, or reparation orders that can be used for the benefit of victims.[29] This factor has not been found to be present in any case to date. In relation to the former category, the cooperation must be both early *and* continuing.[30] Significantly, and similarly to RSCSL practice, this means cooperation in relation to prosecutions and investigations will only weigh in favour of sentence reduction if it continues *after* the end of trial and sentence imposition.[31] Cases to date have consistently applied this requirement: both pre-sentencing cooperation (which can include cooperation considered in sentence mitigation)[32] and post-sentencing cooperation must be present for this factor to weigh in favour of sentence reduction,[33] though the impact of any cooperation is to be considered on a case-by-case basis.[34]

2.3 Gravity

Despite the divergences in approaches between the various international courts, the approach to temporal eligibility and cooperation has remained fairly constant within the policy and practice of individual courts. The same cannot be said in relation to the weight accorded to the gravity of the crimes the individual was convicted of in release decision-making. Not only are there differences in the legal framework of the various courts, but the strong Presidential discretion at the MICT and RSCSL has resulted in varying approaches depending on who is in office at a particular point in time. At the MICT, this has resulted in a significant retributive shift that has centralised gravity considerations in conditional release decisions.

Gravity is not a feature of sentence reduction reviews at the ICC, either in terms of the governing legal provisions or their application. The judges of consecutive panels have consistently confirmed that the explicit statutory and regulatory provisions comprise the totality of the legal framework to be applied in the consideration of sentence reduction – and this does not permit

---

28 Art. 110(4) ICCSt.

29 Art. 110(4)(b) ICCSt.

30 See Art. 110(4)(a) ICCSt.

31 *Katanga* Sentence Review, para. 34.

32 *Katanga* Sentence Review, paras 28–31. See also Rule 145(2)(a)(ii) ICC RPE.

33 See *Al Mahdi* Sentence Review, paras 26–27, 31.

34 *Lubanga* First Sentence Review, paras 30, 36; *Katanga* Sentence Review, paras 26, 32.

consideration of gravity. Votja agrees with this approach, arguing that taking gravity into account in release decision-making is 'unnecessarily stigmatising since it has already been acknowledged as an important factor in determining the length of the sentence'.[35]

Gravity does not feature in the statute, rules, or practice direction as a distinct factor for consideration in RSCSL release decisions. Nor did gravity feature as a distinct ground of assessment in the *Kondewa* or *Senessie* decisions. Yet in *Fofana*, President Waki discussed gravity separately and at length (citing from the Trial and Appeal judgments), referring to the need to respect the totality principle and the fact that gravity is a paramount consideration in sentencing.[36] This discussion went beyond recalling the harm caused by the committed offences, as he decided that 'the high gravity of the crimes' weighed against release.[37] Despite the lack of any clear legal basis for doing so, President Kamanda adopted the same approach in *Gbao*, recounting the detail and impact of the applicant's offences.[38] Kambanda's approach can be differentiated from Waki's to the extent that the former's discussion of gravity was restricted to recalling the offences, rather than stating if this weighed for or against release. Further, the discussion was situated within a rehabilitation context (asking whether it was safe for him to serve the remainder of his sentence in the community).[39] These cases demonstrate the differentiated approaches that can emerge on account of the preference or views of the President in office.

Release decisions under former President Meron at the MICT discussed the gravity of the offences in detail, often containing lengthy extracts from judgments. The gravity section of decisions outlined relevant elements such as the scale of the crimes, the convicted person's level of responsibility and role in planning or committing the crimes, and the impact of the offences on victims.[40] The inclusion of gravity in release decision-making enabled the President to acknowledge and recount the reason why the person had been convicted and imprisoned by an international criminal tribunal for some of the most serious crimes known to mankind. Yet, the gravity factor, by itself, *did not* result in the denial of release at the MICT under President Meron. In every case, President Meron noted that the (very) high gravity of the applicants' crimes militated

[35] Votja, note 22, 418.

[36] *Prosecutor v Fofana and Kondewa*, Decision of the President on Application for Conditional Early Release, SCSL-04-14-ES, 11 August 2014, paras 15, 45–46.

[37] Ibid, para. 17.

[38] *Prosecutor v Gbao*, Decision of the President on Application for Conditional Early Release, RSCSL-04-15-ES, 8 September 2020, paras 22–28.

[39] Ibid, paras 21, 28.

[40] See Chapter 2, section 3.3.

against the grant of release. Release was usually granted, notwithstanding the gravity of the offences the applicant had been convicted of, if the applicant had served the requisite period.[41]

For former President Agius, the assessment of the severity of the convicted person's conduct, a primary consideration in determining the length of the sentence imposed, was also a 'factor of fundamental importance' in release decision-making.[42] He dismissed arguments that gravity should not be used to deny release on the basis that it was already considered in sentencing. Agius argued that it was appropriate to include gravity on the basis that other factors considered in mitigation in sentencing could also be taken into account in favour of release, such as cooperation with the Prosecutor and expressions of remorse.[43] Despite the detailed analysis of gravity, and its stated weight against release in his decisions, Agius, like Meron, granted release 'notwithstanding' the high gravity of the offences committed.[44] Where Agius, and later Santana, departed from Meron's approach was in relation to the interplay between the consideration of gravity and rehabilitation. For them, 'the graver the criminal conduct ... the more compelling a demonstration of rehabilitation should be'.[45]

3. REHABILITATION RECONCEPTUALISED FOR INTERNATIONAL CRIMINAL LAW

Rehabilitation is both a rights-based and consequentialist penal objective.[46] A rehabilitative penal system should offer offenders treatment and support to enable them, as rational actors, to address their criminal behaviour and become law-abiding citizens upon re-entry into society. Human rights law posits that it should be the primary goal of any penitentiary system.[47]

---

41 Ibid.

42 *Prosecutor v Dordević*, Decision on the Applications for Early Release of Vlastimir Dordević, MICT-14-76-ES, 30 November 2021, para. 36.

43 *Prosecutor v Kunarac*, Decision on Dragoljub Kunarac's Application for Early Release, MICT-15-88.ES.1, 31 December 2020, paras 37–38.

44 See *Prosecutor v Lukić*, Decision on the Application for Early Release of Sreten Lukić, MICT-14-67-ES.4, 7 October 2021, paras 48, 93, 95–96.

45 See *Prosecutor v Krstić*, Decision on the Application for Early Release of Radislav Krstić, MICT-13-46-ES.1, 15 November 2022, para. 34.

46 See Marina Maier, 'Offender Rehabilitation in International Criminal Justice: Towards Implementation of Tailored Rehabilitation Programs' (2021) 53 *Case W. Res. J. Int'l L.* 269 at 278.

47 See Art. 10(3) International Covenant on Civil and Political Rights, 1966; Rule 4 Nelson Mandela Rules, Annex, A/Res/70/175, 15 December 2015; Preamble, OAS Principles and Best Practices on the Protection of Persons Deprived of Liberty in the Americas, 2008.

Consequently, any prison system that is solely retributory is not rights compliant.[48] This rights approach to punishment is applicable to international punishment, whether directly (through Article 21(3) ICCSt, for example) or indirectly (through the rights obligations of enforcing States). Former President Meron recognised that, in line with a rights-based approach, the enforcement of sentences imposed by the ICTR, ICTY and Mechanism should be 'focused on the rehabilitation of these convicted persons with the goal of their eventual return to and reintegration into society'.[49]

Despite this, the 'dominant emphasis on punishing … and the anti-impunity discourse' in international criminal justice has seriously reduced the space for critical and constructive discussions about rehabilitation for a long time.[50] Further, the conceptual clarity required to situate a rehabilitative-focused penal system within (and after the conclusion of) a retribution-focused judicial process is often missing in international criminal discourse. The fundamental basis of these two objectives conflict. As Riccardi posits, rehabilitation 'denies the main assumption of retribution': claiming that the punishment (alone) restores the harm caused by the crime to society.[51] The retention of retribution and deterrence as the primary sentencing goals does not, however, negate the value of prioritising rehabilitation as the primary penal management objective. Sentence imposition and sentence implementation are distinct stages of the international criminal justice process that should be governed by appropriate and relevant objectives.[52] To understand how rehabilitation is understood in the international penal context, it is necessary to explore the paradigmatic shift in the Presidential interpretations and applications of rehabilitation within the MICT early release jurisprudence, before examining the approaches adopted by the ICC and RSCSL.

---

[48] Human Rights Committee General Comment No. 21 (1992), CCPR/C/21/Rev.1/Add.7, para. 10.

[49] Meron, note 5, 266.

[50] Barbora Holá and Maja Munivrana, 'There is Something Special about War Criminals: Constructing and Assessing the Rehabilitation of War Criminals at the ICTY/IRMCT and in Croatia' (2023) *Journal of International Criminal Justice* 1–23 at 7.

[51] Alice Riccardi, 'The Sentencing Principle of 'Internationalised' Rehabilitation in the Practice of International Criminal Courts and Tribunals Sentence Enforcement' in R Mulgrew and M Christensen, *Research Handbook on the Punishment of Atrocity Crimes* (Edward Elgar Publishing, 2024) at 144.

[52] Róisín Mulgrew, *Towards the Development of the International Penal System* (CUP, 2013) at 211–213.

3.1 The Presidential Reconceptualisation of Rehabilitation at the MICT

At both the ICTY and the ICTR, rehabilitation was discussed in early release decisions in relation to a wide range of factors including behaviour, work and education in detention, acknowledgements of responsibility, the risk of recidivism and ability to reintegrate. This ad hoc range of factors were not deemed 'equally important nor considered systemically'.[53] Despite the scope of factors addressed, rehabilitation tended to have very little impact on release decisions *if* the sentenced person had served two-thirds of their sentence. The factor only became impactful if less than two-thirds had been served.[54]

3.1.1 President Meron

When the supervision of sentences imposed by the UN Tribunals shifted to the MICT, rehabilitation became a more prominent feature in terms of the content of release decisions.[55] The fact remained, however, that in the vast majority of cases, at least some signs of rehabilitation were found, and accordingly, this factor almost always weighed in favour of granting early release. Under Meron, as consideration of rehabilitation 'almost never hindered early release,' it seemed as though the system was highly effective at rehabilitating international prisoners.[56] Closer scrutiny of release decisions from this period, however, reveals that the decisive factor was (virtually always) sufficient service of sentence. Up to 2017, 93% of applications were granted, with rejections resting on a failure to serve two thirds.[57]

---

53 Kelder, Holá and van Wijk arranged 16 identified factors into four categories:

- *Period in prison*: conduct, prison integration, participation in programmes, changes in prison, prison regime, attitude towards other nationalities
- *Future perspectives*: family ties, relationship with home country, career prospects, explicit intention not to reoffend
- *Reflection on crimes*: showing regret/remorse, acceptance of responsibility
- *Personal characteristics*: Mental health, personality traits, conduct prior to crimes, age.

See Jessica M. Kelder, Barbora Holá and Joris van Wijk, 'Rehabilitation and Early Release of Perpetrators of International Crimes: A Case Study of the ICTY and ICTR' (2014) 14 *Int'l Crim L Rev* 1177 at 1185–1186.

54 See Chapter 2, section 3.

55 See Chapter 2, section 3.3.

56 Kelder, Holá and Van Wijk, note 53, 1178.

57 Holá and Munivrana, note 50, 9.

3.1.2 President Agius

This light-touch approach to rehabilitation changed drastically under the Presidency of Carmel Agius.[58] Even prior to his Presidency, Agius had argued that in the international criminal justice context, a focus on conduct in detention for rehabilitation assessments, while perhaps acceptable at a domestic level, constituted a 'disservice to international criminal law' and did not make sense 'in a context of the gravest crimes against humanity, war crimes and genocide'.[59]

One aspect in which President Agius's approach diverged sharply from his predecessor's was the requirement for the applicant to *demonstrate remorse* for the crimes they had been convicted of. President Meron felt strongly that, as it was not a requirement in the applicable legal framework, remorse should not be used as a factor to determine if early release was appropriate.[60] He pointed out that many convicted persons had been granted early release despite a lack of any remorse or even express denials that they had committed the crimes.[61] President Agius, in contrast, felt this was a significant element of any rehabilitation assessment and, therefore, a key consideration in deciding whether to grant release.

A lack of remorse, and denials of responsibility featured in many decisions in which President Agius declined to grant release, on the grounds (inter alia) of insufficient rehabilitation. From February 2020 onwards, release decisions featured a distinct analysis of an applicant's acceptance of responsibility, signs of critical reflection, and genuine expressions of remorse. This assessment was detailed and demanding: statements deflecting responsibility, vague or abstract expressions of empathy, unsupported claims to support reconciliation, and any questioning of the appropriateness of the conviction or sentence were all highlighted and named as factors underpinning a finding of insufficient rehabilitation.[62] Such findings carried significant weight: they were found to undermine positive findings of rehabilitation and reintegration and even pose a threat to peace and security if release was granted.

Agius drew attention to the fact that general and/or private expressions of remorse did not demonstrate acceptance of responsibility for, or sufficient

---

[58] 19 January 2019 until 30 June 2022.

[59] *Prosecutor v Ćorić*, Further Redacted Public Redacted Version of the Decision of the President on the Early Release of Valentin Ćorić and Related Motions, MICT-17-112-ES.4, 16 January 2019, para. 62.

[60] *Prosecutor v Simba*, Public Redacted Version of the President's 7 January 2019 Decision on the Early Release of Aloys Simba, MICT-14-62-ES.1, 7 January 2019, para. 44.

[61] Ibid.

[62] See Chapter 5, section 6.3.2.

critical reflection on, offences. Specific, sincere and public statements carried greater weight. In *Lukić*, a public and genuine apology to victims during his trial, critical reflection on crimes while in prison, and the denunciation of politics that glorifies ICTY convicted persons constituted cumulative and positive indicators of a 'fair level' of rehabilitation.[63] According to Agius, remorse could be demonstrated by accepting moral blameworthiness, even if this fell short of accepting criminal responsibility.[64] However, this stands in contrast to the emerging requirement that convicted persons accept the international judicial record and findings in relation to culpability in their totality.

Hola and Munivrana note that President Agius 'attempted to take a different stance from predecessors' by developing 'a *sui generis* approach to constructing and assessing the level of rehabilitation of international prisoners,' one that would reframe and reform release decision-making.[65] Agius had argued that in the context of international criminal justice, 'a different paradigm was required' for defining and applying rehabilitation.[66] Maier warns, however, that this change of policy is likely to be disadvantageous for those still serving their sentences and raises questions of equality of treatment.[67] It is clear that this new approach has resulted in increased release denial rates. Other than the grant of release in one case,[68] denials have been based primarily on the failure to demonstrate sufficient rehabilitation or an ability to peacefully reintegrate into a given society.[69]

3.1.3 President Santana

Agius, through his release jurisprudence, created 'an elaborate mechanism for the assessment of rehabilitation'.[70] President Santana endorsed the position

---

63 *Prosecutor v Lukić*, Decision on the Application for Early Release of Sreten Lukić, MICT-14-67-ES.4, 7 October 2021, paras 71–72.

64 *Prosecutor v Dordević*, Decision on the Applications for Early Release of Vlastimir Dordevic, MICT-14-76-ES, 30 November 2021, para. 60.

65 Holá and Munivrana, note 50, 4–5, 10.

66 See *Prosecutor v Bralo*, Decision on the Early Release of Miroslav Bralo, MICT-14-78-ES, 31 December 2019, paras 37–38.

67 Maier, note 46, 304.

68 *Prosecutor v Lukić*, Decision on the Application for Early Release of Sreten Lukić, MICT-14-67-ES.4, 7 October 2021, paras 93–94.

69 See for example *Prosecutor v Kunarac*, Decision on Dragoljub Kunarac's Application for Early Release, MICT-15-88.ES.1, 31 December 2020, para. 86; *Prosecutor v Brdanin*, Decision on the Application of Radoslav Brdanin for Early Release, MICT-13-48-ES, 28 February 2020, paras 96–97; *Prosecutor v Krstić,* Decision on the Application for Early Release of Radislav Krstić, MICT-13-46-ES.1, 15 November 2022, paras 69, 92.

70 Maier, note 46, 299.

adopted by Agius in relation to the need for a different approach in the context of international criminal justice. She accepted that the 'graver the criminal conduct in question, the more compelling a demonstration of rehabilitation should be'[71] and accepted Agius's non-exhaustive list of indicators of rehabilitation, which included critical reflection upon crimes, expressions of remorse, and actions to foster reconciliation or seek forgiveness.[72] Santana's rehabilitation assessment in *Krstić* was conducted under three headings: behaviour in prison; acceptance of responsibility, signs of critical reflection and expressions of genuine remorse or regret; and mental state and prospects of social reintegration into society. Like Agius, she concluded that good behaviour alone is not sufficient for persons convicted of the most heinous international crimes.[73]

Santana considered acceptance of responsibility to be an important factor in assessing rehabilitation. Like Agius, she asserted that it did 'not constitute a legal requirement… and is not a precondition for early release'.[74] She likewise claimed that partial acceptance of responsibility would 'merit positive weight' but 'any notable differences' between the role the convicted person ascribed to themselves and the role 'actually played' – in other words, the role the trial or appeals chamber ascribed to them - would 'suggest insufficient critical reflection'.[75] For example, in *Krstić*, Santana felt that while a letter expressing remorse revealed 'evidence of progress,' the generic nature of the statements, and the failure to elaborate on the offences that he was held responsible for and his role in those events, combined with vague expressions of remorse, indicated that he was unable to articulate why he felt remorseful and therefore failed to demonstrate adequate critical reflection.[76] Further, these statements were not 'substantiated by positive actions' that would indicate sufficient critical reflection on his crimes.[77] These factors ultimately proved decisive in the overall assessment of Krstić's rehabilitation.

3.2 A Paradigmatic Shift?

These jurisprudential pronouncements resulted in a paradigmatic shift in MICT release decision-making whereby rehabilitation was framed and applied through a retributive and victimological lens. This normative re-positioning

---

[71] *Prosecutor v Krstić,* Decision on the Application for Early Release of Radislav Krstić, MICT-13-46-ES.1, 15 November 2022, para. 69.

[72] Ibid, paras 46–47.

[73] Ibid, paras 49, 55.

[74] Ibid, para. 56.

[75] Ibid.

[76] Ibid, paras 59–61.

[77] Ibid, paras 61, 69.

coincided with the reversal of the presumption for release. The current, explicit position is that there is a presumption against release for persons under MICT supervision and that release will be exceptional.[78] Unsurprisingly, a backward-looking, gravity-focused review of release worthiness, and the influence this approach has had on the threshold required for rehabilitation assessments, has resulted in higher rates of release denial. MICT practice has gone from one extreme to another – from virtually all prisoners being deemed rehabilitated to virtually all prisoners being found to be insufficiently rehabilitated following a change in President. Holá and Munivrana have contemplated whether this new conceptualisation of rehabilitation can be attributed to external political pressures, 'personal proclivities' or simply the coming of age of international criminal justice.[79] What is clear however, is that this 'new' approach at the MICT is in fact consistent with the approach applied by the ICC and RSCSL.

What differs at the ICC is that the approach to rehabilitation is dictated by the explicit provisions of the Rules of Procedure and Evidence, not the jurisprudential musings of the President. Pursuant to (elements of) several rules, Sentence Review Panels must determine if convicted persons have dissociated from their crimes through conduct in detention, acknowledged responsibility for their crimes, and/or expressed remorse.[80] Conduct in detention must demonstrate a genuine dissociation from the crimes convicted of.[81] Sentence review decisions to date have shown that generalised or abstract expressions of remorse will not suffice. Further, convicted persons must demonstrate how they will return to a crime-free life in society upon release.[82] The ICC rules also add a reparative element, with panels required to assess 'any significant action taken by the sentenced person for the benefit of the victims'.[83] This assessment differs from the dissociation from crime analysis: while the assessment may involve the same actions, the analysis of the (benefit or significance of the) actions is from the victims' perspective.[84] Decisions caution, however, against over-emphasising subjective victims' views in order to avoid arbitrary outcomes: assessments are to be taken on a case-by-case basis and require the adoption of a reasonableness (objective) evaluation of victims' rejections of

---

78 See *Prosecutor v Dordević*, Decision on the Applications for Early Release of Vlastimir Dordevic, MICT-14-76-ES, 30 November 2021, para. 36; *Prosecutor v Krstić*, Decision on the Application for Early Release of Radislav Krstić, MICT-13-46-ES.1, 15 November 2022, para. 33.

79 Holá and Munivrana, note 50, 10.

80 Rule 223(a) ICC RPE.

81 See *Katanga* Sentence Review, paras 40, 46.

82 Rule 223(b) ICC RPE.

83 Rule 223(d) ICC RPE.

84 *Katanga* Sentence Review, para. 90.

the benefit of any actions.[85] This assessment only includes *actions* that have occurred since sentencing (as prior acts would have been considered in mitigation in sentencing). Aligning with Santana's view at the MICT, real action for the benefit of victims, not proposals or intentions, is required at the ICC.[86] ICC decisions have also stressed the need to ensure that apologies are adequate in victims' eyes and that crafting an acceptable apology may require that convicted persons enter into dialogue with the victims of their crimes.[87] Similar to MICT practice, ICC judges have also distinguished between the significance of abstract rejections of crimes and events and the acceptance of responsibility and expressions of remorse for the specific criminal acts a person was convicted of.[88] Accepting the Court's findings, expressing regret to direct victims, and recording an apology for victims after sentencing were considered to be significant, whereas non-public apologies and an address to victims during a sentence review hearing were not sufficient.[89]

Presidential decisions at the RSCSL also align with this recently adopted position at the MICT. Presidents have held that applicants requesting early release must acknowledge their crimes and demonstrate remorse with clear and convincing evidence.[90] Gbao, for example, issued a written apology to his direct victims and the people of Sierra Leone (broadcast nationally on radio and at community meetings), expressed regret for participating in the conflict and for his crimes, and renounced the ideology of the Revolutionary United Front (all of which weighed in favour of release).[91] Unlike the MICT, however, where the weight attributed to these factors can vary depending on the exercise of Presidential discretion, at the RSCSL, consideration of these factors is a requirement at both the eligibility and the consideration for release stages.[92]

85 *Katanga* Sentence Review, para. 91; *Al Mahdi* Sentence Review, para. 64.

86 *Lubanga* Second Sentence Review, paras 85–86; *Katanga* Sentence Review, para. 94.

87 *Katanga* Sentence Review, para. 99.

88 *Lubanga* First Sentence Review, para. 45. See also *Katanga* Sentence Review, para. 47; *Lubanga* Second Sentence Review, para. 54.

89 See Chapter 3, section 5.4.

90 *Prosecutor v Gbao*, Decision of the President on Application for Conditional Early Release, RSCSL-04-15-ES, 8 September 2020, para. 69.

91 Ibid, paras 70, 72–75.

92 See Chapter 4, sections 2 and 5.

4. OPERATIONALISING REHABILITATION IN THE INTERNATIONAL PENAL SYSTEM

The application of the rehabilitation principle in domestic penal practice has evolved from therapeutic interventions to 'cure' criminality, to a modern rights-based focus on resocialisation that aims to change the offender's way of thinking and a reintegration focus that addresses life in society.[93] While these components of a modern rehabilitative penal policy are intuitively important, they have proved difficult to operationalise in the international criminal justice context.

4.1 Addressing Criminal Behaviour

International crimes are typically committed in situations of extreme, collective and state-sponsored violence: in such situations, perpetrators may not be acting in a socially deviant manner but have in fact been socialised into committing crimes in abnormal and extraordinary circumstances.[94] 'Conventional' rehabilitation programmes will, therefore, not typically be appropriate to address this form of criminality.[95] As Hola and Munivrana argue, the different criminogenic needs of perpetrators, the unique character of international criminal offences, and the 'multi-faceted harms' that result, dictate that the rehabilitation of international prisoners needs to be 'reimagined'.[96] That being said, it must be recognised that international prisoners are not a homogenous group. In her typology, Smeulers identifies nine classifications of international perpetrators, distinguished on the basis of the causes of criminal behaviour.[97] International prisoners have different criminogenic needs, profiles and reintegration plans that influence their rehabilitative needs.[98]

Some national rehabilitation programmes may be suitable for persons convicted of international crimes. For example, programmes tailored to address violent or sexual offences or overcoming addiction may be helpful for some

---

[93] Gert Vermeulen and Eveline Dewree, *Offender Reintegration and Rehabilitation as a Component of International Criminal Justice?* (Antwerpen, Maklu 2014) at 72–73.

[94] See Mark Drumbl, *Atrocity, Punishment and International Law* (CUP, 2007) at 26.

[95] Kelder, Holá and Van Wijk, note 53, 1197.

[96] Holá and Munivrana, note 50, 8.

[97] Alette Smeulers, 'Perpetrators of International Crimes: Towards a Typology' in A Smeulers and R Haveman (eds) *Supranational Criminology: Towards a Criminology of International Crimes* (Intersentia, 2008) 237–260.

[98] See Maier, note 46, 293; Vermeulen and Dewree, note 93, 74.

individual prisoners. However, the 'status aparte'[99] of persons convicted by international criminal courts and tribunals can create significant obstacles that prevent access to such programmes. As foreign national prisoners, their linguistic abilities and immigration status often bar access to programmes reserved for native speakers that will be reintegrated into the detaining State's society upon release.[100] Their status as international criminals may also prevent access to programmes that focus on 'domestic' crime.[101] Kunarac, for example, was informed that he could not access rehabilitation programmes in Germany, in part, due to his inability to speak the language and, further, as there were no 'special programmes for war criminals'.[102]

Since 2013, academics have been calling for the creation of specialised rehabilitation programmes to address the nature of international crime, confront perpetrators with the 'shortcomings and effects of destructive nationalist or ethnic ideologies' and create space for reflection on the consequences of their crimes with the focus on healing relationships.[103] Despite the longstanding recognition of the need for more tailored approaches to international sentence enforcement,[104] it is also clear that the design and delivery of specialist rehabilitation programmes is not a responsibility that enforcing States with one or two international prisoners are likely to accept as an appropriate use of public funds.[105] Creating a tailored programme for international criminals is not 'economically justiciable or sustainable' for domestic authorities.[106] Those that serve their entire sentences in international detention facilities do not fare much better.[107] At the ICC, for example, the Registrar justified the lack of rehabilitation programmes on the ICC Detention Centre's mandate to house suspects and accused persons.[108]

---

99 Kelder, Holá and Van Wijk, note 53, 1179; Mulgrew, note 52, chapters 6 and 7.

100 See Róisín Mulgrew, 'The Role of Oversight in Foreign-National-Only Prisons: Countering the Disapplication of Rehabilitation' (2018) 70 *Crime Law Soc Change* 77–92; Kelder, Holá and Van Wijk, note 53, 1179; Maier, note 46, 287–288.

101 Kelder, Hola and Van Wijk, note 53, 1190.

102 *Prosecutor v Kunarac*, Public Redacted Decision of the President on the Early Release of Dragoljub Kunarac, MICT-15-88-ES.1, 2 February 2017, paras 48, 57, 67.

103 Kelder, Holá and Van Wijk, note 53, 1200–1201.

104 Mulgrew, note 52, 218–270.

105 Maier, note 46, 293.

106 Holá and Munivrana, note 50, 3; see also Mulgrew, note 52, 266–272.

107 Mulgrew, note 52, 152.

108 *Lubanga* First Sentence Review, para. 49; *Katanga* Sentence Review, para. 52.

Despite the high threshold international judges have imposed for assessing progress towards rehabilitation, the reality is that very few internationally convicted persons ever have their criminal behaviour addressed during the service of their sentence. Maier draws attention to the reality that 30% of ICTY convicted persons served their sentences at the UN Detention Unit with no access to rehabilitation programmes, and of those transferred to serve their sentences in domestic prison systems, most had served a substantial proportion of their sentences in remand custody (on average, they served only a third of their sentence in prison 'proper').[109]

4.2 Delayed Release for Training at the RSCSL

It seems that the RSCSL has been the only international court involved in the design and delivery of tailored, individualised rehabilitation programmes. Despite the rehabilitative framing of these initiatives, the RSCSL's practice in this regard is controversial. A practice of granting release subject to further training has emerged at the RSCSL with worrying liberty implications for convicted persons. In three decisions, Presidents have delayed the release of sentenced persons in order for them to complete (additional) 'training'. In *Fofana, Kondewa* and *Gbao,* conditional release was granted 'subject to' and 'conditional upon' the completion of additional periods of time in custody to facilitate further specific training.[110] The periods required and the topics suggested varied from six months for training on international crimes and responsibility for Fofana,[111] to ten months on human rights and the correct behaviour of a citizen of Sierra Leone for Kondewa,[112] to three months for further training

109 Maier, note 46, 273, 275, 282–284, 309, 322.

110 *Prosecutor v Fofana and Kondewa,* Decision of the President on Application for Conditional Early Release, SCSL-04-14-ES (1270-1291), 11 August 2014, paras 47, 49; *Prosecutor v Kondewa,* Decision of the President on Application for Conditional Early Release, RSCSL-04-14-ES (1581–1604), The Hague, 29 May 2017, paras 59, 61; *Prosecutor v Gbao,* Decision of the President on Application for Conditional Early Release, RSCSL-04-15-ES, 8 September 2020, para. 82(a).

111 *Prosecutor v Fofana and Kondewa,* Decision of the President on Application for Conditional Early Release, SCSL-04-14-ES (1270-1291), 11 August 2014, paras 47, 49.

112 *Prosecutor v Kondewa,* Decision of the President on Application for Conditional Early Release, RSCSL-04-14-ES (1581–1604), The Hague, 29 May 2017, paras 59, 61(a).

for Gbao to help him understand and accept responsibility for the harm he had inflicted on individuals and to the peace process.[113]

The approach adopted by the RSCSL is problematic due to its post-hoc and arbitrary nature and the fact that the training requirements were imposed after previous findings by Presidents and detaining authorities that the applicants had demonstrated rehabilitation, accepted responsibility for their crimes, and expressed remorse.[114] Further, responsibility for a lack of access to suitable or tailored rehabilitation programmes lies squarely with the Court. The Sub-Committee that created the conditional early release scheme at the RSCSL stressed the need to ensure convicted persons had access to rehabilitation specific to atrocity crimes.[115] Consequently, tailored programmes should have been available to enable convicted persons to demonstrate (the required form of) rehabilitation prior to applications for release being submitted. The subject matter of requested additional training appears broad and vague, and it is unclear how the time required for undertaking such programmes was calculated (or differed so significantly) given that the programmes had not yet been designed. For these reasons, it is hard to escape the conclusion that the periods of additional custody imposed were arbitrary. The allocation of offenders to specific programmes and interventions should be guided by explicit criteria.[116] The imposition of additional periods in custody due to a prison authority's failure to create and implement the correct form of training seems disproportionate, particularly given that the training could have continued in the community during the period of supervision.[117] This is particularly true given that the need for further training was identified in the first release decision for core crimes. Delayed release should not then have been necessary in subsequent cases. Gbao, who completed the RSCSL-designed specialist programmes on international humanitarian law, international crimes, human rights, and respect for

---

[113] *Prosecutor v Gbao*, Decision of the President on Application for Conditional Early Release, RSCSL-04-15-ES, 8 September 2020, para. 82(a)–(b).

[114] *Prosecutor v Fofana and Kondewa*, Decision of the President on Application for Conditional Early Release, SCSL-04-14-ES, 11 August 2014, paras 37–38, 42–43; *Prosecutor v Kondewa*, Decision of the President on Application for Conditional Early Release, RSCSL-04-14-ES, 29 May 2017, paras 37–38, 42–43, 50–51, 54; *Prosecutor v Gbao*, Decision of the President on Application for Conditional Early Release, RSCSL-04-15-ES, 8 September 2020, paras 72, 79.

[115] Teresa Anne Doherty and Shireen Avis Fisher, 'Enforcement of Sentences and Oversight of Prisoners Convicted by the SCSL' in R. Mulgrew and D. Abels (eds) *Research Handbook on the International Penal System* (Edward Elgar Publishing, 2016) 355–380 at 368.

[116] Rule 38 ERCSM.

[117] Rule 13.1 Tokyo Rules.

law and order, was still detained for an additional period of three months to receive 'training'.

These additional periods in custody seem to have less to do with rehabilitative needs or risk and, in reality, seem to have been a direct consequence of and response to consultations with other judges in *Fofana* and the Prosecutor and witnesses in *Kondewa*.[118] In *Kondewa*, in particular, the unsubstantiated and *de minimis* fears of one witness (that could have been (and were in fact) addressed with tailored conditions) seem to have acted as a bar to release for 10 months. It is difficult to understand how this approach can be justified on penological grounds. This case illustrates the danger of adopting an expansive approach to consultations and the potential detrimental influence external voices can have on liberty rights.[119] While convicted persons do not have any entitlement to release prior to the complete service of their original sentence, the extension of the custodial period within this conditional early release scheme seems to have been unnecessary and disproportionate. The practice of granting release subject to additional (unpredictable) periods in custody undermined and contradicted previous judicial determinations and the findings of penal experts from national prison authorities in relation to rehabilitation. Prolonging custody to provide training on these grounds appears to rely on a 'pretence' or 'misuse' of rehabilitation to mask the reality that the goal was in fact incapacitation.[120]

4.3 Deflection of Responsibility for Providing Programmes

From a traditional perspective, rehabilitation entails both a *process* that addresses the offenders' criminogenic risk factors and reintegration *outcomes*.[121] Analysis of international release jurisprudence, policy and practice shows that international courts have greatly expanded expected rehabilitation outcomes without providing (timely) access to (appropriate) rehabilitative processes. Hola and Munivrana have highlighted that the lack of any 'tailored penitentiary programmes' focusing on the specific criminogenic risks or reintegrative needs of persons convicted of core crimes has resulted in a 'considerable incoherence' between demanding judicial expectations in relation to reflection and dissociation from crime and contemporary international penal practice.[122] A failure to provide programmes to address international criminality creates heightened risks to societal safety and security as prisoners

118 See Chapter 4, section 6.2.
119 See Chapter 8, section 3.
120 See Riccardi, note 51.
121 Kelder, Holá and Van Wijk, note 53, 1179.
122 Holá and Munivrana, note 50, 23.

will be released without having had their criminogenic propensities or peace-threatening tendencies addressed.

Despite the higher threshold for establishing rehabilitation, contemporary international criminal courts and tribunals have remained hesitant to accept any responsibility for designing or delivering programmes that would enable internationally convicted persons to prove their progress in light of required indicators. The RSCSL is perhaps the outlier in this regard. The adoption of a 'delayed release for training' model resulted in Special Court officers being directly involved in and considered jointly responsible for the design, delivery and evaluation of training provided for RSCSL convicted persons serving their sentences in a domestic prison system (Rwanda).[123] The MICT and ICC should also provide tailored programmes for convicted persons, whether they are housed in international remand centres or serving their sentences in enforcing states. The lack of suitable programmes has foreseeable liberty consequences as applicants cannot demonstrate sufficient rehabilitation and are therefore being denied release. International courts' responsibility for the design and delivery of atrocity crime-relevant programmes is necessary to prevent arbitrary detention. With ultimate authority for custody, and the power to keep individuals in custody for failing to demonstrate rehabilitation, it would seem logical to place the duty to develop and implement suitable rehabilitation programmes on international courts, not cooperating States.

5. REINTEGRATION

Under both a rights-based approach and, indeed, the approach taken in international release jurisprudence and policy, reintegration is a core component of rehabilitation assessments. In the international criminal context, reintegration assessments go beyond discussions of financial stability and social capital. As

---

[123] *Prosecutor v Fofana and Kondewa*, Decision of the President on Application for Conditional Early Release, SCSL-04-14-ES (1270-1291), 11 August 2014, paras 47–49; First Annual Report of the President of the RSCSL, January 2014–December 2014 at 23; *Prosecutor v Fofana and Kondewa*, Presidential Order for Detention and Transfer and for Hearing Pursuant to Article 12(F) of the Practice Direction on Conditional Early Release of Persons Convicted by the SCSL, RSCSL-04-14-ES (1297–1300), The Hague, 9 March 2015 at 2–3; Second Annual Report of the President of the RSCSL, January 2015–December 2015 at 20; *Prosecutor v Kondewa*, Decision of the President on Application for Conditional Early Release, RSCSL-04-14-ES (1581–1604), The Hague, 29 May 2017, para. 61(b); Fourth Annual Report of the President of the RSCSL, January 2017–December 2017 at 19, 28; and Fifth Annual Report of the President of the RSCSL, January 2018–December 2018 at 20.

there is empirical support for the proposition that international criminals are rarely recidivists,[124] in the international context, risk assessment focuses on the impact of an individual's release on local and regional stability and security. This section explores the approaches taken to reintegration at the MICT, ICC and RSCSL.

5.1 Reintegration at the MICT

In addition to the assessment of resocialisation, Presidents have also assessed prospects for successful and peaceful reintegration into a given society.[125] The assessment of reintegrative readiness and preparedness includes an analysis of post-release plans, often in relation to an envisaged place of residence. If the indicated place of residence is in the region where the crimes were committed, extra scrutiny is increasingly being applied due to the fact that the MICT and its predecessor institutions were established under Chapter VII of the UN Charter to contribute to the restoration and maintenance of peace and security.[126] As a general rule, former President Agius did not feel that it was appropriate 'to enable convicted persons to return to the affected region before they have served their full sentence, without having demonstrated a certain degree of rehabilitation, including that their release will not endanger peace and security in the envisaged place of residence'.[127] To facilitate this assessment, MICT applicants have been required to name a proposed location for residence post-release.[128] In fact, the Practice Direction was amended in 2020

124 Maier, note 46, 318–319.

125 *Prosecutor v Brdanin*, Decision on the Application of Radoslav Brdanin for Early Release, MICT-13-48-ES, 28 February 2020, para. 50; *Prosecutor v Bralo*, Decision on the Early Release of Miroslav Bralo, MICT-14-78-ES, 31 December 2019, para. 39; *Prosecutor v Semanza*, Decision on Laurent Semanza's Application for Early Release, MICT-13-36-ES.2, 17 September 2020, para. 47.

126 U.N. Security Council Resolution 1966, 22 December 2010 at 1; U.N. Security Council Resolution 955, 8 November 1994 at 1; U.N. Security Council Resolution 808, 22 February 1993 at 2; *Prosecutor v Brdanin*, Decision on the Application of Radoslav Brdanin for Early Release, MICT-13-48-ES, 28 February 2020, para. 50; *Prosecutor v Semanza*, Decision on Laurent Semanza's Application for Early Release, MICT-13-36-ES.2, 17 September 2020, para. 47.

127 *Prosecutor v Bralo*, Decision on the Early Release of Miroslav Bralo, MICT-14-78-ES, 31 December 2019, para. 39; *Prosecutor v Brdanin*, Decision on the Application of Radoslav Brdanin for Early Release, MICT-13-48-ES, 28 February 2020, para. 50; *Prosecutor v Semanza*, Decision on Laurent Semanza's Application for Early Release, MICT-13-36-ES.2, 17 September 2020, para. 47.

128 *Prosecutor v Krstić*, Decision on the Application for Early Release of Radislav Krstić, MICT-13-46-ES.1, 15 November 2022, para. 8.

to facilitate requests to the convicted person for information on where they wished to live upon release in order to assess any (possible) impacts on local communities.[129] This approach also requires the proposed state of relocation to support the release application and to commit to monitoring any conditions imposed on release.[130]

This approach assumes, however, that applicants will have an identifiable place to which they *can* return. The challenge with adopting a coherent position on reintegration at the MICT is that it fails to recognise the dichotomy of receptions persons convicted by the ICTY (hero) and the ICTR (international pariah) may face.[131] The fall-out from the de facto statelessness that followed ICTR prosecutions and convictions has been well documented.[132] The relocation of ICTR released persons has caused considerable legal, political and diplomatic challenges, creating 'a heavy responsibility for the institution' that has lasted for over two decades.[133] The continued failure to resolve these issues has resulted in extremely serious, life-changing and often surreal realities that gravely affect the lives of released persons. The issue is not confined to ICTR convicted persons. Some ICTY convicted persons have sought residency rights elsewhere due to fears for their safety should they return to their original residence.[134]

Reintegration may be difficult for legal and immigration status reasons. Further, choosing to nominate a place of residence in the region in which the crimes were committed will result in a higher threshold being applied for rehabilitation assessments.[135] Kelder et al argue that rehabilitation assessments are often too focused on individual rehabilitation and thereby fail to address the collective nature of international criminality, the destroyed social fabric and profound divisions of a post-conflict or post-genocide society.[136] A reintegration assessment based on victims' views of reintegration may ignore the reality that the society to which they return 'does not consist exclusively of their

---

129 Maier, note 46, 298.

130 *Prosecutor v Krstić,* Decision on the Application for Early Release of Radislav Krstić, MICT-13-46-ES.1, 15 November 2022, paras 12, 76, 78.

131 Meron, note 5, 263.

132 See Cécile Lecolle, 'Relocation Issues of Released and Acquitted at International Criminal Courts and Tribunals: A Defence Perspective' (2023) 21(1) *JICJ* 167–184. See also Chapter 6, section 6.

133 Annual Report of the IRMCT to the Security Council, 30 July 2021, A/76/248; S/2021/694, para. 83.

134 See Kelder, Holá and Van Wijk, note 53, 1199.

135 *Prosecutor v Krstić,* Decision on the Application for Early Release of Radislav Krstić, MICT-13-46-ES.1, 15 November 2022, para. 50.

136 Kelder, Holá and Van Wijk, note 53, 1199.

victims' but also their 'supporters and admirers' who look for heroes 'to justify … the rightfulness' of the actions of that group.[137] As Hola et al stress, the reintegrative potential for internationally convicted persons may actually be enhanced if they do not acknowledge the crimes they were convicted for and reject attempts to make them express remorse.[138] However, under the conditional release system, applicants must commit to keeping a low public profile and staying out of politics. For Agius, rehabilitation is first and foremost a process through which a convicted person can show that they will be able to successfully and peacefully integrate into a given society.[139] This MICT focus on re-entry, framed in peace and security terms, aligns with the approach adopted by the ICC and RSCSL.

5.2 Reintegration at the ICC

ICC judges must also consider the impact of release on the proposed society for relocation. The ICC Rules obligate the sentence reduction panel to assess 'whether the early release of a sentenced person would give rise to significant social instability'.[140] Considerations to date have included the timing of elections, links with political and military groups, and the views of the local community.[141] Panels have also referred to the potential value of information that release would undermine public safety, cause riots or ethnic-based violence, lead to the commission of new international crimes by the convicted persons' supporters, or undermine confidence in domestic legal orders.[142] It is difficult to understand, however, how some of these factors can be objectively and empirically demonstrated, or how factors beyond the control of the prisoner can be allowed to negatively affect their chances of regaining liberty. Indeed, Estrada refers to this factor as 'one of the most problematic preconditions' and notes that it is specific to the international criminal justice process.[143]

---

137 Maier, note 46, 272.

138 Barbora Holá, Joris van Wijk, Francesca Constantini and Armi Korhonnen, 'Does Remorse Count? ICTY Convicts' Reflections on Their Crimes in Early Release Decisions' (2018) 28(4) *International Criminal Justice Review* 349–351 at 350.

139 *Prosecutor v Brdanin*, Decision on the Application of Radoslav Brdanin for Early Release, MICT-13-48-ES, 28 February 2020, para. 50.

140 Rule 223(c) ICC RPE.

141 *Lubanga* First Sentence Review, paras 54–57; *Katanga* Sentence Review, paras 63–65.

142 *Katanga* Sentence Review, para. 74; *Al Mahdi* Sentence Review, para. 58.

143 Cristina Fernández-Pacheco Estrada, 'What We Talk About When We Talk About Early Release in International Criminal Law: The Sui Generis Nature of the

The relevance of this factor remains to be seen. To date, submissions on this ground from national authorities and victims have tended to focus on their opposition to *any* grant of release due to their dissatisfaction with the original sentence[144] and have included unsubstantiated claims that release could lead to the resumption of conflict or the commission of new international crimes.[145] Convicted persons, in response, have stressed the need to avoid reliance on unverified claims and opinions in the absence of objective evidence of a risk to stability.[146]

The ICC has dismissed the relevance of opinions on the adequacy of the sentence length under this ground and unsubstantiated 'bald' assertions.[147] The Prosecution has often brought balance to the analysis, highlighting that there was no indication of an increased threat of conflict if released.[148] However, in *Katanga*, the timing of elections was, arguably unnecessarily, taken into account given the unproven link between election timing, his release and any potential instability that could result.[149]

Overall, ICC sentence review panels have treated the 'social stability' factor with the caution that it deserves, recognising the challenges of (a) considering domestic political conditions within an international sentence reduction review, (b) basing such assessments on what will invariably be inconclusive and conflicting information, and (c) the fact that these conditions are beyond the convicted person's control.[150] Erring on the side of caution, panels have been willing to accept that some degree of social instability may result from a sentence reduction and subsequent release. However, the explicit inclusion of the word 'significant' in the rule has given the panel a way to reduce the effect of this factor on decisions (by either not finding it to be present or categorising it as a neutral factor).[151] Any risks or possibilities of instability to date have been found to be local and controllable by national or international forces.[152]

Reduction of Sentence Under the Rome Statute' (2022) 22 ICLR 539–567 at 566.

144 *Lubanga* First Sentence Review, para. 58; *Katanga* Sentence Review, paras 71–72.

145 *Lubanga* First Sentence Review, para. 62.

146 *Lubanga* First Sentence Review, paras 59–60; *Katanga* Sentence Review, paras 66–67.

147 *Katanga* Sentence Review, paras 77–78.

148 *Katanga* Sentence Review, para. 70.

149 *Katanga* Sentence Review, para. 69.

150 *Lubanga* First Sentence Review, paras 54, 63–64; *Lubanga* Second Sentence Review, paras 63–64, 73; *Katanga* Sentence Review, paras 62, 747-5.

151 *Lubanga* First Sentence Review, para. 64; *Katanga* Sentence Review, paras 76, 79; *Lubanga* Second Sentence Review, para. 73.

152 *Lubanga* First Sentence Review, para. 57.

This approach means that the discussion of this factor in the sentence reduction context, in the absence of credible evidence of a specific threat posed by the convicted person to social stability, will allow states, victims and the Prosecutor to air their concerns. Opening up this discursive space for discussions of possible post-release threats to stability may only (further) amplify the lack of conditional release options under the Rome Statute. For example, in the *Al Mahdi* sentence reduction decision, victims expressed fears that the convicted person might renew ties with armed groups if released.[153] Al Mahdi suggested that the possibility of disturbance to society could be reduced by his relocation to another country.[154] These types of concerns could be more adequately dealt with by a conditional form of release to ensure supervised re-entry. Moreover, general concerns should be addressed in relation to the suitability of the proposed area of relocation rather than taken as decisive factors that determine whether it is appropriate or not to grant a sentence reduction.[155]

5.3 Reintegration at the RSCSL

An important aspect of the conditional release scheme introduced by the RSCSL was the assessment of the *suitability* of the proposed area for post-release residence. Presidential analysis in cases to date has focused on whether the releasee can be subject to monitoring in the nominated area, whether the residents of this community will accept the convicted person as a co-resident,[156] and since 2016, an assessment of the views, concerns, willingness and acknowledgements of this community in relation to the guilt of the individual for the crimes they were convicted for and the harm caused to victims.[157] To acquire the information needed to make such assessments, RSCSL

153 *Al Mahdi* Sentence Review, para. 54.

154 Ibid, para. 57.

155 R. Mulgrew, 'Releasing International Prisoners' in M. Herzog-Evans (ed.) *Offender Release and Supervision: The Role of Courts and the Use of Discretion* (Wolf Legal Publishers: The Netherlands, 2014) 21–51 at 43.

156 See Art. 8(C)(ii) PDCER. This was also discussed under the heading 'Views of Victims, Witnesses, Their Families and Others at Risk' in *Kondewa*. See *Prosecutor v Kondewa*, Decision of the President on Application for Conditional Early Release, RSCSL-04-14-ES (1581–1604), The Hague, 29 May 2017, para. 31; See *Prosecutor v Fofana and Kondewa*, Decision of the President on Application for Conditional Early Release, SCSL-04-14-ES (1270-1291), 11 August 2014, para. 21; *Prosecutor v Senessie*, Decision of the President on Application for Conditional Early Release, SCSL-11-01-ES (580–589), 4 June 2014, para. 18.

157 Art. 8(D)(vi) PDCER. See *Prosecutor v Kondewa*, Decision of the President on Application for Conditional Early Release, RSCSL-04-14-ES (1581–1604), The Hague, 29 May 2017, para. 20.

officials and counsel contact a diverse range of stakeholders (civil society, local government officials and police, traditional and religious leaders, women and youth groups, victims, former combatants and members of the applicant's family) through a variety of means including interviews, questionnaires, phone-in radio programmes and town hall meetings.[158] In all cases to date, consulted community members have expressed overall support for the release of applicants.[159] This support stemmed from beliefs that the individuals were sorry for and would not repeat their crimes, they could be reintegrated into society, and that they understood that they would be released under conditions and supervision. This positive response may be attributed to the extensive release-focused outreach and sensitisation activities conducted by the RSCL[160] and/or the national experience with transitional reconciliation processes geared towards peace and harmony (the Truth and Reconciliation Commission) that seem to have generated increased receptiveness to reintegration following punishment.[161]

[158] *Prosecutor v Fofana and Kondewa*, Decision of the President on Application for Conditional Early Release, SCSL-04-14-ES (1270–1291), 11 August 2014, paras 23, 25; *Prosecutor v Senessie*, Decision of the President on Application for Conditional Early Release, SCSL-11-01-ES (580–589), 4 June 2014, paras 21, 23; *Prosecutor v Kondewa*, Decision of the President on Application for Conditional Early Release, RSCSL-04-14-ES (1581–1604), The Hague, 29 May 2017, para. 20; *Prosecutor v Gbao*, Decision of the President on Application for Conditional Early Release, RSCSL-04-15-ES, 8 September 2020, para. 57.

[159] *Prosecutor v Fofana and Kondewa*, Decision of the President on Application for Conditional Early Release, SCSL-04-14-ES (1270–1291), 11 August 2014, para. 24; *Prosecutor v Kondewa*, Decision of the President on Application for Conditional Early Release, RSCSL-04-14-ES (1581–1604), The Hague, 29 May 2017, paras 19, 21, 24; *Prosecutor v Gbao*, Decision of the President on Application for Conditional Early Release, RSCSL-04-15-ES, 8 September 2020, paras 41, 43–48, 50, 52, 59, 61.

[160] See *Prosecutor v Gbao*, Decision of the President on Application for Conditional Early Release, RSCSL-04-15-ES, 8 September 2020, paras 49, 54, and 82(c), (e).

[161] See *Prosecutor v Kondewa*, Decision of the President on Application for Conditional Early Release, RSCSL-04-14-ES (1581–1604), The Hague, 29 May 2017, paras 22–23, 34; *Prosecutor v Gbao*, Decision of the President on Application for Conditional Early Release, RSCSL-04-15-ES, 8 September 2020, para. 51.

6. THE RISK OF OVER-REACH: MANDATORY MORALISATION AND JUDICIAL CENSORSHIP

Numerous scholars have advocated for careful consideration of how rehabilitation is framed and applied in the international criminal justice context.[162] Calls for a more sophisticated approach that encompasses both an individualised, rights-based approach to resocialisation, and more collective, reparative and reconciliatory elements to enhance reintegration, societal healing and peace maintenance in post-conflict settings seem to have been translated into international release policy.[163] The assessment of rehabilitation has been 'reframed and gained elevated importance' as a release factor, with the contemporary model generating expectations that released persons will have reflected critically on their crimes, accepted responsibility and expressed remorse for them, and undertaken commitments not to jeopardise fragile peace or reconciliation processes when they return to the community.[164]

The difficulty lies in striking the correct balance between what may be conflicting interests.[165] The model adopted should be able to incorporate components relevant for international criminal justice but only to the extent permitted by legal, penological and rights principles. The preceding analysis of the evolution of the rehabilitation principle in international release policy and practice has highlighted positive changes but also flagged more controversial aspects of its reimagining – delayed release to facilitate additional training, the failure to take responsibility for the design and delivery of tailored programmes, and the questionable merit of taking subjective, unverified opinions on the potential impact of release on political and security stability into account. Questions have also been raised in relation to the increasingly rigid requirements to express remorse in precise and public ways and for convicted persons to fully accept all aspects of the international judicial record.

Making remorse and acceptance of responsibility mandatory may prove to be counter-productive: 'remorse cannot be genuine if it is compelled … nor

---

162 See Drumbl, note 94; Mulgrew, note 52; Kelder, Hola and Van Wijk, note 53.

163 See Riccardi, note 51; Edith Riegler, 'Rehabilitating Enemies of Mankind: An Exploration of the Concept of Rehabilitation as a Sentencing Aim at the ICTY and the ICC' (2020) 20 *Int Criminal Law Review* 701 at 726–727.

164 Holá and Munivrana, note 50, 20.

165 See Elena Maculan and Alicia Gil Gil, 'The Rational and Purposes of Criminal Law and Punishment in Transitional Contexts' (2020) 40(1) *Oxford Journal of Legal Studies* 132–157, 135.

can positive moral convictions be dictated'.[166] Do people have a 'right to feel innocent' or should release be reserved for 'repentant' perpetrators?[167] Former President Meron was highly sceptical of the idea that convicted persons should be legally required to express remorse or accept responsibility for crimes to demonstrate rehabilitation or as a pre-condition for release.[168] Defending his inclusion of such factors in his list of indicators of rehabilitation, former President Agius argued that they did not constitute legal requirements for demonstrating rehabilitation or preconditions for release.[169] In reality, however, these considerations have acted as bars to release: their absence will result in a finding of insufficient rehabilitation. Analysis of release practice under Agius at the MICT led Holá and Munivrana to conclude that inducing moral change had become an elevated or primary goal of rehabilitating international prisoners: a failure to acknowledge responsibility (fully and publicly), reflect on crimes or express genuine remorse was construed as an attempt to rationalise, minimise or deny criminal behaviour.[170] The mandatory and rigid nature of the requirement undermines and reduces its victimological and reconciliatory potential. Making remorse a crucial component of release decision-making has resulted in Prosecutors and victims viewing apologies and statements accepting responsibility as cynical, self-serving strategies to gain early release.[171] The heightened focus on these elements has reduced their credibility and impact. Release policy should move away from creating demands for forced apologies towards the creation of 'a conscious framework of encouragement' that promotes reconciliation efforts and denunciation of extremist ideologies.[172]

According to Riccardi, the international conception of rehabilitation also refers to the willingness and capacity of offenders to contribute to the development of a culture of respect for international criminal law values and to

---

[166] Navanethem Pillay, Keynote address at the International Criminal Justice Sentencing and Post-Conflict Societies, Cape Town, South Africa, 13 October 2011, at http://www.ohchr.org/en/NewsEvents/Pages/DisplayNews.aspx?NewsID=11630&LangID=E (accessed 21 November 2023).

[167] Maier, note 46, 304.

[168] *Prosecutor v Brdanin*, Decision on the Application of Radoslav Brdanin for Early Release, MICT-13-48-ES, 28 February 2020, para. 94.

[169] Ibid, paras 70, 95.

[170] See Holá and Munivrana, note 50, 11–12.

[171] *Katanga* Sentence Review, para. 45; *Prosecutor v Semanza*, Decision on Laurent Semanza's Application for Early Release, MICT-13-36-ES.2, 17 September 2020, para. 65; *Prosecutor v Fofana and Kondewa*, Decision of the President on Application for Conditional Early Release, SCSL-04-14-ES (1270-1291), 11 August 2014, para. 39.

[172] Pillay, note 166. See also Mulgrew, note 52, 218–262.

internalise the international rule of law.[173] While Presidents Agius and Santana have indicated that a partial acceptance of responsibility may merit positive weight in rehabilitation assessments,[174] any notable difference between the role the convicted person 'ascribes to himself and the role he actually played' would suggest that the convicted person has 'not sufficiently engaged in crucial reflection upon his crimes'.[175] Holá and Munivrana worry that this need to show 'complete and utter deference' to findings leaves both the 'impression and the uneasy feeling of judicial censorship'.[176] This approach is also questionable in light of the high acquittal rate at international courts.[177] Despite these reservations, the practice of requiring applicants to affirm the judicial record is becoming embedded in rehabilitation assessments in international release decision-making.

7. CONCLUSION

The retributive reach of international sentences has been extended by judicial pronouncements at the MICT. Not only has the presumption in favour of release been reversed, but rehabilitation assessments are now undertaken using a more rigorous and gravity-informed lens. Both the ICC and RSCSL systems require a wide range of factors to be taken into account in sentence reduction and conditional release decisions. Despite the growing expectations to demonstrate numerous indicators to establish progress towards rehabilitation and proof of potential to successfully reintegrate into society, international criminal courts and tribunals are not providing convicted persons with access to the programmes that could help convicted persons understand or establish these components during their time in prison.[178] Persons convicted of international crimes have no right to be released before the end of the sentence imposed on them. They do, however, have the right to apply for early release or sentence reduction. Release decisions should be reached on the basis of clear

---

173 Riccardi, note 51.

174 *Prosecutor v Dordević*, Decision on the Applications for Early Release of Vlastimir Dordevic, MICT-14-76-ES, 30 November 2021, paras 65, 67.

175 Ibid, para. 70.

176 Holá and Munivrana, note 50, 21.

177 See R. Mulgrew, 'The Costs of Suspicion: A Critical Analysis of the Compensation Scheme Established by Article 85(3) of the Rome Statute' in Mulgrew and Abels (eds), *Research Handbook on the International Penal System* (Edward Elgar Publishing, 2016) 445–491.

178 For previous arguments in this regard, see R. Mulgrew, 'On the Enforcement of Sentences Imposed by International Courts: Challenges Faced by the SCSL' (2009) 7(2) *JICJ* 373–396; Mulgrew, note 52, 213–217.

criteria that seek to achieve specific and achievable objectives and are applied consistently. While criteria can evolve, they should not be subject to dramatic change on the basis of the interpretative whims of particular judges or external political influence. The balance of interests must also be considered carefully when release systems allow a broad range of possible stakeholders to express subjective views on the merits or impacts of release.

8. Influences on release decisions: the judicial role, victim input and other voices

1. INFLUENCES ON RELEASE DECISIONS

In addition to the form of release and the substantive factors taken into consideration in release decision-making, it is important to understand and analyse other influences on release. This chapter begins by exploring the fundamental importance of the judicial role in release decision-making. Consultation requirements and judicial presumptions in relation to release are examined, before a more critical eye is turned to the integrity implications that may arise when release decisions are viewed as judicial activism and release procedures that may create (or avoid) perceptions of unilateral and/or partial decision-making.

International release decision-making processes increasingly allow judges to consider input from a growing range of stakeholders that includes victims, prosecutors and states. The impact and merit of considering victims' views in release or sentence reduction decisions remain open to debate, and the policy and practice facilitating their participation vary significantly between the international courts. This chapter compares the limited engagement with witnesses at the MICT, the broad community-based consultation with victims and their families at the RSCSL, and the standing granted to victims (through their legal representatives) at the ICC. The chapter concludes with a review of the extent and effect of participation by and input from prosecutors and States.

2. THE JUDICIAL ROLE IN RELEASE DECISIONS

The processes used to consider eligibility and appropriateness of release and sentence reduction vary significantly between contemporary international criminal courts and tribunals. At the MICT, early release decisions are made by the President following receipt of an application (initiated by either an enforcing state or a sentenced person).[1] At the ICC, a panel of judges appointed by the Appeals Chamber decides on the appropriateness (and extent) of (any) sentence reduction on a mandatory and *proprio motu* basis for initial reviews at statutorily fixed temporal points, and either on a *proprio motu* basis or following receipt of applications from sentenced persons for subsequent reviews.[2] The RSCSL, in contrast, has a two-stage process. The President must first decide if a prisoner is eligible for consideration for conditional release, and second, if they should be granted conditional release. At all three contemporary courts, there is no avenue to appeal release or sentence reduction decisions.[3] Rather, unsuccessful applicants can re-apply when there is a significant change of circumstances, or following a statutorily or judicially determined interval.[4]

In contrast to the variety of processes involved, the judicial nature of release decision-making is consistent.[5] What is not consistent is whether the decision lies with one judge, or a group of judges. The concentration of decision-making power in the Presidents of the UN Tribunals, Mechanism and RSCSL has not been replicated within the ICC system. The ICC may, therefore, avoid the criticisms that have been levied at the MICT in relation to the perceived unilateral and partial nature of Presidential decision-making, as well as accusations of judicial legislation.

---

1 See Chapter 2, section 4 and Chapter 5, section 4.

2 See Chapter 3, section 3.

3 See para. 12 MICT PDER; Art. 8(E) PDCER.

4 See Rule 224(3) ICC RPE; *Prosecutor v Thomas Lubanga Dyilo*, Decision on the review concerning reduction of sentence of Mr Thomas Lubanga Dyilo, ICC-01/04-01/06, 22 September 2015, para. 2 (*Lubanga* Sentencing Review); *Prosecutor v Lubanga*, Second Decision on the review concerning reduction of sentence of Mr Thomas Lubanga Dyilo, ICC-01/04-01/06, 3 November 2017, para. 95 (*Lubanga* Second Sentence Review); para. 10 MICT PDER; Art. 9(B) PDCER; *Prosecutor v Musema*, Decision on the Request for Reconsideration of the Decision Denying Early Release, MICT-12-15-ES.1, 10 January 2020; *Prosecutor v Simba*, Public Redacted Version of the President's 7 January 2019 Decision on the Early Release of Aloys Simba, MICT-14-62-ES.1, 7 January 2019, para. 4; *Prosecutor v Brdanin*, Decision on the Application of Radoslav Brdanin for Early Release, MICT-13-48-ES, 28 February 2020, paras 1, 5–6; *Prosecutor v Bralo*, Decision on the Early Release of Miroslav Bralo, MICT-14-78-ES, 31 December 2019, para. 84.

5 Suggestions to establish an international parole board or more executive decision-making within the Assembly of States Parties at the ICC were not adopted. See Cristina Fernández-Pacheco Estrada, 'What we talk about when we talk about early release in international criminal law: the sui generis nature of the reduction of sentence under the Rome Statute' (2022) 22 ICLR 539–567 at 546.

2.1 Consultation with Other Judges

By its nature and structure, the ICC sentence reduction process results in the issuance of a joint decision from three judges. In contrast, the Presidents of the UN Tribunals and the RSCSL were endowed with the sole power to make early release decisions. They were, however, required to consult with other judges during the decision-making process. This requirement to consult with other judges may have been seen as an important constraint on this concentrated Presidential power. While this requirement was placed on a statutory basis for the UN Tribunals,[6] it was not at the MICT, where it could be found in the Rules.[7] Meron felt strongly that as the Statute vested sole decision-making power in the President and did not refer to consultations with other judges, consultation was not always required.[8] Strong criticisms of this view and practice ultimately resulted in changes to the detail and scope of this obligation to ensure that sufficient consultation with other judges actually occurred.[9] MICT Presidents must now always consult with at least two other judges, even if judges that were part of the sentencing chamber are no longer available.[10] This consultation requirement is reflected in the RSCSL Practice Direction: the President must consult with the Judges who imposed the sentence, or others if these judges are not available.[11]

The requirement, however formulated, does not alter the fact that the Presidents of these courts are not bound by views expressed during these discussions. Consulted judges have disagreed with Presidents' views and decisions, and the grounds for the disagreements are sometimes outlined in release decisions. It is not explicit what weight these views should have. However, Agius described the consultations as forming 'a meaningful part' of Presidential decisions, and it does seem that a *de facto* majority rule approach has been adopted.[12] It is unclear what the position will be at the ICC as all sentence reduction decisions to date have been reached unanimously.[13] The legal

---

[6] Article 28 ICTYSt; Article 27 ICTRSt.

[7] Rule 150 MICT RPE; para. 7 MICT PDER.

[8] Theodore Meron, *Standing Up for Justice: The Challenges of Trying Atrocity Crimes* (OUP 2021) at 265.

[9] See Chapter 2, section 4.

[10] See para. 16 PDCER, Rev. 3.

[11] Art. 8(A)-(B) PDCER.

[12] *Prosecutor v Ćorić*, Further Redacted Public Redacted Version of the Decision of the President on the Early Release of Valentin Ćorić and Related Motions, MICT-17-112-ES.4, 16 January 2019, para. 59. See Chapter 2, section 4.

[13] *Lubanga* First Sentence Review, preamble; *Prosecutor v Katanga*, Decision on the review concerning reduction of sentence of Mr Germain Katanga,

framework does not stipulate whether decisions require consensus, or can be adopted on a majority basis.

2.2 Presumptions For or Against Release

At the MICT, consultations have taken place against the Presidential view on whether there is a presumption for or against release. Meron and Agius held diametrically opposed views in this regard. For Meron, the possibility of release is required by human rights principles generally and pursuant to the rehabilitative principle and the right to respect for human dignity in particular. On this basis, prisoners have a right to a review of their sentence *and* prospects for release.[14] In addition to this principled approach, Meron argued that the rights obligations of states that voluntarily offered to implement sentences of imprisonment meant that ensuring prospects for release also served a pragmatic purpose: the facilitation of cooperation on sentence enforcement.[15] The logical conclusion of this line of reasoning was that Meron supported a *presumption in favour of release.* In *Ćorić*, Meron noted that the Mechanism had 'inherited a long-standing practice of granting requests for early release upon completion of 2/3 of a sentence absent particular circumstances that warrant against it'.[16]

In complete disagreement, Agius strongly supported a *presumption against granting release.* In his view, the general rule should be that sentences should be served in full.[17] In sharp contrast to the rights underpinnings of Meron's approach, Agius focused on the seriousness of the offences that had resulted in the conviction and sanction. Under his approach, the *gravity* of offences would 'determine the threshold that the arguments in favour of early release should

ICC-01/04-01//07, 13 November 2015, preamble (*Katanga* Sentence Review); *Lubanga* Second Sentence Review, preamble; *Prosecutor v Al Mahdi*, Public Redacted Version of the Decision on the review concerning reduction of sentence of Mr Ahmad Al Faqi Al Mahdi, ICC-01/12-01/15-434-Red3, 25 November 2021, preamble (*Al Mahdi* Sentence Review).

14 *Prosecutor v Galić*, Reasons for the President's Decision to Deny the Early Release of Stanislav Galić and Decision on Prosecution Motion, MICT-14-83-ES, 23 June 2015, para. 22.

15 Meron, note 8 at 264.

16 *Prosecutor v Ćorić*, Further Redacted Public Redacted Version of the Decision of the President on the Early Release of Valentin Ćorić and Related Motions, MICT-17-112-ES.4, 16 January 2019, paras 38–39.

17 *Prosecutor v Dordević*, Decision on the Applications for Early Release of Vlastimir Dordevic, MICT-14-76-ES, 30 November 2021, para. 36.

reach'.[18] Meron drew attention to these divergent views and resulting practice in 2021, stating that while his model of consistently granting early release followed the approach adopted by his predecessors, his successor (Agius) had 'adopted a distinctly different approach' and that no early release had 'been granted on his watch so far'.[19]

Despite this complete change in practice, the presumption against release was also adopted by Agius' successor. Santana has perhaps gone further than Agius. Framing her approach in gravity terms, Santana relayed that in her personal opinion, 'the early release of persons convicted … for genocide, crimes against humanity or war crimes should be *exceptional*'.[20] This would mean that, during her tenure, the baseline is that early release, even with conditions, would be rare and unlikely. She reiterated the approach adopted by Agius in his release jurisprudence: sentences should be served in full as a general rule given the gravity of the crimes under the Mechanism's jurisdiction unless the convicted person can demonstrate that they should be granted release.

The presumption in favour of release constructed by Meron on principled and pragmatic grounds has been reversed by Agius (and endorsed by Santana) on gravity grounds. Underpinning a release system with gravity considerations alters the normative frame towards a fundamentally more punitive approach. The subsequent impact on both gravity and rehabilitation assessments has and will continue to reduce possibilities for release, despite the introduction of the option of granting release on a conditional basis.

2.3 Beyond Semantics

This paradigmatic shift in release policy and practice illustrates the extraordinary levels of discretion awarded to Presidents at the ICTY, ICTR and MICT, and how fundamentally and arbitrarily the underpinnings of a release system can change based solely on the views of one judge. As a consequence of the reversal of the presumption by Agius and the endorsement of this approach by Santana, release has been repeatedly denied on the basis of gravity and the failure to sufficiently demonstrate rehabilitation. Presidents, through their decisions, have made other significant changes to release policy by introducing temporal eligibility rules (that were not in the statute or rules) and reconceptualising core factors.[21] As Maier observes, by giving the President sole responsibility for designating enforcing states, changing the location of enforcement,

---

[18] Ibid.

[19] Meron, note 8 at 263.

[20] *Prosecutor v Krstić,* Decision on the Application for Early Release of Radislav Krstić, MICT-13-46-ES.1, 15 November 2022, para. 33.

[21] See Chapter 7.

deciding whether and how to accept victim observations on release, etc., the Statutes have placed concentrated decision-making power in relation to critical aspects of 'the life of a convicted person post-sentence ... purely in the hands of one single judge'.[22]

Using this power, Presidents have created significant and far-reaching penal policies by codifying their approach to release in Practice Directions. Practice Directions, written and amended by Presidents, have become the explicit policy basis for introducing conditional early release at both the MICT and RSCSL. Practice Directions should be based on consultations with the Registrar and Prosecutor (MICT), or the Prosecutor and Defence staff (RSCSL) and their contents should be consistent with the Statute and Rules.[23] However, these requirements do not prevent the introduction of new provisions or amendments based on the President's interpretation of these legal documents. The Rules, therefore, fail to prevent arbitrary changes based on personal opinions that can significantly affect the consistency, fairness and foreseeability of the procedure, factors and presumptions that underpin release. Unforeseen and externally influenced changes to expectations to be considered eligible for release, and the introduction of conditional release, for example, have increased the punitive reach of international sentences to the detriment of sentenced persons.

Judges of international criminal courts are often required to play a creative role in the 'interpretation, development and crystallisation' of legal norms; not only due to the lack of a functioning legislature, but also because of the 'laconic provisions' they must apply in often 'untested situations'.[24] Powderly draws a distinction, however, between judicial creativity on the one hand, which proposes to fill lacunae through reliance on pre-existing principles and public policy considerations, and judicial activism on the other, which he describes as an arbitrary form of rule creation based on personal and subjective preferences.[25] It is clear that by situating policy development and decision-making power with a single judicial officer at the MICT and RSCSL, changes to international penal practice risk being viewed as the latter.

---

[22] Marina Maier, 'Offender Rehabilitation in International Criminal Justice: Towards Implementation of Tailored Rehabilitation Programs' (2021) 53 *Case W. Res. J. Int'l L* 269, 301.

[23] Rule 23(B) MICT RPE; Rule 19(B) RSCSL RPE. The RSCSL rules also require that Practice Directions be consistent with the terms of the Agreement between the UN and the Government of Sierra Leone on the Establishment of a Special Court for Sierra Leone, 16 January 2022.

[24] Joseph Powderly, *Judges and the Making of International Criminal Law* (Brill Nijhoff, Leiden 2020), 4–6.

[25] Ibid, 10.

2.4 (Perceived) Integrity Implications at the MICT

In addition to resulting in accusations of judicial activism, concentrating decision-making power with the President has also led to concerns in relation to partiality. A former ICTR prosecutor, Gregory Gordon, was highly critical of Meron's approach to release decision-making, questioning the (perceived) integrity and partiality of his decision to grant early release to Ferdinand Nahimana on account of (a) his failure to consult with any other judge and (b) the fact that Meron had disagreed with the basis of liability underpinning the applicant's conviction and advocated for a lesser sentence[26] during the appeal stage.[27] Despite the fact that the Rules only required the President to consult with judges that were part of the sentencing chamber, and none were judges of the Mechanism at that time, Gordon argued that Meron had failed to comply with the 'spirit' of the rules and had 'hung his hat on a technicality'.[28] Further, in Gordon's view, Meron should have either held a hearing with input from victims, prosecutors, UN officials, government officials and NGOs, or recused himself from the release decision on professional conduct grounds.[29] Gordon, refers to the 'deontological normative framework' for judicial decision-making set out in the Mechanism's rules and codes of conduct (designed to ensure public confidence in a fair and transparent judicial process) to imply that Meron should have withdrawn from the release decision-making role due to his previous association with the case that (he claimed) affected his partiality and (presumably) assigned another judge.[30]

The potential for unilateral decision-making was resolved with the 2019 amendment to the Rules that resulted in the requirement to consult with two other judges.[31] The Practice Direction repeats and stresses that 'in all circumstances' the President must consult with at least two other judges and that consulted judges should receive information from the enforcing state, the

---

26 See *Nahimana, Barayagwiza and Ngeze v Prosecutor*, AC, Judgment, ICTR-99-52-A, 28 November 2007, Partially Dissenting Opinion of Judge Theodor Meron, 374-380, para. 22.

27 Gregory S. Gordon, 'Integrity in International Criminal Law: Post-Conviction Proceedings' in Morten Bergsmo and Viviane E. Dittrich (eds), *Integrity in International Justice* (Torkel Opsahl Academic EPublisher, Brussels 2020), 984–985, 1010, 1016.

28 Ibid, 1002-3.

29 Ibid, 985.

30 Gordon refers to Rule 18(A), (D) MICT RPE; Preamble and Article 3(1) MICT Code of Professional Conduct for the Judges of the Mechanisms (2015) in note 27 at 1010-1.

31 Rule 150, MICT/1/Rev.5, amended on 4 March 2019.

Prosecution, comments from the convicted person, and any other third-party submissions or information the President considers relevant.[32]

However, the legal framework does not provide any mechanism for MICT (or RSCSL[33]) Presidents to recuse themselves from making release decisions. The procedure for applying for the withdrawal and disqualification of judges in cases where their impartiality is affected or doubted involves the President receiving applications, appointing a three-judge panel to decide the application, and deciding on the replacement judge.[34] Though the Rules do foresee a situation in which the President may in fact be the judge in question, the solution (appointing the next most senior Judge) is not feasible as they must be 'able to act' – the Statute does not grant any other judge power to make release decisions.[35] Other Rules do provide for the Duty Judge to assume Presidential functions until a new President is appointed, if the President is permanently or temporarily unable to carry out their functions.[36] However, this is a qualitatively different scenario that involves substitution and the appointment of an interim President, and not a form of recusal and delegation or transfer of power process envisaged by Gordon.

Would the same arguments have been advanced had Meron previously supported the grounds for liability or argued for a higher sentence? The partiality debate only seems to have been invoked as Meron's previous interventions in the case had been perceived to be potentially beneficial to the convicted person. Further, the requirement to consult with other judges, under the Tribunals' and RSCSL's legal frameworks, has always focused on consultation with judges directly involved in the convicted person's sentencing.[37] Not only does this potentially centre discussions on gravity (again) but this procedural requirement may also create issues of (perceived) partiality. This approach of consulting with the sentencing chamber has not been adopted at the ICC.

---

32 Paras 16–17 MICT PDER Rev. 3.

33 The same level of criticism does not seem to have been directed at the RSCSL Presidents. This may be due to the widespread consultation processes that resulted in support for the grant of conditional release and the familiarity of consulted persons with transitional justice processes.

34 Rule 18(A), (B)(i)–(ii) MICT RPE.

35 Rule 18(B)(iv) MICT RPE.

36 Rule 24(A)-(B) MICT RPE.

37 See Rule 124 ICTY RPE; Rule 125 ICTR RPE; para. 5, ICTY PDER, Rev. 1 1999; para. 6 ICTY PDER, Rev. 2, 2009; paras 6, 8 ICTY PDER, Rev. 3, 2010; para. 8(A) PDCER.

2.5 Ensuring Impartiality at the ICC

Perceptions of partiality are reduced significantly by the fact that ICC sentence reduction reviews are conducted by three judges appointed by the Appeals Chamber.[38] The Rome Statute requires judges to perform duties and exercise their powers in an impartial manner.[39] Further, under the Rome Statute, the Presidency may excuse any judge from the exercise of any function.[40] Judges cannot participate in any 'case' in which their 'impartiality might reasonably be doubted on any ground'.[41] A judge may be disqualified from the 'case' if the judge was previously 'involved in any capacity'.[42] Further, under the rules, judges can request their excusal from 'functions' by submitting a written request to the Presidency.[43]

The Presidency must determine whether the nature and degree of prior involvement give rise to an objective appearance of bias.[44] Moreover, judges are obliged to request their excusal if there are reasonable grounds to believe a ground for disqualification exists.[45] Given this legal framework, judges have a strong ethical duty to proactively safeguard the integrity of proceedings by preventing perceptions of partiality arising.[46] Indeed, a failure to comply with the duty to request excusal can constitute a serious breach of duty and result in disciplinary measures or removal from the bench.[47]

While it is not obvious that the statutory provisions on disqualification apply to the constitution of sentence review panels (as they refer to investigation and prosecution explicitly), a plenary of ICC judges convened to discuss a disqualification request in relation to *Lubanga's* sentence review accepted that they do. They felt that a broader reading was necessary to ensure the process could be applied to 'all phases of a case before the Court' and was required by 'the interests of fairness… to uphold the principle of impartiality' and prevent 'conflict with the principle of equality of arms'.[48]

---

[38] Rule 224 ICC RPE.
[39] Rule 5(1)(a) ICC RPE.
[40] Art. 41(1) ICCSt.
[41] Art. 41(2)(a) ICCSt.
[42] Art. 41(2)(a) ICCSt.
[43] Rule 33(1) ICC RPE.
[44] Powderly, note 24 at 138.
[45] Rule 35 ICC RPE.
[46] Powderly, note 24 at 135.
[47] Art. 46(1)(a) ICCSt.
[48] *Prosecutor v Lubanga*, Annex I of Notification of the Decision of the Plenary of Judges on the Defence Application for the Disqualification of Judge

It was stressed, however, that the threshold for overcoming the presumption that judges were impartial would be high given the 'limited pool of judges' available.[49] It is interesting that the Majority of judges in this decision tried to justify this high threshold by referring to the MICT practice of permitting Presidents to review sentences regardless of their involvement in the appeals phase of the case.[50] Some members of the Majority were cautious, however, about the potential for doubts as to impartiality given Judge Fernández de Gurmendi's prior role within the Office of the Prosecutor. In this particular case, however, her 'strategic, high-level and relatively removed' role meant that there was no concrete evidence to support any claim of partiality.[51] The Minority, in contrast, stressed the seriousness of the matter, classifying the case as one of 'apparent, not actual, bias' and argued that the 'prudent approach' would be for the judge to step aside to 'protect the judicial process' from accusations of partiality.[52]

The Majority also argued that sentence reduction reviews could be distinguished from proceedings dealing with the attribution of responsibility as they were based on consideration of particular facts and circumstances that largely occurred following conviction and sentencing.[53] The Minority urged caution in relation to the Majority's classification of the Article 110 procedure as distinct, highlighting that sentence reviews were 'a fundamentally judicial discretion rather than an administrative or quasi-executive function'.[54] Further, some factors did, in fact, overlap with sentencing considerations: cooperation with Court investigations and prosecutions was a factor directly relevant to consideration of Judge Fernández de Gurmendi's prior involvement with the case.

In practice, however, it seems that these ethical and legitimacy concerns have influenced sentence reduction panel appointments. ICC sentence review panels composed to date have avoided including judges previously involved in either trial or appeal proceedings in the majority of instances. The only exception seems to have occurred in *Katanga*, where Judge Christine Van den Wyngaert acted as both a member of Trial Chamber II that sentenced Germain

---

Silvia Fernández de Gurmendi from the case of The Prosecutor v Thomas Lubanga Dyilo, ICC-01/04-01/06, 3 August 2015, para. 34.

[49] Ibid, para. 35.

[50] Ibid, para. 37.

[51] Ibid, para. 38.

[52] Ibid, para. 39.

[53] Ibid, para. 36.

[54] Ibid, para. 37.

Katanga[55] and the panel appointed by the Appeals Chamber to conduct his sentence review.[56]

2.6 Ensuring Impartiality at the RSCSL?

RSCSL judges also take an oath to serve impartially[57] and they may not sit on a 'trial or appeal' in any case in which their impartiality may be reasonably doubted.[58] The explicit reference to trial and appeal proceedings in the Rules would appear to disapply disqualification provisions from other types of cases before the RSCSL. However, in a sentence enforcement case in 2020, the Chamber held that the combined effect of the statutory right of accused persons to a fair trial and the requirement of judicial impartiality extended the applicability of the Rule 15 disqualification mechanism to the post-sentencing phase.[59]

The RSCSL adopts an objective test to determine if there is an appearance of bias: the view of the accused person is not decisive, though no actual proof of bias is required.[60] Due to the solemn oath judges take, and training to act impartially, a heavy burden of proof is required to rebut the presumption of judicial impartiality.[61] Consequently, prior judicial 'contact with the facts of a case' alone would not typically suffice to result in perceptions of bias given the varying roles judges can perform and their training to distinguish between these tasks.[62] In fact, RSCSL Chambers cross-referenced an ICTR decision which held that only in 'truly extraordinary' cases would prior involvement in

55 *Prosecutor v Katanga*, Decision on Sentence pursuant to Article 76 of the Statute, ICC-01/04-01/07, 23 May 2014.

56 *Prosecutor v Katanga*, Decision on the review concerning reduction of sentence of Mr Germain Katanga, ICC-01/04-01/07, 13 November 2015.

57 Rule 14(A) RSCSL RPE.

58 Rule 15(A) RSCSL RPE, see also Rule 15(E).

59 Decision on Principal Defender's Request for the Withdrawal and/or Recusal of Hon. Justice Teresa Doherty of the UK as the Duty Judge on the Application of Charles G. Taylor to be Temporarily Transferred to a Safe Third Country to Continue his Imprisonment Due to the Massive Outbreak of COVID-19 in the UK, RSCSL-03-01-ES, 24 August 2020, para. 27 (hereafter Recusal Request (Taylor)).

60 Recusal Request (Taylor), note 59, paras 28, 31; *Prosecutor v Taylor* Appeals Chamber, Decision on Charles Ghankay Taylor's Motion for partial voluntary withdrawal or disqualification of Appeals Chamber Judges, SCSL-04-15-AR-15, 13 September 2021, para. 16 (hereafter Withdrawal Request (Taylor)).

61 Recusal Request (Taylor), note 59, para. 29; Withdrawal Request (Taylor), note 60, para. 19.

62 Recusal Request (Taylor), note 59, para. 28; Withdrawal Request (Taylor), note 60, paras 17, 36.

decisions be sufficient to establish actual bias.[63] Further, the Rules establish a threshold in relation to prior involvement – the approval of an indictment, or involvement in pre-trial or interlocutory matters, would not suffice for disqualifications purposes.[64] However, as with the MICT system, the Statute grants sole power to the President to make release decisions. No mechanism exists, therefore, to enable the President to stand down and appoint another judicial officer to grant or deny applications for conditional release.

2.7 The Judicial Role in International Release Decision-making

Release is a judicial decision in the international criminal justice process. Whether the decision should be made by the President or a panel of Appeals Chamber judges, over one or two stages, following consultation or not, remains open to debate. Analysis of practice to date, however, shows that concentrating decision-making power with one judge results in extraordinary levels of discretion that can result in far-reaching change. At the MICT, differing views on whether there was a presumption in favour or against release, for example, significantly increased the punitive reach of the original sanction imposed. Arbitrary changes to the fundamental underpinnings of the release system affect consistency, foreseeability, and ultimately, fairness. This form of judicial activism, informed by personal views, undermines the integrity and legitimacy of judicial decision-making. Another aspect of release decision-making that is marked by both variation between international courts and inconsistent approaches within the practice of a single international court is the degree to which victim participation in release decision-making should be permitted.[65]

3. VICTIM INPUT

The victims' rights movement resulted in victims increasingly securing roles in domestic sentencing and release decision-making processes from the 1980s onwards, with the stated goal of influencing the severity of criminal sanctioning. Until recently, the discussion in international criminal law has focused

---

63 *Prosecutor v Sesay, Kallon and Gbao*, Decision on Sesay and Gbao Motion for Voluntary Withdrawal or Disqualification of Hon. Justice Bankole Thompson from the RUF case, SCSL-04-15-T-909, 6 December 2007.

64 Rule 15(F) RSCSL RPE.

65 Julian V Roberts, 'Listening to the Crime Victim: Evaluating Victim Input at Sentencing and Parole' (2009) 38(1) *Crime and Justice* 347-412 at 350; Kathryn Morgan and Brent L. Smith, 'Victims, Punishment and Parole: The Effect of Victim Participation on Parole Hearings' (2005) 4(2) *Criminology and Public Policy* 333–360, 334, 336.

more on facilitating victim participation in trial and sentencing proceedings than in release decision-making. Presidential positions at the MICT, practice at the RSCSL and the legal framework at the ICC have, however, resulted in increasing space for the inclusion of victims' views in early release and sentence reduction processes.

3.1 Limited Attempts to Include the Views of Victim Witnesses on Release at the MICT

Practice at the UN Tribunals has also evolved with respect to the range of persons who can make submissions on the merits (or otherwise) of granting early release. This evolution also resulted from the appointment of Carmel Agius as President. Meron had repeatedly rejected requests to grant standing to victims to submit their views on release on account of the lack of a legal basis for doing so and the lack of precedent in UN Tribunal practice; Meron argued that the rules would need to be formally amended to permit consideration of victim views.[66] Other judges supported his position, pointing to the broader MICT role that required focus beyond victim suffering, to look to the future and the reintegration of convicted persons.[67]

In contrast, Agius felt that consideration of victim views was permitted within the President's discretion.[68] The MICT Practice Direction now facilitates the acceptance or request of submissions from third parties.[69] On this basis, Agius and Santana have sought information about witnesses and (any) risks posed to them by (potential) release.[70] However, given the logistical and ethical challenges posed by undertaking such consultations, their analyses of victims' views have been limited to internal requests for information about

66 See *Prosecutor v Ćorić*, Further Redacted Public Redacted Version of the Decision of the President on the Early Release of Valentin Ćorić and Related Motions, MICT-17-112-ES.4, 16 January 2019, paras 21–23, 25; *Prosecutor v Simba*, Public Redacted Version of the President's 7 January 2019 Decision on the Early Release of Aloys Simba, MICT-14-62-ES.1, 7 January 2019, paras 72–73.

67 *Prosecutor v Ćorić*, Further Redacted Public Redacted Version of the Decision of the President on the Early Release of Valentin Ćorić and Related Motions, MICT-17-112-ES.4, 16 January 2019, para. 26.

68 *Prosecutor v Brdanin*, Decision on the Application of Radoslav Brdanin for Early Release, MICT-13-48-ES, 28 February 2020, para. 89; *Prosecutor v Dordević*, Decision on the Applications for Early Release of Vlastimir Dordevic, MICT-14-76-ES, 30 November 2021, para. 10; *Prosecutor v Lukić*, Decision on the Application for Early Release of Sreten Lukić, MICT-14-67-ES.4, 7 October 2021, para. 12.

69 Para. 14 MICT PDER, Rev. 3.

70 See Chapter 5, section 4.4.2.

risks posed to witnesses, which the witness support section has repeatedly claimed it was not in a position to provide.[71] Attempts to contact victim associations have also proven unsuccessful.[72] Yet neither Agius nor Santana felt it was necessary 'to disturb former witnesses' by contacting them directly for their views on release.[73]

Santana has been willing, however, to accept unsolicited victim views. For example, she was 'mindful' in her considerations of the views expressed in a letter received from the Association of the Mothers of Srebrenica and Žepa Enclaves and the Association of Victims and Witnesses of Genocide when deciding on Krstić's application for release.[74] Their view that he had failed to demonstrate remorse or engage with victims on the crimes at Srebrenica or to help locate missing persons or graves,[75] may have partially influenced Santana's finding that Krstić was insufficiently rehabilitated due to his lack of positive actions to demonstrate critical reflection on his crimes.[76] In this case, these unsolicited victims' views may have had an impact that went beyond an expressivist function: they may have (partially) influenced the decision to deny release.

As Palmer notes, 'the Presidential stance on the admission of victim statements has shifted from one extreme to the other, based on the discretion of the judge holding the position' and that the scope of any role for victims is 'subject

[71] See *Prosecutor v Brdanin*, Decision on the Application of Radoslav Brdanin for Early Release, MICT-13-48-ES, 28 February 2020, para. 90; *Prosecutor v Dordević*, Decision on the Applications for Early Release of Vlastimir Dordevic, MICT-14-76-ES, 30 November 2021, paras 87–88; *Prosecutor v Lukić*, Decision on the Application for Early Release of Sreten Lukić, MICT-14-67-ES.4, 7 October 2021, para. 85; See *Prosecutor v Krstić,* Decision on the Application for Early Release of Radislav Krstić, MICT-13-46-ES.1, 15 November 2022, paras 81–82.

[72] *Prosecutor v Brdanin*, Decision on the Application of Radoslav Brdanin for Early Release, MICT-13-48-ES, 28 February 2020, para. 91; *Prosecutor v Lukić*, Decision on the Application for Early Release of Sreten Lukić, MICT-14-67-ES.4, 7 October 2021, para. 86.

[73] *Prosecutor v Brdanin*, Decision on the Application of Radoslav Brdanin for Early Release, MICT-13-48-ES, 28 February 2020, paras 84, 90; *Prosecutor v Dordević*, Decision on the Applications for Early Release of Vlastimir Dordević, MICT-14-76-ES, 30 November 2021, para. 88; *Prosecutor v Lukić*, Decision on the Application for Early Release of Sreten Lukić, MICT-14-67-ES.4, 7 October 2021, para. 85; *Prosecutor v Krstić,* Decision on the Application for Early Release of Radislav Krstić, MICT-13-46-ES.1, 15 November 2022, para. 83.

[74] *Prosecutor v Krstić,* Decision on the Application for Early Release of Radislav Krstić, MICT-13-46-ES.1, 15 November 2022, paras 11, 84, 86.

[75] Ibid, para. 84.

[76] Ibid, paras 61, 69.

entirely to the determination of the President'.[77] In practice, there have been only limited attempts by the MICT to reach out to victims in society, and only the views of those who have given testimony or evidence to support convictions have been sought.[78] Reliance on internal enquiries in relation to witness concerns has resulted in superficial and tokenistic engagement with victim views. Overall, the broader, inclusive approach seemingly advocated by Agius has not translated into meaningful, direct or community-based consultations with victims.

3.2 Broad Community-based Consultations at the RSCSL

This can be contrasted sharply with the law, policy and practice of the RSCSL. The interests of prosecution witnesses and victims must be taken into account by the President when making release decisions.[79] The Registrar is mandated by the Practice Direction to inform witnesses of impending conditional release decisions and to collect the views of victims, witnesses and their families from both the Prosecutor and the Witnesses and Victims section of the Registry.[80] The Registrar must provide the President with information from the enforcing state on the convicted person's empathy towards and willingness to make amends with victims (individually and collectively).[81] Further, the Registrar must provide the President with information on the impact of release on their well-being and safety, any perceived threats to their safety, the suitability of proposed areas of residence for the releasee, and any recommendations for conditions on release and supervision.[82] The President's decision must include an evaluation of the safety, views and concerns of victims, witnesses and their families (if any).[83] Relevant victims and witnesses must be notified if release is granted, prior to its execution.[84] Given the detailed nature of these requirements, and the large number of victims involved, it is unsurprising that these

---

77 Yasmine Palmer, 'Amplifying Voices and Fighting Impunity: A Case for Incorporating Victim Impact into Early Release Decisions at the International Residual Mechanisms for Criminal Tribunals' (2020) 27 *Wm & Mary J Race Gender & Soc Just* 233, 248–249.

78 *Prosecutor v Krstić,* Decision on the Application for Early Release of Radislav Krstić, MICT-13-46-ES.1, 15 November 2022, para. 15.

79 Rule 124 RSCSL RPE.

80 Para. 5(E)–(F) PDCER.

81 Para. 5(D)(ii)(d)–(e) PDCER.

82 Para. 5(F) PDCER.

83 Para. 8(D)(i)–(ii)) PDCER.

84 Para. 10(G) PDCER.

consultations can lead to delays in release decision-making.[85] However, these consultations have, in contrast to the MICT experience, resulted in overall support for the grant of conditional release in individual cases.

Despite this, the RSCSL Prosecutor has consistently opposed release, requesting that applications for release be denied, inter alia, on the basis of the security fears of prosecution witnesses.[86] This position did not reflect the stated views of consulted witnesses. In every case, the majority of consulted witnesses did not completely oppose release.[87] In *Gbao*, for example, only 10% of prosecution witnesses consulted by the Prosecutor and 20% of prosecution witnesses consulted by the Registry's Witness and Victims Section completely opposed release.[88] Whilst recognising the legitimacy and importance of witness fears in relation to release, RSCSL Presidents have rightly pointed out that concerns could be sufficiently addressed, and potential risks reduced, through the imposition of appropriate conditions.[89] Significantly, this judicial view was shared by the majority of consulted witnesses and victims.[90] Reliance on the supervision of conditional release is a more appropriate approach (than allowing concerns to act as a bar to release) given that consulted prosecution

---

[85] See Third Annual Report of the President of the RSCSL, January 2016–December 2016 at 15.

[86] *Prosecutor v Fofana and Kondewa*, Decision of the President on Application for Conditional Early Release, SCSL-04-14-ES (1270–1291) 11 August 2014, para. 29; *Prosecutor v Kondewa*, Decision of the President on Application for Conditional Early Release, RSCSL-04-14-ES (1581–1604), The Hague, 29 May 2017, para. 25; *Prosecutor v Gbao*, Decision of the President on Application for Conditional Early Release, RSCSL-04-15-ES, 8 September 2020, para. 14.

[87] *Prosecutor v Fofana and Kondewa*, Decision of the President on Application for Conditional Early Release, SCSL-04-14-ES (1270-1291) 11 August 2014, para. 29; *Prosecutor v Kondewa*, Decision of the President on Application for Conditional Early Release, RSCSL-04-14-ES (1581-1604), The Hague, 29 May 2017, paras 26–27.

[88] *Prosecutor v Gbao*, Decision of the President on Application for Conditional Early Release, RSCSL-04-15-ES, 8 September 2020, paras 12, 30–31.

[89] *Prosecutor v Fofana and Kondewa*, Decision of the President on Application for Conditional Early Release, SCSL-04-14-ES (1270-1291) 11 August 2014, paras 27, 34; *Prosecutor v Gbao*, Decision of the President on Application for Conditional Early Release, RSCSL-04-15-ES, 8 September 2020, para. 32.

[90] *Prosecutor v Fofana and Kondewa*, Decision of the President on Application for Conditional Early Release, SCSL-04-14-ES (1270–1291) 11 August 2014, para. 32; *Prosecutor v Kondewa*, Decision of the President on Application for Conditional Early Release, RSCSL-04-14-ES (1581–1604), The Hague, 29 May 2017, para. 33; *Prosecutor v Gbao*, Decision of the President on Application for Conditional Early Release, RSCSL-04-15-ES, 8 September 2020, paras 12, 14, 31.

witnesses typically did not live in the community to which the person was being released.[91]

3.3 Victim Participation in Sentence Reduction Reviews at the ICC

Unlike the RSCSL process, it does not seem that local communities were directly consulted about their views on the impact of the release of particular individuals by the ICC.[92] Instead, the ICC Rules permit panels to invite, to the extent possible, victims or their legal representatives who participated in proceedings to either participate in the sentence reduction review hearing or to submit written observations.[93] Victims have been represented at all ICC sentence reduction review hearings to date by a Legal Representative of Victims (LRV) and, at times, the Office of the Public Counsel for Victims (OPCV). These representatives are requested to submit written observations on the release criteria set out in Article 110(4)(a) to (c) and Rule 223(a) to (e) prior to the hearing[94] (though they do not always do so).[95] The LRV may also be invited to address particular issues in oral submissions.[96]

Lubanga's second sentence review demonstrates the potential for victim participation to be disruptive. Both LRVs and the OPVC wrote to Mr Lubanga's counsel requesting that he make a public declaration on his responsibility for the crimes for which he was convicted, to which Mr Lubanga responded in writing.[97] His response led to the LRV requesting a postponement of the scheduled sentence review for six months to facilitate meetings between Lubanga and victims to discuss possible forms of public apology to enhance the success of reconciliation and reparations processes.[98] The OPCV

---

[91] *Prosecutor v Kondewa*, Decision of the President on Application for Conditional Early Release, RSCSL-04-14-ES (1581-1604), The Hague, 29 May 2017, paras 26–27, 29–30; *Prosecutor v Gbao*, Decision of the President on Application for Conditional Early Release, RSCSL-04-15-ES, 8 September 2020, paras 12, 30.

[92] *Lubanga* Sentencing Review, para. 57; *Katanga* Sentencing Review, para. 65.

[93] See Rule 224(1) ICC RPE for initial reviews and Rule 224(4) ICC RPE for subsequent reviews.

[94] See Lubanga Sentencing Review, para. 4. *Lubanga* Second Sentence Review, para. 5; *Prosecutor v Katanga*, Decision on the request to modify the schedule for written submissions, ICC-01/04-01/07-3581, 31 August 2015, paras 6, 11; *Al Mahdi* Sentence Review, paras 3, 6–7.

[95] *Lubanga* Sentencing Review, para. 8.

[96] *Al Mahdi* Sentence Review, para. 8.

[97] *Lubanga* Second Sentence Review, para. 6.

[98] Ibid, paras 12–15.

and Prosecutor opposed any postponement.[99] Lubanga did not and seemed open to discussing ideas for a ceremony in which he could meet victims of his crimes.[100] The Panel, however, was not convinced that Lubanga's disclosure of future and uncertain intentions was sufficient to warrant the postponement of its decision.[101]

Victims have tended to be sceptical in their analysis of criteria that may favour possible sentence reductions. They have categorised good behaviour in detention and the withdrawal of appeals as strategic moves, doubted the sincerity of expressions of remorse and apologies, rejected submissions that the convicted person had support from the community they would be released to or observed that the convicted person should serve their sentence in full.[102] Adopting an objective stance, and noting the diverging views among consulted victim groups, Panels have, however, been cautious not to attribute excessive weight to subjective victim views or rejections of acts, statements or claims by convicted persons.[103]

The inclusion of victim views in sentence reduction reviews has highlighted a victim's desire for the management of potential risks to their safety that may result from sentence reductions and for measures to be implemented to prevent recidivism.[104] Significantly, it has been conveyed that the availability of post-release measures to prevent recidivism could enhance victim support for 'early release'.[105] ICC judges do not, however, have recourse to any legal mechanism that would enable them to impose conditions that would take effect following a sentence reduction and the subsequent release of a convicted person.[106] ICC Sentence Review panels are, however, required to communicate their decisions, with reasons, for both initial and subsequent sentence reduction reviews to victims and their legal representatives who participated in the review proceedings.[107]

---

99 Ibid, paras 16–17.

100 Ibid, para. 18.

101 Ibid, paras 20–23.

102 *Katanga* Sentence Review, paras 44–45, 54, 56; *Al Mahdi* Sentence Review, paras 60, 62.

103 See *Katanga* Sentence Review, paras 50, 59; *Al Mahdi* Sentence Review, para. 67.

104 *Al Mahdi* Sentence Review, para. 60.

105 Ibid, para. 62.

106 See Chapter 3, section 7.

107 Rule 224(2), (5) ICC RPE.

3.4 The Impact and Merit of Including Victim Views in Release Decision-making?

It is clear that decision-making bodies in domestic criminal justice systems often take the likely effect of release on victims into account when making (conditional) release decisions, and that (some) victims are notified about release if granted. However, despite growing participation rights during trial proceedings, victims do not tend to have standing to directly participate in release hearings or to make submissions on the appropriateness of release or conditions that may be imposed.[108] Even where participation rights are specifically granted in domestic victim charters, these are often limited to an opportunity to read out a statement and offer opinions on the conditions that should attach, but not to comment on the appropriateness of release itself.[109]

Victim groups are often 'vocal opponents' of early release as it is viewed as an indicator of leniency towards offenders.[110] As research on domestic practice shows, victim procedural rights can (and are intended to) have punitive effect(s).[111] In fact, there is often a demonstrable positive correlation between victim participation (where they oppose release) and higher rejection rates for release applications.[112] As victims often argue for the focus to be on the seriousness of the offences underpinning the sentence, it is important to exercise caution to ensure the integrity of the decision-making process and the liberty interests of convicted persons are upheld.[113]

Some arguments for including victim views in international release decision-making are unconvincing. These include the assertion that a failure to do so would contravene the very purpose of international criminal justice or weaken impunity[114] or that victims deserve finality in terms of the sentence imposed and therefore release or sentence reductions should not be granted as this would represent 'tacit acceptance of … past crimes'.[115] Victims in

---

108 Braun outlined the very limited participation permitted in decision-making for victims post-sentencing in Germany, Sweden, France and Denmark. Kerstin Braun, *Victim Participation Rights: Variation Across Criminal Justice Systems*, Palgrave Studies in Victims and Victimology (Palgrave Macmillan, 2019) at 182.

109 Ibid at 190-3 (practice in England and Wales, and Australia).

110 Anika Ades, 'Unconditional Injustices: Victim Participation and Early Release in International Criminal Law' (2020) 42 *NYU J Int'L & Pol* 593 at 596–597.

111 Roberts, note 65 at 350, 385.

112 Morgan and Smith, note 65 at 334, 351, 355.

113 Roberts, note 65 at 382, 385–386, 390.

114 Palmer, note 77 at 249–251.

115 Ades, note 110 at 609, 630–631; Palmer, note 77 at 246.

international criminal cases can express outrage and staunch opposition to release in evocative, emotionally and morally charged statements.[116] How do passionate calls by victims for convicted persons to serve their full sentences impact upon release and sentence reduction decision-making? At the MICT, Meron claimed that he had resisted requests to consult with victims, inter alia, on the basis that it 'would have changed the balance of considerations to the disadvantage of the prisoners as … victims would typically oppose all early releases'.[117] The balance of considerations may also be affected by the levels of representation permitted during decision-making processes. In other words, if victim participation is a codified right, this may result in equality of arms issues. For example, in both the first and second Lubanga sentence reduction reviews at the ICC, while six representatives acted for victims and two representatives for the Prosecutor participated, two representatives spoke on behalf of the convicted person.

Victim input may more beneficially inform release decision-making when it relates to security and recidivism concerns linked directly to reintegration in a particular community.[118] Even then, care must be taken. Analysis of international jurisprudence has revealed instances in which *de minimis* witness fears were relied upon to oppose applications or were overstated to stave off criticism that release denials may have been swayed by political considerations.[119] On the whole, however, it seems that international judges have exercised caution in relation to the weight that should be attributed to fears in relation to recidivism, particularly where conditions can be imposed post-release to reduce this risk. Judges have also maintained a reintegration focus, by carefully scrutinising this risk in relation to where the victims and releasee (will) live.

4. OTHER VOICES

4.1 Prosecution Views

Another significant change to stakeholder input occurred recently at the MICT. In 2019, the MICT Prosecutor argued that the practice of rejecting prosecution submissions (under Meron) had departed from international practice at the

---

[116] Barbora Holá, 'Early Release of ICTR Convicts: The Practice Beyond the Outrage' 5 July 2019, at https://www.justiceinfo.net/en/41861-early-release-of-ictr-convicts-the-practice-beyond-the-outrage.html (accessed 24 February 2024).

[117] Meron, note 8 at 264.

[118] Roberts, note 65 at 387, 401.

[119] See for example Chapter 4, section 6.2.

ICC and RSCSL.[120] This was true. At the RSCSL, the Registrar is required to request, and the President must take into account, the Prosecutor's views on conditional release and a wide range of factors that affect release decisions (such as the impact on the safety of the community, evidence of threats, suitability of the proposed area of residence, recommendations for conditions and supervision etc).[121] The inclusion of prosecutorial views on sentence reduction is also required and routine at the ICC. Under the Rules, the appointed Appeals Chamber judges must invite the Prosecutor to participate in both initial and subsequent sentence reduction reviews.[122] The ICC Prosecutor has been invited to participate in hearings and/or to submit written observations on the factors set out in Article 110(4) and Rule 223.[123]

Throughout his Presidency at the MICT, in contrast, Meron repeatedly denied Prosecutors standing to make submissions or recommendations on release at the MICT, other than to comment on the cooperation provided by applicants. He was, however, willing to point to his statutory discretion to permit submissions of relevant information if the Prosecutor could demonstrate compelling and special circumstances in specific cases.[124] Meron claimed that he had 'resisted requests to consult the Prosecutors' on the same grounds that he denied standing to victims: a lack of a legal basis for doing so and his opinion that the inclusion of their views on release 'would have changed the balance of considerations to the disadvantage of the prisoners as the Prosecutors ... typically oppose' early release.[125]

Agius, in sharp contrast, permitted Prosecutor submissions on sentence enforcement matters on the basis of a fundamentally different interpretation and application of the same legal framework. While Meron had argued that Prosecutorial submissions would only be acceptable following a formal amendment of the Rules, Agius argued in 2019 that Presidents could accept Prosecutorial submissions under their broad statutory discretion. Further, he felt that as part of a broader consultation process required by the interests of justice, the Prosecutor may possess important information relevant to core assessments (rehabilitation and gravity) and could identify potentially

120 *Prosecutor v Bralo*, Decision on the Early Release of Miroslav Bralo, MICT-14-78-ES, 31 December 2019, para. 65.

121 Articles 5(G), 6(B)–(D) PDCER.

122 Rule 224(1), (4) ICC RPE.

123 See *Lubanga* Sentence Review, paras 4, 8; Second *Lubanga* Sentence Review, paras 5, 9–10.

124 See Chapter 2, section 4 and Chapter 5, section 4.4.1.

125 Meron, note 8 at 264.

vulnerable witnesses that could be affected if release was granted.[126] Agius stressed, however, that a cautious approach was required to avoid 'unreasonable imbalance to the detriment of the convicted person': the President would have to decide on a case-by-case basis which Prosecution submissions were relevant 'mindful of the rights of the convicted person'.[127]

President Santana has endorsed both Agius' view that the President can consider comments and information provided by the Prosecutor in relation to early release applications and the need to proceed cautiously, adopting a case-by-case approach to avoid unreasonable imbalance to the convicted person's detriment.[128] It is unclear what weight permitted submissions have had or will have in practice. For example, Agius took 'note' of the Prosecution's submissions and opposition to release in *Semanza*.[129] Santana gave 'due regard' to Prosecutor views that release should not be granted due to the gravity of the crimes, insufficient rehabilitation, and a lack of cooperation in *Krstić*.[130] The actual impact Prosecution submissions will have on the ultimate decision of whether to grant conditional release at the MICT remains unclear. Prosecutor views on the types of conditions that could or should be attached to release may be more persuasive.

4.2 State Views

State submissions on the release of internationally convicted persons can come from the state of origin of the victims, the state of origin of the convicted person, or third states willing to accept released persons. There can be a strong divergence in levels of support for release depending on which category the submitting state falls into. Rwanda, for example, has repeatedly

126 *Prosecutor v Bralo*, Decision on the Early Release of Miroslav Bralo, MICT-14-78-ES, 31 December 2019, para. 68.

127 *Prosecutor v Bralo*, Decision on the Early Release of Miroslav Bralo, MICT-14-78-ES, 31 December 2019, para. 69; *Prosecutor v Brdanin*, Decision on the Application of Radoslav Brdanin for Early Release, MICT-13-48-ES, 28 February 2020, para. 83; *Prosecutor v Semanza*, Decision on Laurent Semanza's Application for Early Release, MICT-13-36-ES.2, 17 September 2020, para. 75; *Prosecutor v Kunarac*, Decision on Dragoljub Kunarac's Application for Early Release, MICT-15-88.ES.1, 31 December 2020, para. 76.

128 *Prosecutor v Krstić,* Decision on the Application for Early Release of Radislav Krstić, MICT-13-46-ES.1, 15 November 2022, para. 72.

129 *Prosecutor v Semanza*, Decision on Laurent Semanza's Application for Early Release, MICT-13-36-ES.2, 17 September 2020, para. 77.

130 *Prosecutor v Krstić,* Decision on the Application for Early Release of Radislav Krstić, MICT-13-46-ES.1, 15 November 2022, paras 73–75.

and publicly objected to the early release of its nationals that were convicted by the ICTR.[131] The Rwandan Government has made numerous public statements and complained to the UN Security Council that it had not been consulted on, or notified about, release decisions in advance, calling the decision-making process opaque, secretive and lacking in credibility.[132]

Responding to the release decision in *Simba*, the Rwandan Government issued a statement calling the MICT release procedure secretive and lacking in transparency, labelling the procedure a form of 'unchecked, underhanded unilateralism'.[133]

These claims were perhaps more directed to the outcome of the process: given the legal framework, the stated procedure, consistent practice of granting release, and the lack of any obligation to consult with the Rwandan Government, the process adopted did not diverge from policy or practice. Further, Meron consistently stated that Rwanda had not demonstrated compelling reasons to depart from the longstanding practice of not considering submissions from states to be relevant for release decisions.[134] In contrast, Agius was open to considering the views of states, arguing they may be relevant to his determinations. However, he noted that he would 'carefully assess, on a case-by-case basis, which submissions are of relevance in any given case, and I will attach particular importance to the convicted person's comments'.[135]

What has gained more significance in international practice, with the trend towards granting conditional forms of release, have been submissions from the proposed states of relocation. The support of these states for release, former President Agius explained, was relevant to considerations of the convicted person's reintegrative potential, the overall merit of their release application,

---

131 See *Prosecutor v Simba*, Public Redacted Version of the President's 7 January 2019 Decision on the Early Release of Aloys Simba, MICT-14-62-ES.1, 7 January 2019, paras 67, 70; *Prosecutor v Semanza*, Decision on Laurent Semanza's Application for Early Release, MICT-13-36-ES.2, 17 September 2020, paras 79–84.

132 See Palmer, note 77 at 247.

133 Statement from the Minister of Justice on the early release of Aloys Simba by Judge Theodor Meron, Kigali, 17 January 2019, at: https://www.minijust.gov.rw/news-detail/statement-from-the-minister-of-justice-on-the-early-release-of-aloys-simba-by-judge-theodor-meron (accessed 24 February 2024).

134 *Prosecutor v Simba*, Public Redacted Version of the President's 7 January 2019 Decision on the Early Release of Aloys Simba, MICT-14-62-ES.1, 7 January 2019, para. 74.

135 *Prosecutor v Semanza*, Decision on Laurent Semanza's Application for Early Release, MICT-13-36-ES.2, 17 September 2020, para. 78.

and the conditions to impose on this form of release.[136] In many instances, this form of state support has been forthcoming. However, it is clear that for some convicted persons seeking to return to their country of origin or a third state, whether under the terms of a conditional release agreement or following the completion of a (reduced) sentence, this support will not be forthcoming or sufficient. The extreme gulf in state approaches has been demonstrated in particular by MICT sentence enforcement supervision. The lack of state support for relocation may mean that release is not possible.[137] While Serbia has indicated its support for applicants seeking to return to serve the remainder of their sentence in the community,[138] some persons convicted by the ICTR have found themselves in an enduring state of de facto statelessness and house arrest.[139] State support, and subsequent international judicial support, for the return or relocation of released international prisoners may be heavily dependent on the current political and security climate in the requested state.[140] Challenges may also arise due to states failing to respond to relocation requests[141] or an inability to identify a state of relocation due to the immigration or residency status

---

[136] See *Prosecutor v Lukić*, Decision on the Application for Early Release of Sreten Lukić, MICT-14-67-ES.4, 7 October 2021, para. 83; *Prosecutor v Brdanin*, Decision on the Application of Radoslav Brdanin for Early Release, MICT-13-48-ES, 28 February 2020, para. 88.

[137] See Chapter 6, section 6.

[138] See *Prosecutor v Brdanin*, Decision on the Application of Radoslav Brdanin for Early Release, MICT-13-48-ES, 28 February 2020, para. 86; *Prosecutor v Lukić*, Decision on the Application for Early Release of Sreten Lukić, MICT-14-67-ES.4, 7 October 2021, paras 29–31, 82; *Prosecutor v Dordević*, Decision on the Applications for Early Release of Vlastimir Dordevic, MICT-14-76-ES, 30 November 2021, para. 85.

[139] See Cécille Lecolle, 'Relocation Issues of Released and Acquitted at International Criminal Courts and Tribunals – a Defence Perspective' (2023) 21(1) *JICJ* 167-184; Kate Gibson and Bonnie Johnston, 'Acquitted, released and homeless: The crisis of stateless former defendants' in R Mulgrew and M J Christensen (eds) *Research Handbook on the Punishment of Atrocity Crimes* (Edward Elgar Publishing, forthcoming 2024).

[140] See *Prosecutor v Al Hassan Ag Abdoul Aziz Mohamed Ag Mahmoud*, Public Redacted version of 'Decision of the Defence request for interim release' ICC-01/12-01/18, 29 May 2020, paras 65–75, 78–79; *Prosecutor v Ahmad Al Fazi Al Mahdi,* Public Redacted Version of the Decision on the review concerning reduction of sentence of Mr Ahmad Al Faqi Al Mahdi, ICC-01/12-01/15-434-Red3, 25 November 2021, paras 54–59.

[141] *Prosecutor v Semanza*, Decision on Laurent Semanza's Application for Early Release, MICT-13-36-ES.2, 17 September 2020, para. 17.

of the applicant.[142] The significance of geopolitical, security and transitional justice factors are likely to continue to have a major practical effect on international release decision-making and operationalisation.

5. CONCLUSION

At all international courts, release and sentence reduction decisions are made by judges. Procedural variations, however, raise important questions that can impact significantly on the legitimacy of release decision-making. Is decision-making power concentrated with one judge? Does this judge have to consult with other judges? Can a judge decide on release if they were previously involved in the case? Who makes release decisions, and how release decisions are made, can have significant integrity implications. The concentration of release decision-making power with one individual can also have significant consequences for the penal policy and practice of a particular court. At the MICT, Meron's presumption of release at two-thirds of the sentence was overturned and replaced with a presumption against release (Agius) and Santana's view that release should only be granted in exceptional cases. Concerns about unilateral decision-making and judicial activism seem to have been mostly avoided so far at the ICC through the adoption of a three-judge panel model, and the decision not to create penal policy beyond the explicit provisions of the Statute and the Rules.

Policy and practice on victim input remain varied, ranging from tokenistic engagement with witnesses at the MICT to the broad community-based consultations at the RSCSL and the opportunity to participate in sentence review hearings through legal representatives at the ICC. Irrespective of whether the practice is policy-based or codified, the weight attributed to victim views seems to be limited. In particular, victim views on whether or not release is appropriate seem to be less influential than submissions on how specific conditions or measures might be used to address particular fears or concerns. This cautious approach reflects the need to ensure an appropriate balance of considerations. This careful, case-by-case analysis of the relevance of submissions appears to have been extended to Prosecution and state submissions, except in cases of conditional release, where the support of the state of relocation is of utmost importance.

Submissions from stakeholders should be accepted, but only to the extent that they do not impinge on the liberty interests of convicted persons and their

142 See Maarten P. Bolhuis and Joris van Wijk, 'The Aftermath of Dutch International Crime Cases: Post-prosecution scenarios for Nationals and Non-Nationals' (2023) 21(1) *JICJ* 137–165.

right to equality of arms, and do not undermine or interfere with the judicial duty to undertake their functions independently and impartially.[143] Release processes should ensure that decisions are made impartially (free from the judges' personal convictions, prejudices and bias) and independently (free from undue, external political pressures, with decisions based on fact and legal principle).[144] While the range of influences that can be brought to bear on such decisions has increased over time, it remains unclear what weight these voices have or should have. Whatever the merits or dangers of wider stakeholder input into release decisions, international judges often treat permitted submissions cautiously, adopting objective and case-by-case assessments of their relevance and validity, mindful of the rights of convicted persons.

143 See Meron, note 8 at 263.

144 See Art. 8(1) MICTSt. See also Art. 11(2) RSCSLSt; Art. 40(1) ICCSt; Powderly, note 24 at 115, 118, 120.

9. Health and advanced age in release decision-making: compassionate release and palliative care considerations

1. HEALTH AND ADVANCED AGE IN RELEASE DECISIONS

International criminal courts and tribunals permit consideration of ill-health and advanced age as possible grounds for release or sentence reduction.[1] Despite this, legal, practical and political hurdles may delay or prevent release. The UN Office of Drugs and Crime has highlighted the importance of devising 'appropriate policies and strategies' to address the medical care of terminally ill prisoners and formulate criteria and procedures for release on compassionate grounds.[2] This chapter explores the jurisprudence, policy and practice relevant to the treatment and release of ill and older prisoners, in light of contemporary rights, penal and medico-ethical principles, multi-disciplinary scholarship and the international criminal justice operational context. Given the foreseeable obstacles to granting release in some cases, it is important to examine the implications of a delayed response to or denial of compassionate release requests. Specifically, international criminal courts and tribunals are obliged to provide adequate palliative care for terminally ill prisoners. Release requests will also arise as a consequence of the older profile of international prisoners on account of age-associated degenerative conditions and disabilities. This chapter examines the possibilities for and obstacles to the grant of compassionate release at the MICT, ICC and RSCSL,[3] the challenges posed

---

1 See Chapter 2, sections 3.1, 3.3, Chapter 3, section 5.5, Chapter 4, section 3, and Chapter 5, section 7.1.

2 See UNODC, *Handbook on Prisoners with Special Needs* (Vienna, 2009) 143–156, at 143.

3 This section builds on the findings and recommendations of Róisín Mulgrew, 'Terminal Illness and Compassionate Release: Lessons for the ICC from the UN Tribunals and National Jurisdictions' (2023) 21(1) *JICJ* 61–87.

by providing palliative care in the (international) custodial context, and the impact of advanced age on release decision-making.

2. COMPASSIONATE RELEASE

Compassionate release is 'an ethical and just response to managing terminal illness'.[4] International standards require authorities to put efficient judicial procedures in place to consider applications from seriously ill prisoners for release to facilitate treatment at home or in the community.[5] Compassionate release has a long history in the international criminal justice context: persons convicted by the Nuremberg Tribunal were released from Spandau Prison following their diagnosis with terminal illness.[6] Internationally convicted persons can apply for early release or sentence reduction on the grounds of health and advanced age. Despite this, such prisoners can face significant legal and practical obstacles that may delay or prevent the grant of such release, particularly if they have not served the requisite period of time in custody. This section begins by outlining the judicial approaches adopted by President Meron when faced with applications for compassionate release prior to the introduction of conditional release at the MICT. It proceeds to make recommendations for possible normative, legal, substantive and procedural bases for a compassionate release system at the ICC and methods of incorporating a new compassionate release model into its statutory or regulatory framework. It concludes with an assessment of the possibilities and obstacles to compassionate release at the RSCSL.

2.1 Compassionate Release at the MICT

While not an enumerated factor for consideration in release decisions, MICT Presidents have accepted and considered information on humanitarian factors when making release decisions. In practical terms, under paragraph 10(f) of the Practice Direction, the President can direct the Registry to collect *any*

---

[4] M. Stensland and S. Sanders, 'Detained and Dying: Ethical Issues Surrounding End-of-life Care in Prison' (2016) 12(3) *Journal of Social Work in End-of-life and Palliative Care,* 259–276 at 269.

[5] See Rule 14, Council of Europe Recommendation No. R(93)6 concerning prison and criminological aspects of the control of transmissible diseases including AIDS and related health problems in prison; Rule 51, Council of Europe Recommendation No. R(98)7 on the ethical and organisational aspects of health care in prison.

[6] See N. Goda, *Tales from Spandau: Nazi Criminals and the Cold War* (CUP, 2007) 132, 193.

other information that they feel will assist with the determination of the release application.[7] In line with judicial precedent, release can be granted if the applicant's medical condition or a serious illness makes continued detention inappropriate.[8] This is unproblematic when an applicant has served the requisite two-thirds of their sentence (or more than 30 years of a life sentence).[9] If a convicted person applies for release on health grounds prior to this point, however, they must demonstrate the existence of *exceptional and compelling circumstances*.[10]

This process was more complicated prior to the introduction of conditional early release at the MICT in 2018. Key decisions in 2015 and 2017 demonstrated considerable judicial reluctance to grant unconditional release, even in cases of terminal illness, when the applicants had only served a short portion of their sentences. To overcome these obstacles, President Meron opted to grant release on humanitarian grounds, not on the basis of unconditional early release, but on the basis of provisional release in *Nikolić* (from the UN Detention Unit) and conditional release (before it was introduced at the MICT) in *Beara* (from an enforcing state).

2.1.1 Provisional release

The *Nikolić* decision in 2015 demonstrated the priority that was accorded to the maintenance of the strict temporal eligibility threshold, even in a clear case of impending death. Despite finding that there were compelling humanitarian considerations, the President opted to deny the request for early release as the convicted person had not served two-thirds of his sentence.[11] For Meron, the need to uphold 'equal treatment' and to respect the sentence imposed by Chambers took precedence over the need to show compassion and 'deference

---

7 Practice Direction on the procedure for the determination of applications for pardon, commutation of sentence, and early release of persons convicted by the ICTR, the ICTY and the Mechanism (hereafter PDER) (MICT/3/Rev.3) 15 May 2020, para. 10(f).

8 See *Prosecutor v Munyakazi*, Public Redacted Version of the 22 July 2015 Decision of the President on the Early Release of Youssof Munyakazi, MICT-12-18-ES.1, 22 July 2015, para. 22; *Prosecutor v Krstić,* Decision on the Application for Early Release of Radislav Krstić, MICT-13-46-ES.1, 15 November 2022, paras 87, 90.

9 See Chapter 2, sections 2.1.3 and 2.2; Chapter 5, section 3.

10 See *Prosecutor v Galić*, Decision on the Early Release of Stanislav Galić, MICT-14-83-ES, 26 June 2019, para. 46; *Prosecutor v Bralo*, Decision on the Early Release of Miroslav Bralo, MICT-14-78-ES, 31 December 2019, para. 82.

11 *Prosecutor v Nikolić*, Public Redacted Version of the 20 July 2015 Decision of the President on the Application for Early Release or other Relief of Drago Nikolić, MICT-15-85-ES.4, 13 October 2015, paras 31, 33, 35.

to the highest humanitarian principles'.[12] Instead, provisional release was granted. This was a surprising decision given that only Chambers (not the President) can grant provisional release and it may only be granted to accused persons or those with cases under appeal, and not for sentenced persons (as Meron himself had ruled).[13] In this case, however, Meron felt that there were cogent reasons to justify departing from earlier decisions and to permit provisional release after final sentence if there were *particularly compelling circumstances*.[14] As the Prosecutor later argued, this decision was likely *ultra vires* the President's powers.[15] Without this controversial categorisation, however, Nikolić would have passed away in custody at the UN Detention Unit. All of the consulted judges found that the requirements for early release had not been met.[16] Meron granted Nikolić provisional release for a period of six months (when the order would be reassessed).[17] During this time, Nikolić was obliged to remain at home or in hospital under 24-hour armed guard, and to comply with numerous conditions, including bans on association and requirements to comply with orders from national authorities and the MICT.[18] Nikolić died at home less than three months after his provisional release was granted.[19]

2.1.2 Conditional release

In January 2017, the MICT received a request from the German authorities to terminate the enforcement of Beara's sentence as expeditiously as possible, as his poor health prevented its continued enforcement.[20] The urgency of the matter was clear: the notification warned that Beara's 'precarious health condition'

---

[12] Ibid, para. 34.

[13] See Rule 68 MICT RPE; *Prosecutor v Radic*, Decision on Request for Provisional Release, IT-98-3011-A, 13 July 2005, para. 3.

[14] *Prosecutor v Nikolić*, Public Redacted Version of the 20 July 2015 Decision of the President on the Application for Early Release or other Relief of Drago Nikolić, MICT-15-85-ES.4, 13 October 2015, para. 38.

[15] See *Prosecutor v Nikolić*, Prosecution Appeal of the Decision Granting Provisional Release to Drago Nikolić, MICT-15-85-ES.4, 27 July 2015, paras 3, 9-13.

[16] *Prosecutor v Nikolić*, Public Redacted Version of the 20 July 2015 Decision of the President on the Application for Early Release or other Relief of Drago Nikolić, MICT-15-85-ES.4, 13 October 2015, para. 19.

[17] Ibid, para. 44.

[18] Ibid, paras 41, 44.

[19] *Prosecutor v Nikolić*, Decision on the Prosecution Appeal of the Decision Granting Provisional Release, MICT-15-85-ES.4, 22 October 2015.

[20] *Prosecutor v Beara*, Public Redacted version of the 7 February 2017 Decision of the President on the Early Release of Ljubiša Beara, MICT-15-85-ES.3, 16 June 2017, paras 7, 16.

required 'very quick action without any undue delay' given that there was no domestic detention facility that could cater for his condition.[21] The German authorities did not apply for his early release (nor did Beara), nor did they specify that he was eligible for release under domestic law. This communication clearly requested the termination of sentence enforcement on the basis of terminal illness. In spite of this clarity, Meron considered that this request, in light of the Medical Officer's report mentioning early release, constituted notification of eligibility for early release.[22]

Meron reiterated the principled position that health may be considered in the early release context, particularly if the seriousness of the prisoner's condition made continued detention inappropriate.[23] However, given that Beara was only 13 years into his life sentence and would only become eligible for early release after he had served more than 30 years, it was considered necessary to request that the UNDU Medical Officer travel to Germany to independently verify his life expectancy.[24] This assessment revealed that 'curative medical care' was 'no longer medically indicated' and that as he was only expected to live for a few weeks, at best, keeping him in custody would be 'tantamount to a violation of Beara's internationally guaranteed human right not to be subjected to inhuman or degrading treatment or punishment'.[25] In other words, it was evident that the severe and rapid deterioration of Beara's condition was 'irreconcilable with having his prison sentence executed at a correctional facility'.[26] Though both the gravity of his crimes and the fact that he had only served a limited amount of the sentence imposed, Meron ruled that his 'highly abbreviated' life expectancy and rights norms meant it was no longer appropriate for him to remain in prison.[27]

When consulted, other judges agreed with this view, but recommended that release be granted on a conditional basis to enable the MICT to be informed if there were any changes in his health status that would necessitate the revocation of release and his return to custody.[28] As the legality of the application of provisional release in these circumstances remained uncertain,[29] humanitarian

---

[21] Ibid, para. 7.
[22] Ibid, paras 17–18.
[23] Ibid, para. 33.
[24] Ibid, para. 36.
[25] Ibid, para. 45.
[26] Ibid, para. 45.
[27] Ibid, para. 47.
[28] Ibid, para. 48.
[29] Ibid, para. 48, footnote 74; *Prosecutor v Nikolić*, Decision on the Prosecution Appeal of the Decision Granting Provisional Release, MICT-15-85-ES.4, 22 October 2015.

release was granted on a conditional basis, to take effect immediately or as soon as practicable thereafter.[30] Though conditional release was a new approach at this stage in MICT operations, it offered the most appropriate means to facilitate discharge from detention, bearing in mind the gravity of offences, the limited amount of sentence served, and the possible need to recall Beara if his condition evolved in a 'non-terminal fashion'.[31] Despite efforts to expedite the usual procedure given the urgency of the situation,[32] the decision-making process (given the need to verify the medical prognosis and consult with other judges) took a few weeks.[33] Beara died, aged 77, in a Berlin prison hospital the day after he was granted conditional, humanitarian release.[34]

2.1.3 Dependence on state cooperation

The unique context in which international criminal courts and tribunals operate creates additional challenges in the release context. There are often political sensitivities surrounding the early release of persons convicted of atrocity crimes, and the need to independently verify the medical prognosis in a decentralised enforcement system and consult with other judges can result in delayed decision-making.[35] The legal obstacles to granting conditional release encountered by Meron in the decisions discussed above have now been removed. With the introduction of a simple sentence in the MICT's Practice Direction, early release may now be granted 'subject to conditions'.[36] Compassionate release can now be granted, subject to conditions (and potential recall). Since the introduction of the conditional release scheme, Presidents have continued to adopt the position that 'the condition of a convicted person's health may be taken into account in the context of an application for early release especially

---

[30] *Prosecutor v Beara*, Public Redacted version of the 7 February 2017 Decision of the President on the Early Release of Ljubiša Beara, MICT-15-85-ES.3, 16 June 2017, paras 49–50.

[31] Ibid, paras 48–49. See also paras 20–21, 26–27.

[32] The MICT Practice Direction was amended in 2020 to introduce an expedited procedure. Paragraph 21 states that 'in cases of extreme urgency, the President may dispense with the procedural steps set forth in this Practice Direction to the extent required to meet the urgency, accelerate the consultation with other Judges, and, if necessary, issue a decision with reasons to follow'.

[33] *Prosecutor v Beara*, Public Redacted version of the 7 February 2017 Decision of the President on the Early Release of Ljubiša Beara, MICT-15-85-ES.3, 16 June 2017, paras 36, 39–42.

[34] New York Times, 'Ljubiša Beara, Who Oversaw Massacre at Srebrenica, Dies at 77', at https://www.nytimes.com/2017/02/10/world/europe/ljubisa-beara-dead-srebrenica-genocide.html (accessed 24 February 2024).

[35] See Mulgrew, note 3 at 71–73.

[36] PDER, para. 20.

when the seriousness of the condition makes it inappropriate for the person to remain in prison any longer'.[37] This is based, however, on Presidential discretion, not a statutory or regulatory provision or a specific and tailored policy.

The challenge facing the MICT going forward is that the implementation of conditional release relies completely on the voluntary cooperation of the requested state of relocation. In the two examples above, the requested Governments gave political guarantees that they would comply with orders to make the convicted person accessible to the MICT at any time, pay for transfers and the armed guard, and submit regular reports on adherence to the conditions of release.[38] This support and cooperation will not be forthcoming in all cases. Given that states have no obligation to enforce international sentences of imprisonment,[39] it is unsurprising that there is also no duty to enforce community sanctions or measures. The recent and ongoing Niger controversy highlights the challenges created by dependency on such cooperation.[40] Niger concluded a bilateral agreement with the MICT to accept de facto stateless persons released and acquitted by the ICTR, living in a safe house in Tanzania, for relocation purposes. Before the agreement could be implemented, one of the men, Bicamumpaka, died from cancer in hospital in Nairobi after spending 23 years in the safe house in Arusha following his acquittal at the ICTR.[41] Shortly after the other men arrived in Niger, they were issued with deportation

---

[37] *Prosecutor v Simba*, Public Redacted Version of the President's 7 January 2019 Decision on the Early Release of Aloys Simba, MICT-14-62-ES.1, 7 January 2019, para. 51; *Prosecutor v Ćorić*, Further Redacted Public Redacted Version of the Decision of the President on the Early Release of Valentin Ćorić and Related Motions, MICT-17-112-ES.4, 16 January 2019, para. 56; *Prosecutor v Kunarac*, Decision on Dragoljub Kunarac's Application for Early Release, MICT-15-88.ES.1, 31 December 2020, para. 79; *Prosecutor v Brdanin*, Decision on the Application for Early Release of Radoslav Brdanin, MICT-13-48-ES, 3 September 2022 at 2.

[38] *Prosecutor v Nikolić*, Decision of the President on the Application for Early Release or other Relief of Drago Nikolić, MICT-15-85-ES.4, 13 October 2015, paras 36, 41–44; *Prosecutor v Beara*, Decision of the President on the Early Release of Ljubiša Beara, MICT-15-85-ES.3, 16 June 2017, para. 49, footnote 75; See also *Prosecutor v Brdanin*, Decision on the Application for Early Release of Radoslav Brđanin, MICT-13-48-ES, 3 September 2022 at 4.

[39] See R. Mulgrew, *Towards the Development of the International Penal System* (CUP, 2013) at 34.

[40] See Cécile Lecolle, 'Relocation Issues of Released and Acquitted at the International Criminal Courts and Tribunals: A Defence Perspective' (2023) 21(1) *JICJ* 167–184.

[41] See L'Hora, 'The death today of Mr. Jérôme Bicamumpaka in Nairobi', at https://l-hora.org/en/deces-aujourdhui-de-m-jerome-bicamumpaka-a-nairobi-john-philpot-rappr-19-05-2022/ (accessed 24 February 2024).

orders, in a clear and direct violation of the terms and purpose of the relocation agreement.[42] They remain under (armed) house arrest, with the International Committee for the Red Cross providing financing for medical treatment.[43] One relocated person under house arrest, Tharcisse Muvunyi, died in June 2023 'after an appeal for medical assistance in Britain went unanswered'.[44] President Santana stressed, the same month, that the MICT could not resolve the predicament alone and urged the Security Council 'to appreciate how the status quo is untenable in every respect'.[45]

It is foreseeable, therefore, that a de facto stateless status could significantly impact upon the MICT's ability to grant compassionate release. Numerous persons convicted by the ICTR have died while serving their sentences (in both the Tribunal's host state and enforcing states). Joseph Serugendo died in August 2006 aged 60 at a hospital in Arusha following a long illness. Clement Kayishema died in 2016, Eliézer Niyitegeka in 2018, Yussuf Manyakazi in 2020 and Théoneste Bagosora in 2021 while serving their sentences in Mali. In Benin, Jean Bosco Barayagwiza and Georges Rutaganda both died in 2010, as did Callixte Kalimanzira in 2015 and Ephrem Setako in 2016. Though the bilateral enforcement agreements with these enforcing states provide for the termination of sentence enforcement on the grounds of the impossibility of continued detention,[46] it can be presumed that the de facto stateless status of terminally ill prisoners convicted by the ICTR would have presented a significant obstacle had they applied for compassionate release. The MICT experience demonstrates the reality that international criminal courts and tribunals

---

42 *In the Matter of François-Xavier Nzuwonemeye, Propsper Mugiraneza, Protais Zigiranyirazo, Anatole Nsengiyumva, Alphonse Nteziryayo, André Ntagerura, Tharcisse Muvunyi and Innocent Sagahutu*, Decision on the motions regarding the relocation agreement with Niger and Order for the Transfer of the Relocated Persons to the Arusha Branch, MICT-22-124, 7 February 2022.

43 Balthazar Nduwayezu, 'The Punishment of the Stateless ICTR "Migrants"' 9 June 2022, at: https://www.justiceinfo.net/en/93462-punishment-stateless-ictr-migrants.html (accessed 23 November 2023).

44 Sonia Rolley, 'Soldier guilty in Rwanda's genocide dies in Niger' 10 June 2023, Reuters, at: https://www.reuters.com/world/africa/soldier-guilty-rwandas-genocide-dies-niger-2023-06-10/ (accessed 23 November 2023).

45 MICT Press Release, 'President Gatti Santana briefs the UN Security Council on the progress of Mechanism's work' 12 June 2023, at: https://www.irmct.org/en/news/president-gatti-santana-briefs-un-security-council-progress-mechanism-work-0 (accessed 23 November 2023).

46 See Art. 10, Agreement between the UN and Mali on the Enforcement of Sentences, 30 June 2016; Art. 11, Agreement between the UN and Benin on the Enforcement of Sentences, 12 May 2017.

are entirely dependent on the political will of requested states to facilitate compassionate release.

This dependency is also likely to pose problems for the ICC. This was illustrated in March 2023 when the Court noted, with regret, that it had been forced to deny a request for interim release as all requested states had either declined, often without (relevant) reasons to accept the individual, or simply did not respond.[47] Release, that would otherwise have been granted, could not be effected due to a complete lack of state willingness to cooperate.

2.2 Compassionate Release at the ICC

The ICC faces (other) significant challenges in relation to compassionate release. The Rome Statute does not provide for the grant of conditional early release. Though persons remanded in custody during their trial can be granted conditional release,[48] the Rome Statute only provides for unconditional release following sentence reduction post-conviction. While sentence reductions can be based on 'a worsening state of physical or mental health or advanced age',[49] the Rome Statute *only* permits review *after* two-thirds (or 25 years of a life sentence) has been served.[50] Article 110(3)'s explicit direction that sentence reviews 'shall not be conducted before' the statutorily determined temporal eligibility threshold is a significant curtailment on judicial discretion. In addition, prisoners cannot petition the Court for sentence reduction prior to this initial, *proprio motu* judicial review. The ICC's legal framework does not, therefore, permit judges to grant release on health grounds prior to the service of a substantial and fixed portion of the sentence. Further, even if it did, the framework does not provide a mechanism for recalling prisoners granted a sentence reduction on health grounds should their condition progress in a non-terminal manner. This lacuna sits uneasily with the Rome Statute's acceptance of the applicability of rights norms to its operations.[51] A rights-approach necessitates the development and implementation of a compassionate release scheme. To make recommendations for the creation of such a scheme at the ICC, it is crucial to explore the normative and legal foundations of compassionate release schemes, necessary substantive and procedural components, and means for incorporating compassionate release into the current legal framework.

---

[47] *Prosecutor v Maxime Jeoffroy Eli Mokom Gawaka*, Public redacted version of 'Decision on Interim Release' ICC-01/14-01/22, 8 March 2023, paras 59–60.

[48] See Art. 60(1)–(3) ICCSt; Rule 119 ICC RPE.

[49] Rule 223(e) ICC RPE.

[50] Art. 110(3) ICCSt.

[51] Art. 21(3) ICCSt.

2.2.1 Normative and legal foundations of compassionate release

In contrast to penological justifications that underpin sentence execution, compassionate release should be determined by whether or not continued detention is possible on the basis of legal (right to protection from torture, inhuman and degrading treatment and punishment) and medical/practical reasons (access to adequate palliative care). As Stensland and Sanders argue, persons who are 'so ill or cognitively impaired that they lose awareness of the punishment they are being subjected to and are too functionally impaired to actually pose a safety threat to larger society' should no longer be detained.[52] In such circumstances, the punishment would no longer be justified on penological grounds.[53]

The prohibition on torture, inhuman or degrading treatment or punishment[54] provides the fundamental legal basis for compassionate release. This right does not generate a general obligation for authorities to release detained persons on health grounds. It may make release necessary, however, in the exceptional circumstances where the detainee's state of health is absolutely incompatible with detention,[55] or if detention conditions exacerbate the suffering caused by an illness.[56] The compatibility of a prisoner's health with continued detention can be determined by assessing the condition of the prisoner, the quality of care that can be provided, and the advisability of continuing detention in view of the prisoner's state of health.[57] A rights-based approach recognises that terminal illness should be accepted as 'permanently incompatible with continued detention'.[58] The ICC relies on states to implement its sentences. These states are legally bound by this non-derogable prohibition on inhumane treatment and punishment. Consequently, they may not be able to continue to enforce the sentence if a prisoner is seriously or terminally ill in light of its rights obligations.[59] Germany included the specific possibility of terminating the enforcement of sentences imposed by the ICTY on health grounds due to the impossibility of continued enforcement in its ad hoc bilateral enforcement

---

[52] Stensland and Sanders, note 4 at 269.

[53] His Majesty's Prison and Probation Service (HMPPS), Early Release on Compassionate Grounds Policy Framework: Guidance on applying for the early release of a sentenced prisoner, child or young person on compassionate grounds, 13 May 2022, paras 1.2, 4.41.

[54] See Art. 7 ICCPR, Art. 3 ECHR.

[55] *Rozhkov v Russia* (Application no. 64140/00) 19 July 2007, para. 104.

[56] *Paposhvili v Belgium* (Application no. 41738/10) 13 December 2016, para. 175.

[57] *Farbtuhs v Latvia* (Application no. 4672/02) 2 December 2004, para. 53.

[58] Article 720-1-1 Code of Criminal Procedure (France).

[59] See *Mouisel v France* (Application no. 67263/01) 21 May 2003, para. 48.

agreements.[60] The ICC, itself bound by rights principles, would find it difficult to justify detaining prisoners in the same situation or organising for a transfer to facilitate the continued enforcement of the sentence.

Continued detention following a medical prognosis of a limited life expectancy risks being unlawful on the grounds of the prohibition on torture and the prohibition on arbitrary detention. Prison physicians are obliged by contemporary penal standards to inform prison directors as soon as they consider that a prisoner's physical or mental health will be 'injuriously affected by' or 'put seriously at risk' by continued imprisonment,[61] an obligation reflected in the rules governing detention in the remand facilities of the MICT and ICC.[62] Ultimately, decisions on whether and when to transfer a prisoner with a short-term fatal prognosis to hospital or to consider them for compassionate release should be based solely on medical grounds.[63]

2.2.2 Substantive and procedural considerations for a compassionate release scheme

To operationalise a compassionate release scheme, it is necessary to consider the procedure that would apply, eligibility requirements and the ability to recall released prisoners.

Due to the risk of rapid deterioration, and the legal and practical challenges this would present, it should be possible for the ICC (Presidency, Registrar or Detention Centre officials), the enforcing state, and the prisoner (or their family or legal representatives) to initiate a compassionate release process. Procedures for compassionate release should be 'accessible to prevent the unnecessary prolongation of the waiting period, resulting in the death of patients in prison, while a decision on release is still being considered'.[64] To prevent this from occurring, sentence enforcement supervision should entail identifying prisoners who may be eligible for compassionate release, and a file should be opened to collect relevant information as soon as a diagnosis of

---

[60] Art. 2(5) Agreement between Germany and the IRMCT in relation to Ljubiša Beara, 26 June 2015. See also Articles 2(5) in the enforcement agreements in relation to Vujadin Popović (26 June 2015) and Stanislav Galić (11 February 2015).

[61] Rule 33 Nelson Mandela Rules; Rule 43(3) Recommendation Rec(2006)2-rev on the European Prison Rules.

[62] Rules 49(2), 50(1) MICT Rules of Detention, 5 November 2018; Regulations 162(1) 223, ICC Regulations of the Registry, ICC-BD/03-03-13.

[63] Rule 51, Recommendation No. R(98)7 on the ethical and organisational aspects of health care in prison.

[64] See UNODC, *Handbook on Prisoners with Special Needs* (Vienna, 2009) 143-156 at 153; Mulgrew, note 3 at 83–84.

terminal illness is made. The MICT appears to have regularised the assessment of prisoners' health and compatibility with continued detention in the consideration of early release applications, with the Practice Direction requiring medical reports and information on whether 'the convicted person is capable of serving his sentence in the enforcement state'.[65] Diagnosis with a terminal condition, rather than an application for release, should trigger the compassionate release procedure.

Eligibility for the two forms of release (sentence reduction and compassionate release) can and should be distinguished. Compassionate release, founded on humanitarian concerns, should be available to *all* prisoners irrespective of the time they have served.[66] This contrasts with former President Meron's prioritisation of the requirement to serve a fixed period of time to ensure equality of treatment. What should be prioritised is what Ashworth and Player term 'equality of impact'. This approach advocates the assessment of the impact of imprisonment upon particular prisoners, including persons suffering from illness.[67] Prisoners may experience illnesses that result in suffering that is 'greater than the deprivation of liberty intended by the punishment'.[68] In other words, dying in prison would constitute an additional punitive burden that was not intended or indeed justified by the rationales for imposing the original sentence. Compassionate release systems are designed to cater for those prisoners who cannot satisfy typical criteria for early release, particularly in terms of time spent behind bars.[69] Eligibility should not be defined in relation to time served, but in relation to the time remaining until the prisoner's expected death.

This low threshold for eligibility for consideration is counterbalanced by the need to have the medical prognosis independently verified and the power to recall prisoners back to detention should their medical condition progress in a non-terminal manner.[70] ICC judges can impose conditions on temporary pre-conviction release, including travel restrictions and a requirement to surrender

---

[65] PDER, para. 10(c).

[66] See Art. 720-1-1 Code of Criminal Procedure (France); HMPPS, note 53, paras 1.1, 4.1, 4.2; Art. 91(1) Organic Act 10/1995, Criminal Code (Spain).

[67] See A. Ashworth and E. Player, 'Sentencing, Equal Treatment and the Impact of Sanctions' in A. Ashworth and M. Wasik (eds) *Fundamentals of Sentencing Theory* (OUP, 1998) 253–261.

[68] HMPPS, note 53, para. 4.17.

[69] See E. Steiner, 'Early Release for seriously ill and elderly prisoners: Should French practice be followed?' (2003) 50(3) *Probation Journal* 267–276 at 269.

[70] See for example *Prosecutor v Brdanin,* Decision on the Application for Early Release of Radoslav Brdanin, MICT-13-48-ES, 3 September 2022, at 4 and paras 3(G), 6–7 Conditional Early Release Agreement.

travel documents.[71] There is potential for developing this power to facilitate post-conviction conditional release on humanitarian grounds before a prisoner has served the requisite period for consideration for sentence review.

2.2.3 Incorporating a compassionate release scheme into the ICC's legal framework

Due to the statutory prohibition on sentence reduction review prior to the fixed temporal points, it is necessary for the ICC to develop a distinct mechanism for compassionate release and a procedure for doing so. Either Article 105 (enforcement of sentences) or 106 (supervision of enforcement) could be amended to include a judicial power to grant compassionate release and develop a procedure and criteria for decision-making. Two-thirds of the members of the Assembly of States Parties (ASP) would have to agree to the inclusion of a new statutory provision.[72] Alternatively the rules could be amended to include the new system, again requiring adoption by two-thirds of ASP members.[73] In urgent cases, prior to any statutory or regulatory change, judges, acting on a two-thirds majority, could draw up a provisional rule permitting compassionate release that would apply until formally adopted, amended or rejected at the next ASP meeting.[74] In addition to changing the Court's legal framework, it will also be necessary to include a specific reference to this distinct form of release in bilateral enforcement agreements, in light of the importance of continuing and close cooperation between the ICC and the detaining authorities of enforcing states to ensure the early identification of potential cases.

2.3 Compassionate Release at the RSCSL

While health and advanced age are not explicit factors for consideration in the RSCSL release process, the Registrar can include medical reports on the prisoner's general and mental health in the information provided to the President.[75] Further, as with the UN Tribunals, the President can request any other information he or she considers relevant.[76] The issue has not arisen in the release jurisprudence of the RSCSL. To date, one sentenced person has died while serving their sentence.[77] Brima's death, however, was preventable: he

---

71 See Rule 119(1) ICC RPE.

72 Art. 121(3) ICCSt.

73 Art. 51(2)(a)–(c) ICCSt.

74 Art. 51(3) ICCSt.

75 Art. 5(C) PDCER.

76 Art. 5(D)(iii)(vi) PDCER.

77 Two indicted persons died while in remand custody. Foday Sankoh experienced serious health problems following a stroke in August 2002. After being

died due to his refusal to accept medical treatment.[78] Further, he did not apply for early release.

A review of the relevant legal framework reveals that the RSCSL may face similar constraints in relation to compassionate release as the ICC. An amendment to the SCSL Rules in 2011 resulted in the introduction of a rigid temporal threshold: early release can '*only* occur *after* the prisoner has served a minimum of two-thirds of his original sentence'.[79] This direction is further embedded in the Practice Direction, which adds that the process for applying for release can only be initiated five months prior to the service of two-thirds of the sentence.[80] Applications for release prior to this temporal threshold will be rejected on the grounds of prematurity.[81] This would seem to prevent applications for compassionate release prior to this point. Yet, the solution may actually lie within Rule 124 itself, as it makes explicit reference to the Presidential discretion to grant pardon or commutation of sentence, measures which do not appear to be constrained by the requirement to serve two-thirds of the

---

taken into the custody of the Special Court on 10 March 2003, he was transferred to hospital on 29 March 2005. He died on 29 July 2005 at Choithram Hospital in Freetown aged 66 (SCSL Press Releases, 'Registrar Announces the Death of Foday Sankoh' 30 July 2003, at: https://s3.eu-west-1.amazonaws.com/rscsl.org/Documents/Press/2003/pressrelease-073003.pdf) (accessed 24 February 2024). Samuel Hinga Norman died on 23 February 2007 in a military hospital in Dakar, Senegal while recuperating from surgery. See SCSL Press Release, 'Special Court Principal Defender Regrets the Death of Samuel Hinga Norman' 23 February 2007, at: https://s3.eu-west-1.amazonaws.com/rscsl.org/Documents/Press/2007/pressrelease-022307b.pdf (accessed 24 February 2024).

[78] Brima died after serving 13 years of his 50-year sentence in King Faisal Hospital in Kigali at the age of 44. The autopsy revealed that his death was caused by 'thrombotic peripheral arterial disease with gangrene of both feet'. Brima was advised when hospitalised on 1 May 2016 that his feet should be amputated in order to save his life. Although this procedure was available in Rwanda, Brima would only accept treatment if he was transferred to Europe or North America to undergo the procedure. He died on 9 June 2016. See SCSL Press Releases 'Alex Tamba Brima dies in Rwanda' 9 June 2016, at: https://rscsl.org/press-releases/afrc-prisoner-alex-tamba-brima-dies-in-rwanda/ (accessed 24 February 2024); 'Alex Tamba Brima's Body Returned to Sierra Leone, Cause of Death Established' 21 June 2016, at: https://rscsl.org/press-releases/alex-tamba-brimas-body-returned-to-sierra-leone-cause-of-death-established/ (accessed 24 February 2024).

[79] Rule 124 SCSL RPE, amended 16 November 2011.

[80] See Arts 2(A) and 3(C) PDCER.

[81] See *Prosecutor v Fofana and Kondewa*, Decision of the President on Application for Conditional Early Release, SCSL-04-14-ES (1270–1291) 11 August 2014, para. 3.

sentence. The grant of a medical pardon, or the commutation of the sentence on medical grounds, may fall within the President's statutory discretion at any stage of the sentence.

Another possible obstacle lies in the fact that convicted persons cannot directly petition the President for release; they can only initiate the process by applying to the enforcing state.[82] Direct applications from sentenced persons have been rejected due to non-compliance with the relevant procedure.[83] The Rules and Practice Direction should be amended to allow for direct petitions involving compassionate release requests.

The RSCSL position may be distinguished from the ICC, however, in two respects. Firstly, the RSCSL has a well-established conditional release system and procedure for recall. Secondly, these systems have been supported by the country of origin of the majority of sentenced persons (Sierra Leone). Further, in general, the communities consulted in the context of early release decision-making processes have been receptive to release.[84] Though things may be different for Charles Taylor (a Liberian citizen serving his sentence in the UK), the majority of sentenced persons still serving their sentences in Rwanda are likely to be supported should they request compassionate release to receive palliative care at home or in a hospital in Sierra Leone. What is unclear is whether the RSCSL would be willing to contribute to the cost of (continuing) care in the community for terminally ill prisoners released conditionally. A lack of financial means can result in a denial of conditional early release.[85] Further, a condition of Gbao's release was that he had to undertake financial responsibility for his own medical bills, even though he had to submit to the Court's monitoring of his health condition.[86]

3. PALLIATIVE CARE

Even if a compassionate release system is in place, some applicants will be denied release for legal and practical reasons. In addition, despite being an 'unlikely preferred place to die,' the alternative of an isolated and unsupported death in the community may lead to some prisoners opting to die in prison.[87]

---

[82] Art. 3(A), (C) PDCER.

[83] *Prosecutor v Senessie*, Decision of the President on Application for Conditional Early Release, SCSL-11-01-ES (580–589) 4 June 2014, para 7.

[84] See Chapter 7, section 5.3.

[85] Art. 8(C)(iii) PDCER.

[86] *Prosecutor v Gbao*, Decision of the President on Application for Conditional Early Release, RSCSL-04-15-ES, 8 September 2020, para. 83(ix).

[87] Mary Turner, Shelia Payne, and Zephyrine Barbarachild, 'Care or Custody? An Evaluation of Palliative Care in Prisons in North West England' (2011) 25(4)

Some international prisoners, who have served lengthy sentences in a country with which they have little or no connection and, in some cases, with limited abilities to be relocated or reunited with their families, may choose not to apply for compassionate release. Irrespective of whether compassionate release is requested, delayed or denied, international courts and tribunals are under a positive obligation to ensure policies, procedures and funds are in place to ensure the provision of adequate palliative care for the prisoners they are responsible for.

3.1 The Right to Palliative Care

UN Security Council Resolutions have highlighted the importance of the MICT ensuring that persons are detained in accordance with international standards, including those relating to healthcare.[88] These standards require that detaining authorities ensure access to the 'highest' or 'best' attainable standard of healthcare and medical treatment.[89] Further, the principle of equivalence of care dictates that prisoners must have access to the same health services that are available in the community.[90] Obligations requiring access to equivalent and external healthcare are reflected in rules governing the detention of remand detainees and persons serving sentences at the MICT and ICC detention centres.[91] International standards advocate that detaining authorities put measures in place to ensure the humane treatment and meet the health needs

Palliative Medicine 370–377 at 375.

[88] Security Council Resolution 2529 (2020), 25 June 2020, para. 11; Security Council Resolution 2637 (2022), 22 June 2022, para. 13.

[89] Art. 12(1) International Covenant on Economic, Social and Cultural Rights; Art. 16(1)–(2) African Charter on Human and Peoples' Rights; Art. 39(1) Arab Charter on Human Rights; Art. 10(1) Additional Protocol to the ACHR in the Area of Economic, Social and Cultural Rights (Protocol of San Salvador); *Mouisel v France* (Application no. 67263/01) 14 November 2002, para. 40; *Farbtuhs v Latvia* (Application no. 4672/02) 2 December 2004, para. 51.

[90] Rule 24(1) Nelson Mandela Rules, GA Resolution 70/175 (NMR); Principle 9 UN Basic Principles for the Treatment of Prisoners GA Resolution 45/111; Rule 40(3) Recommendation Rec(2006)2-rev on the European Prison Rules; Rule 19, Recommendation No. R(98)7 on the ethical and organisational aspects of health care in prison; Rule 4, Recommendation No. R(93)6 concerning prison and criminological aspects of the control of transmissible diseases including AIDS and related health problems in prison.

[91] See Rules 46(1), 47(1), (3) MICT Rules of Detention; Regulation 154(1)–(3), ICC Regulations of the Registry, ICC-BD/03-03-13.

of vulnerable groups such as older prisoners or those suffering from terminal illness.[92] In addition to ensuring equal access to preventative and curative healthcare, rights obligations extend to the provision of palliative care.[93] While waiting for transfer to external hospitals to receive such care, terminally ill prisoners must receive 'optimum nursing care' at prison healthcare centres and provision should be made for 'periodic respite care in an outside hospice'.[94] For those who will remain in prison until they die, they should be accommodated in single occupancy cells (to afford the dying prisoner privacy), with access to palliative care and regular visits from close relatives.[95] Detaining authorities must 'respect and protect the dignity of terminally ill or dying persons' and recognise their legal entitlement and equitable access to comprehensive and appropriate palliative care.[96] International criminal courts must ensure that terminally ill prisoners are provided with access (without undue delay) to free palliative care before they become eligible for or are granted compassionate release, or in situations where compassionate release is not or cannot be granted.[97] They must therefore adopt policies that can operate to prevent prisoners from dying 'exposed to unbearable symptoms' (pain or suffocation) or the prolongation of death against their will.[98]

---

[92] Principle XI(1), OAS Principles and Best Practices on the Protection of Persons Deprived of Liberty in the Americas; Art. 14(2) Protocol to the ACHPR on the Rights of Older Persons in Africa.

[93] CESCR General Comment No. 14 (2000) on Article 12 ICESCR: The Right to the Highest Attainable Standard of Health, para. 34.

[94] Rule 51, Recommendation No. R(98)7 on the ethical and organisational aspects of health care in prison.

[95] See CPT Report on the visit to Latvia, CPT/Inf (2001) 27, para. 169.

[96] Parliamentary Assembly Recommendation 1418 (1999) Protection of the human rights and dignity of the terminally ill and the dying, 25 June 1999, paras 9.1.1 and 9.1.2.

[97] See Council of Europe, Recommendation CM/Rec(2014)2 of the Committee of Ministers to Member States on the promotion of human rights of older persons, Rule 45; Recommendation Rec (2003)24 of the Committee of Ministers to member States on the organisation of palliative care, 12 November 2003, Rules III(8) and 118.

[98] See COE Parliamentary Assembly Recommendation 1418(1999) Protection of the human rights and dignity of the terminally ill and the dying, 25 June 1999, para. 8.

3.2 The Challenges of Providing Palliative Care in Custodial Contexts

The Inter-American Convention on Protecting the Rights of Older Persons explains that palliative care involves the 'active, comprehensive and interdisciplinary care and treatment of patients whose illness is not responding to curative treatment or who are suffering avoidable pain, in order to improve their quality of life until the last day of their lives'.[99] According to the World Medical Association, the objective of palliative care is 'to maintain patient dignity and freedom from distressing symptoms' so as to make the patient 'as comfortable as possible' by controlling their pain and attending to their social, psychological and spiritual needs.[100]

The rapid 'greying' of national prisoner populations, in terms of both the number and proportion of older and the 'oldest old' prisoners, has forced national prison systems to develop policies and practices to manage deaths in prisons.[101] This demographic change, referred to as a 'silver tsunami,' and the low number of compassionate releases granted, have resulted in prisons providing hospice care.[102] In many cases, however, end-of-life care is often not available due to the difficulties involved in its provision in custodial environments.[103] Effective end-of-life care should provide 'physical, psychological, social and spiritual care to those with life-limiting conditions'.[104] The provision

---

[99] Art. 2, Inter-American Convention on Protecting the Human Rights of Older Persons (A-70), entered into force on 11 January 2017.

[100] World Medical Association Declaration on Terminal Illness (Adopted by the 35th World Medical Assembly, Venice, Italy, October 1983, and revised by the WMA General Assembly, Pilanesberg, South Africa, October 2006, and by the 73rd WMA General Assembly, Berlin, Germany, October 2022), para. 1.

[101] Mary Turner, Marian Peacock, Sheila Payne, Andrew Fletcher, and Katherine Froggatt, 'Ageing and dying in the contemporary neoliberal prison system: Exploring the "double burden" for older prisoners' (2018) 212 *Social Science and Medicine* 161–167 at 161–162; Meghan A. Novisky, Chelsey S. Narvey, Stephanie Grace Prost, 'Older Adults' perspectives on death and dying in prison' (2022) 83 *Journal of Criminal Justice* 101930.

[102] Casey N. Ferri, 'A Stuck Safety Valve: The Inadequacy of Compassionate Release for Elderly Inmates' (2013) 43(1) *Stetson Law Review* 197–243 at 197; Turner et al., note 101, at 163.

[103] See Voila Handtke, Tenzin Wangmo, Bernice Elger and Weibke Bretschneider, 'New Guidance for an Older Problem: Early Release for Seriously Ill and Elderly Prisoners in Europe' (2017) 97(2) *The Prison Journal* 224–246 at 225.

[104] Katie Stone, Irena Papadopoulos and Daniel Kelly, 'Establishing Hospice Care for Prison Populations: An Integrative Review Assessing the UK and USA

of palliative care in prisons is, however, challenging due to the incompatibility of the health and social requirements of managing death with prison regimes and infrastructure.[105] Scholarship provides ample examples of practical problems: trying to fit hospital beds into prison cells, prison beds being too small for pressure mattresses, a lack of space for equipment, the absence of ensuite facilities, a lack of privacy, noise levels and access barriers for healthcare staff at night.[106] As Dawes notes, prison life generates security, operational and legal obstacles 'to the provision of good patient care for dying prisoners'.[107]

The provision of medication for dying prisoners poses a significant challenge. Problems range from fears of the misuse or trafficking of such drugs among prisoners to the practical challenges of having prescriptions filled in a timely manner.[108] Morphine-based painkillers are often prohibited in prison settings. The UN Office on Drugs and Crime has warned that the inability to provide 'basic pain control' can lead to prisoners experiencing 'unnecessary, prolonged suffering' that may constitute a 'harshening of the prison sentence'.[109] Significantly, a number of UN experts have noted that 'the denial of palliative care and pain relief is a human rights violation' that undermines the fundamental right to health and the prohibition on inhuman and degrading treatment.[110] A former UN Special Rapporteur on torture explicitly urged states to 'overcome regulatory and attitudinal obstacles that restrict availability to essential palliative care medications, especially oral morphine'.[111] These recommendations have been repeated by the Council of Europe: States must ensure 'the adequate availability and accessibility of palliative care

---

Perspective' (2011) 26(8) *Palliative Medicine* 969–978 at 969.

105 Lynn Saunders, 'End-of-life care in prisons' PRI Blog 21 February 2022, at https://www.penalreform.org/blog/end-of-life-care-in-prisons/9 (accessed 24 February 2024).

106 Ibid; Turner et al., note 101 at 165; Stone, Papadopoulos, and Kelly, note 104, 974–995.

107 John Dawes, 'Dying with Dignity: Prisoners and Terminal Illness' (2002) *Illness, Crisis and Loss* 188–203 at 191.

108 Turner, Payne and Barbarachild, note 87 at 376.

109 See UNODC, *Handbook on Prisoners with Special Needs* (Vienna, 2009) 143–156 at 145–146.

110 'Older persons deprived of liberty', Report of the Independent Expert on the enjoyment of all human rights by older persons, Claudia Mahler (A/HRC/51/27), 9 August 2022, para. 59; Report of the Special Rapporteur on torture and other cruel, inhuman and degrading treatment, or punishment, Juan E. Méndez, A/HRC/22/53, 1 February 2013, para. 56.

111 See Report of the Special Rapporteur on torture and other cruel, inhuman and degrading treatment, or punishment, Juan E. Méndez, A/HRC/22/53, 1 February 2013, para. 86(b).

medicines'[112] and that patients who wish to, can 'receive adequate pain relief … even if this … may contribute to the shortening of the individual's life'.[113] The principle is further echoed by the World Medical Association. In 2020, it stated that access to pain management is a human right, and its denial violates the right to health and is medically unethical.[114] Further, it stated that 'the clinical management of pain in patients at the end of life is of paramount important [sic] in terms of alleviating suffering'.[115]

Prison hospices (usually no more than 2–3 beds) have been created in national systems to overcome these problems and to enable terminally ill prisoners with less than six months to live to 'approach death with dignity'.[116] The creation of a prison hospice or palliative care suite within a prison enables the provision of end-of-life care away from the prison wing regime but within the prison. It facilitates access for specially trained medical and family liaison staff, provides more space, and enables the safe storage of medication.[117] Difficult ethical questions remain: Do prison hospices simply create isolated units with few amenities within a security-focused regime? Can admission be based on informed consent (particularly if a do-not-resuscitate order is required for admission)? Does their existence undermine the right to compassionate release?[118] Further, it is important to ask if it is 'really possible to provide genuine hospice care in a correctional setting' and whether compassionate release should be preferred and advocated for.[119] The security environment

112 Council of Europe, Recommendation CM/Rec(2014)2 of the Committee of Ministers to Member States on the promotion of human rights of older persons, Rule 49.

113 Parliamentary Assembly Recommendation 1418(1999) Protection of the human rights and dignity of the terminally ill and the dying, 25 June 1999, para. 9.1.7.

114 World Medical Association Resolution on the Access to Adequate Pain Treatment, adopted by the 62nd WMA General Assembly, Uruguay, October 2011, and amended by the 71st WMA General Assembly, October 2020.

115 World Medical Association Declaration of Venice on End of Life Medical Care (Adopted by the 35th World Medical Assembly, Venice, Italy, October 1983, and revised by the 57th WMA General Assembly, Pilanesberg, South Africa, October 2006, and by the 73rd WMA General Assembly, Berlin, Germany, October 2022), para. 2.

116 Stone, Papadopoulos and Kelly, note 104, 970.

117 Saunders, note 105.

118 Dawes, note 107, 193–194; Stone, Papadopoulos and Kelly, note 104, 975–996; Turner et al., note 101 at 165; Stensland and Sanders, note 4 at 261.

119 Dawes, note 107, 192.

and philosophy of a prison can mean that the 'contrast between dying in prison and dying in a hospice are stark'.[120]

3.3 Palliative Care in the International Penal System

In 2022, the MICT identified a budgetary need to cater for the medical treatment of an ageing population serving long sentences.[121] There have already been examples of persons convicted by the UN Tribunals being transferred to public hospitals to receive end-of-life care in enforcing states. For example, Barayagwiza was transferred from prison to the Centre Hospitalier Départemental de l'Ouéme in Porto Novo, 20 days before he died aged 60 following a long illness.[122] Mile Mrkšic died in a public hospital in Portugal aged 68 while serving his sentence following a 'progressive and irreversible disease'.[123]

The UNODC noted in 2022, that as 'access to high cost clinical resources and ongoing palliative care, which most prisoners with a terminal illness are in need of, are simply unavailable in most prison systems … prisoners may suffer unnecessarily or receive aggressive medical treatment that is neither justified nor likely to be beneficial'.[124] Further, the risk of 'rapid change or deterioration necessities 24 hour 7 day medical supervision and nursing services which most prisons systems are unlikely to be able to provide'.

The obligation to treat prisoners with humanity and respect for their dignity is not dependent on available resources.[125] Due to their dependency, prisoners

120 Turner, Payne and Barbarachild, note 87 at 370, 372, 276.

121 Proposed Budget for the IRMCT for 2021, A/75/383, 9 October 2022, paras 32–34.

122 MICT Press Release 'Death of convict Jean Bosco Barayagwiza' 25 April 2010, at https://unictr.irmct.org/en/news/death-convict-jean-bosco-barayagwiza; 'Genocide Convict Barayagwiza dies in Benin' Justiceinfo.net, 26 April 2010, at https://www.justiceinfo.net/en/22424-en-en-260410-deathbarayagwiza-genocide-convict-barayagwiza-dies-in-benin1323113231.html (accessed 24 February 2024).

123 New York Times, 'Mile Mrksic, a Serb Army Officer Convicted of War Crimes, Dies at 68' 17 August 2015, at https://www.nytimes.com/2015/08/18/world/europe/mile-mrksic-a-serb-army-officer-convicted-of-war-crimes-dies-at-68.html (accessed 24 February 2024).

124 See UNODC, *Handbook on Prisoners with Special Needs* (Vienna, 2009) 143–156, at 145.

125 HRC General Comment No. 21 (1992) on Article 10: Humane Treatment of persons deprived of their liberty, para. 4.

should be able to access healthcare free of charge when needed.[126] The Council of Europe's Parliamentary Assembly has called on states to ensure sufficient funds and resources are provided for adequate supportive care.[127] The provision of palliative care, whether in prison or in hospital, will create direct financial implications for the MICT and ICC in detention centres, but also in some enforcing states. For example, the UN has agreed to cover (pre-agreed) costs for the medical care of persons convicted by the ICTR or MICT in Benin and Mali.[128] In addition to medical care, the UN may also have to pay for adaptations required by a prisoner's deteriorating health in some countries.[129] The UN and ICC are responsible for the costs of adjustments to accommodation necessitated by a detainee's medical condition at their respective detention centres.[130] The cost of incarcerating seriously or terminally ill prisoners can represent a significant proportion of a prison budget;[131] it is estimated to cost at least double or triple that for a typical prisoner.[132] International courts must

---

126 Principle 9 UN Basic Principles for the Treatment of Prisoners GA Resolution 45/111; Rule 24(1) Nelson Mandela Rules; Principle 24 Body of Principles of Persons under any form of Detention or Imprisonment, GA Resolution 43/173; Principle XI(1), OAS Principles and Best Practices on the Protection of Persons Deprived of Liberty in the Americas; Rule 39 Recommendation Rec(2006)2-rev on the European Prison Rules.

127 Parliamentary Assembly Recommendation 1418(1999) Protection of the human rights and dignity of the terminally ill and the dying, 25 June 1999, para. 8.

128 Art. 11(2)(c) Agreement between the UN and Mali on the Enforcement of Sentences, 30 June 2016; Art. 11(2)(c) Agreement between the UN and Benin on the Enforcement of Sentences, 12 May 2017. The Senegal agreement refers to 'sundry medical expenses' – Art. 11(1)(d) Agreement between Senegal and the UN on the Enforcement of Sentences, 22 November 2010.

129 Art. 11(2)(d) Agreement between the UN and Mali on the Enforcement of Sentences, 30 June 2016; Art. 11(d) Agreement between the UN and Benin on the Enforcement of Sentences, 12 May 2017; Art. 11(1)(c) Agreement between Senegal and the UN on the Enforcement of Sentences, 22 November 2010.

130 Rule 49(1) MICT Rules of Detention; Regulation 160, ICC Regulations of the Registry, ICC-BD/03-03-13.

131 Handtke et al., note 103 at 226.

132 Ferri, note 102, 197; Novisky, Narvey and Prost, note 101; Tiffany Albanese, 'The Adoption and Implementation of Compassionate Release for Terminally Ill and Elderly Inmates: Comparing the United States' and China's Guidelines for Medical Parole Petitions' (2019) 42(1) *Suffolk Transnational Law Review* 169–200 at 184.

ensure that sufficient budgetary resources are allocated to provide the appropriate levels of palliative care.[133]

The resource and cost implications of providing this care are not, however, alone, legitimate grounds to justify release.[134] If an appropriate level of palliative care cannot be provided for in an enforcing state, the international court may have to consider transferring the prisoner to its detention centre or another enforcing state. The MICT recently stated that it is investing resources to increase its pool of potential enforcing states in Africa to ensure it can facilitate the movement of prisoners to another state if this is required for health reasons.[135] The ICC may need to conclude a new form of cooperation agreement to facilitate transfer to a country that can provide palliative care for prisoners who cannot be released to their country of origin or a third country. Such agreements could be modelled on the interim release agreement concluded by the ICC with Argentina. This agreement allows for revocation by the ICC, the payment of costs if the prisoner is indigent, and ensures the host state will grant visas for at least three visits per year from family.[136] Even if release is granted, the authorities must 'address another critical issue, namely, where to transfer the prisoner?' [137] Though intended to provide residency rights to released persons prior to transfer to a third state, current provisions in some bilateral enforcement agreements with the UN may provide a means for enforcing states to permit persons granted compassionate release to remain on their territory to receive palliative care.[138]

4. ADVANCED AGE

International criminal courts and tribunals will supervise the sentences of an older prisoner population due to a combination of the age of prosecuted persons entering the system and the lengthy or indeterminate sentences that

---

[133] Rule 15, Recommendation No. R(93)6 concerning prison and criminological aspects of the control of transmissible diseases including AIDS and related health problems in prison.

[134] See HMPPS, note 53, para. 4.20.

[135] Proposed Budget for the International Residual Mechanism for Criminal Tribunals for 2021, Report of the Secretary-General, A/75/383, 9 October 2020, para. 14 at 14.

[136] Arts. 5(2), 6(5), 7(2) Framework agreement between the Argentine Republic and the ICC on interim release, ICC-PRES/25-01-18.

[137] Handtke et al., note 103 at 226.

[138] See Art. 12(1), (3) Agreement between the UN and Mali on the Enforcement of Sentences, 30 June 2016; Art. 12 Agreement between Senegal and the UN on the Enforcement of Sentences, 22 November 2010.

have been applied. For example, when a recent case at ICC on the situation in Darfur commenced, the accused person (Ali Muhammad Ali Abd-al-Rahman) was 72.[139] Advanced age, alone, will seldom justify release. However, it is well documented that prisoners often 'display biological signs of ageing earlier than those that continue living in community' and that due to this phenomenon of 'accelerated ageing,' many prison systems consider people to be older by the age of 50 or 55.[140] Given the known higher rate of medical deaths among older prisoners at a younger chronological age compared to the general population, it is critical that international criminal courts and tribunals 'incorporate the trajectory of palliative, end-of-life and hospice care for incarcerated persons' into policy and financial planning.[141]

Older prisoners often have complex medical and social needs due to their physical health and age-related frailty.[142] The costs associated with detaining older persons are high due to the need to provide 'age-appropriate' healthcare (geriatric, palliative and other specialised care) which remains 'scare [sic] and limited worldwide'.[143] Corwin estimates that 'senoritis' results in costs '3 times' higher than imprisoning younger persons and double the cost of nursing home care. She notes that the unique and complex health and psychosocial needs of this group; prisoners have an average of three chronic illnesses, require approximately 24 medical visits a year, and need additional support including 'corrective aids, prosthetic devices … dentures, hearing aids, ambulatory equipment, orthopaedic shoes'.[144]

The Inter-American Convention highlights the need to ensure access to social and health care for chronic degenerative diseases that may affect older prisoners, such as dementia and Alzheimer's disease.[145] A recent MICT case

139 Case Information Sheet, at: https://www.icc-cpi.int/sites/default/files/2023-06/abd-al-rahmaneng.pdf.

140 'Older persons deprived of liberty', Report of the Independent Expert on the enjoyment of all human rights by older persons, Claudia Mahler (A/HRC/51/27), 9 August 2022, para. 26.

141 Tina Maschi, Suzanne Marmo and Junghee Han, 'Palliative and End-of-Life Care in Prisons: A Content Analysis of the Literature' (2014) 10(3) *International Journal of Prisoner Health* 172–197 at 173.

142 Turner et al., note 101 at 162; Novisky, Narvey and Prost, supra note 101.

143 'Older persons deprived of liberty', Report of the Independent Expert on the enjoyment of all human rights by older persons, Claudia Mahler (A/HRC/51/27), 9 August 2022, para. 45.

144 Patricia S Corwin, 'Senoritis: Why Elderly Federal Inmates are Literally Dying to Get out of Prison' (2001) 17 *Journal of Contemporary Health Law and Policy* 687–714 at 687, 697.

145 Art. 19(i), Inter-American Convention on Protecting the Human Rights of Older Persons (A-70), entered into force on 11 January 2017.

demonstrated this reality. In June 2023, a MICT Trial Chamber, by a majority, declared that Kabuga, a 90-year-old man, was unable to meaningfully participate in his trial (irrespective of trial modality or accommodations) on account of his severe, permanent and irreversible dementia.[146] Despite this finding, and the subsequent decision to implement a controversial 'alternative finding procedure' that would *not* result in a conviction or any custodial punishment, Kabuga was not initially released.[147] Without the prospect of a conviction or custodial punishment, it is unclear on what legal basis the MICT decided to keep a 90-year-old man with severe dementia in detention. As defence counsel argued, the only logical conclusion to such a finding should have been the termination of legal proceedings and his immediate release.[148] In September 2023, after imposing a definite stay of proceedings, it was decided that he should remain in detention at the UNDU pending the arrangement of his provisional release (with the support of the Registry).[149] With the age profile of the international prisoner population, it is foreseeable that age-related conditions will feature in future release and sentence reduction applications and decision-making.

5. CONCLUSION

This chapter focused on the rights-based and ethical imperatives for international courts to devise and implement effective compassionate release policies and procedures, and to put cooperation agreements and funding in place to facilitate appropriate levels of care for ill and ageing prisoners under their care. The UNODC has recommended that such policies should include, at a minimum, clear criteria and procedures for determining the existence of terminal

---

[146] *Prosecutor v Kabuga*, Further Decision on Félicien Kabuga's Fitness to Stand Trial, MICT-13-38-T, 6 June 2023, paras 16, 18, 36, 39. While the Trial Chamber did refer to the Committee on the Rights of Persons with Disabilities Guidelines, which state that declarations of unfitness to stand trial are contrary to the CRPD as they deprive persons of the right to due process and safeguards, the TC felt this was not sufficient to depart from the binding precedent of the ICTY – see paras 26–27.

[147] *Prosecutor v Kabuga*, Further Decision on Félicien Kabuga's Fitness to Stand Trial, MICT-13-38-T, 6 June 2023, paras 45, 57–58.

[148] *Prosecutor v Kabuga*, Defence Request for Certification to Appeal the 'Further Decision' on Félicien Kabuga's Fitness to Stand Trial issued on 6 June 2023, 13 June 2023, para. 8. The decision was appealed by both the Prosecution and the Defence – see Decision on Motions for Certification to Appeal the Further Decision on Félicien Kabuga's Fitness to Stand Trial, MICT-13-38-T, 16 June 2023.

[149] *Prosecutor v Kabuga*, Decision Imposing an Indefinite Stay on Proceedings, MICT-13-38-T, 8 September 2023.

illness, providing healthcare to prisoners with terminal illnesses in prison, transferring terminally ill prisoners to civilian hospitals, for compassionate release and for continuing health care in the community following release.[150] This minimum requirement does not appear to be met by the current (public) policy approach of contemporary international courts. Approximately 15% of ICTR prisoners have died while serving their sentences,[151] while around 10% of ICTY prisoners died following the finalisation of their sentences.[152] With the increasing age profile of the prisoners under the supervision of international courts, it is clear that this issue is only going to increase in significance over time. Though some indications have emerged of attempts to prepare for the 'greying' of the international prisoner population at the MICT, there remains no (public) dedicated policy on compassionate release or the provision of palliative care. The ICC and SCSL need to make more fundamental changes to their legal frameworks to ensure the timely and effective management of requests for release or care from convicted persons whose conditions are incompatible with continued detention.

Contemporary standards governing compassionate release and palliative care in prisons are ultimately founded upon the recognition of the need to ensure dignity in dying.[153] While it is clear that compassionate release decisions should depend solely on 'medical eligibility and authorisation by a legal entity',[154] the reality is that numerous other considerations can complicate decision-making. End-of-life care is 'rife with ethical dilemmas in the community so dying in the context of incarceration … adds to this complexity'.[155] It becomes even more complicated in the international criminal justice context, given that a prisoner's nationality and immigration status can frustrate plans at a time when urgent care and decisions are needed. Release and care decisions will be affected and complicated by legal, penological, political, humanitarian, rights, medical, ethical and logistical factors. Compassionate release may be considered a 'cost-efficient alternative for reducing the expense

---

150 See UNODC, *Handbook on Prisoners with Special Needs* (Vienna, 2009) 148.

151 Joseph Serugendo, Jean Bosco Barayagwiza, Callixte Kalimanzira, Clément Kayishema, Eliézer Niyitegeka, Georges Rutaganda, Ephrem Setako, Édouard Karemera and Yussuf Munyakazi.

152 Milan Babić, Ljubiša Beara, Rasim Delić, Miroslav Deronjić, Milan Gvero, Mile Mrkšić, Drago Nikolić, Slobodan Praljak, Zdravko Tolimir.

153 Council of Europe, Recommendation CM/Rec(2014)2 of the Committee of Ministers to Member States on the promotion of human rights of older persons, Rule 44; Handtke et al., note 103 at 237–238.

154 Handtke et al., note 103 at 239.

155 Stensland and Sanders, note 4 at 260.

of caring for dying prison inmates'.[156] However, compassionate release should only be granted if adequate supports and care are available and accessible in the community.[157] If a terminally ill international prisoner cannot be released, the international court must ensure that either the international detention facility or the enforcing state can provide access to free palliative care of sufficient quality to ensure it does not violate the absolute prohibition on inhuman and degrading treatment and punishment – whether in the prison, the prison hospital or in the community.

156 Maschi, Marmo and Han, note 141 at 187.
157 See HMPPS, note 53, para. 4.28.

10. Conclusion

While early release serves an important function in 'a dynamic penal system', Guiney notes that it can also represent 'a highly contested form of symbolic communication where the anxieties and contradictions of contemporary penality begin to coalesce'.[1] These 'anxieties and contradictions', often amplified and accentuated in the international criminal justice context, provide a fitting frame to discuss and contextualise some of the key findings of this book. This concluding chapter draws out and analyses issues related to the evolving form, function and reach of international punishment; the influences on release decisions; the impact of age and illness; the effect of security and legacy expectations; and the impossibility of release for some convicted persons.

1. THE EVOLVING FORM, FUNCTION AND REACH OF INTERNATIONAL PUNISHMENT

Custodial punishment remains the sanction of choice in international criminal law. Despite this common position on the primary penalty, all international courts to date have adopted different substantive, procedural and punitive approaches to early release. Further, these approaches have evolved over time and, in so doing, altered the form of release that can be granted. Until 2018, persons sentenced by the UN ad hoc Tribunals or MICT were almost routinely granted unconditional release after serving two-thirds of their sentence, creating a system of de facto sentence reduction.[2] The ICC Statute introduced a scheme whereby the fundamental basis of sentence review was to permit changes to the original sentence and, therefore, for successful applicants, also facilitated unconditional release.[3] At the SCSL, in contrast, it was decided that 'an early release programme that reduces the sentence is not acceptable'.[4]

[1] Thomas C Guiney, 'Parole, Parole Boards and the Institutional Dilemmas of Contemporary Prison Release' (2022) *Punishment and Society* 1–20 at 1–2.

[2] See Chapter 2.

[3] See Chapter 3.

[4] See Teresa Anne Doherty and Shireen Avis Fisher, 'Enforcement of Sentences and Oversight of Prisoners Convicted by the SCSL' in R. Mulgrew and

A detailed system and procedure for granting conditional early release was introduced by the judges.[5] Following political pressure from the UN Security Council in 2018, the MICT changed course and introduced a system of conditional release. It did so without the detailed policy and paperwork, clear legal basis to support recall, or enumerated potential consequences for breach of conditions that was so clearly embedded in the SCSL's conditional early release policy framework.[6]

Community-based sanction supervision is now a core task of the residual mechanisms for the UN ad hoc tribunals (MICT) and the SCSL (RSCSL). Yet with desistance and reintegration support lacking, conditional early release remains risk-centred and control-focused under international criminal law. The introduction of conditional release systems has also raised questions about the suitability of conditions, the efficacy of monitoring mechanisms, the legal basis for recall, and the appropriate consequences for breaches of conditions.[7] Further, conditional early release, from both a normative and operational perspective, has altered the predictability of international penality and has the potential to increase the penal reach and depth of international punishment. Despite these issues, it is clear that the ICC needs to consider developing a conditional release system to facilitate humanitarian and compassionate release for persons not eligible for sentence reduction under the Rome Statute.

Though international sentences are operationalised and concretised through enforcement, they are shaped and given further significance through release decision-making. The expanded penal reach of international custodial sanctions is attributable to not only the form of release granted, but also to the factors that are taken into consideration in release decision-making. This has been made particularly clear at the MICT, where an increased focus on gravity in release decision-making has resulted in the reversal of the presumption in favour of release, and the introduction of a heightened, retribution-informed threshold for rehabilitation assessments.[8] Persons convicted by the ICTY, ICTR and MICT are now serving their sentences under a presumption against release. The pattern of rejections of early release requests at the MICT has continued, justified by the high gravity of crimes and a heightened threshold for determining whether rehabilitation has been sufficiently demonstrated.[9]

D. Abels (eds) *Research Handbook on the International Penal System* (Edward Elgar Publishing, 2016) 355–380 at 355, 361, 364.

5 See Chapter 4.

6 See Chapters 5 and 6.

7 See Chapter 6.

8 See Chapter 5.

9 *Prosecutor v Župljanin*, Decision on the Application for Early Release of Stojan Župljanin, MICT-13-53-ES.1, 18 January 2024, paras 62, 79–80; *Prosecutor*

President Santana, for example, has expressed doubts about the sincerity of the acceptance of responsibility from applicants, highlighting the lack of (sufficient) critical reflection and a failure to express remorse.[10] Further, a lack of positive action is increasingly viewed as problematic: 'mere assertions' will no longer satisfy release requirements, particularly for an applicant wishing to reintegrate into the region where the crimes were committed.[11] For President Santana, 'the mere passage of time cannot constitute sufficient grounds for early release:' she has rejected any form of automatic release as this would 'give insufficient weight to the judicially determined sentence of the convicted persons … [and] … undermine the *exceptionality* of being released early' (emphasis added).[12] Even with the possibility of conditions being imposed upon release, President Santana rejected an application to spend the few months remaining on a sentence in the community on the basis of insufficient rehabilitation.[13] This release practice seems to reflect the trend at the sentencing stage whereby gravity and aggravating factors are directly and significantly affecting sentence length, but mitigating factors that focus on diplomatic and policy objectives are not.[14]

Rehabilitation is the primary rights-based, penological goal of sentence implementation and prison management.[15] Yet, it has long been recognised that the decentralised system of sentence enforcement relied on by international criminal courts and tribunals 'creates a real correctional dilemma' as

---

v Miletić, Decision on the Application for Early Release of Radivoje Miletić, MICT-15-85-ES.5, 18 January 2024, para. 85.

10 *Prosecutor v Stojić*, Decision on the Application for Early Release of Bruno Stojić, MICT-17-112-ES.3, 17 January 2024, paras 71, 101; *Prosecutor v Miletić*, Decision on the Application for Early Release of Radivoje Miletić, MICT-15-85-ES.5, 18 January 2024, para. 66; *Prosecutor v Župljanin*, Decision on the Application for Early Release of Stojan Župljanin, MICT-13-53-ES.1, 18 January 2024, para. 77.

11 *Prosecutor v Župljanin*, Decision on the Application for Early Release of Stojan Župljanin, MICT-13-53-ES.1, 18 January 2024, para. 62

12 *Prosecutor v Stojić*, Decision on the Application for Early Release of Bruno Stojić, MICT-17-112-ES.3, 17 January 2024, para. 100.

13 *Prosecutor v Miletić*, Decision on the Application for Early Release of Radivoje Miletić, MICT-15-85-ES.5, 18 January 2024, paras 67, 85.

14 See Joseph W. Doherty and Richard H. Steinberg, 'Punishment and Policy in International Criminal Sentencing: An Empirical Study' (2016) 110(1) *AJIL* 49–81 at 76.

15 See Róisín Mulgrew, *Towards the Development of the International Penal System* (CUP, 2013) at 208–209.

it fails to provide 'a career plan' for prisoners from the outset of their sentence.[16] Despite decades of experience in sentence enforcement, international prisoners are now regularly failing to demonstrate that they are sufficiently rehabilitated. This highlights the failings of international criminal courts and tribunals to design, implement or support rehabilitation programmes in enforcing states (or international detention facilities) to help convicted persons work towards and try to achieve rehabilitative goals. Contemporary release practice demonstrates the need for international criminal courts to move away from a warehousing approach to imprisonment and to recognise their direct responsibility for ensuring that modes and regimes of enforcement facilitate progress towards the achievement of release criteria from the outset of the sentence.

There has been a growing focus on the definition and application of rehabilitation as a release decision-making factor in international criminal law. This can be observed in presidential pronouncements at the MICT, the invocation of rehabilitation as a justification for delayed release at the RSCSL, and the emphasis on reintegration during ICC sentence reduction reviews.[17] This rehabilitative revival has been accompanied by increasingly precise requirements about the manner in which applicants should apologise, express remorse and take positive actions for victims. This judicially imposed precision brings with it the danger of mandatory and counter-productive moralisation. While remorse is often invoked in release applications to demonstrate transformation, diminished criminality and capacity for change, Kapoor's study highlights the 'deep underlying difficulty in the detection of and allocation of consequences of remorse'.[18] Overcoming this challenge by providing 'remorse-scripts' can create incentives for convicted persons to engage in performative remorse.[19] Diggelman also stresses that the judicial practice of requiring planned and tailored remorse can foster a culture of fake and strategic remorse on the one hand, and an over-estimation of the recidivism effect of remorse and apology in the context of atrocity crimes on the other.[20] This is not surprising, as criminological studies have shown that prisoners will learn to navigate (changing) release systems without necessarily engaging in a genuine manner.[21] Forced

---

[16] Patricia M. Wald 'Punishment of War Crimes by International Tribunals' (2002) 69(4) *Social Research* 1119–1134 at 1133.

[17] See Chapter 7, section 3.

[18] Radhika Kapoor, '"Is it Too Late Now to Say Sorry": Remorse at International Criminal Tribunals' (2023) 21 *JICJ* 877–902 at 877–881.

[19] Ibid at 886–887.

[20] See Oliver Diggelmann, 'International Criminal Tribunals and Reconciliation' (2016) 14 *JICJ* 1073–1097 at 1077.

[21] Nicola Carr and Ester Blay, 'Parole and prisoner release: Exploring rationalities across time and place' (2019) 11(3) *European Journal of Probation* 119–123

remorse can be counter-productive if it is (perceived to be) provocative to victims who doubt its sincerity. This approach also fails to take account of the fact that there will come a point at which the convicted person will complete their sentence and be free to retract 'required' statements without consequence.[22]

2. INFLUENCES ON EARLY RELEASE DECISIONS

2.1 Judicial Influence

Powderly has highlighted the 'unavoidable and barely contested reality' that judges have made international criminal law.[23] Early release is and will remain an international judicial decision. The statutes of the UN Tribunals, the MICT and the (R)SCSL placed release decision-making power in the hands of the President, tempered by fluctuating requirements to consult with other judges. Presidents of these ad hoc courts were therefore able to shape release policy through decisions, jurisprudential pronouncements on the interpretation of statutory and regulatory provisions and the issuance of Practice Directions. This concentrated power, and its use to effect change, has resulted in critique in relation to perceived partiality and reduced certainty in relation to sentence enforcement.[24] The form of release, presumptions about release, and the (thresholds for) determining factors at the MICT, for example, have depended on the views of the President and, at times, it seems, external political influence. The procedure for release and the substantive factors involved can have significant implications for perceptions of legitimacy, partiality and predictability. Unilateral decision-making and (perceived) judicial activism can be avoided by adopting the model used by the ICC. The ICC appears to have sidestepped the problem, not only by creating a three-judge panel to decide on sentence reviews, but also by limiting the scope of the applicable legal framework to the explicit provisions of the statute and rules of procedure and evidence.[25]

at 122.

[22] The average age of perpetrators at the time of release is 52 – see Marina Maier, 'Offender Rehabilitation in International Criminal Justice: Towards Implementation of Tailored Rehabilitation Programs' (2021) 53 *Case W. Res. J. Int'l L.* 269 at 308.

[23] Joseph Powderly, *Judges and the Making of International Criminal Law* (Brill Nijhoff, Leiden: 2020) at 9.

[24] See Chapter 8, section 2.

[25] See Chapter 3, sections 1 and 3.

2.2 Victims' Influence

There are a number of questions that can be asked about victim influence in early release decisions. Should victims participate in release procedures? If they should, how can such participation be facilitated? And, finally, what impact should victims' views have on the final decision whether or not to grant release? All international criminal courts and tribunals now answer the first question in the affirmative. The policy and practice in relation to how to facilitate victim participation in release decision-making procedures, however, varies significantly from tokenistic engagement with victim-witnesses at the MICT, to extensive community consultations at the RSCSL, to formal standing to participate in sentence review hearings through legal representation at the ICC.[26] The MICT approach has expanded more recently with President Santana considering (unsolicited) written submissions from victim associations opposing release.[27]

Despite the 'centrality of victims and victimhood in and for international criminal justice', Lohne warns that the risk of violating rights and principles of legality necessitates careful procedural balancing.[28] Beyond permitting victim participation, international judges have treated victim submissions on the merits of release carefully, adopting objective and case-by-case assessments of the relevance and validity of such views.[29] International judges have, rightly, adopted a cautious approach to ensure the maintenance of an appropriate balance of considerations, careful not to impinge on fundamental fair trial rights or liberty interests of convicted persons. Overall, it seems that the weight attributed to victims' views on whether or not release should be granted has been limited in international criminal law. Submissions from victims on the

---

[26] See Chapter 8, section 3.

[27] For example, the Victims' Association, Association of Camp Inmates of Bosnia and Herzegovina, Association of Citizens Civilian Victims of War Mostar, Mostar Association of Prison Camp Inmates, Association of the Victims and Witnesses of Genocide, Association of Mothers of the Srebrenica and Žepa Enclaves. See *Prosecutor v Stojić*, Decision on the Application for Early Release of Bruno Stojić, MICT-17-112-ES.3, 17 January 2024, paras 87–91, 93; *Prosecutor v Miletić*, Decision on the Application for Early Release of Radivoje Miletić, MICT-15-85-ES.5, 18 January 2024, paras 77–78; *Prosecutor v Župljanin*, Decision on the Application for Early Release of Stojan Župljanin, MICT-13-53-ES.1, 18 January 2024, paras 70, 72.

[28] Kjersti Lohne, 'Penal Welfarism "Gone Global"? Comparing International Criminal Justice to the Culture of Control' 23(1) (2021) *Punishment and Society* 3–23 at 13, 16.

[29] See Chapter 8, section 3.

conditions that could be imposed to address particular concerns may be more influential on decision-making than views on the merits of release itself.

3. AGE AND ILLNESS

International criminal justice institutions pursue justice for atrocity crimes. The historic nature of offences, the senior positions of accused persons, combined with the lengthy procedures and sanctions that can be imposed, have created a greying international detention population. The supervision of sentences being served by older prisoners will inevitably and foreseeably result in applications for release based on advanced age-associated conditions and disabilities. While the punishment and imprisonment of elderly persons may 'further retributive, utilitarian and expressive aims', Davidson notes that it is not age itself, but the 'accessories of old age' that may engage human rights obligations to grant release or consider alternatives to custody.[30] Radko Mladić, for example, is serving his life sentence in the UN Detention Unit for genocide, crimes against humanity and war crimes.[31] Yet a recent unsuccessful application for conditional release to receive treatment for a potentially life-threatening condition in Serbia portrays the deteriorating physical health and cognitive function of the 82-year-old, who is entirely dependent on others for care around the clock.[32] Age aside, release policies should also provide for compassionate release based on terminal illness.

While there have been indications of UN attempts to prepare for this greying of the prisoner profile,[33] there is still no specific (public) policy for compassionate release or the provision of palliative care for those denied release at the MICT. The ICC and RSCSL need to instigate more fundamental changes to their legal frameworks to ensure the timely and effective management of requests for release or care from convicted persons whose conditions are

---

[30] Caroline Davidson, 'Aging Out: Elderly Defendants and International Crimes' (2020) 61 *Va J Int'l L* 57–110 at 60–61.

[31] The life sentence was affirmed by the Appeals Chamber. *Prosecutor v Mladić*, Judgment, MICT-13-56-A, 8 June 2021, para. 592.

[32] See *Prosecutor v Mladić,* Urgent Defence Motion for Provisional Release of Ratko Mladić based on Compassionate and Humanitarian Grounds or in the Alternative Allowing Him to Serve the Remainder of this Sentence in Serbia, MICT-13-56-ES, 1 May 2024, paras 1–2, 4, 23; *Prosecutor v Mladić*, Decision on the Application for Release of Ratko Mladić, MICT-13-56-ES, 10 May 2024, paras 46–47.

[33] See UN Security Council Resolution 2529 (2020), 25 June 2020, para. 11; UN Security Council Resolution 2637 (2022), 22 June 2022, para. 13.

incompatible with continued detention.[34] To ensure the human rights of terminally ill prisoners are protected, including their right to receive medical care equivalent to that in the community, it is vital that both court and prison authorities incorporate clear rules and procedures relating to the treatment and release of prisoners with a terminal illness into their enforcement agreements and prison management policies.[35]

Contemporary international criminal courts do permit consideration of ill-health and advanced age as possible grounds for release or sentence reduction.[36] The reality is that numerous additional considerations may complicate decision-making in the international criminal justice context. Nationality and immigration status may frustrate planning at a time when urgent decision-making is required. Release and care decisions may be further delayed and/or complicated by legal, penological, political, humanitarian, rights, ethical and logistical factors. Nevertheless, human rights law requires international courts, and states enforcing sentences on their behalf, to recognise that there will come a point when continued detention will become inhumane and therefore unlawful. Contemporary standards governing compassionate release and palliative care in prisons are ultimately founded upon the recognition of the need to ensure dignity in dying. Such decisions should be based solely on medical grounds.

However, the rights recognition that continued detention in certain health or age-associated circumstances can be inhumane exists alongside a maximalist approach to victims' rights to justice and punishment, which views persons convicted of international crimes as less eligible (or ineligible) for compassionate release.[37] Justice advocates are issuing warnings about the risk of 'biological impunity' by which they mean the risk of accused persons dying following indictment, during trial and enforcement of sentence, or an inability to proceed with trial due to age-related cognitive impairments.[38] Indeed, recent MICT cases provide pertinent examples. In the final case on the MICT's docket, Kabuga's 'state of health proved fatal to the costly ambitions of UN justice'.[39] Remanding the case to the Trial Chamber with an instruction to

[34] See Chapter 9, sections 2.2–2.3.

[35] See UNODC, *Handbook on Prisoners with Special Needs* (Vienna, 2009) 143–156 at 148.

[36] See Chapter 9, section 2.

[37] Davidson, note 30 at 86, 103.

[38] See Trial International, *Universal Jurisdiction Annual Review*, 2024 at 14–15.

[39] Balthazar Nduqayezu, 'Final Curtain Falls on Kabuga Trial' on Justiceinfo.net, 22 August 2023, at: https://www.justiceinfo.net/en/120523-final-curtain-falls-on-kabuga-trial.html.

impose an indefinite stay on proceedings due to unfitness to stand trial on account of dementia,[40] the Appeals Chamber stressed that priority consideration had to be given to release 'under conditions most appropriate in the circumstances'.[41] Compassionate release was granted to Franko Simatović three months after the conclusion of the longest trial process in international criminal law history. Though released on compelling humanitarian grounds due to a serious deterioration in health, subject to 24-hour surveillance and ongoing independent medical verification of his life expectancy,[42] the Croatian Prime Minister informed the MICT President that he was unhappy about the temporary release granted to the former Serbian state security official.[43] The Extraordinary Criminal Chambers of Cambodia also grappled with the impact of advanced age and had to support the 'transition of a detention facility into a hospice' and witness the deaths of Khmer Rouge figures in detention or during the service of their sentences.[44] Drumbl and Fournet have described this process as a quest to keep the 'barely alives'[45] alive to ensure they could be prosecuted, punished, and 'serve as much sentence as can be eked out'.[46] Fisher notes that prosecuting older persons in poor health 'presents new expressive challenges' given the potential for sympathy and perceptions of the futility of this course of action as older convicted persons are unlikely to serve (much of) their sentence.[47]

It is clear that persons convicted of international crimes are often seen as less eligible for release.[48] De Guzman argues that while 'there is nothing in

---

40 *Prosecutor v Kabuga*, Decision on Appeals of Further Decision on Félicien Kabuga's Fitness to Stand Trial, MICT-13-38-AR80.3, 7 August 2023, para. 74.

41 Ibid, para. 75.

42 *Prosecutor v Simatović*, Decision on the Application for Early Release of Franko Simatović, MICT-15-96-ES.1, 29 August 2023 at 4, 5 and Annex, Conditional Early Release Agreement, paras 3(E), (H), 6 and 7(e), (k).

43 Vuk Tasija, 'Croatian PM Protests Temporary Release of Serbian War Criminal' 4 September 2023, Balkan Transitional Justice at https://balkaninsight.com/2023/09/04/croatian-pm-protests-temporary-release-of-serbian-war-criminal/.

44 Mark Drumbl and Caroline Fournet, 'The Visualities and Aesthetics of Prosecuting Aged Defendants' (2022) 22 *International Criminal Law Review* 1–21 at 3, 4, 6.

45 Davidson, note 30 at 61–62.

46 Drumbl and Fournet, note 44 at 9–10.

47 Kirsten J Fisher, 'The Expressive Value of Prosecuting Aged Defendants: A Rebuke of Ageism' (2021) 22(1–2) *International Criminal Law Review* 63–85.

48 See Róisín Mulgrew, 'Terminal Illness and Compassionate Release: Lessons for the ICC from the UN Tribunals and National Jurisdictions' (2023) 21(1) *JICJ* 61–87 at 71.

punishment theory that mandates harsh punishment for international crimes … gravity rhetoric, as well as the narratives of monstrosity … have the potential to … lead to over-punishment'.[49] Dubray observes that counter-impunity discourse can result in an insistence on adequate punishment, which often translates into resistance to the grant of (compassionate) early release: insistence on the effective enforcement of sentences has underpinned an evolution from a 'culture of conviction' towards a 'culture of (severe) punishment'.[50] Pardons granted to those who had been convicted of atrocity crimes have generated controversy and resulted in applications for interventions by human rights courts, even when (purportedly) granted on health or humanitarian grounds.[51] This advocacy for the complete service of the sentence imposed has manifested itself in presidential pronouncements at the MICT, with statements to the effect that persons convicted of atrocity crimes should ordinarily serve their sentences in full. In other words, sentences are served under a presumption against release. Grounding international punishment in a 'purely retributionist and maximalist standpoint', Maculan and Gil Gil warn, risks permanently ostracising such persons, contrary to reconciliation objectives.[52]

In contrast, a rights-based approach appreciates that compassionate release is not early release in a traditional sense. In the words of the Grand Chamber of the European Court of Human Rights, it is correct to 'doubt whether compassionate release for the terminally ill or physically incapacitated could really be considered release at all, if all it meant was that a prisoner died at home or in a hospice rather than behind prison walls'.[53] All international criminal courts and tribunals need to develop concrete and feasible policies on humanitarian release that include options for palliative care for those who cannot be released. This requires consideration of the medical, legal, ethical, logistical, financial

---

49 Margaret M deGuzman, 'Harsh Justice for International Crimes' (2014) 39(1) *Yale Journal of International Law* 1–36 at 34.

50 See Marion V Dubray, 'Impunity and Atrocity Punishment after Mass Violence and Conflict: Questioning the Admissibility of Leniency Measures in (Post)Transition Contexts' in R Mulgrew and MJ Christensen, *Research Handbook on the Punishment of Atrocity Crimes* (Edward Elgar Publishing, 2024).

51 Leiry Cornejo Chavez, Juan-Pablo Pérez-León-Acevedo and Jemima García-Godos, 'The Presidential Pardon of Fujimori: Political Struggles in Peru and the Subsidiary Role of the Inter-American Court of Human Rights' (2019) 13 *Int J Transitional Justice* 328–348.

52 Elena Maculan and Alicia Gil Gil, 'The Rationale and Purposes of Criminal Law and Punishment in Transitional Contexts' (2020) 40(1) *Oxford Journal of Legal Studies* 132–157 at 153.

53 *Vinters and Others v UK*, Application Nos 66069/09, 130/10, 3896/10, Grand Chamber, 9 July 2013, para. 127.

and pragmatic factors relevant to managing older prisoners and end-of-life care. This includes the need to recognise the rights and ethical imperatives to devise and implement effective compassionate release policies and procedures and to put cooperation agreements and funding in place to facilitate appropriate levels of care for ill and ageing prisoners under their care.[54]

4. THE COOPERATION DEFICIT AND RELEASE IMPOSSIBILITY

Lohne posits that international criminal justice has constituted 'new geographies of penal power'.[55] An inverse reality also exists. International criminal justice has created geographies of penal power deficits. Practice has repeatedly demonstrated that international criminal courts and tribunals can find themselves in a situation whereby they cannot effectively exercise release powers. The challenges of finding states to accept persons detained by international criminal courts and tribunals, thereby thwarting judicial efforts to grant release from custody, are well documented.[56] In March 2023, for example, Pre-Trial Chamber I of the ICC regretted that it could not grant interim release that it would have otherwise granted, due to the failure to identify a cooperating State or secure the agreement of the Host State to permit temporary transfer onto its territory.[57] The Court's refusal to return Mokom to the Central African Republic due to the life sentence with hard labour imposed on him following a trial in absentia has resulted in his prolonged detention in a hotel room, temporarily and exceptionally designated as a premises of the Court.[58] In August 2023, the MICT Appeals Chamber acknowledged that identifying a State to accept Kabuga onto its territory following the termination of proceedings

---

[54] See Chapter 9.

[55] Kjersti Lohne, 'Penal Humanitarianism Beyond the Nation State: An Analysis of International Criminal Justice' (2020) 24(2) *Theoretical Criminology* 145–162 at 147.

[56] See Róisín Mulgrew, 'Temporary Transfer of Persons in Custody' in H Ruiz Fabri (ed), *Max Planck Encyclopaedia of International Procedural Law* (OUP, 2022); Róisín Mulgrew, 'International Prisoners and the Pandemic: Seeking Release, Improved Conditions and Family Contact Before International Criminal Courts' in F Dünkel, S Harrendorf and D van Zyl Smit (eds) *The Impact of Covid-19 on Prison Conditions and Penal Policy* (Routledge, 2022) 581–595 at 589–591.

[57] *Prosecutor v Maxime Jeoffroy Eli Mokom Gawaka*, Public Redacted Version of 'Decision on Interim Release' ICC-01/14-01/22, 8 March 2023, paras 59–60.

[58] *Prosecutor v Maxime Jeoffroy Eli Mokom Gawaka*, Public Redacted Version of 'Appeal against "Decision pursuant to Rule 185 of the Rules of Procedure and Evidence"' ICC-01/14-01-22-318-Red, 8 February 2024, paras 4, 7, 37.

'may present obstacles' but as there was no basis for continued detention, the Trial Chamber had to 'expeditiously consider appropriate modalities and conditions for release'.[59] International indictment and punishment have long been blamed for the de facto statelessness of persons tried or convicted by the ICTR following their long-term liberty deprivation in Tanzania and later house arrest in Niger.[60]

It is entirely foreseeable, therefore, that early and compassionate release will not be an available option for all internationally convicted persons due to a lack of state cooperation or unstable security conditions in proposed states of relocation. This creates a further level of disparity among persons sentenced or supervised by the same international court or tribunal. The stigma of international punishment is increasingly being compounded by the serious implications of risk-centred applications of immigration and refugee law, and a lack of countries willing to facilitate resettlement. Van Sliedregt, for example, has warned that 'until the asymmetry or mismatch of standards between ICL and international refugee law … has been fixed, refugee exclusion is a perfectly lawful way to hamper the relocation and resettlement of …sentenced persons'.[61] Further, she notes that there is a normative assumption that labels such persons as both deserving of punishment and undeserving of protection, a label that creates a space for persons to be considered outlaws or rightless.[62] Tripković cautions that denationalisation and statelessness 'subject individuals to volatile forms of penality beyond any country's control', creating 'ungoverned subjects … exposed to harmful consequences in spaces devoid of formal state control'.[63] This has been borne out in international sentence enforcement and release practice. For those left in legal limbo, without a (Host) State willing to take responsibility for them or grant (temporary) residence rights, the indicting international court remains physically, legally and financially responsible for affected individuals. These post-release consequences extend the punitive reach of international punishment in deeply affecting and potentially irreversible ways. From a legal and liberty perspective, for some convicted persons, it may not be possible for an international court to give effect to judicial orders to grant release (in a timely or appropriate manner).

59 *Prosecutor v Kabuga*, Decision on Appeals of Further Decision on Félicien Kabuga's Fitness to Stand Trial, MICT-13-38-AR80.3, 7 August 2023, paras 76, 79.

60 See Chapter 6, section 6.

61 Elies van Sliedregt, 'International Outlaws' (2020) *LJIL* 535–540 at 536.

62 Ibid at 539.

63 Milena Tripkovic, 'No Country for "Bad" Men, Volatile Citizenship and the Emerging Features of Global Neo-colonial Penality' (2023) 63(6) *The British Journal of Criminology* 1351–1367 at 1352.

5. THE IMPACT OF SECURITY AND LEGACY EXPECTATIONS

The legitimacy of a given criminal justice system is often 'linked to the political dimensions of prisoner release' and 'wider penal crises and systemic concerns'.[64] Further, as former MICT President Meron noted in 2021, while early release is often 'delicate and controversial' in domestic systems, 'the political, national, ethnic and religious context makes early releases even more difficult and contentious' for international criminal courts and tribunals.[65] The often contested nature of release in international criminal law introduces reintegration issues that extend beyond traditional penological considerations. Ad hoc tribunals also consider the implications of release decisions for the community and wider society to which the individual will be released, and the (perceived) legacy of these institutions.[66]

International punishment is based on and determined by individual responsibility despite the fact that the crimes were committed during periods of collective violence and inverted societal values and norms.[67] Concerns about institutional legacy, and the failure to achieve aims of peace maintenance through the imposition of individual accountability, may be acting as barriers to release in situations of increased societal tension. Release, a core remaining function of the MICT and a key aspect of the ICTY's legacy, is firmly under the spotlight at the moment. The legacy worry is that not only has international punishment failed to rehabilitate some convicted persons, but that peace and security may actually be threatened by allowing such persons to re-enter society before serving their full sentence. Release policies are increasingly viewed as having the potential to destabilise the region and undermine peace. Victim and survivor disappointment with sentences is being aggravated by the grant of early release in a context of 'hate speech, genocide denial, glorification of convicted war criminals' in a region that may 'be on the brink of another conflict'.[68] There have been warnings that the involvement of former ICTY prisoners in public and political life may pose a security risk in the current

---

64 Carr and Blay, note 21 at 122.

65 Theodore Meron, *Standing Up for Justice: The Challenges of Trying Atrocity Crimes* (OUP, 2021) at 263.

66 See Chapter 6, section 2.2.

67 Mark Drumbl, *Atrocity, Punishment and International Law* (CUP, 2007); Lohne, note 28 at 7.

68 David Pettigrew, 'Mandate Interrupted: The Problematic Legacy of the United Nationals International Criminal Tribunal for the Former Yugoslavia' (2020) 19(3) *Wash U Global Stud L Rev* 381–404 at 389–390.

climate of ethno-nationalist bias and extremism.[69] The former Commissioner for Human Rights of the Council of Europe specifically warned about the risk posed by releasing convicted war criminals and permitting them to re-enter public and political life at a time when 'reconciliation and social cohesion remain elusive and even peace seems threatened', in particular due to the growing glorification of war crimes.[70] The problem was linked directly to ICTY convicted war criminals who had not admitted responsibility, failed to express remorse or reject ideological positions that led to the crimes.[71] Buljabašic and Veljan also warn that overlooking the potential for renewed violence or offences is problematic given that 'most convicts return to a society that has not addressed the deep-seated ideologies that led to the atrocities in the first place'.[72]

Beyond the UN ad hoc tribunals, however, a different approach emerges. The judges of the ICC have adopted a highly cautious approach to allowing considerations of release on societal stability to impinge on sentence reduction decision-making, noting the inconclusive and speculative nature of information available and the fact that the security situation is beyond the convicted person's control.[73] Further, the widespread consultations with relevant communities in the release procedures of the RSCSL have consistently shown widespread support for release, based perhaps on the knowledge that residency requirements, conditions on release, and recall processes can adequately address concerns and fears about reintegration.[74] This may be attributable to the specific transitional context of Sierra Leone. As Sirleaf noted a decade ago, the combined use of truth and punishment mechanisms can produce mutually reinforcing effects, which are further enhanced by hosting both types of mechanisms in the country where the crimes were committed: proximity not

69 Filip Vojta, 'From West Berlin, with Love: The Legacy of the Spandau Prison in the Contemporary International Sentence Enforcement Practice' Leuven Transitional Justice Blog, 2 November 2021; see also Lina Strupinskienė, 'Life after Conviction at the International Criminal Tribunal for the former Yugoslavia' (2023) 21 *JICJ* 113–135.

70 Council of Europe Commissioner for Human Rights, *Dealing with the Past for a Better Future: Achieving Justice, Peace and Social Cohesion in the Region of the Former Yugoslavia*, Issue Paper (2023), at 9, 12, 55.

71 Ibid at 56, 61.

72 Mirza Buljabašić and Nejra Veljan, 'Securitisation of Punishment for Atrocity and Terrorism Crimes in Bosnia and Herzegovina' in R Mulgrew and MJ Christensen (eds), *Research Handbook on the Punishment of Atrocity Crimes* (Edward Elgar Publishing, 2024).

73 See Chapter 3, section 5.3; Chapter 7, section 5.2.

74 See Chapter 7, section 5.3.

only optimises possibilities for participation but also for processing the mechanisms' outcomes.[75] In other words, the 'geographies of justice' matter.[76] The opposite is true in the Balkans; the failure to establish a truth and reconciliation commission in the region has been blamed for the creation of space for atrocity denial and historical revisionism.[77] These differing approaches to and worries about the societal and legacy impact of release are therefore important dimensions of discussions about how to address atrocity crime.

6. CONCLUDING OBSERVATIONS

In one sense, it is astonishing that it has been possible to write a book on the law, policy and practice of early release in international criminal law given that it is not a power granted by the statute of any international criminal court or tribunal. The statutes of the UN ad hoc tribunals and the Special Court for Sierra Leone referred to pardon and commutation of sentence, powers that have never been used. Over time, judicial practice and policymaking introduced early release, and later conditional early release. With no further cases on their dockets, a core function of the residual mechanisms for these courts will be to make and supervise release decisions. The ICC Statute also does not grant judges the power to grant early release. At the ICC, sentences are reviewed in order to ascertain whether it is appropriate to grant a sentence reduction. However, it is apparent that the ICC should consider introducing a form of conditional early release for particular humanitarian situations.

Early release does not only impact upon convicted persons, victims and affected societies: it is important for the credibility of judicial institutions.[78] For the ad hoc courts and tribunals, the camera and critical lens have moved from arrests, trial and sentencing to focus on the outcome and impact of release decisions. The success of international criminal law is no longer measured in terms of the number of outstanding warrants, the spectacle of the trial, or the determination of guilt and sentence length – but in relation to the impact of the custodial sanction on the person held individually accountable and how that person can reintegrate into society. Scholarship has also moved from its prioritisation of substantive and procedural international criminal law towards

---

[75] Matiangai V S Sirleaf, 'Beyond Truth and Punishment in Transitional Justice' (2013) 54(2) *Virginia Journal of International Law* 223–294 at 229.

[76] Ibid at 289.

[77] COE Commissioner for Human Rights, note 70 at 11, 13.

[78] See Cristina Fernández-Pacheco Estrada, 'What We Talk About When We Talk About Early Release in International Criminal Law: The Sui Generis Nature of the Reduction of Sentence Under the Rome Statute' (2022) 22 *ICLR* 539–567 at 541.

a more sustained and critical engagement with questions of sanctioning and how sentences have been operationalised in the international criminal justice context.[79]

Punishment is a speech act.[80] Constructed during sentencing (to reflect gravity and culpability), punishment is then given 'concrete and tangible content' during sentence enforcement.[81] It is vital, therefore, that the import and impact of early release are recognised and reflected upon in order to fully understand international punishment. Release is important as it moulds and concludes international criminal law's reach and purpose, with implications for wider understandings of punishment, rights, justice and transition.

The findings of this book align with Carr and Blay's observation that release mechanisms can find themselves 'caught in the bind of competing and oscillating penal logics' and become 'a key site of policy contestation'.[82] This chapter has highlighted the tensions between rights, penological and transitional goals on the one hand, and retributivist, security and (counter-impunity) justice objectives on the other in the context of release. The limited NGO and civil society attention on the rights of defendants and convicted persons in international criminal law begs the important question: who will 'speak truth to penal power' in the context of international criminal law.[83] Particularly when the form of punishment can be altered, and penal power extended, at the whim of one judicial officer or following input from a political organ. Rights advocates should remain cognisant of the long-lasting consequences that may result from international punishment and release policies.[84]

---

79 See Róisín Mulgrew and Mikkel J Christensen, 'Researching the Punishment of Atrocity Crimes' in R Mulgrew and MJ Christensen (eds), *Research Handbook on the Punishment of Atrocity Crimes* (Edward Elgar Publishing, 2024).

80 Joachim J Savelsberg, 'Punitive Turn and Justice Cascade: Mutual Inspiration from Punishment and Society and Human Rights Literature' (2018) 20(1) *Punishment and Society* 73–91 at 86.

81 Maculan and Gil Gil, note 52 at 148.

82 Carr and Blay, note 21 at 120.

83 Lohne, note 28 at 16.

84 See, for example Natasa Mavronicola's critique of human rights law being used to foreground punishment and carceral approaches in 'The Case Against Human Rights Penality' (2024) *Oxford Journal of Legal Studies* at 2.

Index